Lecture Notes in Computer Sci

Edited by G. Goos, J. Hartmanis and J. van

T0237764

Springer

Berlin
Heidelberg
New York
Barcelona
Hong Kong
London
Milan
Paris
Singapore
Tokyo

Alexander Romanovsky   Christophe Dony
Jł rgen Lindskov Knudsen   Anand Tripathi (Eds.)

Advances in Exception Handling Techniques

Springer

Series Editors

Gerhard Goos, Karlsruhe University, Germany
Juris Hartmanis, Cornell University, NY, USA
Jan van Leeuwen, Utrecht University, The Netherlands

Volume Editors

Alexander Romanovsky
University of Newcastle upon Tyne, Department of Computing Science
Newcastle upon Tyne, NE1 7RU, UK
E-mail: alexander.romanovsky@ncl.ac.uk

Christophe Dony
University of Montpellier-II, LIRMM Laboratory
161 rue Ada, 34392 Montpellier Cedex 5, France
E-mail: dony@lirmm.fr

Jł rgen Lindskov Knudsen
University of Aarhus, Department of Computing Science
Aabogade 34, 8200 Aarhus N, Denmark
E-mail: jlk@daimi.au.dk

Anand Tripathi
University of Minnesota, Department of Computer Science & Engineering
Minneapolis, MN 55455, USA
E-mail: tripathi@cs.umn.edu

Cataloging-in-Publication Data applied for

Die Deutsche Bibliothek - CIP-Einheitsaufnahme

Advances in exception handling techniques / Alexander Romanovsky ...
(ed.). - Berlin ; Heidelberg ; New York ; Barcelona ; Hong Kong ;
London ; Milan ; Paris ; Singapore ; Tokyo : Springer, 2001
    (Lecture notes in computer science ; 2022)
    ISBN 3-540-41952-7

CR Subject Classification (1998): C.2.4, D.1.3, D.1.5, D.2, D.3, D.4, F.3, I.2.11

ISSN 0302-9743
ISBN 3-540-41952-7 Springer-Verlag Berlin Heidelberg New York

Springer-Verlag Berlin Heidelberg New York
a member of BertelsmannSpringer Science+Business Media GmbH

http://www.springer.de

' Springer-Verlag Berlin Heidelberg 2001
Printed in Germany

Typesetting: Camera-ready by author, data conversion by PTP-Berlin, Stefan Sossna
Printed on acid-free paper   SPIN: 10782337   06/3142   5 4 3 2 1 0

Foreword

For years exception handling has been a side issue in language and system design. I could not be more pleased to see the recent surge of interest in this topic, as reflected in recent special issues of Transactions on Software Engineering, the workshop yielding the papers in this volume, and future planned workshops. Moreover, in reading through these papers, I was surprised at the breadth of topics covered. Programming language issues are no longer the central focus; researchers are looking into broader topics such as workflow processes, distributed systems, system design, etc.

This broad interest is understandable. Although exception handling originated with sequential programming languages, today's distributed, component-oriented computing world raises new language design and implementation issues as well as new concerns about how to deal with exceptions in system design. I am glad to see such vigorous exploration of these issues.

Several of the papers deal with system design, but there are still issues that remain to be explored. For example, I have long (but quietly) advocated dealing with exception handling issues early in the design of a system. Unfortunately, there is a natural tendency to focus on the main functional flow of a system, ignoring the impact of exceptional situations until later. Design guidelines for using exceptions are lacking; indeed, there is little appreciation of the *need* for such guidelines. For example, even leaving aside distributed and concurrent programming issues, what design guidelines exist to help decide which preconditions should be checked inside a module and which should be the caller's responsibility? For which exception situations should a module provide a Boolean function such as At_End_of_File so a programmer can test for the existence of the situation without calling the method that raises the exception? When an exception occurs, what additional information should be provided to the handler (even at the cost of a breach in information hiding), and what system-wide conventions define what information will be provided and how it will be provided?

Another topic that concerns me is the interaction between exceptions and optimization. Long ago, a PL/I implementer observed that the existence of exceptions raised by language-defined operations could kill many optimizations. For example, if code is reordered to optimize usage of a pipelined floating point processor, some textually-later operations may be performed in parallel with the floating point computations. Suppose a complex assignment that occurs textually later in the code is actually started while waiting for the floating point processor to finish. If an overflow exception is raised after the assignment is completed, the handler may not expect the variable to be updated. If the assignment is interrupted, the variable may be left in a partially updated state. When a language permits such reorderings, then the state seen at an exception handler is less defined than a programmer might think. When a language does not permit such reordering, then code may run slower. Deciding what computational states are allowed after occurrence of an exception raised by a language-defined operation is a tricky proposition; it occupied a lot of discussion during the Ada design.

I raise these points only to suggest that despite the swell of papers and work on exception handling, there are still technical nuggets to be mined by the adventurous explorer. The nuggets that can be found in this book are still only the beginning.

January 2001   John B. Goodenough
                                                                                    Carnegie Mellon University

Preface

Modern software systems are becoming more complex in many ways (including their size, modules, components, distribution, concurrence, interoperability) and have to cope with a growing number of abnormal situations which, in their turn, are increasingly more complex to handle. The most general way of dealing with these problems is by incorporating exception handling techniques in software design. In the past, various exception handling models and techniques have been proposed, many of which are part of practical languages (e.g. PL/I, Ada, CLU, LISP, Smalltalk, Eiffel, BETA, C++, Java) and software composition technologies (e.g. CORBA, COM, or Enterprise Java Beans).

In spite of these developments and a better understanding of exception handling techniques by todays software designers, many problems still persist because the mechanisms embedded in exception handling systems and the methodologies of using them are often error-prone due to the complexity of exception code. Moreover, specification, analysis, verification, and testing of programs and systems intended for coping with exceptional situations are far from being straightforward. Finally, very often the exception handling features used are not compatible with the programming language features or the methodology in which they are employed, thus creating a gap that can cause mistakes or unnecessary complications. Developing new exception handling techniques should go together with developing advanced models, languages, and paradigms and take into account various specific application domains as well as users experience of employing the existing ones.

In the early 1970s John Goodenough[1] was the first to define the seminal concepts for exception handling models, techniques, and applications. He defined exception conditions and handling as follows: "Of the conditions detected while attempting to perform some operation, *exception conditions* are those brought to the attention of the operation invoker. ... Bringing an exception condition to invokers attention is called *raising* an exception. The invokers response is called *handling* the exception." Knudsen[2] defined exception conditions in a more general sense: "an exception occurrence is a computational state that requires an extraordinary computation". This book brings together a collection of 17 papers addressing a wide range of issues in exception handling techniques, reflecting this broad view and the importance of exception handling in todays software systems.

This collection aims at discussing important topics of developing advanced exception handling techniques and of applying them in building robust and dependable systems. The papers presented describe well-established results, recent developments on

---

[1] Goodenough, J.B.: Exception Handling, Issues and a Proposed Notation. Communications of ACM, **18**, 12 (1975) 683-696

[2] Knudsen. J.L.: Better Exception Handling in Block-structured Systems, IEEE Software, May (1987) 40-49

specific issues, and practical experience. The research problems addressed include linguistic issues and programming constructs, integration of exception handling models with object-oriented programming principles, and methodologies for employing exception handling in software designs incorporating concurrent and distributed components. The book offers an exposition of techniques and experiences concerning exception handling in mission-critical systems, databases, and workflow process management systems.

This book is composed of five parts, which deal with topics related to exception handling in the context of programming language models, design methodologies, concurrent and distributed systems, applications and experiences, and large-scale systems such as databases and workflow process management systems.

The first part focuses on language support for exception handling. It comprises three papers which describe how exception handling systems are integrated into statically and dynamically typed programming languages. These systems differ in how exceptions are represented; what kind of control structures are provided to signal and handle exceptions; the semantics of these control structures and its effect on the expressive power and the program quality and, finally, how the exception handling primitives can be implemented. The paper by Jt rgen Lindskov Knudsen presents a new design for augmenting the static exception handling model in BETA by a dynamic exception handling model, and discusses how these two models can coexist and interact. Finally, the strengths of both models are discussed. Christophe Dony describes the design and implementation of a fully object-oriented exception handling system for Smalltalk which incorporates class handlers. And finally, Kent M. Pitman presents the rationale and evolution of exception handling models in the LISP language family.

The second part deals with the design and modeling of exception handling structures. So far, there have not been enough studies which consider the most effective ways of using the existing systems, their limitations, and how to overcome them. Bjarne Stroustrup discusses the effective and practical use of exception handling libraries in C++. The paper by Yolande Ahronovitz and Marianne Huchard is concerned with the design of exception class hierarchies and their connection with predefined exception hierarchies. Finally, the paper by Anna Mikhailova and Alexander Romanovsky describes the evolution of application programs and, in particular, the issues raised by the integration of new exceptions in module interfaces, and proposes some effective solutions.

The papers in the third part focus on exception handling issues in concurrent and distributed computing. With cooperative concurrency, an exception encountered by one component may require actions by the components cooperating with it. Also, exceptions concurrently raised by different components need to be resolved together to determine the global handling action to be undertaken. The paper by Valℓie Issarny presents a programming language level support addressing these problems. Several particular problems arise when the cooperating autonomous components of an application are distributed. Thus, in agent-based systems components can migrate in the network. Anand Tripathi and Robert Miller propose a framework for exception handling in agent-based systems. Many concurrent and distributed systems are structured using shared objects and atomic actions. Such systems support both competitive and cooperative models of concurrency. The exception handling approaches based on action-oriented structuring of such concurrent systems are outlined in the survey paper by Alexander Romanovsky and J rg Kienzle. Finally, Marta Patiæo-Martinez, Ricardo JimØhez-Periz, and Sergio ArØvalo discuss exception handling mechanisms developed for replicated object groups, employing the transactional model of atomic actions.

The papers in the fourth part of the book focus on practical problems and experience of integrating exception handling techniques in real-world systems. The topics addressed include techniques for building dependable systems, integration of distributed components using COM, and implementation mechanisms for checkpointing the state of partially executed programs for reliability or mobile computing. Integration of exception handling in software system design is essential for building mission-critical and dependable systems. The paper by Charles Howell and Gary Vecellio presents various patterns of exception handling derived from building mission-critical systems using Ada. Alessandro F. Garcia and Cec lia M.F. Rubira propose a reflective architecture for systematically integrating exception handling mechanisms at various stages of designing an object-oriented dependable system. The paper by Bjł rn Eigil Hansen and Henrik Fredholm presents techniques for adapting the C++ exception handling model to the COM exception model. And, finally, Tatsurou Sekiguchi, Takahiro Sakamoto, and Akinori Yonezawa show how an exception handling system can be used to develop a portable implementation of control operators which allows the manipulation of program continuations in imperative languages.

The last part is concerned with exception handling techniques for information systems, with a special focus on database and workflow management systems. The paper by Elisa Bertino, Giovanna Guerrini, and Isabella Merlo discusses the issues related to exceptions in object-oriented databases. These exceptions can arise in two situations: when the data not conforming to the prescribed schema are stored in the database, and when the abnormal conditions occur during data processing. Workflow process management systems support the modeling and enactment of enterprise-wide processes. Such processes can sometimes encounter exceptional conditions during their execution due to errors in the modeling of business activities, mistakes made by the people involved in a process, or failures in the underlying computing infrastructure. Fabio Casati and Gianpaolo Cugola discuss how such exceptions and failures occurring in business process applications, which model and mimic human group activities, can be classified and handled by higher-level dedicated exception handling systems. The paper by Dickson K.W. Chiu, Qing Li, and Kamalakar Karlapalem presents an overview of a workflow management system integrating several original approaches to exception handling: the automated and cooperative resolution of expected exceptions, handling via workflow evolution, and developing support for user-driven handling of unexpected exceptions.

The starting point of our work on this book was the workshop on Exception Handling in Object-Oriented Systems that we organized at ECOOP 2000[3]. Later on we decided to widen the scope of the book and, after inviting several workshop participants to prepare chapters for this book, extended this invitation to a number of other leading researchers working on different aspects of exception handling. It is only natural that the choice of contributors to this book reflects our personal views on this research area. However, we are hopeful that reading this volume will prove rewarding to all computer scientists and practitioners who realise the importance of dealing with abnormal events in building robust and safe systems.

Our thanks go to all authors, whose work made this book possible. Many of them also helped during the review process. We also would like to thank Prof. John Goodenough for contributing the foreword to this book. Finally, we would like to thank Alfred Hofmann of Springer-Verlag for recognising the importance of the project and publishing this book.

January 2001

Alexander Romanovsky
Christophe Dony
Jł rgen Lindskov Knudsen
Anand Tripathi

---

[3]   Romanovsky, A., Dony, C., Knudsen, J.L., and Tripathi, A.: Exception Handling in Object-Oriented Systems. In Malenfant, J., Moisan, S., and Moreira, A., (eds.): Object-Oriented Technology. ECOOP 2000 Workshop Reader. Lecture Notes in Computer Science Vol. 1964. Springer-Verlag, Berlin (2000) 16-31

Table of Contents

Part 4 Applications of Exception Handling Techniques

Part 5 Exception Handling in Information Systems

Fault Tolerance and Exception Handling in BETA

Jørgen Lindskov Knudsen

Computer Science Department, Aarhus University
Aabogade 34, DK-8200 Aarhus C, Denmark
Tel.: +45 89 42 31 88 – Fax.: +45 89 42 56 24
E-mail: jlknudsen@daimi.au.dk

Abstract. This paper describes the fault tolerance and exception handling mechanisms in the object-oriented programming language BETA. Exception handling in BETA is based on both a static and dynamic approach to exception handling in contrast to most other languages only supporting a dynamic approach.

The BETA approach to static exception handling is based on a static termination model. Exceptions and their handlers may be defined both on the program, class, method, and instruction level, and default handlers for exceptions are defined as part of the definition of the ordinary handler. Exception propagation is under the control of the programmer.

The BETA approach to dynamic exception handling is similar to other traditional dynamic exception handling models. Exception handlers are associated with blocks in the code, and in the case of an exception occurrence, the dynamic call-chain is scanned to find the dynamically nearest block with a handler matching the exception occurrence.

1 Exception Handling and Fault Tolerance

When studying error handling, there seem to be two different, but closely related problems, namely that of exception handling and that of fault tolerant programming. This applies both when studying the issues of error handling in programming and the many different proposals for language constructs for error handling. To clarify, we would like to characterize the concepts *exception handling* and *fault tolerance* in the context of error handling:

Exception handling

Exception handling is the technique by which the designer of a piece of software – an abstraction (library, module, class, etc.) can define possible exceptional occurrences that are expected to occur in the abstraction. Moreover, these exceptional occurrences are part of the definition of the abstraction in the sense that the users of the abstraction knows about the possibilities of these exceptional occurrences, and thereby are able (or forced) to deal with these occurrences when using the abstraction.

A. Romanovsky et al. (Eds.): Exception Handling, LNCS 2022, pp. 1-17, 2001.
© Springer-Verlag Berlin Heidelberg 2001

Fault tolerant programming

Fault tolerant programming, on the other hand, is the techniques to cope with exceptional occurrences that are not defined as part of the abstraction definition. Examples of such occurrences are programming errors in the code of the abstraction, unhandled exceptions, and unexpected system states (e.g. the disk system suddenly becomes inaccessible) as illustrated in Fig. 1.

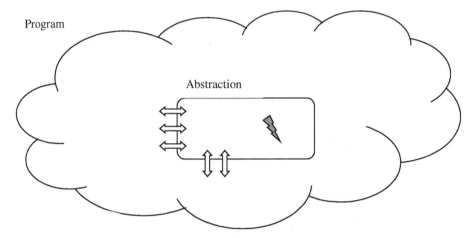

Fig. 1: Exception occurrences inside abstractions with interface

If the error occur within the abstraction, and is completely handled by the abstraction itself, we will call this exception handling. Likewise if the error occur within the abstraction and is propagated through the interfaces of the abstraction by means of exceptions known in the interface definition of the abstraction (as indicated in the picture above by the arrows). However, if errors occur within the abstraction, and the error is not handled internally in the abstraction and propagated through the interface by exceptions not known in the interface to the abstraction, we will call this a fault (thus calling for mechanisms for fault tolerance). We call this a fault since the user of the abstraction has no means to foresee the error in any reasonable way. An example is a communication abstraction in which the programmer of the abstraction forgets to make provisions for the situation where the communication line breaks down for some reason (e.g. the cable is broken). In this case a communication error will occur within the abstraction, and this error will somehow be propagated to the users of the abstraction, but they have no direct way to handle this situation.

Language mechanisms for error handling have mostly used the dynamic model of exception handling, as initiated by the work by Goodenough [1], and realized in languages like C++ and Java.

Interestingly, the trend in dynamic exception handling (as exemplified by Java) is to introduce more static analysis in order to make exception handling more safe (exceptions are declared in the interfaces, and the language compiler enforces static checks to ensure, that these exceptions are handled). This gives a static verifiability of an otherwise dynamic mechanism. On the other hand, the static model of exception handling (as exemplified by BETA [6]) have realized that there are cases, where the static nature of the model makes it very difficult to ensure that a program never terminates due to an unhandled exception.

Looking more closely at the Java exception handling mechanism [2], one will find an interesting change in the rules of the game when we investigate the rules concerning the very basic exceptions (such as numeric exceptions). While the compiler enforces the handling of all exceptions in an interface, the compiler does not enforce this rule on the basic exceptions.

Looking more closely into the arguments for this, it is interesting to see that sentences like "it would become tedious to properly declare them all, since practically any method can conceivably generate them" are given. And an example is "every method running on a buggy Java interpreter can throw an InternalError exception".

One interpretation of these differences in semantics is exactly that regular exceptions (i.e. Throwables) are handled using exception handling, whereas non-Throwables are handled using fault tolerance. In the Java case, this implies that the exception type system is used to differentiate between exception handling and fault tolerance.

In the BETA case, the type system of exceptions does not introduce any differentiation between exceptions for exception handling and exceptions for fault tolerance. This is actually a deliberate design decision. The reason is, that in some parts of a system, a given exceptional case might be known as a part of the definition of an abstraction, whereas the same exceptional case may occur in other places, where it is unreasonable to define it as part of the abstraction. In the Java case, this situation implies that the system must have two exception types defined – one for the exception handling case, and another for the fault tolerance case. In BETA, this is handled by the same exception definition. If the exception is raised using the static exception handling system, then the exception is handled using exception handling, whereas if the exception is raised using the dynamic exception handling mechanisms, then the exception is handled using fault tolerance.

It should be noted, that the BETA mechanisms are actually connected, such that if an exception is raised as a static exception, but unfortunately not handled by anyone, then the exception handling system will automatically convert it into a dynamic exception. This implies that the error is converted to a fault to be handled through fault tolerance mechanisms.

In conclusion, the relationship between exception handling and fault tolerance needs further investigation, and there is a need for further development in the area and language constructs for supporting both exception handling and fault tolerance. However, it seems important not to do this through separate language constructs, but to develop interconnected language constructs, enabling these two approaches to error handling to be integrated, improving the stability of future system designs.

2   The BETA Error Handling Mechanisms

Error handling in BETA is based on both a static and dynamic approach in contrast to most other languages only supporting a dynamic approach.

The BETA approach to static exception handling is based on the static termination model (i.e. the termination level of raising an exception is understood through the static structure of the program). This implies that the extent of exceptions and handlers are defined by the static structure. The static termination model is based on a language construct called *sequel*, presented by R. D. Tennent in [8]. The static approach to exception handling was first presented in [3] and further developed in [4]. Hereafter, the static approach was adapted by the BETA language [6] implementation in the Mjølner System [7].

Exceptions and their handlers may be defined both at the level of the program, class, method, and statement, and default handlers for exceptions are defined as part of the definition of the exception itself. Exception propagation is under the control of the programmer. Static exception handling is realized using virtual patterns in BETA.

The BETA approach to dynamic exception handling is similar to other traditional dynamic exception handling models. Exception handlers are associated with blocks in the code, and in the case of an exception occurrence, the dynamic call-chain is scanned to find the dynamically nearest block with a handler matching the exception occurrence.

The BETA exceptions allow for both termination, resumption and retry models of exception handling, and the programmer has full control over the model chosen.

The BETA exception handling model is implemented within the BETA language to the extent that a programmer may choose to implement an exception handling model that is particular suited for the specific applications. BETA has no special built-in language mechanisms for exception handling. Only a slight runtime system support is needed in the BETA implementation.

The static exception handling model in BETA is "free-of-charge". That is, there is no runtime overhead on programs that do not utilize static exception handling. Programs using the static exception handling model will only experience little extra runtime overhead when an exception actually occur (except that of course the actual execution of the handler code). That is, the time used to locate handlers etc. is essentially zero.

The dynamic exception handling model in BETA is not totally "free-of-charge". A slight runtime overhead is imposed on the execution of those blocks that have associated exception handlers. In the case of an exception occurrence, the dynamic search for a matching handler is an extra execution overhead.

The introduction of exceptions into the BETA language is done in two steps. Firstly, we introduce the static exception handling model in BETA, leading to a very simple, and very efficient exception handling technique, where no runtime overhead are induced on programs utilizing this approach.

Following the introduction to the static approach, we will introduce dynamic exception handling into BETA. The dynamic exception handling model is inspired by the dynamic exception handling model in C++.

3   Static Exception Handling in BETA

In the following sections, the technique for static exception handling in BETA will be presented. It should be noted that the implementation of static exception handling in BETA is not identical to the original static approach as described in [3] and [4]. The most significant difference is that when implementing the static approach in BETA, it was decided to do this without changing the core BETA language and thus implement static exception using the existing language facilities of BETA. This implied that the introduction of sequels as defined by R. D. Tennent in [8] and utilized for the original proposal for static exception handling was abandoned. Instead the BETA version of static exception handling is realized by using virtual patterns and by extensive usage of the ability to bind virtual exception patterns to concrete exception handlers.

3.1 Exception Handling Terminology

A virtual pattern dealing with an exception is called an exception pattern, or just an exception. The invocation of an exception pattern is called an exception occurrence. An exception is raised when an exception pattern is invoked. The code associated with an exception pattern is called a handler or an exception handler.

The code associated with a specialization of the exception pattern will be the default handler for the exception in the case where no further binding of it is made. A sub-pattern may extend the default handler by a further binding. A specific instance handler may be associated with each instance by instantiating a singular object with a further binding of the exception pattern.

3.2 The Exception Pattern

The exception pattern is defined in Fig. 2. The text object msg is intended to hold the text to be displayed to the user in case the exception leads to termination of the program. In sub-patterns of exception, it is possible to specify the termination message.

The default action of an exception is to stop execution. The rationale behind this is that an exception is an error that must explicitly be dealt with by the programmer. If the exception should not result in the termination of the application (i.e. the execution should be resumed after the exception have been handled), then the exception have to specify an explicit true->continue.

The exception pattern defines two local patterns: error, and notify. Error is a pattern to be used when defining the individual exceptions in a category, and notify is for defining the individual notifications in the category.

The static exception handling mechanism for BETA as presented here is an updated version of the static exception handling mechanism described in [6] – we refer to [6] for details. The updated version presented here has been available in the Mjølner System [7] from release r5.0.

The benefits of the static approach to exception handling is a very declarative exception handling style, where the consequences of raising an exception can be deduced from the static properties of the program. This also implies that the cost of these mechanisms are extremely low, both in the case of the exceptions never being raised, but also in the case of an exception being raised. The cost of static exception handling is fully comparable with ordinary programming.

It is our experience, that static exception handling is the exception handling model per se for well-designed object-oriented systems. The focus is on the use-relation between objects: it is the responsibility of the user (or client) of an object (or a service) to specify explicitly the consequences of exception occurrences in the object.

```
exception:
  (# msg:
        (* append text to this 'msg' variable to specify
         * the exception error message for
         * this(exception)
         *)
        @text;
     continue: @boolean
        (* the value of this variable determines the
         * control-flow behaviour of this(exception):
         *     true:  continue execution after exception
         *     false: terminate execution by calling
         *            'stop'; default
         *);
     error:
        (* used to define local exception conditions
         * which can be handled separately.  All error's
         * that are not handled separately will be
         * handled by this(exception)
         *)
        (#
        do false->continue;
           INNER;
           '**** Error processing\n'->msg.prepend;
           (if not continue then this(exception) if)
        #);
     notify: error
        (* used to define local notification conditions
         * which can be handled separately.  All
         * 'notify's that are not handled separately
         * will be handled by this(exception)
         *)
        (# do true->continue; INNER #);
  do INNER exception;
     (if not continue then
         '**** Exception processing\n'->msg.prepend;
         (* Terminate program execution:
          * Details not given here *)
     if)
  #);
```

Fig. 2: The exception pattern

The static exception handling model gives the ability for an object (through its pattern declaration) to specify the exception occurrences that may occur within it (by declaring virtual attributes, that are specialization's of the exception pattern).

The static exception handling model offers the ability for the client of the object (or service) to explicitly (and statically) specify the handling of such exception occurrences through virtual bindings of these exception patterns. This is in contrast to the usual dynamic approaches, where the handler is found through dynamic search in the runtime stack. Dynamic exception handling thus ignores the static structure of the program.

The effectiveness of static exception handling is demonstrated by the fact, that the entire Mjølner System is programmed entirely using static exception handling as the only exception handling model.

4   Dynamic Exception Handling in BETA

The static exception handling model is based on three assumptions, namely perfect implementation, perfect design, and local object creation. We will elaborate a little on these assumptions in the following:

Perfect Implementation

There is an underlying assumption that all implementers of a given pattern makes a complete handling of all low-level errors that can originate from the implementation code, and that the implementers do not make implementation errors (e.g. dereference a null reference).

Nearly by definition, implementers will forget to handle some low-level errors and they will make programming mistakes, giving rise to unanticipated errors.

Perfect Design

There is an underlying assumption that all users of a given pattern with exception specifications makes a complete handling of the exceptional occurrences (i.e. further binds the proper virtual).

Nearly by definition, designers will make mistakes, forgetting to take care of some exceptional occurrences, giving rise to the program being terminated.

Local Object Creation

There is also an underlying assumption that the objects being used by the application are also created by that application (making it possible to handle the exceptional occurrences in these objects through static exception handling).

In a persistent or distributed environment, objects are not created only by the running application, but also by other applications and made available to the running application.

4.1 Introducing Fault Tolerant Mechanisms

These assumptions imply that there is a need for offering an additional model for exception handling in order to be able to support truly fault-tolerant systems.

Exception handling deals with the handling of well-defined error conditions within a well-defined system or framework. And fault tolerant programming deals with error handling in all other cases: ill-designed systems, faults in the exception handling code, errors originating from outside the system or framework.

Our experience with the static exception handling mechanisms of BETA have proved static error handling as an effective exception handling mechanism, but also that it is difficult (and in some cases impossible) to use for fault tolerant programming.

We therefore propose the introduction of a dynamic error handling mechanism to be used for effective fault tolerant programming.

We would like to stress that the static exception handling model should be used almost exclusively, since it gives the most well-designed exception handling, integrated with the object-oriented tradition, and reserve dynamic exception handling only to those case where no other error handling solution can be found. One could say, that the relation between static and dynamic exception handling is fairly similar to the relation between structured programming and the GOTO controversy.

In the dynamic approach, there is no static connection between the definitions of an exception, the raising of an exception, and the actual handling of an exception. Exceptions are defined anywhere in the program, and may be raised anywhere where these exceptions are visible in the program text. Handling of the exception is on the other hand possible in all parts of the program (even places where the exact definition of the exception is unknown).

4.2 Dynamic Exception Handling Model in BETA

The dynamic model for exception handling for BETA is heavily inspired by the C++ model for exception handling, which in turn is inspired by the ML model for exception handling.

The dynamic exception handling model for BETA is concentrated around the following four main concepts: exception objects, throwing exceptions, try blocks, and exception handlers.

Exception Objects

An exception object is a regular BETA object. The purpose of an exception object is to act as a messenger between the point where the exception occurrence have been identified, and the place where the exception is handled. The exception object may have attributes, carrying information from the exception occurrence to the exception handler, but it may also act merely as a signal (without attributes).

Throwing Exceptions

When an exception occurrence have been identified, the dynamic exception model offers the possibility of throwing an exception object. When an exception object is thrown, the intuition is that the exception object 'travels' back the dynamic call-chain until an exception handler for this exception object type have been located. When located, the particular exception handler is given access to the exception object, and may then initiate proper exception handling processing, possibly based on the information brought to it by the exception object. During the processing of the exception object, the exception handler may decide on the proper continuation of execution of the application.

If the entire dynamic call chain have been exhausted in the search for an exception handler and no matching exception handler have been found, then the exception is automatically converted into an instance of the predefined exception unknown. This unknown exception object contains a reference to the original exception object and is automatically thrown at the same spot as the original exception object. If no handlers on the dynamic call chain handle this unknown exception object, the unknown exception object is raised as a static exception occurrence, giving raise to termination of the entire application.

Try Blocks

The BETA model for dynamic exception handling is based on try blocks as the means for specifying the extent of exception handlers. A try block is a special kind of nested blocks (similar to nested blocks in ALGOL, PASCAL and C/C++). The purpose of a try block is to function as a definition place for exception handlers, and a try block is capable of handling those exceptions for which there are defined a handler. In the description of the semantics of throwing an exception object, it was mentioned that a handler was sought. To be more specific: during a throw of an exception object, the dynamic call-chain is scanned to find the first try block with an exception handler, matching the exception object. If no matching exception handler is found in a try block, the exception is automatically propagated to the next try block in the dynamic call chain.

Exception Handlers

As described above, dynamic exception handlers are defined in try blocks. An exception handler is capable of handling a series of exceptions through the specification of a series of when-clauses. Each when-clause is capable of handling one particular exception object type (or any subtype hereof).

The sequence of when-clauses in a handler is important, since more than one when-clause in a handler may match a given exception object (the two subtypes overlap). The handler handles this potential ambiguity by choosing the first when-clause that matches the particular exception object.

During the handling of an exception in a when-clause, the when-clause has access to the exception object being handled.

Execution Control

During the handling of an exception object, the chosen when-clause has four different possibilities for controlling the execution of the program, namely continue, retry, propagate, and abort.

- *Continue*: If continue is chosen, the exception occurrence have been fully recovered, and the execution may continue from the spot, where the exception object was originally thrown.
- *Retry*: If retry is chosen, the execution is resumed from the beginning of the try block in which the chosen when-clause is specified. Retry implies that the best way to continue the application is to re-execute the entire execution from which the exception occurrence arose. Usually this implies that the exception handling has brought the application back to a stable state.
- *Propagate*: If propagate is chosen, the exception object is propagated further backwards along the dynamic call chain in order to be further handled by some other try block. Propagation is the default for exception objects for which no exception handlers are found in a try block. Propagation is also the default for exception objects with a matching when-clause if no other execution control is specified in the when-clause. Propagation implies that the exception handling have only partially been concluded.
- *Abort*: If abort is chosen, the execution is resumed after the try block in which the chosen when-clause is specified. Abort implies that the actions of the exception handler have replaced the remained of the try block (i.e. the actions after the spot, where the exception object was thrown).

4.3 The BETA Framework for Fault Tolerance

The following is a short introduction to the BETA framework of the above model for dynamic exception handling. The description will not present all details, but sufficient details to get solid understanding of the framework.

As mentioned previously, exception objects can be any BETA objects, implying that the model for dynamic exception handling does not require any special exception pattern. The only exception pattern used by the dynamic approach, is the predefined unknown exception, which is used to handle dynamic exception objects otherwise not handled. The unknown exception pattern is defined by:

```
unknown: exception
  (# original: ^object
  do INNER
  #)
```

In order to enable throwing exception objects, the following pattern is supplied:

```
throw:
  (# current: ^object;
     ...
  enter current[]
  ...
  #);
```

Throwing an exception object can then be done as follows:

```
(# fe: ^fileError;
do &fileError[]->fe[]; 'someFileName'->fe.n[];
   fe[]->throw;
#)
```

where fileError is, e.g., defined as:

```
fileError: exception
   (# n: ^text do 'fileError Exception'->msg.puttext;
INNER #);
```

Note that in this case, the dynamic exception object is an instance of a specialization of the static exception pattern exception, but that is just a coincidence.

In order to enable the definition of try blocks, handlers, and when-clauses, the following patterns are defined as part of the BETA framework for dynamic exception handling:

```
try:
  (# handler:<
        (# when:
                (# type:< object; current: ^type;
                   continue: (# ... #);
                   retry: (# ... #);
                   propagate: (# ... #);
                   abort: (# ... #);
                 ...
                #);
           ...
        ...
        #);
     ...
  #);
```

A try block is specified by:

```
do ...
      try
        (# ...
        do ...
           ...
        #);
      ...
```

In order to specify when-clauses, a handler needs to be defined in the try block:

```
do ...
   try
   (# handler::
          (#
          do ...
```

```
        #)
do ...
        ...
#);
    ...
```

When-clauses are specified in the do-part of the handler of a try block. An exception object is matched against the when-clauses in the sequence they are specified in the do-part:

```
handler::
  (#
do when(# ... do ... #);
    when(# ... do ... #);
    when(# ... do ... #);
  #)
```

Each when-clause handles one exception type (and all subtypes hereof).

The type of exception objects handled by a when-clause are specified by a final binding of the type virtual in the when-clause:

```
when
  (# type:: fileError;
  do ...
  #);
```

The execution control resulting from handling an exception object is specified in the do-part of the when-clause by means of the imperatives continue, retry, propagate and abort:

```
when
  (# type:: fileError;
  do ...; retry
  #);
```

These execution control actions should be placed as the last imperative in the do-part of the when-clause.

4.4 Handler Matching on Object Identity and Object State

In the above framework, only when-clauses capable of handling exception object types are presented. It is easy to extend the handler mechanisms with facilities for allowing when-clauses to match particular exception objects, and not only exception object types.

At least two possible special cases might be interesting. The first one is a when-clause, that only tests for the object identity of the exception object thrown (making the when-clause only match if the identity of the exception object thrown is exactly the exception object, expected by the when-clause. The second interesting case is where the actual state of the exception object is investigated in order to validate whether the exception object thrown matches the when-clause.

Both cases can be handled by a simple extension to the when pattern, namely the introduction of a predicate virtual:

```
when:
   (# predicate:< booleanValue;
      ...
   do ...
   #)
```

We can now make exception object identity testing by e.g.:

```
when:
   (# predicate::
         (# do (current[]=specificObject[])->value #)
   do ...
   #)
```

and exception object state testing by e.g.:

```
when:
   (# type:: fileError;
      predicate::
         (# do ('some text'->current.n.equal)->value #)
   do ...
   #)
```

4.5 Implementation Issues

Experimental implementations of this dynamic exception handling mechanisms have been done. This implementation demands a few extra efforts from the programmer using the facilities in order for it to be working reliable in all cases. A fully reliable implementation can fairly easy be facilitated with a little help from the runtime system. The prime problem is to be able to support non-local leave/restart, and to locate the dynamically nearest try block. However, on some implementations of the Mjølner System, these facilities are available.

4.6 Fault Tolerance Example

The following is a minor example illustrating the facilities of the dynamic exception handling model in BETA.

```
(# fileError: exception
      (# n: ^text
      do 'fileError Exception'->msg.puttext;
         INNER
      #);
   fileOSerror: fileError
      (# do '\nfileOSerror Exception'->msg.puttext #);
```

```
    P: (# fe: ^fileError;
       do &fileError[]->fe[]; 'someFileName'->fe.n[];
          fe[]->throw;
       #)
do ...
   try
      (# handler::
            (#
            do when(# type:: fileError;
                   do retry
                   #);
               when(# type:: exception
                  do 'Exception'->putline
                  #)
            #)
      do ...
         try
            (# handler::
                  (#
                  do when(# type:: fileOSError
                         do propagate
                         #);
                  #)
            do P
            #);
            ...
      #);
   ...
#)
```

5   Integrating Static and Dynamic Exception Handling in BETA

As the static and dynamic exception handling models have been presented above, they appear as totally separate mechanisms. In order to ensure fault tolerance with respect to exception handling, it is important that static exceptions can be handled through the dynamic exception handling mechanisms if they are not handled properly (i.e. if we are dealing with a poorly designed system).

Fortunately, we can integrate these two models by a fairly minor change in the definition of the static exception model, namely by making a slight change to the exception pattern.

In the definition given in Section 3.2, the consequence of not handling an exception is specified to be termination of the entire application. Instead, we could convert the static exception into a dynamic exception, and then try to leave the fault tolerance handling of these exceptions to the dynamic exception handling mechanisms. This can be accomplished by the new definition of the exception pattern given in Fig. 3.

```
exception:
  (# msg: @text;
     continue: @boolean;
  do INNER exception;
     (if not continue then
          (* throw the static exception as a dynamic
           * exception object
           *)
          this(exception)[]->throw;
     if)
  #);
```

Fig. 3: The exception pattern with dynamic throwing

With this new definition, we can now protect a given part of our code against poorly designed exception handling by catching all such static exceptions by means of a try block like:

```
try
  (# handler::
        (#
        do when:
             (# type:: exception
             do (* handle any static exception *)
                . . .
             #)
        #)
     . . .
  #)
```

And we can handle specific static exceptions by e.g.:

```
try
  (# handler::
        (#
        do when:
             (# type:: register.overflow;
             do (* handle register.overflow exception *)
                . . .
             #)
        #)
     . . .
  #)
```

Please note that the above do-part of the exception pattern is a little too simple since it does not take care of the details of avoiding the unknown exception to become thrown repeatedly. However, taking care of this is simple.

6 Handling Runtime Faults in BETA

The current version of the Mjølner System (release 5.2, Dec. 2000) does not offer any support for handling runtime faults (such as numeric errors, etc.). This is primarily due to the inability of the static approach to deal with faults (as explained in Section 4.1).

However, with the addition of the dynamic exception handling model, it is possible to introduce abilities for fault tolerant programming in the presence of e.g. runtime faults. The basic runtime system for BETA in the Mjølner System is being prepared for the introduction of dynamic exception handling in the presence of runtime faults. It is expected that the next major release of the Mjølner System will contain support for both dynamic exception handling in general, and specifically the handling of runtime faults.

In this work will also be the definition of a hierarchy of exceptions, modeling the different categories of runtime faults, that can occur (related for numeric computation, memory management, etc.). As part of this work will properly be a thorough investigation into the matter of execution control after the handling of an runtime fault. In some cases, it does not make sense e.g. to resume computation (e.g. if memory is exhausted). This investigation might reveal the need for supporting restrictions of the possible execution control, that is allowed for certain exceptions (e.g. that resumption is not allowed for memory exhausted exceptions). This is similar to the original Goodenough classification of exceptions into notifications, signals, etc. However, it is expected that the solution in BETA will be of a more dynamic nature, but time will tell.

Acknowledgements. The exception handling mechanism presented here has been developed during the implementation of The Mjølner System [7]. We greatly acknowledge the contributions made by all the members of the Mjølner System development team over the years.

Part of this work was presented at the ECOOP'2000 workshop on Exception Handling in Object-Oriented Systems [5], and the discussions at that workshop have help in clarifying some of the issues.

References

1. Goodenough, J.B.: Exception Handling: Issues and a Proposed Notion, *Comm. ACM*, 18(12), December 1975.
2. Gosling, J., Joy, B., Steele, G.: *The Java Language Specification*, Addison-Wesley, August 1996.
3. Knudsen, J.L.: Exception Handling – A Static Approach, *Software – Practice & Experience*, May 1984.
4. Knudsen, J.L.: Better Exception Handling in Block-structured Systems, *IEEE Software*, May 1987.

5. Knudsen, J.L.: Exception Handling versus Fault Tolerance. Presented at workshop on Exception Handling in Object-Oriented Systems (EHOOS'2000) at European Conference on Object-Oriented Programming (ECOOP'2000), France, June 2000, and reported in Romanovsky, A., Dony, C., Knudsen, J.L., Tripathi, A. (Eds.): Exception Handling in Object Oriented Systems. In J. Malenfant, S. Moisan, A. Moreira. (Eds.): *Object-Oriented Technology. ECOOP 2000 Workshop Reader.* LNCS-1964. pp. 16-31, 2000.

6. Madsen O.L., Møller-Pedersen, B., Nygaard, K.: *Object-Oriented Programming in the BETA Programming Language*, Addison Wesley, June 1993.

7. *The Mjølner System*: http://www.mjolner.com/mjolner-system.

8. Tennent, R.D.: Language Design Methods based on Semantic Principles, *Acta Infor matica*, 8(2), 1977.

A Fully Object-Oriented Exception Handling System: Rationale and Smalltalk Implementation

Christophe Dony

Montpellier-II University - LIRMM Laboratory
161 rue ADA, 34392.Montpellier Cedex 05.
dony@lirmm.fr
http://www.lirmm.fr/~dony

Abstract. This paper motivates and presents the specification and the implementation of an exception handling system for an dynamically typed object-oriented language. A full object-oriented representation of exceptions and handlers, a meta-object protocol to handle using either termination or resumption makes the system powerful as well as extendible and solves various exception handling issues. Three kind of dynamic scope handlers (expression handlers, class handlers and default ones) make it possible to define reusable and fault-tolerant software modules. The implementation of the system is readable and simple to understand because achieved entirely in Objectworks Smalltalk, thanks to the reflective facilities of this language.

1 Introduction

The program structures for handling exceptional events [7] [12] [13] [2] [24] [9] have been designed to implement software entities able to return well defined and foreseen answers, whatever may happen while they are active, even though an exceptional situation occurs. The end of the 1970s saw the development of exception handling systems dedicated to procedural programming. All specifications have all been influenced by Goodenough's seminal paper [7]. Well known implementations include MESA [15], CLU [13] or ADA [8]. Exception handling systems have later been integrated into object-oriented languages at the end of the 1980s (Zetalisp+Flavors [17], CommonLisp(+CLOS) [19], Eiffel [14], Objectworks Smalltalk [21], C++ [11], or more recently in Java.

This papers presents an overview of the specification and implementation of an exception handling system initially conceived [3] for the Lore Object-Oriented Language and adapted to Smalltalk [4]. The key-ideas of this system are (1) to apply object-oriented design to the whole system, to define a reusable and open class library for exception handling allowing systems designers to reuse it to produce dedicated exception handling systems and (2) to take into account the specificity of object-oriented programming by integrating expression and class handlers allowing users to define functional, class-based or even component-based fault tolerant modules.

Implementations of exception handling systems are rarely presented because they are generally done at a low level (compilers, virtual machines) and hard to describe in the context of a paper. The implementation of this system is reasonably readable and

A. Romanovsky et al. (Eds.): Exception Handling, LNCS 2022, pp. 18-38, 2001.

simple to understand because achieved entirely in Objectworks Smalltalk, thanks to the reflective facilities of this language. The main implementation issues detailed in the paper are: the internal representation of handlers, the algorithm for searching them - knowing that both resumption and termination are allowed, the achievement of termination and resumption, which takes into account some possible user-defined unwind protections. Our EHS has been specified and implemented as the same period than Objectworks Smalltalk's one and both share many similarities (except for class and default handlers) but none of their implementations have been published yet.

Section 2 recalls some definitions and introduces our notations. Section 3 presents our EHS specification and motivates the main choices. Section 4 presents the implementation. Point to point comparison with related works is scattered in the different sections. Sections 3 require that readers have a minimal knowledge of the Smalltalk syntax. Section 4 supposes a higher knowledge of that system but should be globally readable by anyone knowing object-oriented languages.

2   Definitions, Terminology, Notation

Software failures reveal either programming errors or the application of correct programs to an ill-formed set of data. An exception can be defined as a situation leading to an impossibility of finishing an operation. The problem of handling exceptions is to provide materials allowing to establish communication between a function or procedure which detects an exceptional condition, while performing an operation, and those functions or objects or modules that are clients of this operation (or have something to do with it) and wish to dynamically handle the situation. An exception handling system (**EHS**) allow users to signal exceptions and to associate handlers to entities (according to the language, an entity may be a program, a class, an object, a procedure, a statement or an expression). To *signal* an exception amounts to identify the exceptional situation, to interrupt the usual sequence of operations, to look for a relevant handler, to invoke it and to pass it relevant information about the exceptional situation, such as the context in which the situation arose. To *handle* means to set the system back to a coherent state. Handlers can usually choose, knowing about their definition context and using arguments provided by the signaler, whether to (1) transfer control to the statement following the signaling one (*resumption*), (2) discard the execution context between the signaling statement and the one to which the handler is attached (*termination*) or (3) signal the same or a new exception, which is generally called *propagation* and should be interpreted as a delegation of responsibility to a more general handler.

For the examples in this paper, we use two different syntax (cf. Figure 1) for handlers declaration and definitions: firstly a general one inspired of what can be found in procedural languages, secondly the Smalltalk syntax used in our system.

3   Specifications

This section discusses the main issues related to the design of an EHS in a non concurrent context, explains our choices and presents the specifications of our system.

"General Syntax":
{protected-instruction1; ...; protected-instructionN;
    {when exception (parameter) do
        {handling-instruction1; ...; handling-instructionN;}}}

"Smalltalk Syntax":
[protected-expression1 ... protected-expressionN]
    when: exception:
    do: [parameter | handling-instruction1 ... handling-instructionN]

Fig. 1. Syntax for associating handlers to instructions.

3.1   Resumption and Termination: a Dual Model

Choosing which control structures are available to write handlers bodies is one of the first crucial decision to be taken when designing an EHS and impacts the whole specification and implementation. Most exception handling systems only propose the termination model, others propose both termination and resumption (let us call this the **dual** model) and a few ones only propose resumption [12]. The respective merits of termination and resumption have already been widely discussed in many papers, e.g. [7, 13]. Let us just recall that to forbid termination is a very specific choice because many exceptions are really fatal. To forbid resumption is a way to produce EHS simple to use and to implement, although reducing the expressive power since some exceptions are really proceedable in some contexts. The resumption model is indeed more expensive in computation time and space, more complex to implement (see section 4) and also makes program static analysis more complex. It is however useful and time-saving in any application in which proceedable exceptions are raised, especially in interactive application in which users or operators, can choose a solution to recover from an exceptional situation. For example, interactive WEB applications can take benefit of resumption to restart calculus after a network interruption.

3.2   Handlers Scope and Fault-Tolerant Encapsulations

The scope of handlers, and as a consequence the way they are searched when an exception is signaled, determines what kinds of fault tolerant modules are offered by a system. The issue is the same whatever kind of modules are considered, classes, methods, etc.

Lexical Scope Handlers. Lexical scope handlers are by definition accessible when located in the program textual part in which they are lexically visible. A handler for an exception raised within an inner module, if not found locally, is searched in a lexically englobing one. Lexical scope handlers allow users to define modules that handle all exceptions raised within their scope, they allow to check statically which handler will be invoked for each exception signaled within the module. Their main drawback is that exceptions are never propagated to modules clients.

Various systems (e.g. Beta [9] or Smalltalk-80 [6, p.102]) provide lexical scope handlers. As an example, let us consider the standard Smalltalk-80 ones (cf. Figure 2). The Smalltalk historical EHS specification only uses the language standard constructions; this is the same for Beta and this is one of the great advantages of this static approach. Exceptions are signaled within methods by sending to *self*, a message (e.g. *error:*). Handlers are standard methods defined on classes (let us call them class handlers) and are invoked by a standard message sending: they can only be found in the class (or one of its super-classes, they are of course inherited) in which the signaling method is defined. This means that, as far as exceptions are never propagated to operations callers, a method has no way to regain control, either to hide the occurrence of an exception (modularity) or to execute some recovery actions, when one of the methods it has invoked failed. We come back in section 3.5 on the potential interest of class handlers in term of expressive power and reusability.

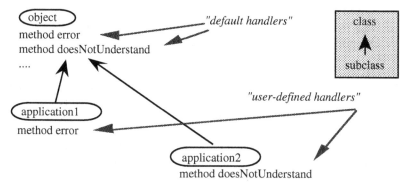

Fig. 2. Smalltalk-80 lexical scope class handlers

Dynamic Scope Handlers. On the other hand, dynamic scope handlers are searched in the execution stack when an exception is raised. They allow standard and exceptional responses to be specified in software modules interfaces. For a given module, internal exceptions are those handled internally, and external exceptions (sometimes called failures) those propagated to the module's clients. Dynamic scope handlers allow clients to retrieve control when the modules they use fail and to give execution context dependent answers to these failures. The semantic of the signaling process is then to transfer the problem from a place where it can only be noted to a place where it could be interpreted. The following example illustrates the first idea: the client module, a procedure *process-yield* correctly encapsulates its private's use of its a list by trapping the exceptions possibly raised by the list manipulation and by propagating an exception (*InactiveProcess*) of the same conceptual level than the achieved service. The second idea (giving caller context dependent answers) is illustrated the *pgcd* example. This is just a toy example, more expensive than the standard version without exception handling, but short enough to be presented here.

All handlers in our system have a dynamic scope. Most of earlier EHS for procedural languages such as *PL/I*, *Clu*, or *Mesa*, and recent ones, for object oriented languages (Clos, C++, Java) are based on a stack-oriented research of dynamic scope

---

procedure process-yeld (a-process)
    {remove(Active-process-list, a-process);
        {when itemNotFound(e) do
            {signal (InactiveProcess)}}}

function pgcd (int a, b)
    {loop {aux := a; a := b ; b := modulo(aux, b)};
        {when division-by-zero(e) do {exit(aux)}}}

---

handlers (limited to one stack level in CLU). New evolution of the *Beta* EHS integrates such handlers [10].

3.3   Status of Exceptions

The next issue to be discussed is the status of exceptions and of exceptional events. How are exceptions represented and referenced? How can they be manipulated or inspected?

Exceptional Events as First-Class Objects. The idea that consists in representing each conceptual exception by a class and each of its concrete occurrences (what we call exceptional events) as an instance (an exception object) of that class can initially be found in Taxis [18], *Zetalisp* [17] or [1] and is now almost a consensus; all todays object oriented systems have integrated it. Let us shortly recall its main interests.
- Exceptions can be organized into a knowledge sharing inheritance hierarchy.
- It is possible trap different events with a single handler.
- Signalers can communicate with handlers [16] pass to handlers the instance of the signaled exception which holds in its slots all the information about the exceptional situation.
- New user-defined exceptions can be created as subclasses of existing ones. There is no distinction between system and user-defined ones, all can be signaled and handled in the same way.

Exceptions as First Class Entities. The systems that pioneered the above idea did not brought it to its limits; for example in Zetalisp, signaling and handling primitive are not standard methods invocable by sending messages to exceptions objects. We have extended the above idea towards a complete object-oriented representation of all entities composing the EHS and towards an EH meta-object protocol to handle exceptions. Another language in which similar ideas can be found is Objectworks Smalltalk. The first step in that direction has led us to make conceptual exception first class entities by defining exception classes as instances of a metaclass. The Figure 3 shows the two kernel classes of our specification for what concerns exceptions representation. Each occurrence of an exception is an instance of a subclass of the class *ExceptionalEvent* that holds basic protocols for handling All exceptions classes are instances of the meta-class *ExceptionClass*[1] that holds basic protocols for signaling

---

[1] When explicitly manipulated, meta-classes are *Class* subclasses. In our *Smalltalk-80* implementation, *ExceptionClass* is implemented by the automatically created meta-class

and are subclass of *ExceptionalEvent*. The next sections detail the advantages of that organization.

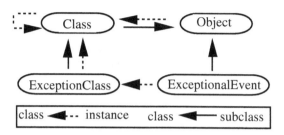

Fig. 3. Kernel exception classes.

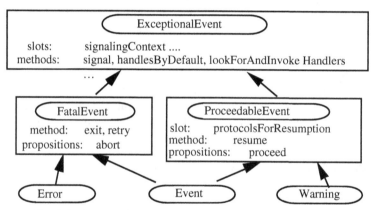

Fig. 4. Basic exception classes, associated attributes and methods.

3.4   Basic Primitives

The dual model of exception handling imposes that primitives for termination and resumption be available to write handler bodies. All our basic primitives to handle exceptions (*exit* and *retry* for termination, *resume* for resumption and *signal* for propagation) are implemented by standard methods defined on a set of kernel exception classes (cf. Figure 4) and constitute a meta-object protocol (following the CLos definition of term) for exception handling.

Kernel Exception Classes and Basic Handling Primitives. *ExceptionalEvent* is then divided into *FatalEvent*, to which are attached termination primitives, and *ProceedableEvent* to which are attached those for resumption. The slot

---

ExceptionalEvent class. Each exception class has its own (automatically created) meta-class subclass of *ExceptionalEvent class.*

signalingContext is to be dynamically bound at each occurrence of an exception to the signaling context. The slot *propositions* (instance variable of the meta-class) is used to store for each exception some propositions for interactive handling as initially proposed in Zetalisp. From the user's viewpoint, the system is then based on three predefined exception classes.

- *Error* is the class of exceptional events for which resumption is never possible whatever the context in which the event is signaled.
- *Warning* is the class of exceptional events for which the termination is impossible.
- Finally, multiple inheritance is simulated to create the exception-class *Event* in order to allow both capabilities.

Basic Signaling Primitive. Within EHSs supporting the dual model, a set of pri mitives is generally provided to support the various signaling cases. E.g., in Goodenough's proposal, signaling with *escape* states that termination is mandatory, *notify* forces resumption and *signal* lets the handler responsible for the decision. In our system, *signal* is the single basic signaling primitive because knowing whether the signaled exception is proceedable or not only depends of its type (its position in the exception hierarchy). To signal an exception amounts to send the exception class the message *signal* whose corresponding method is defined on *ExceptionClass* (i.e. on *ExceptionalEvent class* in the Smalltalk implementation). *Signal* creates the "exception object" and assigns its slots with, on the one hand values given by the signaler and on the other hand, values owned by the system (e.g. *signalingContext*), cf. Figure 5 for an example. *Signal* finally sends to the initialized instance the message *lookForAndInvokeHandler* (cf. Figure 4), which will find and invoke a handler.

3.5   Additional Primitives and Control Structures

Unconditional Restorations. The dual model raises various issues that require additional primitives. The first issue is the restoration of coherent program states. Any method has to ensure that it will leave data, memory and resources in a coherent state whatever happens during its execution. A first solution to that problem, found in many systems is to give programmers the ability to define handlers that trap all exceptions to re-signal (propagate) the trapped one. The following example illustrates that solution, in a procedural-like syntax with the classical file example. It also highlights the fact that this solutions forces programmers to write restoration actions twice, once for normal and once for exceptional exit.

```
File f;.
{open(f); workOn(f);. close(f);
    {when any-exception (e) do
        {close(f); signal(e);}}}
```

However, that solution does not work properly in the dual model because a later handler may entail resumption and put the system back into an incoherent state in which f would be closed but should not be. To avoid writing more complex handlers and the duplication of the *close* instruction, an ad-hoc. primitive (cf. cleanup handlers in [7] or Lisp's *unwind-protect*) is necessary to allow users to write unconditional restoration statements executed whenever the procedure's related stack frame is really discarded. The exception handling system has to take this primitive into account while performing termination, by executing in the right order and in the right environment the restorations (cf. Section 4.5). In our system, the file example can thus be written as follows:

```
f := File new.
[f.open. f.workOn.]
    unwindProtect: [f.close]]
```

Cooperation for Resumption. Resumption raises another important issue: it should not be achieved without the agreement of both the signaler and the handler when, although the handler is responsible for saying what to do, the effective computation restart is performed by the signaler in its environment. In any cases, the signaler should be able to predict which kind of restarts he is ready to achieve. A slot named *protocolForResumption*, defined on *ProceedableEvent* provides a basic solution to this problem[2]. The signaler can use it to indicate, at signaling time, the options among which a handler can choose in order to achieve resumption. Assigning it to *nil* means that resumption is impossible. In conjunction, a handler wanting to entail resumption has to indicate which protocols it has chosen. In the figure 5 example, handlers can for example use the message *messageValue:* which itself entails resumption by using the correct protocol.

```
Event subclass: #DoesNotUnderstand
    instanceVariableNames: 'messageReceiver messageSelector messageArgs '
    methodsFor: 'handling'
        messageValue:               "resume with a message value ..."
        newSelector:                "resume with a new selector ..."
        newReceiver:                "resume with a new receiver ..."
...................
Signaling the exception with propositions for resumption
result :=
    DoesNotUnderstand
        signalWithProtocolsForResumption:
                        #(supplyValue newReceiver newSelector)
                messageReceiver: anObject
                messageSelector: aSymbol
                messageArgs: anArray.
"if control returns here, result is tested and the corresponding actions performed"
```

Fig. 5. Example of definition of a new exception, to represent runtime message sending failure. Its occurrences are either proceedable or fatal; thus it is a subclass of *Event*. While signaling it, the signaler can pass arguments to handlers to indicate which kind of resumption it is ready to achieve.

---

[2][19] has proposed for this problem a more sophisticated solution: some new dedicated control structures (e.g. *restart-case*) provide a user-friendly way (with a case-like syntax) of writing code such as the one in the example and allow users to dynamically create new options for proceeding.

3.6   Various Kind of Handlers

This section deals with issues related to handler definition and shows how to create various kind of handlers in our system. It is first classical to associate handlers to pieces of code (expressions, blocks, procedure or programs). Besides, different researches have investigated the idea of associating handlers with data structures [12] thus controlling exceptional situations arising when manipulating them. Within an object-oriented language, it is also natural to wonder whether it is interesting to associate handlers to objects or to classes and with which semantics Finally many solutions have been proposed in existing systems to store the most general, execution context independent, default handlers

Expression Handlers. For what concerns pieces of code, we offer the possibility to associate handlers to any kind of Smalltalk expressions. This is done by grouping the expressions into a lexical closure[3] (a block in Smalltalk) and by sending this block the message *when:do*. The first argument *<exception-name>* is the exception to be trapped and the second one is the handler. Handlers have one parameter bound at handling-time to the current exception object.

```
[<protected expression>]
    when: <exception-name>
    do: [<handler parameter> | <handler body>]
```

Class Handlers. To associate handlers with individual objects is not compatible with the class-based model in which all instances of a class have to share the same behavior. Besides, we have quoted in section 3.2 the existence of handlers associated with classes in Smalltalk-80 and in Beta. We propose to define equivalent handlers but to give them a dynamic scope. A class handler associated with a class C for an exception E will thus be able to trap all occurrences of E raised anywhere during the execution of any method of C or of C's subclasses. Such class-handlers allow programmers to control which exceptions can be propagated outside of any methods of a class, to control for example, that *overflow* and *EmptyStack* are the only exceptions that can be propagated outside of any method defined on the class *Stack*. These class handlers also induce original reusability schemes based on inheritance. Consider again the class *Stack*. Now suppose that a class of stacks that are able to grow is needed. A simple solution to this consists is creating a *Stack* subclass named *GrowingStack*, on which is defined a handler for *overflow* and a method *grow*, this handler can resume the interrupted method, whatever its name and its location, after having grown the stack buffer. Class-handlers have been widely used in this way in Smalltalk-80 extensions to modify message sending, e.g. to implement *Encapsulator* or to implement asynchronous message sending in the Briot's *Actalk* System.

A few systems provide dynamic scope class handlers (see. e.g. [22]). In our system, class handlers can be attached to any class by using the method *when:do:*, defined on *ClassDescription*, with the following syntax:

---

[3]This is the price to pay to implement handler definition by a message sending.

<protected class>
    <u>when</u>: <exception-name>
    <u>do</u>: '<handler parameter> | <handler body>'

The first argument is the exception to be trapped and the second one is a string. This method *when:do:* first calls the Smalltalk compiler to compile the handler string in the environment of the protected class so that instance and class variables defined on the class can be accessed. Then it inserts the created handler in the handler collection of the class and of its subclasses. For each class, class-handlers are ordered compared to the exceptions they are defined for. Class-handlers cost nothing while exceptions are not signaled; they only are taken into account at signaling time.

Default Handers. Interesting but somehow semantically complex propositions to define default handlers at various program levels can be found e.g. in [20]. We have chosen a simpler point of view in which default handlers are considered as the place where the most general information regarding how to handle an occurrence of an exception, independently of any execution context, should be stored. We propose to associate them to exceptions by defining them as methods (named *defaultHandle*) defined on exception classes. The system most general default handler is defined on *ExceptionalEvent* and can be overridden in subclasses, each exception can thus own its specific default handler. Default handlers are invoked by sending the message *defaultHandle* to the exception object as shown in the top-level loop example (cf. Section 3.7). We have integrated the idea of interactive propositions found in Zetalisp, which exploits exception hierarchies. A proposition is a couple of two method names, one to display a string and one to execute a corresponding action. Propositions are stored for each exception in the slot named *propositions* defined on *ExceptionClass* and displayed when the most general default handler is invoked.

3.7   Writing Handlers Bodies in a Generic Way

All kind of handlers can use the same primitives in the same generic way to put the program execution back into a coherent state. Genericity first means that neither programmers nor implementors have to perform tests to ensure that operations incompatible with the signaled exception will not be invoked - Note that his rule is violated for resumption where the slot *protocolForResumption* is tested by the system. For example, any attempt to send the message *exit:* to an object which is not a *FatalEvent* will fail. Genericity also means that the operations relevant to the current exception object will automatically be selected even though an abstract (multiple) exception has been caught.

Termination Examples. Sending to the exception object the message *exitWith:* entails termination. The execution stack frames located between the signaler and the handler are discarded while recovery blocks are executed. The argument's value becomes the value returned by the expressions to which the handler is attached. Here is our system's version of the above function *pgcd*, now defined on class *Integer*, that uses termination.

"computes the pgcd of a and b"
    [[true] whiletrue: [aux := a.   a := b.   b := aux modulo: b]]
        when: division-by-zero
        do: [:e | e exitWith: aux]

For what concerns a class-handler, which is invoked when an exception is about to be propagated outside of a method *C* defined on a protected class, termination ends *C*'s execution and the exit value becomes the value returned by *C*'s invocation. The following example is an implementation of the growing stack example described in Section 3.6, it highlights the interest of the *retry* primitive.

GrowingStack
    when: Overflow
    do: [:anOverflow | self grow.
                        anOverflow retry].

Finally, default-handlers are conceptually attached to the program main procedure (or to the top-level loop in an interpreted environment), thus termination in a default-handler ends the program execution (or returns to the top-level). Here is an example of applying termination that uses both *exit* and *retry* , to implement a top-level loop. The only way to exit the loop is to signal the exception *LoopExit*. If any other exception is trapped, its default handler is invoked and finally, whatever it does, the loop is re-entered.

[[true] whileTrue: [((aStream.read).eval).print]]
    when: LoopExit
    do: [aLoopExit: | aLoopExit exitWith: #bye]
    when: ExceptionalEvent
    do: [anExcEvent: | anExcEvent defaultHandle.
                        anExcEvent retry]

Resumption Example. Sending to the exception object the message "*resumeWith: <aResumptionOption> with: <aValue>*" entails resumption. The couple *<option, value>* becomes the value returned by the method *signal* provided that the option belongs to the *protocolsForResumption* collection of the signaled exception.

[anObject aMessage]
    when: DoesNotUnderstand
    do: [e: | e resumeWith: #SupplyValue with: 33]

Propagation Example. Signaling a new exception or propagating the trapped one can be done by sending the message *signal* either to a new exception (a class), or to the exception object. Here is an illustration with the previously described *stack* examples (cf. Section 3.5) which shows how to control, with class handlers, which exceptions will be propagated outside of any methods defined on *Stack* or on its subclasses. The second handler for *ExceptionalEvent* traps all exceptions, except *Overflow* and *EmptyStack*, and propagates *StackInternalException*.

Stack
    when: #(Overflow EmptyStack)
    do: ':exceptionObject | exceptionObject signal'   *"propagation"*
    when: ExceptionalEvent
    do: 'exceptObject: | StackInternalException signal' *"new exception signaled"*

4   Implementation

This section describes some key-points of the above specification implementation which is entirely achieved in *Objectworks Smalltalk* without any modification to the virtual machine. This has been possible thanks to the reflective capabilities offered by this programming environment, particularly because methods, lexical closures and the execution stack are or can be made first class objects. The main focus is put on the representation of exceptions, of handlers and on the signaling algorithm taking into account expression, class and default handlers within a context in which both resumption and termination are allowed. The interest of this section is to describe this algorithm in its real implantation context.

Objectworks Smalltalk EHS specification has considerably evolved since the blue book specification and share many common points with our specification, except for what concerns class handlers and less importantly interactive propositions. The implementation of Objectworks EHS, as far as I know never described in any paper, also shares common point with ours but is more efficient because part of it have been moved to the virtual machine. In particular, stack frames are no more reified but are accessed at the virtual machine level.

4.1   Exception Classes

The class *ExceptionalEvent* (cf. Figure 6), the root of our exception classes hierarchy, declares four instance variables, three of them are of interest here. *SignalingContext* is used to store the stack frame (we will frequently call stack frame "contexts" because Smalltalk objects that represent them are called "contexts objects") in which the exception has been signaled. *HandlerContext* is used to store the context in which a handler is found. *ErrorString* allows users to pass a string argument to handlers. *ExceptionalEvent* also declares different class variables, four of which (*BottomStackMethod, HandleMethod, InvokeHandlerMethod* and *UnwindMethod*) designed to store references to particular methods addresses that will be used during handler research and invocation.

Note for example that the method *when:do:* allowing users to define expression handlers is represented by a Smalltalk object that can be retrieved by sending to the class *BlockClosure*, on which the method is defined, the message *compiledMethodAt:*. *SpecialMark* contains a unique mark used to implement the *retry* method Finally, this class also defines an interactive proposition named *askForRetry*.

Object subclass: #**ExceptionalEvent**
   instanceVariableNames: 'errorString signalingContext handlerContext private '
   classVariableNames: 'BottomStackMethod HandleMethod InvokeHandlerMethod
                RetryMark UnwindMethod '

initialize   *"defined on ExceptionalEvent class"*
   HandleMethod := BlockClosure compiledMethodAt: #when:do:.
   UnwindMethod := BlockClosure compiledMethodAt: #unwindProtect:.
   BottomStackMethod
     := SmalltalkCompiler compiledMethodAt: #evaluate:in:to:notifying:ifFail:.
   InvokeHandlerMethod := ExceptionalEvent compiledMethodAt: #invokeHandler:with:.
   RetryMark := #().

Fig. 6. *ExceptionalEvent* class (detail)

4.2   Status and Storage of Handlers

Default handlers are standard methods defined on exceptions classes under the selector *handlesDefault*. They do not raise any structure or storage problems.

Handlers Associated to Expressions. Handlers associated to expressions have to be executed in the environment in which they have been created. The resumption model forbids destroying the stack frames located between the signaler frame and the handler frame in order to allow the calculus to be eventually restarted. To invoke a handler thus supposes to go back to a previously defined environment without destroying the execution stack. A first solutions to this problem is to copy the stack at signaling time (e.g. with an equivalent of the scheme *call-cc* primitive), to destructively search a handler, to execute the handler in its context, now located on top of the stack, and finally to replace the current stack by the copy made at signaling time. We have neither implemented this solution nor seen it implemented. A second solution is to execute the handler on top of the stack but in its definition context, i.e. in such a way that free variables of the handler get their value and are assigned in the handler definition context. This supposes that handlers be lexical closures.

   The method *when:do:* to associate handlers to expressions is defined (cf. below) on the class *BlockClosure* that represents lexical closures in Smalltalk. The receiver (*self*) is a block containing the protected expressions. The method simply sends *self* the message *value*, which entails the execution of the protected expressions. If an exception is raised during this execution, the system will find the handler as the second argument (*handlerBlock*) stored in the stack frame created by the method *when:do:*.

---

when: exception **do:** handlerBlock   *"Defined on BlockClosure"*
   ^self value

Handlers Associated to Classes. Handlers associated to classes are some kind of compiled methods, of which they inherit the basic structure, the specific part of their structure being described by the *ClassHandler* class (see below). The instance variable *domain* stores the class on which the class handler has been defined, for example, the class *GrowingStack* for our Section 3.6 example. The *event* instance variable stores the exception for which the class is protected (*Overflow* in our example). The instance variable *receiver* is to be bound at handler invocation time to the object that is active when the trapped exception is raised.

CompiledMethod subclass: #**ClassHandler**
    instanceVariableNames: 'event domain receiver '
    classVariableNames: 'SortBlock '

Class-handlers are stored for each class into a sorted collection from the most specific to the most general. For that purpose, we have added an instance variable named *classHandlerSet* to the kernel class *ClassDescription* with defines the basic structure of all Smalltalk classes. Albeit they have a compiled method status, class-handlers are not stored in the classes method dictionary for three reasons: they should not to be directly invoked by users, they are not connected to external selectors and they have to be stored in a specific order.

4.3   Signaling

In its simplest form, signaling simply consists in creating the exception object, an instance of the class that receives the *signal* message, in initializing its fields and in sending to the exception object a message to look for handlers. See next section for an explanation about the *thisContext* variable.

---

signal   *"defined on ExceptionalEvent class"*
    ^self new initialize signal

signal   *"defined on ExceptionalEvent "*
    signalingContext := thisContext.
    ^self lookForAndInvokeHandler

4.4   Handler Search

This section describes the method that looks for a handler after an exception has been raised. A simplified version is primarily presented. The complete version is described afterwards.

Accessing the Stack. As far as handlers are searched into the stack, the first issue is to access it. The Objectworks environment is able, when asked, to represent the execution stack frames as first-class objects, instances of various subclasses of the *Context* class. This is powerful example of reflection because that object can not only be viewed but also modified. Modifying the slot sender of such an object effectively produces a non local jump when returning from the method in which the modification is done. At any time during a computation, creating the object representing the current stack frame can be done by accessing the read-only variable called *thisContext*. Its slots contain all the information needed to implement our system:
- the receiver of the message the execution of which has created the frame,
- the method that has been invoked as a consequence of this message,
- the sender of the current frame, i.e. the calling frame lower in the stack.

A Simplified Algorithm for Finding Handlers. Figure 7 describes a simplified algorithm that search a handler without taking into account exceptions signaled within handlers. When a handler is found, it is immediately invoked.

The Implementation of the Simplified Algorithm. Figure 8 shows the method implementing this simplified algorithm. The *lookForAndInvokeHandler* method is defined on *ExceptionalEvent* and invoked while signaling by sending this message to the exception object. Within this method, *self* is the current exception object for which a handler is searched.

- The search starts at the signaling context sender. The signaling context is retrieved in the *signalingContext* instance variable of the exception object (Figure 8, line 1). *UnwindContexts* is a local variable used to monitor the collection of recovery actions found while going down the stack.

- A loop is entered (2) and will be exited, by returning ("^" is the smalltalk's return instruction.) the value of the method *invokeHandler:with:*; control never returns to the instruction following the *invokeHandler:with:* message sending.

Let E be the signaled exception,
Let F initially be the sender of the stack frame in which the message *signal* has been sent,
Let UnwindContexts be an empty ordered collection.

L: **If** F is the bottom of the stack frame
   then invoke default handler for E
   else   **If** the frame F has been established by an invocation of the method *when:do:*
        and if the associated handler H traps the exception E,
        then invoke H.
        else   let C be the class of the receiver of the current frame method.
             If a handler H for the exception E is defined on C,
             then invoke H.
             else if F has been established by an invocation of unwindProtect:,
                  then   append the argument to UnwindContexts **end-if**
                  let F be F 's sender (stack previous frame) and goto L.
             end-if
        end-if
   end-if

Fig. 7. A simplified version of the algorithm to search a handler.

- When a handler is found, this method (cf. section 4.5) is called (lines 5,8,12) with the handler as first argument and the unwind blocks collection monitored during the search as second argument. The handler is either a block or a kind of compiled method. The stack frame in which it is located is stored in the *handlerContext* slot of the exception object (4, 7, 10) and will be used to achieve handling.

- The test in (3) is true when the bottom of the stack is reached. This means that no expression or class handler has been found. A default handler is invoked by sending the message *handlesDefault* to the exception object (5).

---

lookForAndInvokeHandler

    "defined on ExceptionalEvent"
| currentContext classHandler method | *"local variables"*
currentContext := signalingContext sender.   (1)
unwindContexts := OrderedCollection new.
[true] whileTrue: (2)
    [method := currentContext method.
    "if the bottom of the stack is reached, invoke default handlers"
    (method == BottomStackMethod)   (3)
      ifTrue: [handlerContext := currentContext sender.   (4)
          ^self invokeHandler: [:e | e handlesDefault] with: unwindContexts]   (5)
      ifFalse: [
    "looking for an expression handler"
      (method == HandleMethod and:
              [self isKindOf: (currentContext localAt: 1)])   (6)
        ifTrue:
        [handlerContext := currentContext.   (7)
        ^self invokeHandler: (currentContext localAt: 2)
              with: unwindContexts]   (8)
    "looking for a class handler in the class of the current context receiver"
      classHandler := currentContext receiver class isProtectedFor: self.   (9)
      classHandler isNil ifFalse: [
      handlerContext := currentContext.   (10)
      classHandler receiver: currentContext receiver.   (11)
      ^self invokeHandler: classHandler with: unwindContexts]   (12)
    "no handler here, but check if this context contains an unwind blocks"
      (method == UnwindMethod)   (13)
        ifTrue: [unwindContexts addLast: (currentContext localAt: 1)].   (14)
    "no handler here, going down one frame"
      currentContext := currentContext sender   (15)
    ] *"end of ifFalse: method == BottomStackMethod"*
  ] *"end of the while loop*

Fig. 8. An implementation of the simplified algorithm in Fifure 7.

- The test in (6) is true if the current frame method is *when:do:* and if the exception object is an element of the class a reference to which is stored in the first argument of the method (arguments of the current frame method can be accessed by sending the message *localAt:* to the context object). This means that an expression handler has been found. Its body is stored in the second argument of the *when:do:* method(8).

- The method *isProtectedFor:* sent to the class C of the receiver of the current frame method, returns either a class-handler for the current exception if one is present on C or nil. In the first case, the handler is invoked (12). Before that, the receiver in the method that raised the exception is stored in the class handler's *receiver* slot (11).

- Lines 13 and 14 deal with unconditional recovery actions defined in unwind blocks. If only termination was supported, this would be the place to execute these actions. Supporting the dual model (termination and resumption) imposes to monitor all unwind blocks found between the signaling context and the handler context, to pass that collection to the handler and to execute them if the handler entails termination.

- In (15), no handler has been found in the current frame, the loop's body is entered again with the variable *currentContext* pointing to the previous stack frame.

The Complete Version Taking into Account Exceptions Signaled Within Handlers.

The real algorithm is more complex since it supports the dual model (termination and resumption) which imposes that handlers be executed while the signaling context has not been destroyed. The algorithm has thus to ensure that, when an exception is signaled within a handler (either an expression, class or default one), the new search starts just below the frame in which the current handler has been found, thus preventing its recursive invocation. Signaling the exception *InactiveProcess* in the handler for *ItemNotFound* is an example of such as situation as shown in Section 3.2. Figure 9 presents the complete version of the method that looks for and invoke handlers.

- The test in line 9 determines whether the current frame has been created by the invocation of *invokeHandler:with:*. If true, this means that the current exception has been raised within a handler and execution continues in line 9. Otherwise the standard algorithm described in the previous section is executed (line 21).
- In line 9, let e2 be the current exception object and h1 be the handler that as been invoked to trap the first exception e1. The current context objet represents the frame created by the invocation of h1; its *receiver* slot contains the exception object e1.
- It is first necessary to update the *unwindContexts* collection by concatenating ("," is the concatenation operation) (lines 11 and 12) the current recovery action collection to the collection collected during the search for h1 which is stored in the stack as the second argument of the current context method. When found, the handler h2 for e2 will have in hand the whole set of recovery actions found between e1 signaling frame and h2 definition frame, to be executed if h2 entails a termination.
- The handler for e2 now has to be searched below the frame in which h1 has been defined and which is stored in e1's *handlerContext* slot. As specified by the instruction in line 13, the *currentContext* is assigned to h1 definition context.
- Before continuing the search in the previous frame (line 20) a special case has to be handled. If h1 is a default handler, its definition context is the bottom of the stack frame and in such a case, tested in line 14, the search is stopped and the most general default handler has to be invoked (line 18).

4.5   Handler Invocation

The method to invoke handlers is shown in Figure 10. All handlers (either lexical closure or class-handlers) are invoked by receiving the *value:* message with argument the current exception objet (cf. Figure 10, line 5). Two marks are stored in the stack

---

LookForAndInvokeHandler   *"defined on ExceptionalEvent"*
| currentContext classHandler method unwindContexts dejaVus |
unwindContexts := OrderedCollection new.   (2)
currentContext := signalingContext.   (3)
[true] whileTrue: [(4)
  method := currentContext method.   (5)
  (method == BottomStackMethod)   (6)
   ifTrue: [handlerContext := currentContext sender. (7)
      ^self invokeHandler: [:e | e handlesDefault] with: unwindContexts.].   (8)
  "Detection of exceptions signaled within handlers"
  [method == InvokeHandlerMethod   (9)
   ifTrue: [*"The current exception has been raised within a handler"*   (10)
   "a) dealing with unwind-protections"
   dejaVus := (currentContext localAt: 2) copy.   (11)
   dejaVus isNil ifFalse: [unwindContexts := unwindContexts , dejaVus].   (12)
   "b) jump to the handler context"
   currentContext := currentContext receiver handlerContext.   (13)
   "c) Was the exception signaled within a default handler?"
   currentContext method == BottomStackMethod   (14)
    ifTrue: ["*Direct invocation of the most general default handler"*   (15)
     handlerContext := currentContext.   (17)
     ^self invokeHandler:
      [:e | e basicHandlesDefault] with: unwindContexts]   (18)
    ifFalse: ["*search will continue at the handler context sender"*   (19)
      currentContext := currentContext sender]]   (20)
   ifFalse: [(21)
  "same code than lines 6 to 15 in Figure 8"

Fig. 9. The complete version of handler search.

(lines 3 and 5) just below that invocation point using the method *mark:catch:* which is an equivalent of the classical lisp *catch* function.

Termination will be implemented by a non local exit to the mark named *#exit* and resumption by a non local exit to the mark named *#resume* (see next section). If termination is ordered, control reaches line 7. There, all unconditional restorations monitored during the handler search are executed by the method *fastUnwind:*. Then the current execution frame is assigned to the handler context (line 8); this effectively discards all stack frames between the signaling and the handling point. Finally, the given exit value is tested (line 9). If this value equals the retry dedicated special mark, a retry has been ordered and the expressions to which the handler were associated are executed again (line 10), otherwise the exit value is simply returned as the value of these expressions (line 11). If resumption is ordered, control reaches line (12) and the resume value is simply returned as the value of the handler invocation. It is the responsibility of the signaler to examine the returned value and to achieve the selected solution to restart the standard execution.

Termination. Termination is simply implemented within the *exit* primitive (cf. Figure 11) by a destructive non local exit down to the *#exit* mark previously stored in the stack. The method *mark:exit:* is an equivalent of the *throw* classical lisp function. If the retry protocol is chosen, the value passed to *throw* is our registered special mark.

invokeHandler: aHandler **with:** unwindContexts	
"defined on ExceptionalEvent"	
| exitValue resumeValue |	
"local variables"	(1)
resumeValue :=	(2)
self mark: #resume catch:	(3)
[exitValue :=	(4)
self mark: #exit catch:	(5)
[aHandler value: self].	(6)
self fastUnwind: unwindContexts.	(7)
thisContext sender: handlerContext	(8)
exitValue == SpecialMark	(9)
ifTrue: [handlerContext restart]	(10)
ifFalse: [^exitValue]].	(11)
"control reaches that point if resumption has been ordered."	
^resumeValue	(12)

Fig. 10. Handler Invocation.

Resumption. Resumption (cf. Figure 12) is simply implemented by a destructive non local exit towards the #resume mark previously stored in the stack at handler invocation time. The *resumeWith:with:* primitive checks that the handler has chosen a protocol for resumption effectively proposed by the signaler before entailing the non local exit.

"Methods defined on FatalEvent class"
retry
    "exit and execute protected operation again."
    self mark: #exit throw: SpecialMark.
exit
    self exitWith: nil.!
exitWith: aValue
    self mark: #exit throw: aValue.

Fig. 11. Implementing Termination

There is no room to present other aspects of the system such as interactive propositions; however, their implementation does not raise any problem. The complete implementation can be downloaded from the author WEB page.

"Methods defined on ProceedableEvent class"
resume
    self resumeWith: #resume with: nil!
resumeWith: aSymbol **with:** aValue
    (protocolForResumption indexOf: aSymbol) == 0
        ifTrue: [Error signal:
                The proposed option for proceeding is not valid ...']
        ifFalse: [self mark: #resume
                throw: (Association key: aSymbol value: aValue)]

Fig. 12. Implementing resumption.

5   Conclusion

We have presented a specification and implementation of an open and expressive exception handling system for a dynamically typed object-oriented language. It provides a full object-oriented representation of exceptions and handlers. This now classical organization allows users to organize exceptions in an inheritance hierarchy reflecting the possible sharing of structures and behavior, and to trap any subset of exceptions with a single handler. The ability to define handling primitive on classes and to invoke them via message sending to the exception object makes it impossible to perform an inappropriate action for a given exception. The distribution of handling primitives on various abstract exception classes simplifies the signaling process by restricting the number of signaling primitives. Handlers can be associated to expressions and classes. We have shown the interest of associating dynamic scope handlers with classes. Class handlers are more than a powerful shorthand, they induce original ways to use inclusion polymorphism reusability.

This system architecture can also be considered as a framework for developing dedicated exception handling systems. It is for example very easy to use it to generate, by subclassing, other systems in which, for example, resumption or termination are forbidden. Its meta-object protocol for handing, made of a set of methods defined on exception classes, can be used as a basis to add new and dedicated EH control structures. We can see today a renewest interest for open, reflective and dynamically typed languages used for example to assemble components (cf. [5]) or to develop WEB applications that require powerful and flexible exception handling systems similar to the one presented here.

We finally have presented the key issues of the implementation of the dual model of exception handling in the context of a reflective, dynamically.typed object-oriented langage.

References

1.   A.Borgida: Language Features for Flexible Handling of Exceptions in Information Systems. ACM Transactions on Database Systems, Vol. 10, No. 4, pp. 565-603, December 1985.

2.   F.Christian: Exception Handling and Software Fault-Tolerance. IEEE Trans. on Computers, Vol. C-31, No. 6, pp. 531-540, June 1982.
3.   C.Dony: An Exception Handling System for an Object-Oriented Language. Procs of.ECOOP'88, 1988; Lectures Notes in Comp. Sci. 322, pp. 146-161.
4.   C.Dony: Exception handling & Object-Oriented Programming: Towards a Synthesis. Proceedings of the Joint conference ECOOP-OOPSLA'90, Ottawa, Oct. 1990. Special issue of Sigplan Notices, Vol. 25, No 10, pp. 322-330.
5.   A.F. Garcia, C.M.F.Rubira; Architectural-based Reflective Approach to Incorporating Exception Handling into Dependable Software. In [23].
6.   A. Goldberg, D. Robson: SMALLTALK 80, the language and its implementation. Addison Wesley 1983.
7.   J.B.Goodenough: Exception Handling: Issues and a Proposed Notation. Communication of the ACM, Vol. 18, No. 12, pp. 683-696, December 1975.
8.   J.Ichbiah & al: Preliminary ADA Reference Manual. Rationale for the Design of the ADA Programming Language. Sigplan Notices Vol. 14, No. 6, June 1979.
9.   J.L.Knudsen: Better Exception Handling in Block Structured Systems. IEEE Software, pp 40-49, May 1987.
10.   J.L.Knudsen: Exception Handling and Fault Tolerance in Beta. In [23].
11.   A. Koenig, B. Stroustrup: Exception Handling for C++. Proceedings of Usenix'90, pp. 149--176, San Francisco, USA, April 1990.
12.   R.Levin: Program structures for exceptional condition handling. Ph.D. dissertation, Dept. Comp. Sci., Carnegie-Mellon University Pittsburg, June 1977.
13.   B.Liskov, A.Snyder: Exception Handling in CLU. IEEE Trans. on Software Engineering, Vol. SE-5, No. 6, pp. 546-558, Nov 1979.
14.   B.Meyer: Disciplined exceptions. Interactive Software Engineering, TR-EI-22/EX, 1988.
15.   J.G.Mitchell, W.Maybury, R.Sweet: MESA Language Manual. Xerox Research Center, Palo Alto, California, Mars 1979.
16.   R. Miller, A. Tripathi: Issues with Exception Handling in Object-Oriented Systems. ECOOP '97 proceedings, Lecture Notes in Computer Science", Vol. 1241, pp. 85--103, Mehmet Aksit and Satoshi Matsuoka editors, Springer-Verlag 1997.
17.   D. Moon, D. Weinreb: Signaling and Handling Conditions. LISP Machine Manual, MIT AI-Lab., Cambridge, Massachussets, 1983.
18.   B.A.Nixon: A Taxis Compiler. Tech. Report 33, Comp. Sci. Dept., Univ. of Toronto, April 83.
19.   K.Pitman: Error/Condition Handling. Contribution to WG16. Revision 18.Propositions pour ISO-LISP. AFNOR, ISO/IEC JTC1/SC 22/WG 16N15, April 1988.
20.   K.Pitman: Condition Handling in the Lisp Language Family. In [23].
21.   Objectworks for Smalltalk-80, version 2.5. Advanced User's Guide - Exception Handling. ParcPlace systems, 1989.
22.   Jan Purchase, Russel Winder: Message Pattern Specifications: A New Technique for Handling Bugs in Parallel Object Oriented Systems. ACM SIGPLAN Notices, vol. 25, no. 10, pp. 116--125, October 1990.
23.   Advances in Exception Handling Techniques, Alexander Romanovsky, Christophe Dony, Jorgen Knudsen, Anand Tripathy Editors, Springer-Verlag, 2001.
24.   S.Yemini, D.M.Berry: A Modular Verifiable Exception-Handling Mechanism. ACM Trans. on Progr. Languages and Systems, Vol. 7, No. 2, pp. 213-243, April 1985

Condition Handling in the Lisp Language Family

Kent M. Pitman

kmp@alum.mit.edu

1 Introduction

The Lisp family of languages has long been a rich source of ideas and inspiration in the area of error handling. Here[1] we will survey some of the abstract concepts and terminology, as well as some specific language constructs that Lisp has contributed.

Although there are numerous dialects of Lisp, several of which offer the modern concepts and capabilities described herein, we will focus specifically on Common Lisp as described in the ANSI standard, X3.226-1994 [5].

1.1 Condition Systems vs Error Systems

The Common Lisp community typically prefers to speak about its **condition system** rather than its **error system** to emphasize that there are not just fatal but also non-fatal situations in which the capabilities provided by this system are useful.

Not all **exceptional situations** are represented, or sometimes even detected. A situation that *is* represented within the language is referred to in Common Lisp as a **condition**; an object of class CONDITION is used to represent such a situation.

A **condition** is said to be the generalization of an **error**. Correspondingly, within the language the class CONDITION is a superclass of another class ERROR, which represents situations that would be fatal if not appropriately managed.

So the set of all situations involving conditions includes not only descriptions of outright erroneous situations but also descriptions of situations that are merely unusual or questionable. Even in the case of non-error conditions, the programmer may, as a matter of expressive freedom, choose to use the same capabilities and protocols as would be used for "real" error handling.

1.2 Condition Handling is Primarily a Protocol Matter

To properly understand condition handling, it is critical to understand that it is primarily about **protocol**, rather than mere computational ability. The establishment of protocols is a sort of before-the-fact hedge against the "prisoner's dilemma"; that is, it creates an obvious way for two people who are not directly

---

[1] © 2001 Kent M. Pitman. All Rights Reserved.

A. Romanovsky et al. (Eds.): Exception Handling, LNCS 2022, pp. 39–59, 2001.
© Springer-Verlag Berlin Heidelberg 2001

communicating to structure independently developed code so that it works in a manner that remains coherent when such code is later combined.

For example, if we want to write a program that searches a list for an object, returning true if the object is present and false otherwise, we could write the following, but would ordinarily not:

```
(defun search-list (goal-item list-to-search)
  (handler-case
      ;; Main body
      (progn (dolist (item list-to-search)
               (when (eq item goal-item)
                 (return-from search-list t)))
             ;; Search has failed, signal an error.
             (error 'search-failure
                    :item goal-item))
    ;; Upon error, just return false.
    (error () nil)))
```

The reason not to write this is not that it will not work, but that it involves undue amounts of unneeded mechanism. The language already contains simpler ways of expressing transfer of control from point A to point B in a program where the same programmer, acting in the same role, controls the code at both points. For example, the following would suffice:

```
(defun search-list (goal-item list-to-search)
  (dolist (item list-to-search)
    (when (eq item goal-item)
      (return-from search-list t)))
  nil)
```

However, if the intended action in the case of a failing search were not specified, and was to be provided by the caller, the use of condition handling mechanisms might be appropriate. For example, in the following code, only the signaling is occurring, and the handling is being left to the caller. Because of this, the use of condition handling facilities is appropriate because those facilities will provide matchmaking and data transport services between the signaler and the handler.

```
(defun search-list (goal-item list-to-search)
  (dolist (item list-to-search)
    (when (eq item goal-item)
      (return-from search-list t)))
  (error 'search-failure :item goal-item))
```

Protocol is simply not needed when communicating lexically among parts of a program that were written as a unit and that are not called by other programs that are either logically separated or, at minimum, logically separable. The distinction is subjective, but it is nevertheless important.

2   Historical Influences

Before beginning to look in detail at the features of Common Lisp's condition system, it's useful to observe that computer languages, like human languages, evolve over time both to accommodate current needs and to repair problems observed in past experience. The interesting features of the Common Lisp condition system were not suddenly designed one day as a spontaneous creative act, but rather grew from many years of prior experience in other languages and systems.

2.1   Influence of Multics PL/I on Symbolics Zetalisp

The PL/I language, designed at IBM in the early 1960's, included an extensive condition mechanism which had an extensible set of named signals and dynamic handlers running in the dynamic context of the signal. Since PL/I included "downward" lexical closures these handlers had access to the erring environment, and sometimes to the details of the error.

Multics [1], whose official language was PL/I, adapted and extended this, including the addition of `any_other`, `cleanup`, and `unclaimed_signal`, the passing of machine conditions and other arbitrary data, cross-protection-domain signals, and the use of this mechanism to manage multiple suspended environments on one stack.

Multics divided its address space into concentric "rings" of increasing privilege; this technique, now widely accepted, originated with Multics. The Multics operating system relied on their expanded signaling system for several critical system functions, mostly in the user ring, although cross-ring signals were possible, typically in cases of paging or memory errors.

Historically, Multics was an "early" environment, but it was not, by any analysis, a toy. Its condition system was carefully designed, heavily tested, and had many important characteristics that influenced the later design of Lisp:

- It separated the notion of *condition signaling* from *condition handling.*
- It offered the possibility of resuming an erring computation, presumably after correcting the offending situation. A portion of this capability was also available to the interactive user if automatic handling did not succeed through the use of of the `pi` command, which would signal a `program_interrupt` condition, allowing the errant application to regain control by handling that condition; a typical handler for `program_interrupt` might transfer control back to some pending command level, effectively aborting the erring computation.
- It began to deal with the mediation of signaling and handling through not only a *condition type* but also a set of associated data appropriate to that type: By using a system-defined operator called "`signal_`" instead of the normal PL/I "`signal`", a data block could be associated with the condition being signaled, a crude precursor to the idea of object-oriented condition descriptions that followed later in Lisp.

– It began to deal with the notion of default handling, through the use of the `unclaimed_signal` pseudocondition.

Some of these capabilities, in turn, originated with PL/I itself; for example: the notion of a named signal and the notion of running a handler in the dynamic context of the signaler rather than later after a stack unwind. However, these ideas of PL/I had been elaborated in the Multics environment, and it was from that elaborated environment that the transition to Lisp arose.

In the early 1980's, some former users of the Multics system, including Daniel L. Weinreb, Bernard Greenberg and David Moon, harvested the good ideas of the Multics PL/I condition system and recast them into Zetalisp, a dialect running on the Symbolics Lisp Machines. This redesign was called simply the "New Error System" (or sometimes just "NES").

2.2   Influence of Symbolics Zetalisp on Common Lisp

Key elements of the New Error System (NES) in Symbolics Zetalisp were:

– NES had an object-oriented nature.
– NES clearly separated the treatment of exceptional situations into three logically distinct programming activities:
    – Establishing handlers.
    – Managing "proceed types" (what Common Lisp later called "restarts").
    – Detecting exceptional situations and signaling appropriate conditions.
– NES provided for erring programs to be resumed either interactively or non-interactively, separating information about prompting for replacement data from the conduits that would carry such data so that programs wishing to do mechanical recovery could bypass the prompting but use the rest of the recovery pipeline.

NES directly and strongly influenced the design of the Common Lisp condition system. In fact, one initial concern voiced by a number of vendors was that they were fearful that somehow the ideas of the condition system, being taken from the Lisp Machine environment, would not perform well on standard hardware. It took several months of discussion, and the availability of a free public implementation of the ideas, before these fears were calmed and the Common Lisp community was able to adopt them. Even so, numerous small changes and a few major changes were made in the process.

In both Zetalisp and Common Lisp, handlers are functions that are called in the dynamic context of the signaling operation. No stack unwinding has yet occurred when the handlers are called. Potential handlers are tried in order until one decides to handle the condition. Probably the most conspicuous change between NES and the Common Lisp Condition System was the choice of how a handler function communicated its decision to elect a specific mode of recovery for the condition being signaled.

NES used a *passive* recovery mechanism. That is, in all cases, the handler would return one or more values. The nature of the return values would determine which recovery mode (called a "proceed type" in Zetalisp) was to be used. If NIL was returned, the handler had elected no proceed type, and the next handler was tried. Otherwise, the handler must return at least one value, a keyword designating the proceed type, and, optionally, additional values which were data appropriate to that manner of proceeding.

Common Lisp uses an *active* recovery mechanism. That is, any handler that wishes to designate a recovery mechanism (called a "restart" in Common Lisp) must imperatively transfer control to that restart. If the handler does not transfer control, that is, if the handler returns normally, any returned values are ignored and the handler is said to have "declined" (*i.e.*, elected no restart), and the next handler is tried. The Common Lisp recovery mechanism is called active because a signaled condition is said to be handled *only* when an active choice by the handler is made to perform a non-local transfer of control, whether by a low-level means such as a direct use of GO, THROW or RETURN-FROM or by a more abstract means such as a use of INVOKE-RESTART.

2.3   The Maclisp Experience

I am commonly credited with the "creation" of the Common Lisp Condition System, although I hope to show through this paper that my role in the design was largely to take the ideas of others and carefully transplant them to Common Lisp. In doing this, I relied on my personal experiences to guide me, and many of my formative experiences came from my work with Maclisp [2], which originated at MIT's Project MAC (later renamed to be the Laboratory for Computer Science), and which ran on the Digital Equipment Corporation (DEC) PDP10, DEC TOPS20 and Honeywell Multics systems.

Maclisp, had a relatively primitive error system, which I had used extensively. At the time I came to the Lisp Machine's NES, I did not know what I was looking for in an error system, but I knew, based on my experience with Maclisp, what I was *not* looking for. So what impressed me initially about NES was that it had fixed many of the design misfeatures that I had seen in Maclisp.

One important bit of background on Maclisp, at least on the PDP10 implementation that I used, was that it had no STRING datatype. In almost all cases where one might expect strings to be used, interned symbols were used instead. Symbols containing characters that might otherwise confuse the tokenizer were bounded on either end by a vertical bar (|). Also, since symbols would normally name variables, they generally had to be quoted with a leading single quote (') to protect them from the Lisp evaluation mechanism and allow them to be used as pseudostrings.

```
'|This is a quoted Maclisp symbol.|
```

Poor Separation of Signaling and Handling in Maclisp Maclisp had two forms of the function ERROR. In the simple and most widely used form, one merely called **ERROR** with one argument, a description of the error. Such errors would stop program execution with no chance of recovery other than to transfer to the innermost **ERRSET**, the approximate Maclisp equivalent of Common Lisp's **IGNORE-ERRORS**.

```
(error '|YOU LOSE|)
```

It was possible, however, in a limited way, to specify the particular kind of error. There were about a dozen predefined kinds of errors that one could identify that did allow recovery. For example,

```
(error '|VARIABLE HAS NO VALUE| 'A 'UNBND-VRBL)
```

The "keyword" **UNBND-VRBL** was a system-defined name that indicated to the system that this was an error of kind "unbound variable". A specific recovery strategy was permitted in this case. One could, either interactively in a breakpoint or through the dynamic establishment of a handler for such errors, provide a value for the variable. If that happened, the call to **ERROR** would then return a list of that value and the caller of **ERROR** was expected to pick up that value and use it.

This worked fine for the case where the programmer knew the kind of error and was prepared to recover from it. But a strange situation occurred when one knew the kind of error but was not prepared to recover. Sometimes one knew one had an unbound variable, and wanted to call **ERROR**, but was not prepared to recover. In this case, the programmer was forced to lie and to say that it was an error of arbitrary type, using just the short form, to avoid the misperception on the part of potential handlers that returning a recovery value would be useful.

```
(error '|VARIABLE HAS NO VALUE| 'A)
```

One feature of the NES, which I personally found very attractive, was the notion that I could freely specify the class of error without regard to whether I was prepared to handle it in some particular way. The issue of how to handle the error was specified orthogonally.

Error Message Identity In Maclisp In PDP10 Maclisp, error messages were historically all uppercase, since the system's primitive error messages were that way and many users found it aesthetically unpleasant to have some messages in mixed case while others were entirely uppercase. At some point, however, there was pressure to provide mixed case error messages. The decision made by the Maclisp maintainers of the time was not to yield to such pressure.

The problem was that many programs faced with an error message were testing it for object identity. For example:

```
(eq msg '|UNBOUND VARIABLE|)
```

Had we changed the case of all of the error messages in the Maclisp system to any other case, lower or mixed, these tests would have immediately begun to fail, breaking a lot of installed code and costing a lot of money to fix. The change would have been seen to be gratuitous.

The lesson from this for all of us in the Maclisp community, which became magnified later when we confronted the broader community of international users, was that the identity of an error should not be its name. That is, had we to do it over again, we would not have used |unbound variable| nor |Unbound Variable| as the identity of the error, but rather would have created objects whose slots or methods were responsible for yielding the presented string, but whose identity and nature was controlled orthogonally. This was another thing that NES offered that drew me immediately to it.

2.4   Terminological Influences

At the time of the Common Lisp design, Scheme did not have an error system, and so its contribution to the dialog on condition systems was not that of contributing an operator or behavior. However, it still did have something to contribute: the useful term *continuation*. For our purposes here, it is sufficient to see a continuation as an actual or conceptual function that represents, in essence, one of possibly several "future worlds", any of which can be entered by electing to call its associated continuation.

This metaphor was of tremendous value to me socially in my efforts to gain acceptance of the condition system, because it allowed a convenient, terse explanation of what "restarts" were about in Common Lisp. Although Scheme continuations are, by tradition, typically passed by explicit data flow, this is not a requirement. And so I have often found myself thankful for the availability of a concept so that I could talk about the establishment of named restart points as "taking a continuation, labeling it with a tag, and storing it away on a shelf somewhere for possible later use."

Likewise, I found it useful in some circles to refer to some of the concepts of reflective Lisps, such as Brian Smith's 3Lisp [4], and later work inspired by it. I feel that the condition system's ability to introspect (through operators such as FIND-RESTART) about what possible actions are pending, without actually invoking those pending actions, is an important reflective capability. Even though Common Lisp does not offer general-purpose reflection, the ability to use this metaphor for speaking about those aspects of the language that are usefully described by it simplifies conversations.

3   Abstract Concepts

Having now hopefully firmly established that the formative ideas in the Common Lisp Condition System did not all spring into existence with the language itself, and are really the legacy of the community using the continuum of languages of which Common Lisp is a part, we can now turn our attention to a survey of some of the important features that Common Lisp provides.

3.1 Separating Signaling and Handling

Traditionally, "error handling" has been largely a process of programs stopping and the only real question has been "how much of the program stops?" or "how far out do I throw?" It is against that backdrop that modern condition handling can be best understood.

The proper way to think about condition handling is this:

The process of programming is about saying what to do in every circumstance. In that regard, a computer has been sometimes characterized as a "relentless judge of incompleteness". When a program reaches a place where there are several possible next steps and the program is unwilling or incapable of choosing among them, the program has detected an *exceptional situation*.

The possible next steps are called *restarts*. Restarts are, effectively, named continuations.

The process of asking for help in resolving the problem of selecting among the possible next steps is called *signaling*.

The independently contributed pieces of code which are consulted during the signaling process are called *handlers*. In Common Lisp, these are functions contributed by the dynamic call chain that are tried in order from innermost (*i.e.,* most specific) to outermost (*i.e.,* most general). Each handler is called with an argument that is a description of the problem situation. The handler will transfer control (by `GO`, `RETURN` or `THROW`) if it chooses to handle the problem described by its argument.

In describing condition handling, I tell the following story to help people visualize the need for its various parts:

Think of the process of signaling and handling as analogous to finding a fork in a road that you do not commonly travel. You don't know which way to go, so you make known your dilemma, that is, you signal a condition. Various sources of wisdom (handlers) present themselves, and you consult each, placing your trust in them because you have no special knowledge yourself of what to do. Not all sources of wisdom are experts on every topics, so some may decline to help before you find one that is confident of its advice. When an appropriately confident source of wisdom is found, it will act on your behalf. The situation has been handled.

In the case that the situation is not handled, the next action depends on which operator was used to signal. The function `signal` will just return normally when a condition goes unhandled. The function `error` is like signal, but rather than return, it enters the *debugger*. The Common Lisp debugger might allow access to low-level debugging features such as examination of individual storage locations, but it is not required to. Its *primary* role is to be an *interactive handler*; that is, to present the human user interactively with various options about how computation might be resumed. Conceptually, this is the same as if it were acting as the human user's proxy in being the element on the list of handlers, so that the human user is the source of wisdom whose choice will determine how to proceed. Other capabilities that the debugger might offer in support of that human's decision are probably very important in practice, but are conceptually uninteresting to this understanding of the debugger's role in signaling and handling.

Note, too, that in some possible future world, knowledge representation may have advanced enough that handlers could, rather than act unconditionally on behalf of the signaler, merely return a representation of a set of potential actions accompanied by descriptive information respresenting motivations, consequences, and even qualitative representations of the goodness of each. Such information might be combined with, compared to, or confirmed by recommendations from other sources of wisdom in order to produce a better result. This is how consultation of sources of wisdom would probably work in the real world. Consider that even a doctor who is sure of what a patient needs will ask the patient's permission before acting. However, this last step of confirmation, which would allow more flexibility in the reasoning process, is not manifest in Common Lisp as of the time of writing this paper. It is an open area for future research.

Some of these issues are discussed in much greater detail in my 1990 conference paper [3].

3.2 Generalized Conditions

It was mentioned earlier that the space of conditions that can be used in the Common Lisp Condition System is more general than the space of mere errors. Here are some examples.

Serious, non-error Conditions   The superclass of `error` is `serious-condition`. This kind of condition is a subclass of `condition` but is serious enough that conditions of this kind should generally enter the debugger if unhandled. Serious conditions, which the Zetalisp NES called "debugger conditions", exist as a separately named concept from "error conditions" to accommodate things that are not semantic errors in a program, but are instead resource limitations and other incidental accomodations to pragmatics.

Suppose one writes the following:

```
(ignore-errors (open "some.file"))
```

This will trap errors during the file open. However, what if a stack overflow occurs, not for reasons of infinite recursion, but merely because the call is nested very deeply in other code? The answer is that a stack overflow is considered a serious condition, but not an error. The above code is equivalent to:

```
(handler-case (open "some.file")
  (error (c)
    (values nil c)))
```

And since any condition representing a stack overflow is going to be a kind of SERIOUS-CONDITION, but not a kind of ERROR, the use of IGNORE-ERRORS will succeed in trapping a file error but not a stack overflow. If one wanted to catch serious conditions as well, one would write instead:

```
(handler-case (open "some.file")
  (serious-condition (c)
    (values nil c)))
```

Non-serious conditions Some conditions are not at all serious. Such conditions might be handled, but there is an obvious default action in the case of their going unhandled.

Consider a program doing line-at-a-time output to a console. One might assume the screen to have infinite height, and the output might look like:

```
(defvar *line-number* 0)
(defun show-lines (lines)
  (dolist (line lines)
    (show-line line)))
```

However, it might be useful to specify screen line height, and to have the console pause every so many lines for a human reader to confirm that it's ok to proceed. There are, of course, a number of ways such a facility could be programmed, but one possible such way is to use the condition system. For example,

```
(defvar *line-number* 0)
(defvar *page-height* nil)
(define-condition end-of-page (condition))
(defun show-lines (lines)
  (dolist (line lines)
    (incf *line-number*)
    (when (and *page-height*
               (zerop (mod *line-number* *page-height*)))
      (restart-case (signal 'end-of-page)
        (continue () ;no data arguments needed
        ;; nothing to do in the continue body
        )))))
```

In the above, there is only one way to proceed. A restart named CONTINUE is offered as a way of imperatively selecting this option (imperatively bypassing any other pending handlers), but if the handler declines and the condition goes unhandled, the same result will be achieved.

A similar kind of facility could be used to manage end of line handling. There, it's common to allow various modes, and so a corresponding set of restarts has to be established, which handlers would choose among. If no handler elected to handle the condition, however, no great harm would come. Here's an example of how that might look:

```
(defvar *line-length* nil)
(define-condition end-of-line (condition))
```

```
(defun show-line (line)
  (let ((eol (or *line-length* -1)) (hpos 0))
    (loop for pos below (length line)
          for ch = (char line i)
          do (write-char char)
          when (= hpos eol)
            do (restart-case (signal 'end-of-line)
                 (wrap ()
                   (terpri) ; output a newline char
                   (setq hpos 0))
                 (truncate ()
                   (return))
                 (continue ()
                   ;; just allow to continue
                   ))
          else do (incf hpos))))
```

3.3   Independent, Reflective Specification of Restarts

It has long been the case that Lisp offered the ability to dynamically make
the decision to transfer to a computed return point using the special operator
THROW. However, without reflective capabilities, there has not been the ability
for a programmer to determine if there was a pending CATCH to which control
could be thrown other than relatively clumsy idioms such as the following:

```
(ignore-errors (throw 'some-tag 'some-value))
```

The problem with the above idiom is that while it "detects" the presence or
absence of a pending tag, it only retains local control and the ability to reason
about this knowledge in the case of the tag's non-existence. The price of detecting
the tag's existence is transfer to that tag.

The Common Lisp Condition System adds a limited kind of reflective capability in the form of a new kind of catch point, called a *restart*, the presence
or absence of which can be reasoned about without any attempt to actually
perform a transfer. A restart can also have associated with them a descriptive
textual string that a human user can be shown by the debugger to describe the
potential action offered by the restart.

Restart points that require transfer of control but no data can be established
straightforwardly with WITH-SIMPLE-RESTART. For example:

```
(defun lisp-top-level-loop ()
  (with-simple-restart (exit "Exit from Lisp.")
    (loop
      (with-simple-restart (continue "Return to Lisp toplevel.")
        (print (eval (read)))))))
```

Restarts that require data can also be established using a slightly more elaborate syntax. This syntax not only accommodates the programmatic data flow to the restart, but also enough information for the Common Lisp function INVOKE-RESTART-INTERACTIVELY to properly prompt for any appropriate values to be supplied to that restart. For example:

```
(defun my-symbol-value (name)
  (if (boundp name)
      (symbol-value name)
    (restart-case (error 'unbound-variable :name name)
      (use-value (value)
        :report "Specify a value to use."
        :interactive (lambda ()
                       (format t "~&Value to use: ")
                       (list (eval (read))))
        value)
      (store-value (value)
        :report "Specify a value to use and store."
        :interactive (lambda ()
                       (format t "~&Value to use and store: ")
                       (list (eval (read))))
        (setf (symbol-value name) value)
        value)))))
```

Code that inquires about such restarts typically makes use of FIND-RESTART to test for the availability of a restart, and then INVOKE-RESTART to invoke a restart. For example:

```
(handler-bind ((unbound-variable
                 (lambda (c) ;argument is condition description
                   ;; Try to make unbound variables get value 17
                   (dolist (tag '(store-value use-value))
                     (let ((restart (find-restart tag c)))
                       (when restart
                         (invoke-restart restart 17)))))))
  (+ (my-symbol-value 'this-symbol-has-no-value)
     (my-symbol-value 'pi))) ;pi DOES have a value!
=> 20.141592653589793
```

Absent such a handler, the restart would be offered interactively by the debugger, as in:

```
(+ (my-symbol-value 'this-symbol-has-no-value)
   (my-symbol-value 'pi))
Error: The variable THIS-SYMBOL-HAS-NO-VALUE is unbound.
Please select a restart option:
  1 - Specify a value to use.
```

```
2 - Specify a value to use and store.
3 - Return to Lisp toplevel.
4 - Exit from Lisp.
Option: 1
Value to use: 19
=> 22.141592653589793
```

3.4   Handling in the Context of the Signaler

A key capability provided by Common Lisp is the fact that, at the most primitive
level, handling can be done in the dynamic context of the signaler, while certain
very critical dynamic state information is still available that would be lost if a
stack unwind happened before running the handler.

This capability is reflected in the ability of the operator `handler-bind` to
take control of a computation *before* any transfer of control occurs. Note that
the Common Lisp operator `handler-case`, which is more analogous to facilities
offered in other languages, does not allow programmer-supplied code to run until
after the transfer of control; this is useful for some simple situations, but is less
powerful.

Consider a code fragment such as:

```
(handler-case (main-action)
  (error (c) (other-action)))
```

In this example, the expression (`other-action`) will run *after* unwinding
from wherever in (`main-action`) signaled the error, regardless of how deep into
`main-action` that signaling occured.

By contrast, `handler-bind` takes control *inside* the dynamic context of the
call to `SIGNAL`, and so is capable of accessing restarts that are dynamically
between the call to `SIGNAL` and the use of `HANDLER-BIND`. Consider this example:

```
(with-simple-restart (foo "Outer foo.")
  (handler-case (with-simple-restart (foo "Inner foo.")
                  (error "Lossage."))
    (error (c) (invoke-restart 'foo))))
```

In the above, the outer `FOO` restart will be selected, as contrasted with the
following, where the inner `FOO` restart will be selected:

```
(with-simple-restart (foo "Outer foo.")
  (handler-bind ((error ; any condition of class ERROR
                  (lambda (c) (invoke-restart 'foo))))
    (with-simple-restart (foo "Inner foo.")
      ;; Now signal an error.
      (error "Lossage."))))
```

This is important because error handling tends to want to make use of all available restarts, but *especially* those that are in that code region that HANDLER-BIND can see but HANDLER-CASE cannot. Consider another example:

```
(handler-case (foo)
  (unbound-variable (c)
    (let ((r (find-restart 'use-value c)))
      (if r (invoke-restart r nil)))))
```

The above example will not achieve its presumed intent, which is to supply NIL as the default value for any unbound variable encountered during the call to FOO. The problem is that any USE-VALUE restart that is likely to be found will also be within the call to FOO, and will no longer be active by the time the ERROR clause of the HANDLER-CASE expression is executed.

Use of HANDLER-BIND allows this example to work in a way that is not possible with HANDLER-CASE and its analogs in other programming languages. Consider:

```
(handler-bind ((error ; any condition of class ERROR
                (lambda (c)
                  (let ((r (find-restart 'use-value c)))
                    (if r (invoke-restart r nil))))))
  (foo))
```

3.5   Default Handling

Zetalisp contained a facility not only for asserting handlers to be used for conditions, but also an additional facility for asserting handlers that should be provisionally used only if no normal handlers were found. In effect, this meant there were two search lists, a handlers list and a default handlers list, which were searched in order.

In my use of Zetalisp's NES, I became convinced that it was conceptually incorrect to search the default handlers list in order; I felt it should be searched in reverse order. I had reported this as a bug, but it was never fixed. In all honesty, I'm not sure there was enough data then or perhaps even now to say whether I was right, although I continue to believe that default handling is something that should proceed from the outside in, not the inside out. Nevertheless, whether I was right or not is not so much relevant in this context as is the fact that it was a point of controversy that ended up influencing the design of Common Lisp's condition system. I was distrustful of the operator condition-bind-default that was offered by NES, and so I omitted it from the set of offerings that I transplanted from Common Lisp.

The Common Lisp Condition System *does* provide a way to implement the concept of a default handler, but it is idiomatic. And, perhaps not entirely coincidentally, it has the net effect of seeking default handlers from the outside in rather than the inside out, as I had always felt was right.

The Zetalisp mechanism looked like this:

```
(condition-bind-default ((error
                          (lambda (c)
                          ...default handling...)))
  ...body in which handler is in effect...)
```

The corresponding Common Lisp idiom looks like this:

```
(handler-bind ((error ; any condition of class ERROR
                 (lambda (c)
                  (signal c) ;resignal
                  ...default handling...)))
  ...body in which handler is in effect...)
```

In effect, the Common Lisp idiom continues the signaling process but without explicitly relinquishing control. If the resignaled condition is unhandled, control will return to this handler and the default handling will be done. If, on the other hand, some outer handler does handle the condition, the default handling code will never be reached and so will not be run.

3.6   Unifying "Signals" and "Exceptions"

In some systems, such as Unix, "signals" are an asynchronous mechanism primarily used for implementing event-driven programming interfaces, but are not generally used within ordinary, synchronous programming.

While it is beyond the scope of the ANSI Common Lisp standard to address the issue of either interrupts or multitasking, most Common Lisp implementations have a convergent manner of coping with these issues that is sufficiently stable as to be worth some mention. The approach has been to separate the notion of "interrupting" from the notion of "signaling".

That is, in Common Lisp, all signaling is synchronous. *However,* such synchronous behavior can be usefully coupled with a process interruption to produce interesting effects.

In this separation, process interruptions without signaling might be done for any reason that involved the need to read or modify dynamic state of another process. Here is an example that merely reads the dynamic state of another process:

```
(defvar *my-dynamic-variable* 1)

(let ((temporary-process
        (mp:process-run-function "temp" '()
           ;; Launch a temporary process that
           ;;   merely dynamically binds a
           ;;   certain variable and then
           ;;   sleeps for a minute.
           (lambda ()
```

```
          (let ((*my-dynamic-variable* 2))
            (sleep 60)))))
    (result-value nil))
;; Now interrupt our temporary process
;; to see the value of the variable
(mp:process-interrupt temporary-process
  (lambda ()
    (setq result-value *my-dynamic-variable*)))
;; Now wait for the interrupt to occur
(mp:process-wait "not yet assigned"
  (lambda () result-value)) ;tests for a non-null value
;; If we get this far, the result-value has been assigned
;; and can be returned.
result-value)
```

=> 2

Note that this merely examines the dynamic state of our temporary process, but does not invoke any signaling mechanism at all. And while the process of interruption is inherently asynchronous, the actions to be done in the interrupted process are synchronous.

If we instead intertwine the notion of process interruption with signaling, we get what some systems might call "asynchronous signaling", but which Common Lisp views as just the composition of two orthogonal facilities. So, for example, a keyboard interrupt to a process might be accomplished by:

```
(define-condition keyboard-interrupt ()
  ((character :initarg :character :reader kbd-char))
  (:report (lambda (condition stream)
             (format t "The character ~@:C was typed."
                     (kbd-char condition)))))

(defun keyboard-interrupt (character process)
  (mp:process-interrupt process
    (lambda ()
       ;; Offer the process a chance to handle the condition.
       ;; If the condition is not handled, the call to SIGNAL
       ;; returns and the interrupt is completed.  Normal
       ;; process execution then continues.
       (signal 'keyboard-interrupt :character character))))
```

Using such a facility, a keyboard process (itself a synchronous activity) can asynchronously interrupt another process (presumably, the window selected at the point an interrupt character is seen).

```
(defvar *selected-window* nil)
```

```
(defun keyboard-process (raw-keyboard-stream)
  (loop (let ((char (read-char raw-keyboard-stream)))
          (when *selected-window*
            (if (is-interrupt-character? char)
                (keyboard-interrupt char
                  (window-process *selected-window*))
                ;; otherwise...
                (add-to-input-buffer *selected-window* char))))))
```

Although the KEYBOARD-PROCESS shown here will interrupt the window process, an understanding of what happens at that point does not require any special knowledge of asynchrony. It merely requires observing that at the time of interruption, the other process was about to execute some expression (exp) and will now execute instead

```
(progn (funcall the-interrupt-function) (exp))
```

This kind of structured approach removes much of the mystery and unpredictability normally associated with asynchronous interrupts in other systems, where the description of the effect is often not linguistic at all but deals in overly concrete terms of bits and registers in a way that only career experts can hope to navigate. The sense in the Common Lisp community is that a correct conceptual treatment of these issues makes these sorts of capabilities something that "mere mortals" can safely and conveniently employ in their programming.

4   Open Issues

The Dylan language patterned its efforts after the Common Lisp Condition System, but made some interesting changes. I probably lack the appropriate experience and surely the appropriate objectivity to conclude whether their changes are clear improvements over the Common Lisp approaches. But it's plain that by making divergent decisions in some places, the Dylan community has identified certain areas of the Common Lisp design as "controversial".

4.1   Restarts vs Handlers

Common Lisp provides parallel but unrelated operators such as HANDLER-BIND and HANDLER-CASE for dealing with handlers, and, similarly, RESTART-BIND and RESTART-CASE for dealing with restarts. It was thought that these were orthogonal operations, requiring unrelated dataflow, that really didn't belong intermingled. The Dylan community has sought to coalesce these by making restarts into a kind of condition, and eliminating special binding forms for them.

4.2   The "Condition Firewall"

Probably the most controversial semantic component of the Common Lisp condition system is what has come to be called the "condition firewall". The idea behind the condition firewall is that a given handler should be executed in an environment that does not "see" intervening handlers that might have been established since its establishment.

So, for example, consider this code:

```
(handler-case
    (handler-bind ((error ; any condition of class ERROR
                     (lambda (condition)
                       (declare (ignore condition))
                       (error 'unbound-variable :name 'fred))))
        (handler-case ;; Signal an arbitrary error:
                      (error "Not an UNBOUND-VARIABLE error.")
          (unbound-variable (c) (list 'inner c))))
  (unbound-variable (c) (list 'outer c)))
```

This sets up two handlers for conditions of class UNBOUND-VARIABLE, one outside of the scope of the general-purpose handler for conditions of class ERROR and one inside of its scope. At the time the "arbitrary" error signaled, both handlers are in effect. This means that if the error being signaled *had* been of class UNBOUND-VARIABLE, it would have been caught by the inner HANDLER-CASE for UNBOUND-VARIABLE. However, as the search for a handler proceeds outward, the handlers that are tried are executed in a context where the inner handlers are no longer visible. As such, the above example yields

```
(OUTER #<ERROR UNBOUND-VARIABLE 12A39B87>)
```

By contrast, the following code:

```
(handler-case
    (handler-bind ((error ; any condition of class ERROR
                     (lambda (condition)
                       (declare (ignore condition))
                       ;; Recursively invoke the signaling
                       ;; system by signaling UNBOUND-VARIABLE
                       ;; from within a handler...
                       (error 'unbound-variable :name 'fred))))

        (handler-case ;; The main form of this HANDLER-CASE
                      ;; expression just signals an error.
                      (error 'unbound-variable :name 'marvin)

          ;; Handler clauses for inner HANDLER-CASE
          (unbound-variable (c) (list 'inner c)))
```

```
   )
;; Handler clauses for outer HANDLER-CASE
(unbound-variable (c) (list 'outer c)))
```

yields

```
(INNER #<ERROR UNBOUND-VARIABLE 12A39B87>)
```

It is interesting to note as an aside that the "resignaling trick" used earlier in the discussion of default handling relies implicitly on the condition firewall in order to avoid infinite recursion. Without the condition firewall, a different mechanism for implementing default handling is needed.

The designers of the Dylan language chose to eliminate the condition firewall, perhaps out of necessity since the most useful restarts almost always occur in the dynamic space near the point of signal, and the handlers usually occur farther out. If handlers could only see the restarts farther out than where they were established, they would not see the most useful restarts. (I am personally doubtful of this argument, and am more inclined to believe that this why restarts should not have been turned into a kind of condition in Dylan, but I could be wrong and time will tell.)

The Dylan notation is different in many ways from Common Lisp, but the approximately equivalent code to the above two examples would *both*, I believe, return

```
(INNER #<ERROR UNBOUND-VARIABLE 12A39B87>)
```

5   Summary

Language features don't originate spontaneously out of nowhere. We have surveyed some of the origins of the Common Lisp Condition System in an effort to demonstrate how prior experiences, both good and bad, have influenced the present design. Nor is this the end of the story. The ideas in Common Lisp have had some influence on other languages and will, I hope, continue to do so, since there are a number of things the Common Lisp makes easy through its condition system that other languages do not.

We have also seen that good terminology is important both to the specification of a programming language and to its community acceptance.

Programming is not only a technical endeavor, but a social one. So much of so many lives is spent doing programming, that it is critical that we have good terminology, beyond the terms of the language itself, for talking among each other about what we are doing within the language.

And we have surveyed some of the key features that distinguish Common Lisp's condition system from those offered by other languages, and highlighted some open issues, where Common Lisp's answers to certain problems have already met with challenges.

5.1   A Personal Footnote

During the design of Common Lisp, I headed the committee that produced the design of the condition system. At that time, there were many questions and doubts about the design: Were the decisions sound? Were all of the alternatives explored, or were there better ways we might later wish we'd tried? Were there problems lurking under the surface, waiting to bite someone when used under heavier stress?

It wasn't that people doubted our committee's competence, but rather many qould-be reviewers lacked the relevant experience to critically analyze our proposals. Yet the design seemed mostly right to me, and my larger concern was that if we didn't at some point release it to a community of users to try, we'd be back at the same design table a few years later with the same questions and the same lack of community experience to answer them. A leap of faith seemed to be required to move ahead. So I and my committee nodded our collective heads and said we stood by the design. Personally, I had some doubts about some details, but I found it counterproductive to raise them because I believed the risk of not trying these things out was higher than the risk of trying them.

In my experience, much of language design is like this. We *think* we know how it will all come out, but we don't always. Usage patterns are often surprising, as one learns if one is around long enough to design a language or two and then watch how expectations play out in reality over a course of years. So it's a gamble. But the only way not to gamble is not to move ahead.

I once saw an interview on television with a font designer from Bitstream Inc. about how he conceptualized the process of font design. It is not about designing the shape of the letters, he explained, much to my initial surprise. Then he went on to explain that it was really about the shape of words. The font shapes play into that, but they are not, in themselves, the end goal. Programming language design is like that, too. It's not about the semantics of individual operators, but about how those operators fit together to form sentences in programs.

Unlike the situation with fonts, where whole books can be viewed instantly in a new font to see how the design works, we don't know in advance what sentences will be made in a programming language. We have to wait and see what people choose to write. Common Lisp took a step forward, and while we can quibble endlessly over whether any given design decision was right, the one design decision I'm most certain was right was to offer the community a rich set of capabilities that would empower them not only to write programs, but also to have a stake in future designs. Never again will I fear sending out e-mail to a design group asking for advice about what the semantics of HANDLER-BIND should be and finding that no one has an opinion! To me, that kind of progress, the evolution of a whole community's understanding, is the best kind of progress of all.

Acknowledgements. I would like to thank Keith Corbett, Christophe Dony, Bernard Greenberg, and Erik Naggum for reviewing drafts of this text. Any lingering errors after they got done looking at it are still my responsibility, but

I'm quite sure the editorial, technical, and historical quality of this text was improved measurably through their helpful scrutiny.

References

1. Multicians: The 'Multicians' web site. http://www.multicians.org/
2. Pitman, Kent M.: The Revised Maclisp Manual. Technical Report 295, MIT Laboratory for Computer Science, Cambridge, MA (May 1983).
3. Pitman, Kent M.: Exceptional Situations in Lisp. Proceedings for the First European Conference on the Practical Application of Lisp (EUROPAL'90), Churchill College, Cambridge, UK, (March 27-29, 1990) http://world.std.com/ pitman/Papers/Exceptional-Situations-1990.html
4. Smith, Brian C.: Reflection and Semantics in a Procedural Language. Technical Report 272, MIT Laboratory for Computer Science, Cambridge, MA (January 1982).
5. ANSI working group X3J13: American National Standard for Information Systems–Programming Language–Common Lisp. X3.226-1994 http://www.xanalys.com/software_tools/reference/HyperSpec/FrontMatter/
6. Weinreb, D.L., Moon, D.A.: Lisp Machine Manual. MIT Artificial Intelligence Laboratory, Cambridge, MA (July 1981).

Exception Safety: Concepts and Techniques

Bjarne Stroustrup

AT&T Labs – Research

Florham Park, NJ 07932, USA

http://www.research.att.com/~bs

Abstract. This paper presents a set of concepts and design techniques that has proven successful in implementing and using C++ libraries intended for applications that simultaneously require high reliability and high performance. The notion of exception safety is based on the *basic guarantee* that maintains basic invariants and avoids resource leaks and the *strong guarantee* that ensures that a failed operation has no effect.

1 Introduction

This paper, based on *Appendix E: Standard-Library Exception Safety* of *The C++ Programming Language (Special Edition)* [1], presents

(1) a few fundamental concepts useful for discussion of exception safety

(2) effective techniques for crafting exception-safe and efficient containers

(3) some general rules for exception-safe programming.

The discussion of exception safety focuses on the containers provided as part of the ISO C++ standard library [2] [1]. Here, the standard library is used to provide examples of the kinds of concerns that must be addressed in demanding applications. The techniques used to provide exception safety for the standard library can be applied to a wide range of problems.

The discussion assumes an understanding of C++ and a basic understanding of C++'s exception handling mechanisms. These mechanism, the fundamental ways of using them, and the support they receive in the standard library are described in [1]. The reasoning behind the design of C++'s exception handling mechanisms and references to previous work influencing that design can be found in [3].

2 Exception Safety

An operation on an object is said to be *exception safe* if that operation leaves the object in a valid state when the operation is terminated by throwing an exception. This valid state could be an error state requiring cleanup, but it must be well defined so that reasonable error-handling code can be written for the object. For example, an exception handler might destroy the object, repair the object, repeat a variant of the operation, just carry on, etc.

In other words, the object will have an invariant, its constructors establish that invariant, all further operations maintain that invariant, and its destructor does a final cleanup. An operation should take care that the invariant is maintained before throwing an exception, so that the object is in a valid state.

A. Romanovsky et al. (Eds.): Exception Handling, LNCS 2022, pp. 60–76, 2001.

However, it is quite possible for that valid state to be one that doesn't suit the application. For example, a string may have been left as the empty string or a container may have been left unsorted. Thus, "repair" means giving an object a value that is more appropriate/desirable for the application than the one it was left with after an operation failed. In the context of the standard library, the most interesting objects are containers.

Here, we consider under which conditions an operation on a standard-library container can be considered exception safe. There can be only two conceptually really simple strategies:

(1) *"No guarantees:"* If an exception is thrown, any container being manipulated is possibly corrupted.

(2) *"Strong guarantee:"* If an exception is thrown, any container being manipulated remains in the state in which it was before the standard-library operation started.

Unfortunately, both answers are too simple for real use. Alternative (1) is unacceptable because it implies that after an exception is thrown from a container operation, the container cannot be accessed; it can't even be destroyed without fear of run-time errors. Alternative (2) is unacceptable because it imposes the cost of roll-back semantics on every individual standard-library operation.

To resolve this dilemma, the C++ standard library provides a set of exception-safety guarantees that share the burden of producing correct programs between implementers of the standard library and users of the standard library:

(3a) *"Basic guarantee* for all operations:" The basic invariants of the standard library are maintained, and no resources, such as memory, are leaked.

(3b) *"Strong guarantee* for key operations:" In addition to providing the basic guarantee, either the operation succeeds, or has no effects. This guarantee is provided for key library operations, such as *push_back* ( ), single-element *insert* ( ) on a *list*, and *uninitialized_copy* ( ).

(3c) *"Nothrow guarantee* for some operations:" In addition to providing the basic guarantee, some operations are guaranteed not to throw an exception This guarantee is provided for a few simple operations, such as *swap* ( ) and *pop_back* ( ).

Both the basic guarantee and the strong guarantee are provided on the condition that user-supplied operations (such as assignments and *swap* ( ) functions) do not leave container elements in invalid states, that user-supplied operations do not leak resources, and that destructors do not throw exceptions.

Violating a standard library requirement, such as having a destructor exit by throwing an exception, is logically equivalent to violating a fundamental language rule, such a dereferencing a null pointer. The practical effects are also equivalent and often disastrous.

In addition to achieving pure exception safety, both the basic guarantee and the strong guarantee ensure the absence of resource leaks. That is, a standard library operation that throws an exception not only leaves its operands in well-defined states but also ensures that every resource that it acquired is (eventually) released. For example, at the point where an exception is thrown, all memory allocated must be either deallocated or owned by some object, which in turn must ensure that the memory is properly deallocated. Remember that memory isn't the only kind of resource that can leak. Files, locks, network connections, and threads are examples of system resources that a function may have to release or hand over to an object before throwing an exception.

Note that the C++ language rules for partial construction and destruction ensure that exceptions thrown while constructing sub-objects and members will be handled correctly without special attention from standard-library code. This rule is an essential underpinning for all techniques dealing with exceptions.

3 Exception-Safe Implementation Techniques

The C++ standard library provides examples of problems that occur in many other contexts and of solutions that apply widely. The basic tools available for writing exception-safe code are

(1) the *try-block*, and

(2) the support for the "resource acquisition is initialization" technique.

The key idea behind the "resource acquisition is initialization" technique/pattern (sometimes abbreviated to RAII) is that ownership of a resource is given to a scoped object. Typically, that object acquires (opens, allocates, etc.) the resource in its constructor. That way, the objects destructor can release the resource at the end of its life independently of whether that destruction is caused by normal exit from its scope or from an exception. For details, see Sect. 14.4 of [1]. Also, the use of *vector_base* from Sect 3.2 of this paper is an example of "resource acquisition is initialization."

The general principles to follow are to

(1) don't destroy a piece of information before we can store its replacement

(2) always leave objects in valid states when throwing or re-throwing an exception

(3) avoid resource leaks.

That way, we can always back out of an error situation. The practical difficulty in following these principles is that innocent-looking operations (such as <, =, and *sort* ( )) might throw exceptions. Knowing what to look for in an application takes experience.

When you are writing a library, the ideal is to aim at the strong exception-safety guarantee and always to provide the basic guarantee. When writing a specific program, there may be less concern for exception safety. For example, if I write a simple data analysis program for my own use, I'm usually quite willing to have the program terminate in the unlikely event of virtual memory exhaustion. However, correctness and exception safety are closely related.

The techniques for providing basic exception safety, such as defining and checking invariants, are similar to the techniques that are useful to get a program small and correct. It follows that the overhead of providing basic exception safety (the basic guarantee) – or even the strong guarantee – can be minimal or even insignificant.

Here, I will consider an implementation of the standard container *vector* to see what it takes to achieve that ideal and where we might prefer to settle for more conditional safety.

3.1 A Simple Vector

A typical implementation of *vector* will consist of a handle holding pointers to the first element, one-past-the-last element, and one-past-the-last allocated space (or the equivalent information represented as a pointer plus offsets):

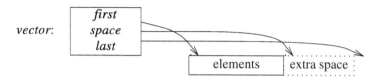

Here is a declaration of *vector* simplified to present only what is needed to discuss exception safety and avoidance of resource leaks:

```
template<class T, class A = allocator<T> > class vector {
public:
      T* v;        // start of allocation
      T* space;    // end of elements, start of space allocated for possible expansion
      T* last;     // end of allocated space
      A alloc;     // allocator

      explicit vector (size_type n, const T& val = T ( ), const A& = A ( ) );
      vector (const vector& a);              // copy constructor
      vector& operator= (const vector& a);   // copy assignment
      ~vector ( );                           // destructor

      size_type size ( ) const { return space-v; }
      size_type capacity ( ) const { return last-v; }

      void push_back (const T&);

      // ...
};
```

Consider first a naive implementation of a constructor:

```
template<class T, class A>             // warning: naive implementation
vector<T,A>::vector (size_type n, const T& val, const A& a)
      :alloc (a)                       // copy the allocator
{
      v = alloc.allocate (n);          // get memory for elements
      space = last = v+n;
      for (T* p=v; p!=last; ++p) a.construct (p, val); // construct copy of val in *p
}
```

There are three sources of exceptions here:

(1) *allocate* ( ) throws an exception indicating that no memory is available;

(2) the allocator's copy constructor throws an exception;

(3) the copy constructor for the element type *T* throws an exception because it can't copy *val*.

In all cases, no object is created. However, unless we are careful, resources can leak.

When *allocate* ( ) fails, the *throw* will exit before any resources are acquired, so all is well. When *T*'s copy constructor fails, we have acquired some memory that must be freed to avoid memory leaks. A more difficult problem is that the copy constructor for *T* might throw an exception after correctly constructing a few elements but before constructing them all. To handle this problem, we could keep track of which elements have been constructed and destroy those (and only those) in case of an error:

```
template<class T, class A>              // elaborate implementation
vector<T,A>::vector(size_type n, const T& val, const A& a)
      :alloc(a)                         // copy the allocator
{
      v = alloc.allocate(n);            // get memory for elements

      iterator p;

      try {
            iterator end = v+n;
            for (p=v; p!=end; ++p) alloc.construct(p, val); // construct element
            last = space = p;
      }
      catch (...) {  // destroy constructed elements, free memory, and re-throw:
            for (iterator q = v; q!=p; ++q) alloc.destroy(q);
            alloc.deallocate(v, n);
            throw;
      }
}
```

The overhead here is the overhead of the *try-block*. In a good C++ implementation, this overhead is negligible compared to the cost of allocating memory and initializing elements. For implementations where entering a *try-block* incurs a cost, it may be worthwhile to test *if*(*n*) before the *try* and handle the empty vector case separately.

The main part of this constructor is an exception-safe implementation of the standard library's *uninitialized_fill*():

```
template<class For, class T>
void uninitialized_fill(For beg, For end, const T& x)
{
      For p;
      try {
            for (p=beg; p!=end; ++p)
                  new (static_cast<void*>(&*p)) T(x); // construct copy of x in *p
      }
      catch (...) {  // destroy constructed elements and rethrow:
            for (For q = beg; q!=p; ++q) (&*q)->~T();
            throw;
      }
}
```

The curious construct &*p takes care of iterators that are not pointers. In that case, we need to take the address of the element obtained by dereference to get a pointer. The explicit cast to *void** ensures that the standard library placement function is used, and not some user-defined *operator new*() for *T**s. This code is operating at a rather low level where writing truly general code can be difficult.

Fortunately, we don't have to reimplement *uninitialized_fill*(), because the standard library provides the desired strong guarantee for it. It is often essential for initialization to either complete successfully, having initialized every element, or fail leaving no constructed elements behind. Consequently, the standard-library algorithms *uninitialized_fill* ( ) , *uninitialized_fill_n* ( ) , and *uninitialized_copy* ( ) are guaranteed to have this strong exception-safety property.

Note that *uninitialized_fill* ( ) does not protect against exceptions thrown by element destructors or iterator operations. Doing so would be prohibitively expensive.

The *uninitialized_fill* ( ) algorithm can be applied to many kinds of sequences. Consequently, it takes a forward iterator and cannot guarantee to destroy elements in the reverse order of their construction.

Using *uninitialized_fill* ( ) , we can write:

```
template<class  T,  class  A>              // messy implementation
vector<T,A>::vector (size_type  n,  const  T& val,  const  A& a)
      : alloc (a)                          // copy the allocator
{
      v = alloc . allocate (n) ;           // get memory for elements
      try {
            uninitialized_fill (v, v+n, val) ;   // copy elements
            space = last = v+n ;
      }
      catch ( . . . ) {
            alloc . deallocate (v, n) ;     // free memory
            throw ;                         // re-throw
      }
}
```

However, I wouldn't call that pretty code. The next section will demonstrate how it can be made much simpler.

Note that the constructor re-throws a caught exception. The intent is to make *vector* transparent to exceptions so that the user can determine the exact cause of a problem. All standard-library containers have this property. Exception transparency is often the best policy for templates and other ''thin'' layers of software. This is in contrast to major parts of a system (''modules'') that generally need to take responsibility for all exceptions thrown. That is, the implementer of such a module must be able to list every exception that the module can throw. Achieving this may involve grouping exceptions, mapping exceptions from lower-level routines into the module's own exceptions, or exception specification.

3.2 Representing Memory Explicitly

Experience revealed that writing correct exception-safe code using explicit *try-blocks* is more difficult than most people expect. In fact, it is unnecessarily difficult because there is an alternative: The ''resource acquisition is initialization'' technique can be used to reduce the amount of code written and to make the code more stylized. In this case, the key resource required by the *vector* is memory to hold its elements. By providing an auxiliary class to represent the notion of memory used by a *vector*, we can simplify the code and decrease the chance of accidentally forgetting to release it:

```
template<class T, class A = allocator<T> >
struct vector_base {
     A alloc;    // allocator
     T* v;       // start of allocation
     T* space;   // end of elements, start of space allocated for possible expansion
     T* last;    // end of allocated space

     vector_base (const A& a, typename A::size_type n)
          : alloc (a), v (a.allocate (n)), space (v+n), last (v+n) { }
     ~vector_base () { alloc.deallocate (v, last-v); }
};
```

As long as *v* and *last* are correct, *vector_base* can be destroyed. Class *vector_base* deals with memory for a type *T*, not objects of type *T*. Consequently, a user of *vector_base* must destroy all constructed objects in a *vector_base* before the *vector_base* itself is destroyed.

Naturally, *vector_base* itself is written so that if an exception is thrown (by the allocator's copy constructor or *allocate* ( ) function) no *vector_base* object is created and no memory is leaked.

We want to be able to *swap* ( ) *vector_base*s. However, the default *swap* ( ) doesn't suit our needs because it copies and destroys a temporary. Because *vector_base* is a special-purpose class that wasn't given fool-proof copy semantics, that destruction would lead to undesirable side effects. Consequently we provide a specialization:

```
template<class T> void swap (vector_base<T>& a, vector_base<T>& b)
{
     swap (a.a, b.a);
     swap (a.v, b.v);
     swap (a.space, b.space);
     swap (a.last, b.last);
}
```

Given *vector_base*, *vector* can be defined like this:

```
template<class T, class A = allocator<T> >
class vector : private vector_base<T,A> {
     void destroy_elements () { for (T* p = v; p!=space; ++p) p->~T(); }
public:
     explicit vector (size_type n, const T& val = T(), const A& = A());
     vector (const vector& a);                // copy constructor
     vector& operator= (const vector& a);     // copy assignment
     ~vector () { destroy_elements (); }

     size_type size () const { return space-v; }
     size_type capacity () const { return last-v; }

     void push_back (const T&);
     // ...
};
```

The *vector* destructor explicitly invokes the *T* destructor for every element. This implies that if an element destructor throws an exception, the *vector* destruction fails.

This can be a disaster if it happens during stack unwinding caused by an exception and *terminate* ( ) is called. In the case of normal destruction, throwing an exception from a destructor typically leads to resource leaks and unpredictable behavior of code relying on reasonable behavior of objects. There is no really good way to protect against exceptions thrown from destructors, so the library makes no guarantees if an element destructor throws.

Now the constructor can be simply defined:

```
template<class T, class A>
vector<T, A>::vector(size_type n, const T& val, const A& a)
        : vector_base<T, A> (a, n)              // allocate space for n elements
{
        uninitialized_fill (v, v+n, val);    // copy elements
}
```

The copy constructor differs by using *uninitialized_copy* ( ) instead of *uninitialized_fill* ( ):

```
template<class T, class A>
vector<T, A>::vector(const vector<T, A>& a)
        : vector_base<T, A> (a.alloc, a.size ( ) )
{
        uninitialized_copy (a.begin ( ), a.end ( ), v);
}
```

Note that this style of constructor relies on the fundamental language rule that when an exception is thrown from a constructor, sub-objects (such as bases) that have already been completely constructed will be properly destroyed. The *uninitialized_fill* ( ) algorithm and its cousins provide the equivalent guarantee for partially constructed sequences.

3.3 Assignment

As usual, assignment differs from construction in that an old value must be taken care of. Consider a straightforward implementation:

```
template<class T, class A>                  // offers the strong guarantee
vector<T, A>& vector<T, A>::operator= (const vector& a)
{
        vector_base<T, A> b (alloc, a.size ( ) );       // get memory
        uninitialized_copy (a.begin ( ), a.end ( ), b.v);  // copy elements
        destroy_elements ( );                            // destroy old elements
        alloc.deallocate (v, last-v);                    // free old memory
        vector_base::operator= (b);                      // install new representation
        b.v = 0;                                         // prevent deallocation
        return *this;
}
```

This assignment is nice and exception safe. However, it repeats a lot of code from constructors and destructors. Also, the "installation" of the new *vector_base* is a bit obscure. To avoid this, we can write:

```
template<class T, class A>              // offers the strong guarantee
vector<T,A>& vector<T,A>::operator=(const vector& a)
{
    vector temp(a);                            // copy a
    swap< vector_base<T,A> >(*this,temp);      // swap representations
    return *this;
}
```

The old elements are destroyed by *temp*'s destructor, and the memory used to hold them is deallocated by *temp*'s *vector_base*'s destructor.

The performance of the two versions ought to be equivalent. Essentially, they are just two different ways of specifying the same set of operations. However, the second implementation is shorter and doesn't replicate code from related *vector* functions, so writing the assignment that way ought to be less error prone and lead to simpler maintenance.

Note the absence of the traditional test for self-assignment:

   if (*this* == &*a*) **return** *this;

These assignment implementations work by first constructing a copy and then swapping representations. This obviously handles self-assignment correctly. I decided that the efficiency gained from the test in the rare case of self-assignment was more than offset by its cost in the common case where a different *vector* is assigned.

In either case, two potentially significant optimizations are missing:

(1) If the capacity of the vector assigned to is large enough to hold the assigned vector, we don't need to allocate new memory.

(2) An element assignment may be more efficient than an element destruction followed by an element construction.

Implementing these optimizations, we get:

```
template<class T, class A>              // optimized, basic guarantee
vector<T,A>& vector<T,A>::operator=(const vector& a)
{
    if (capacity() < a.size()) {       // allocate new vector representation:
        vector temp(a);                        // copy a
        swap< vector_base<T,A> >(*this,temp);  // swap representations
        return *this;
    }

    if (this == &a) return *this;      // protect against self assignment

                                       // assign to old elements:
    size_type sz = size();
    size_type asz = a.size();
    alloc = a.get_allocator();         // copy the allocator

    if (asz<=sz) {  // copy over old elements and destroy surplus elements:
        copy(a.begin(),a.begin()+asz,v);
        for (T* p = v+asz; p!=space; ++p) p->~T();
    }
```

```
else {        // copy over old elements and construct additional elements:
      copy (a . begin ( ) , a . begin ( ) +sz , v ) ;
      uninitialized_copy (a . begin ( ) +sz , a . end ( ) , space ) ;
   }
   space = v+asz ;
   return *this ;
}
```

These optimizations are not free. The *copy* ( ) algorithm does *not* offer the strong exception-safety guarantee. It does not guarantee that it will leave its target unchanged if an exception is thrown during copying. Thus, if $T::operator=$ ( ) throws an exception during *copy* ( ), the *vector* being assigned to need not be a copy of the vector being assigned, and it need not be unchanged. For example, the first five elements might be copies of elements of the assigned vector and the rest unchanged. It is also plausible that an element – the element that was being copied when $T::operator=$ ( ) threw an exception – ends up with a value that is neither the old value nor a copy of the corresponding element in the vector being assigned. However, if $T::operator=$ ( ) leaves its operands in a valid state if it throws an exception, the *vector* is still in a valid state – even if it wasn't the state we would have preferred.

Here, I have copied the allocator using an assignment. It is actually not required that every allocator support assignment.

The standard-library *vector* assignment offers the weaker exception-safety property of this last implementation – and its potential performance advantages. That is, *vector* assignment provides the basic guarantee, so it meets most people's idea of exception safety. However, it does not provide the strong guarantee. If you need an assignment that leaves the *vector* unchanged if an exception is thrown, you must either use a library implementation that provides the strong guarantee or provide your own assignment operation. For example:

```
template<class T, class A>
void safe_assign (vector<T,A>& a, const vector<T,A>& b)  // "obvious" a = b
{
      vector<T,A> temp (a . get_allocator ( ) ) ;
      temp . reserve (b . size ( ) ) ;
      for (typename vector<T,A>::iterator p = b . begin ( ) ; p!=b . end ( ) ; ++p)
            temp . push_back (*p) ;
      swap (a , temp) ;
}
```

If there is insufficient memory for *temp* to be created with room for *b.size* ( ) elements, *std::bad_alloc* is thrown before any changes are made to *a*. Similarly, if *push_back* ( ) fails for any reason, *a* will remain untouched because we apply *push_back* ( ) to *temp* rather than to *a*. In that case, any elements of *temp* created by *push_back* ( ) will be destroyed before the exception that caused the failure is re-thrown.

Swap does not copy *vector* elements. It simply swaps the data members of a *vector*; that is, it swaps *vector_base*s (Sect. 3.2). Consequently, it does not throw exceptions even if operations on the elements might. Consequently, *safe_assign* ( ) does not do spurious copies of elements and is reasonably efficient.

As is often the case, there are alternatives to the obvious implementation. We can let the library perform the copy into the temporary for us:

```
template<class T, class A>
void safe_assign (vector<T,A>& a, const vector<T,A>& b) // simple a = b
{
    vector<T,A> temp (b);     // copy the elements of b into a temporary
    swap (a, temp);
}
```

Indeed, we could simply use call-by-value:

```
template<class T, class A>            // simple a = b (note: b is passed by value)
void safe_assign (vector<T,A>& a, vector<T,A> b)
{
    swap (a, b);
}
```

The last two variants of *safe_assign* () don't copy the *vector*'s allocator. This is a permitted optimization.

3.4 *push_back()*

From an exception-safety point of view, *push_back* () is similar to assignment in that we must take care that the *vector* remains unchanged if we fail to add a new element:

```
template< class T, class A>
void vector<T,A>::push_back (const T& x)
{
    if (space == last) {  // no more free space; relocate:
        vector_base b (alloc, size () ?2*size () :2);  // double the allocation
        uninitialized_copy (v, space, b.v);
        new (b.space) T(x);                    // place a copy of x in *b.space
        ++b.space;
        destroy_elements ();
        swap<vector_base<T,A> > (b, *this);    // swap representations
        return;
    }
    new (space) T(x);                          // place a copy of x in *space
    ++space;
}
```

Naturally, the copy constructor initializing *∗space* might throw an exception. If that happens, the value of the *vector* remains unchanged, with *space* left unincremented. In that case, the *vector* elements are not reallocated so that iterators referring to them are not invalidated. Thus, this implementation implements the strong guarantee that an exception thrown by an allocator or even a user-supplied copy constructor leaves the *vector* unchanged. The standard library offers the strong guarantee for *push_back* ().

Note the absence of a *try-block* (except for the one hidden in *uninitialized_copy* ()). The update was done by carefully ordering the operations so that if an exception is thrown, the *vector* remains unchanged.

The approach of gaining exception safety through ordering and the "resource acquisition is initialization'' technique tends to be more elegant and more efficient than explicitly handling errors using *try-blocks*. More problems with exception safety arise from a programmer ordering code in unfortunate ways than from lack of specific exception-handling code. The basic rule of ordering is not to destroy information before its replacement has been constructed and can be assigned without the possibility of an exception.

Exceptions introduce possibilities for surprises in the form of unexpected control flows. For a piece of code with a simple local control flow, such as the *operator=* (), *safe_assign* (), and *push_back* () examples, the opportunities for surprises are limited. It is relatively simple to look at such code and ask oneself "can this line of code throw an exception, and what happens if it does?" For large functions with complicated control structures, such as complicated conditional statements and nested loops, this can be hard. Adding *try-blocks* increases this local control structure complexity and can therefore be a source of confusion and errors. I conjecture that the effectiveness of the ordering approach and the ''resource acquisition is initialization'' approach compared to more extensive use of *try-blocks* stems from the simplification of the local control flow. Simple, stylized code is easier to understand and easier to get right.

Note that the *vector* implementation is presented as an example of the problems that exceptions can pose and of techniques for addressing those problems. The standard does not require an implementation to be exactly like the one presented here. What the standard does guarantee is described in Sect. E.4 of [1].

3.5 Constructors and Invariants

From the point of view of exception safety, other *vector* operations are either equivalent to the ones already examined (because they acquire and release resources in similar ways) or trivial (because they don't perform operations that require cleverness to maintain valid states). However, for most classes, such ''trivial'' functions constitute the majority of code. The difficulty of writing such functions depends critically on the environment that a constructor established for them to operate in. Said differently, the complexity of ''ordinary member functions'' depends critically on choosing a good class invariant. By examining the ''trivial'' *vector* functions, it is possible to gain insight into the interesting question of what makes a good invariant for a class and how constructors should be written to establish such invariants.

Operations such as *vector* subscripting are easy to write because they can rely on the invariant established by the constructors and maintained by all functions that acquire or release resources. In particular, a subscript operator can rely on *v* referring to an array of elements:

```
template< class T, class A> T& vector<T,A>::operator[] (size_type i)
{
    return v[i];
}
```

It is important and fundamental to have constructors acquire resources and establish a simple invariant. To see why, consider an alternative definition of *vector_base*:

```
template<class T, class A = allocator<T> >        // clumsy use of constructor
class vector_base {
public:
    A alloc;    // allocator
    T* v;       // start of allocation
    T* space;   // end of elements, start of space allocated for possible expansion
    T* last;    // end of allocated space

    vector_base(const A& a, typename A::size_type n)
        : alloc(a), v(0), space(0), last(0)
    {
        v = alloc.allocate(n);
        space = last = v+n;
    }

    ~vector_base() { if (v) alloc.deallocate(v, last-v); }
};
```

Here, I construct a *vector_base* in two stages: First, I establish a "safe state" where *v*, *space*, and *last* are set to *0*. Only after that has been done do I try to allocate memory. This is done out of misplaced fear that if an exception happens during element allocation, a partially constructed object could be left behind. This fear is misplaced because a partially constructed object cannot be "left behind" and later accessed. The rules for static objects, automatic objects, member objects, and elements of the standard-library containers prevent that. However, it could/can happen in pre-standard libraries that used/use placement new to construct objects in containers designed without concern for exception safety. Old habits can be hard to break.

Note that this attempt to write safer code complicates the invariant for the class: It is no longer guaranteed that *v* points to allocated memory. Now *v* might be *0*. This has one immediate cost. The standard-library requirements for allocators do not guarantee that we can safely deallocate a pointer with the value *0*. In this, allocators differ from *delete*. Consequently, I had to add a test in the destructor.

This two-stage construct is not an uncommon style. Sometimes, it is even made explicit by having the constructor do only some "simple and safe" initialization to put the object into a destructible state. The real construction is left to an *init*() function that the user must explicitly call. For example:

```
template<class T>    // archaic (pre-standard, pre-exception) style
class Vector {
    T* v;       // start of allocation
    T* space;   // end of elements, start of space allocated for possible expansion
    T* last;    // end of allocated space
public:
    Vector() : v(0), space(0), last(0) { }
    ~Vector() { free(v); }

    bool init(size_t n); // return true if initialization succeeded

    // ... Vector operations ...
};
```

```
template<class T>
bool Vector<T>::init(size_t n) // return true if initialization succeeded
{
    if (v = (T*) malloc (sizeof(T) *n) ) {
        uninitialized_fill (v, v+n, T() );
        space = last = v+n;
        return true;
    }
    return false;
}
```

The perceived value of this style is
(1) The constructor can't throw an exception, and the success of an initialization using *init* ( ) can be tested by "usual" (that is, non-exception) means.
(2) There exists a trivial valid state. In case of a serious problem, an operation can give an object that state.
(3) The acquisition of resources is delayed until a fully initialized object is needed.
However, this two-stage construction technique doesn't deliver its expected benefits and can itself be a source of problems.

The first point (using an *init* ( ) function in preference to a constructor) is bogus. Using constructors and exception handling is a more general and systematic way of dealing with resource acquisition and initialization errors. This style is a relic of pre-exception C++. Having a separate *init* ( ) function is an opportunity to
(1) forget to call *init* ( ) ,
(2) call *init* ( ) more than once,
(3) forget to test on the success of *init* ( ) ,
(4) forget that *init* ( ) might throw an exception, and
(5) use the object before calling *init* ( ) .
Constructors and exceptions were introduced into C++ to prevent such problems [3].

The second point (having an easy-to-construct "safe" valid state) is in principle a good one. If we can't put an object into a valid state without fear of throwing an exception before completing that operation, we do indeed have a problem. However, this "safe state" should be one that is a natural part of the semantics of the class rather than an implementation artifact that complicates the class invariant.

If the "safe" state is not a natural part of the semantics of the class, the invariant is complicated and a burden is imposed on every member function. For example, the simple subscript operation becomes something like:

```
template< class T> T& Vector<T>::operator [] (size_type i)
{
    if (v) return v[i];
    // error handling
}
```

If part of the reason for using a two-stage initialization was to avoid exceptions, the error handling part of that *operator* [] ( ) could easily become complicated.

Like the second point, the third (delaying acquisition of a resource until is needed) misapplies a good idea in a way that imposes cost without yielding benefits. In many cases, notably in containers such as *vector*, the best way of delaying resource acquisition is for the programmer to delay the creation of objects until they are needed.

To sum up: the two-phase construction approach leads to more complicated invariants and typically to less elegant, more error-prone, and harder-to-maintain code. Consequently, the language-supported "constructor approach" should be preferred to the "*init* ( ) -function approach" whenever feasible. That is, resources should be acquired in constructors whenever delayed resource acquisition isn't mandated by the inherent semantics of a class.

The negative effects of two-phase construction become more marked when we consider application classes that acquire significant resources, such as network connections and files. Such classes are rarely part of a framework that guides their use and their implementation in the way the standard-library requirements guide the definition and use of *vector*. The problems also tend to increase as the mapping between the application concepts and the resources required to implement them becomes more complex. Few classes map as directly onto system resources as does *vector*.

4 Implications for Library Users

One way to look at exception safety in the context of the standard library is that we have no problems unless we create them for ourselves: The library will function correctly as long as user-supplied operations meet the standard library's basic requirements. In particular, no exception thrown by a standard container operation will cause memory leaks from containers or leave a container in an invalid state. Thus, the problem for the library user becomes: How can I define my types so that they don't cause undefined behavior or leak resources?

The basic rules are:

(1) When updating an object, don't destroy its old representation before a new representation is completely constructed and can replace the old one without risk of exceptions. For example, see the implementations of *safe_assign* ( ) and *vector* : : *push_back* ( ) in Sect. 3.

   (1a) If you must override an old representation in the process of creating the new, be sure to leave a valid object behind if an exception is thrown. For example, see the "optimized" implementation of *vector* : : *operator=* ( ) .

(2) Before throwing an exception, release every resource acquired that is not owned by some (other) object.

   (2a) The "resource acquisition is initialization" technique and the language rule that partially constructed objects are destroyed to the extent that they were constructed can be most helpful here.

   (2b) The *uninitialized_copy* ( ) algorithm and its cousins provide automatic release of resources in case of failure to complete construction of a set of objects.

(3) Before throwing an exception, make sure that every operand is in a valid state. That is, leave each object in a state that allows it to be accessed and destroyed without causing undefined behavior or an exception to be thrown from a destructor. For example, see *vector*'s assignment in Sect. 3.2.

   (3a) Note that constructors are special in that when an exception is thrown from a constructor, no object is left behind to be destroyed later. This implies that we don't have to establish an invariant and that we must be sure to release all resources acquired during a failed construction before throwing an exception.

(3b) Note that destructors are special in that an exception thrown from a destructor almost certainly leads to violation of invariants and/or calls to *terminate* ( ) .

In practice, it can be surprisingly difficult to follow these rules. The primary reason is that exceptions can be thrown from places where people don't expect them. A good example is *std* :: *bad_alloc*. Every function that directly or indirectly uses *new* or an *allocator* to acquire memory can throw *bad_alloc*. In some programs, we can solve this particular problem by not running out of memory. However, for programs that are meant to run for a long time or to accept arbitrary amounts of input, we must expect to handle various failures to acquire resources. Thus, we must assume every function capable of throwing an exception until we have proved otherwise.

One simple way to try to avoid surprises is to use containers of elements that do not throw exceptions (such as containers of pointers and containers of simple concrete types) or linked containers (such as *list*) that provide the strong guarantee. Another, complementary, approach is to rely primarily on operations, such as *push_back* ( ), that offer the strong guarantee that an operation either succeeds or has no effect. However, these approaches are by themselves insufficient to avoid resource leaks and can lead to an ad hoc, overly restrictive, and pessimistic approach to error handling and recovery. For example, a *vector<T* >* is trivially exception safe if operations on *T* don't throw exceptions. However, unless the objects pointed to are deleted somewhere, an exception from the *vector* will lead to a resource leak. Thus, introducing a *Handle* class to deal with deallocation and using *vector*<Handle<T> > rather than the plain *vector<T* >* will probably improve the resilience of the code.

When writing new code, it is possible to take a more systematic approach and make sure that every resource is represented by a class with an invariant that provides the basic guarantee. Given that, it becomes feasible to identify the critical objects in an application and provide roll-back semantics (that is, the strong guarantee − possibly under some specific conditions) for operations on such objects.

As mentioned in Sect. 3, the basic techniques for dealing with exceptions, focusing on resources and invariants, also help getting code correct and efficient. In general, keeping code stylish and simple by using classes to represent resources and concepts makes the code easier to understand, easier to maintain, and easier to reason about. Constructors, destructors, and the support for correct partial construction and destruction are the language-level keys to this. ''Resource acquisition is initialization'' is the key programming technique to utilize these language features.

Most applications contain data structures and code that are not written with exception safety in mind. Where necessary, such code can be fitted into an exception-safe framework by either verifying that it doesn't throw exception (as was the case for the C standard library) or through the use of interface classes for which the exception behavior and resource management can be precisely specified.

When designing types intended for use in an exception-safe environment, we must pay special attention to the operations used by the standard library: constructors, destructors, assignments, comparisons, swap functions, functions used as predicates, and operations on iterators. This is best done by defining a class invariant that can be simply established by all constructors. Sometimes, we must design our class invariants so that we can put an object into a state where it can be destroyed even when an operation suffers a failure at an "inconvenient" point. Ideally, that state isn't an artifact defined simply to aid exception handling, but a state that follows naturally from the semantics of the type.

When considering exception safety, the emphasis should be on defining valid states for objects (invariants) and on proper release of resources. It is therefore important to represent resources directly as classes. The *vector_base* (Sect. 3.2) is a simple example of this. The constructors for such resource classes acquire lower-level resources (such as the raw memory for *vector_base*) and establish invariants (such as the proper initialization of the pointers of a *vector_base*). The destructors of such classes implicitly free lower-level resources. The rules for partial construction and the "resource acquisition is initialization" technique support this way of handling resources.

A well-written constructor establishes the class invariant for an object. That is, the constructor gives the object a value that allows subsequent operations to be written simply and to complete successfully. This implies that a constructor often needs to acquire resources. If that cannot be done, the constructor can throw an exception so that we can deal with that problem before an object is created. This approach is directly supported by the language and the standard library.

The requirement to release resources and to place operands in valid states before throwing an exception means that the burden of exception handling is shared among the function throwing, the functions on the call chain to the handler, and the handler. Throwing an exception does not make handling an error "somebody else's problem." It is the obligation of functions throwing or passing along an exception to release resources that they own and to put operands in consistent states. Unless they do that, an exception handler can do little more than try to terminate gracefully.

5 Acknowledgements

The concepts and techniques described here are the work of many individuals. In particular, Dave Abrahams, Matt Austern, and Greg Colvin made major contributions to the notions of exception safety embodied in the C++ standard library.

6 References

[1] Bjarne Stroustrup: *The Design and Evolution of C++*. Addison-Wesley. 1994. ISBN 0-201-54330-3.
[2] Andrew Koenig (editor): *Standard – The C++ Language*. ISO/IEC 14882:1998(E). Information Technology Council (NCITS). Washington, DC, USA. http://www.ncits.org/cplusplus.htm.
[3] Bjarne Stroustrup: *The C++ Programming Language (Special Edition)*. Addison-Wesley. 2000. ISBN 0-201-70073-5.

Exceptions in Object Modeling:
Finding Exceptions from the Elements of the Static Object Model

Yolande Ahronovitz and Marianne Huchard

LIRMM UMR 5506 and Montpellier II University
161 rue Ada, 34392 Montpellier Cedex 5, France
`yolande@lirmm.fr, huchard@lirmm.fr`

Abstract. The problem of modeling exceptions has not been studied much: literature gives good advice, but lacks concepts about how to think up and model exceptions. We propose guidelines, based on static object model elements, on finding exceptions at modeling stage, and on organizing them. Along with this guide, we also present a thought about finding exceptions using constraints, and about composing exceptions. In order to represent the concepts needed above, we propose some additions to the UML metamodel. We conclude by showing how our proposals can solve some subtyping problems, and how they allow to catch exceptions at different levels of accuracy.

1 Introduction

Most of today's object-oriented languages have an exception handling system. Whereas the dynamic mechanisms (signaling, catching, handling) have been and are widely studied, only a few studies about designing exceptions themselves exist. Indeed, modeling and design methods do not tell much about exceptions: maybe because it was generally admitted that they fall into the programming domain. As UML is the most detailed proposal about exceptions in object modeling, it is interesting to study what is proposed in the metamodel, what is proposed in the extensions, and what advice are given in the associated literature.

The point of view of UML The UML metamodel takes into account the only dynamic aspects of exceptions. In the UML metamodel [1], partly shown in Fig. 1, an exception is a *Signal*, dedicated to errors. "A signal represents a named object that is dispatched (thrown) asynchronously by one object and then received (caught) by another" [2]. Different dynamic diagrams allow to represent how a signal is thrown and caught. It is linked by associations to *behavioral features*[1], which catch it and throw it; it is *generalizable* and *specializable*; it may have parameters. Yet, if we strictly follow the metamodel, we can't describe it using attributes, methods, and/or associations. The only provided "feature" is a *body*,

---

[1] UML term, which may refer to an operation or to a method.

A. Romanovsky et al. (Eds.): Exception Handling, LNCS 2022, pp. 77–93, 2001.
© Springer-Verlag Berlin Heidelberg 2001

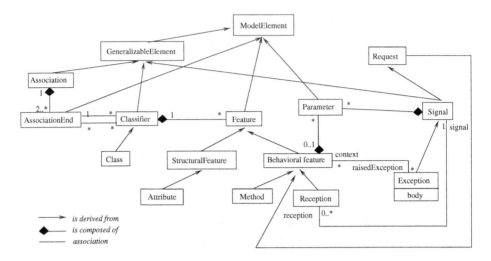

Fig. 1. Extract from UML metamodel

the content of which must be *"a description of the exception in a format not defined in UML"*.

However, UML has extension mechanisms, which add notions not belonging to the metamodel [1]. Among these mechanisms, stereotypes allow to specialize some elements of the metamodel, in order to customize them for a specific problem. UML proposes standard stereotypes, among them we find *<<exception>>*[2]. This stereotype, which specializes *Class*, allows to model exceptions which seem "class-like". We give in Fig. 2 a simple example of the notation. This notation

Fig. 2. *Stack* class and *EmptyStack* exception

hides an ambiguity: *EmptyStack* is both an instance of the metamodel element (metaclass) *Exception*, and an instance of the *<<exception>>* stereotype. We will have further discussion about this point in Sect. 4.

Concerning the design, the authors of [2] suggest to search for exceptions following the place (the operations) where they can be signaled; they also advise the users to organize their exceptions into a hierarchy. These hints are good, but should be developed to be really useful; in particular, they do not propose precise criteria for classifying into the hierarchy.

If we want to find more about design of exceptions, then we have, rather unexpectedly, to look at programming languages, which give us more elaborated answers.

The point of view of programming languages Some of them give predefined hierarchies of classes representing exceptions. Some other offer non reified exceptions, but give advice on how to determine user exceptions.

The content and the organization of the predefined hierarchies show the modeling effort done by the language designers. C++, Java et Python [3] give typical examples of this effort. We review below the proposals of C++ and Java.

As shown in Fig. 3, the C++ predefined hierarchy is very small [4]. It is devised on one hand in order to organize language and standard library exceptions, and on the other hand in order to define general exceptions that the programmer can use or refine. Under the root, we mainly find the subclasses `logic_error`

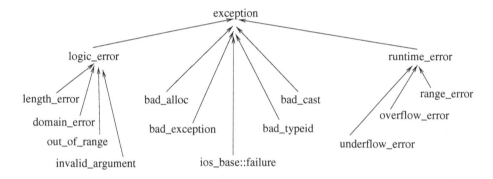

Fig. 3. Complete hierarchy of C++ exceptions

and `runtime_error`. Their subclasses are themselves very general, and should be refined before use. But this is not done for the predefined C++ classes: for example, when the predefined C++ `bitset` class must signal a very specific error in a constructor (in this case that an init string contains other things than zeroes and ones), it throws `invalid_argument`. Moreover, the programmer is not obliged to define his exceptions, or to place them in this hierarchy.

In Java, the predefined hierarchy is more advanced [5,6]. The classes are numerous, precise, and well-documented. They are organized by means of hierarchies, and with packages. The root of the hierarchy is `Throwable`, which has two subclasses `Error` and `Exception`. `Error` is the root of hardware errors and fatal software errors (virtual machine errors, link errors). `Exception` is the root of ordinary software errors. It must be the root of the hierarchies of user defined exceptions. It has several subclasses: `RuntimeException` and `IOException` are roots for important subtrees, while other subclasses are specific. Some exception cases are very detailed: for example, `IndexOutOfBoundsException` has two subclasses `ArrayIndexOutOfBoundsException` and `StringIndexOutOfBoundsException`,

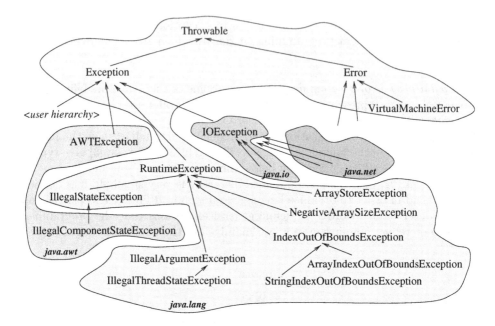

Fig. 4. Extract from the hierarchy of Java exceptions

depending on the type of the object.

But some important questions arise. First, the lack of multiple inheritance prevents the complete classification of some exceptions. For instance, `IllegalComponentStateException` means that "the AWT component is not in the appropriate state for some requested operation"[7]. It is both an AWT component exception, and an exception meaning that a state is not appropriate. So it should have two "natural" superclasses: `AWTException` (subclass of `Exception`), and `IllegalStateException`, subclass of `RunTimeException`; in fact it has only one, the latter. However, it belongs to the *java.awt* package, as the former. Second, the exceptions on arrays could have been grouped together; but then it would have been in conflict with other classifications (see above the subclasses of `IndexOutOfBoundsException`). Third, some exceptions seem to be in a wrong place: `IllegalThreadStateException`, thrown when a thread "is not in a state where it is possible to fulfill the request"[8], is a subclass of `IllegalArgumentException`; it should rather be a subclass of `IllegalStateException`. Finally, the exceptions are put in the packages, but there is no systematically defined exception root for each package. For example, the exceptions of *java.io* are subclasses of the root `IOException`, but there is no exception root in *java.net*, and the exceptions of this package are also subclasses of `IOException`. Another example is the `AWTException` which, despite its name, is not a root for the *java.awt* package exceptions. To sum up, the predefined hierarchies encourage the programmer to define his own exceptions, and to classify them (at least integrating them in the existing hierarchy); but they do not organize the exceptions as systematically as they can do.

As predefined hierarchies are not usual (for example, reified exceptions do not exist in Eiffel and Ada95), it is useful to consult general literature about programming languages: we find there some advice on how to determine and use exceptions. Most of the authors advise to avoid using exceptions in expected situations [5], or in cases "where more local control structures will suffice" [4]. In [9], we find suggestions to determine exceptions according to "what client classes want to catch". Another hint is to study methods' preconditions and postconditions, to define for each object what a consistent state is. This fits with the "contract" notion defined in Eiffel [10].

Towards an object-oriented modeling of exceptions When looking closer, we find the previous proposals unsufficient. Apart from the fact that they are not always precise and clear, the proposed approaches are often more functional than object-oriented. We propose hereafter to follow an object-oriented point of view: we think that it is important to design exceptions in relation to the other parts of an object model (classes, attributes, methods, associations, specialization relations).

Outline of the paper In Sects. 2 and 3, we introduce different ways of finding exceptions based on UML static object model. In Sect. 2, we study how to design exceptions related to the basic elements of the structural model: classes, features, associations, and specialization relations. In Sect. 3, we introduce more advanced notions: using constraints which have been put on the UML diagrams, and making composite exceptions. In Sect. 4, we propose some additions to the UML metamodel, in order to have the means of representing our solutions with this formalism. Finally, we conclude in Sect. 5 by discussing the contributions of our modeling, and the perspectives of this work.

2   Exceptions Based on Static Object Model Elements

In this section, we describe how designing exceptions can be guided by the elements of the structural model: classes, features, associations, and specialization relations.

2.1   Exceptions and Types

We make the assumption that exceptions must be devised in connection with program types, i.e. we study all exceptions associated with every class when building the class. For instance, when we construct the *Stack* class, we must make an inventory of all the problems linked to the state of the stack, and of all the problems which may arise when we use the stack.

We want the exceptions associated with a type to have the same abstraction level as the type itself [11]. For a given type, this leads us to define exceptions which will be used to "encapsulate" low-level exceptions. For example, we create an "impossible push" exception associated with the *Stack* type; such an exception occurs every time a push is impossible, e.g. when a "memory overflow" occurs. That represents, at the conceptual level, what we do in practice when we catch an instance of "memory overflow" and treat it by throwing an instance of "impossible push".

To put to a single hierarchy all the exceptions associated with a given type helps to factorize their features [12]. The previous remarks lead us to the following principle: if X is a type, X 's own exceptions are all rooted under a general exception class $ExcTypeX$.

2.2   Exceptions and Features

According to UML, features of a class can be split up into primitive attributes (this means that the attribute's type is not a class) and methods. For each method $meth$ of X which gives rise to exceptions, we can put, under the main root $ExcTypeX$, an exception class $ExcMeth$, which will be the mother of all the exceptions thrown by $meth$. We can do the same for each primitive attribute $attrP$ of X, assuming that exceptions associated with an attribute mean exceptions its accessor methods can signal.

It looks very heavy. If two methods $meth1$ and $meth2$ can signal the same kind of exception E, there will be one class $E1$ under the root $ExcMeth1$, which represents E in $meth1$'s context, and another class $E2$ under the root $ExcMeth2$, which represents E in $meth2$'s context. Do we need that?

The answer is given when making progress in the design. Either the two contexts are the same, and we can simplify : we remove $E1$, $E2$, even $ExcMeth1$ and $ExcMeth2$, and define only one class E. Or the two contexts are different, and we keep all the classes (and even add E as a superclass for $E1$ and $E2$).

For instance, we can associate an $EmptyStack$ exception with the class $Stack$. The two methods pop and $peek$ (look at the top object without pop) can signal this exception. Must we have an $EmptyStackPop$ exception under $ExcPop$, and an $EmptyStackPeek$ under $ExcPeek$? It depends on the framework in which the stack is used. We can wish to treat differently the $EmptyStack$ problem when trying to pop, or when only wanting to see; if it is the case, then it is better to have the means to catch the two exceptions separately.

2.3   Exceptions and Associations

We now look at associations: can they give rise to exceptions into the classes they link? If so, how and where can we represent them? We find in a class two kinds of exceptions: ones which are generated by an exception defined on the other end of the association (one may say that they "encapsulate" an exception defined on the other end), others which are the result of the association's semantics (of the role the association plays in the class).

Encapsulating Exceptions   When a class X is linked to another class Y, an exception of one of them can generate an exception of the other through the association. Let us take for example a drinks dispenser, containing several compartments. We model this using an "aggregation" between the class *Drinks-Dispenser* and the class *Compartment*. The existence of this aggregation relation, and the existence of an *Empty* exception defined on the *Compartment* class imply the existence of an *AnEmptyCompartment* exception defined on the *DrinksDispenser* class. In the code, we express this by saying that the dispenser catches the instance of the *Empty* exception thrown by a compartment, and treats it by throwing an instance of the *AnEmptyCompartment* exception. On the other hand, a compartment will not catch an exception thrown by the dispenser.

This is typical of a composition relation. To respect the encapsulation, the composite takes responsibility for its components' exceptions, and the opposite would not happen.

For an arbitrary association, there is no such precise rules: some exceptions of X can generate exceptions of Y, some exceptions of Y can generate exceptions of X, and each of the two classes can have exceptions which have no influence at all on the other class. Let us examine the two classes *Person* and *Train*, linked by the *driver* association. This association makes sense as *isDriverOf* from *Person* to *Train*, and *hasForDriver* in the other direction. An error on the person's address must not be transmitted to the train. A person's problem, which implies that the special button has not been pushed for a too long interval, must be transmitted to the train[2].

Exceptions Based on the Association's Semantics   Exceptions can arise in a class as a result of the definition of the association itself. For instance, suppose we have a *birthDate* association between classes *Person* and *Date*. A well-formed date causes no error in the *Date* class. As a *birthDate* for a *Person*, it can cause error, e.g. if it is later than the birthdate of one of the person's children, or if it is later than the current date (see Fig. 5).

In Practice   Implementing an association, if it is not itself reified, means defining attributes and methods in its ends' classes (as they are named in UML terminology). We can thus enrich the hierarchy we talked about in the Sect. 2.1: under the main root *ExcTypeX*, we add roots corresponding to each attribute or method able to have exceptions. As for the primitive attributes, exceptions associated with an attribute means exceptions its accessor methods can signal. For each attribute *attrY* of Y type (or of collection of Y type, according to the multiplicity of the association), we can add under its root *ExcAttrY* two subclasses *ExcCapTypeY*, root of the exceptions which are intended to "encapsulate" Y's exceptions, and *ExcRoleY*, root of the exceptions which result from

---

[2] This is known as a dead man system. In very fast trains, the driver must push a special button at regular intervals. If he doesn't, he is presumed dead, or at least unable to drive, and the train's braking system is automatically started.

UML class diagram   **Implementation**

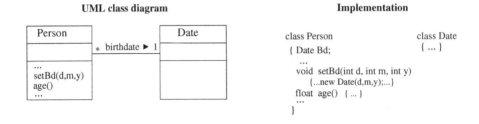

UML sequence diagrams: abnormal cases

Fig. 5. Birthdate example

the role of *attrY* in the *X* class (see Fig. 6 and Fig. 7).

In some cases, it can be useful to insert, between *ExcTypeX* and the roots

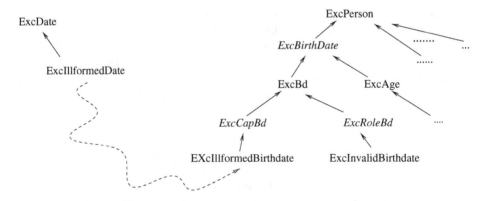

Fig. 6. Birthdate example: associated hierarchy

corresponding to attributes and methods implementing the association, a root *ExcAssoc* which represents the association itself (dotted in Fig. 7).

However, in practice, it is very likely for the *Assoc* association to be reified as an association class (in the UML meaning); thus *ExcAssoc* comes from the rule saying that an exception root is associated with each type.

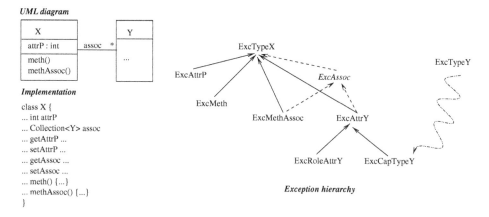

Fig. 7. General diagram of a hierarchy of exceptions associated with a class' features

2.4 Exceptions and Specialization

It seems natural that the hierarchy of the exception classes reflects the hierarchy of the classes of the application. For example, let us consider a *PostObject* class, which has two subclasses *Letter* and *Parcel*; every exception which can occur in every *PostObject*, can a priori occur in a *Letter*, and additional or more specific exceptions can occur in *Letter*.

Figure 8 shows the general diagram of such a hierarchy of exceptions.

In order to refine this first approach, we can split up the exceptions associated

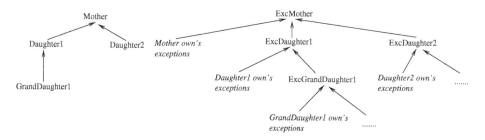

Fig. 8. General diagram of a hierarchy of exceptions associated with a hierarchy of classes

to a *Daughter*[3] class as follows:

1. exceptions associated with *Daughter*'s own features;
2. exceptions associated with features *Daughter* inherits from *Mother*, themselves split up in:

---

[3] The *Mother, Daughter* names refer to the place of the class in the hierarchy.

a) exceptions identical to the *Mother*'s ones, thus not redefined; these exceptions do not necessarily generate classes under the *ExcDaughter* root;

b) exceptions which are specializations of the *Mother*'s ones;

c) exceptions associated with new constraints on the inherited features.

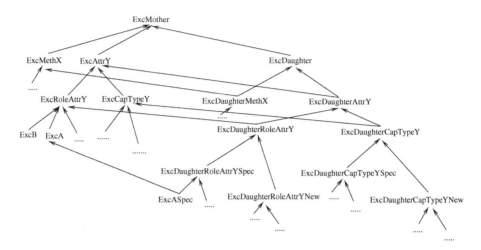

Fig. 9. More detailed diagram for a hierarchy of exceptions associated with *Mother* and *Daughter*

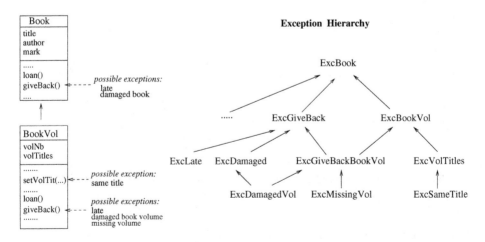

Fig. 10. Example of decomposition

The part of this decomposition showing inherited features is illustrated by the Fig. 9, and Fig. 10 gives a concrete example.

This example describes a *Book* class, which represents library books that we can loan and give back, and the *BookVol* subclass of *Book*, which represents the multivolume books, whose volumes can only be loaned together.

According to the previous decomposition in the case of the *BookVol* class, *ExcSameTitle* is of type 1, *ExcLate* of type 2(a), *ExcDamagedVol* of type 2(b), and *ExcMissingVol* of type 2(c).

3   More Advanced Concepts

3.1   Exceptions Based on Constraints

An exception results of the collision between a system state and an operation: either the operation is not possible in this state, or it leads to an invalid state. If we think to the ways of finding exceptions:

1. to associate exceptions with methods emphasizes the operational aspect: which service may be interrupted by which exception. This contains pre-conditions[4], post-conditions[5], but also what can happen during the course of the method, when it calls another one.
2. to associate exceptions with attributes and associations emphasizes the static (declarative) aspect: which constraint is not satisfied on which object.

To associate exceptions with all the constraints of the system can unify these two approaches. Here, "constraint" has its UML definition, i.e. "an extension of the semantics of a UML element, allowing you to add new rules or modify existing ones" [2]. This includes class invariants, constraints on and between associations, and pre- and post-conditions [2].

In UML notation, constraints can be shown on the diagrams, near the concerned elements, using strings in braces or notes. If the modeling has been precise and exhaustive about constraints, then it is very interesting to use them in order to classify exceptions. It is not easy, because the notation doesn't impose a name on a constraint, nor does it formalize very much the representative string. We give Fig. 11 an example of a "general" constraint (general because it links several attributes of an object) taken from [13]. The constraint specifies the needed ratio between the attributes *width* and *length* of a *Window*, for this window to be "aesthetic".

All that is added to the previously proposed classification: next to the roots of exceptions associated with attributes, methods, and associations constraints, we propose to have exception classes associated with more general constraints. For example, in the *Window* case, we add the exception class *ExcBadRatioLengthWidth*, under *ExcWindow*.

As these constraints may be specialized in the subclasses, we may have a hierarchy of exceptions in order to represent these specializations.

More complicated cases can occur. For example, a constraint can be associated

---

[4] "A constraint that must be true when the operation is invoked" [2].
[5] "A constraint that must be true at the completion of an operation" [2].

{0.8 <= length/width <= 1.5}

Fig. 11. A general constraint about windows.

with several classes; but in this case there is almost always an association *A* between the classes, and the root exception class representing the constraint is naturally a subclass of *ExcA*.

3.2   Composition of Exceptions

Another problem we met is the case of errors which can occur separately or simultaneously. For instance, in a *Date* class, only the day may be wrong, or only the month, or both; in a *DrinksDispenser*, one can lack separately or simultaneously cups, sugar, spoons, drink doses.

When errors occur simultaneously, we can throw an exception corresponding to the first one we detect. However it would be helpful, e.g. for the dispenser manager, to know all the problems which have occurred.

This leads us to add, in some cases of modeling, the notions of single and composite exceptions. These notions are an application of the *Composite* pattern proposed in [14], as shown in Fig. 12. This allows us to represent every single exception (*Leaf* in the *Composite* pattern), and also an exception composed of several exceptions (*Composite* in the *Composite* pattern).

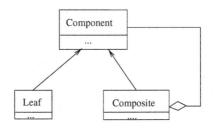

Fig. 12. The UML *Composite* pattern

4   Proposals for UML

In order to represent the concepts needed above, we must have to enrich the UML metamodel. As we have said at the beginning of this paper, exceptions in UML are not recognized as *Classifiers*, so they can't have attributes, methods or associations, unless we use *<<exception>>* stereotype. However, the use of this stereotype leads to a confusion between the static aspect, which uses an object for describing an exceptional problem, and the dynamic one, for which a signal linked to this object is thrown and caught. This confusion is troublesome, because the object has a life independent of its associated signal [15].

A better solution would be to have two separate concepts: an *Exception* meta-class, in order to represent the static aspect, and a *ThrownException* metaclass in order to represent the dynamic aspect. *Exception* would be a *Classifier* specialization, and *ThrownException* a specialization of *Signal*. A *carry* association between *ThrownException* and *Exception* allows to represent the link between a signal and an object.

Still in the metamodel, we would like to add:

1. an *isExceptionFor* association between *Exception* and *Classifier*, meaning that an exception belongs to the exception hierarchy associated with a given type;

2. a *generatesException* ternary association between *Exception* and *Association*; an instance of this association would be defined in a model between two exceptions *E1* and *E2* and one association *A* in order to say that the exception *E1* and the association *A* generate the exception *E2*;

3. an *isCompatibleWith* association on *Exception*, meaning that two exceptions can belong together to a composite exception;

4. a specialization of the *Exception* metaclass by *SingleException* and *CompositeException*, in order to apply the *Composite* pattern cited above.

Figure 13 shows these proposals in the UML metamodel.

This modeling also allows to represent some reifiable aspects of exception handlers, such as class handlers. Such handlers are defined at class level [12,16, 17], whereas most common exception handlers are defined at expression level (*try... catch* structure). A class handler describes the default behaviour to handle a given exception. Depending on the languages, it is defined, either in the class which models the exception, or in the one with which the exception is associated. The two alternatives are acceptable and not exclusive, because this handler falls within their two domains. The UML modeling we proposed above allows us to easily represent this kind of handler as a (possibly reifiable) attribute of the *isExceptionFor* association, proposed above between *Exception* and *Classifier*.

5   Conclusion and Perspectives

We proposed an object-oriented modeling of exceptions mainly based on the elements of the static model. The seek for exceptions involves much modeling

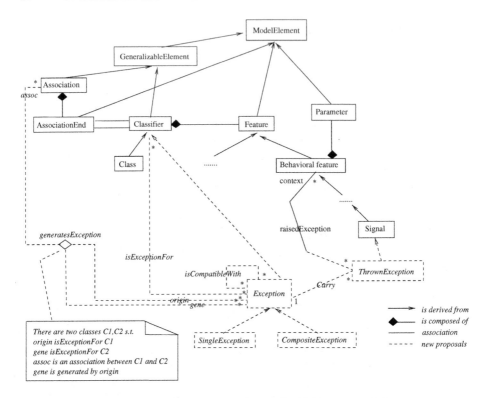

Fig. 13. Some proposals about the UML metamodel

work; the result can be complicated, and difficult to implement in some languages. However, when the final result is complicated, it often means that the problem we wanted to model is complex. This happens particularly when we want a software to be as reliable as possible. For everyday cases, the above proposals make up a kind of guide for modeling: *there's no need to implement everything.* If the final result remains large, it is logically organized, because the hierarchy of exceptions reflects the structure of the static model. Furthermore, even if the implemented hierarchy of exceptions is complex, it is well separated from the hierarchy of the classes of the application. Thus it does not obscure the main development. Moreover, this makes future developments of the software easier: for example, solving problems linked to subtyping, and helping to represent accurately, and also to catch accurately, all error cases, since the exceptions are caught according to their types [5].

Solving a subtyping problem One can define subtyping using substituability: an instance of a *Daughter* subclass must always be able to replace an instance of the *Mother* class. In the case of exceptions, this implies that a method redefined in *Daughter* does not signal exceptions which were not declared as throwable by the original method. For example, Java [5] and C++ [4] respect substituability: they allow the *Daughter*'s method to signal at most the same exceptions as the *Mother*'s method, or exceptions which are subclasses of the exceptions the *Mother*'s method can signal. From the modeling point of view, this is not satisfactory: when specializing a method, we see that constraints can be added, and thus new causes of exceptions can arise. All the "root" exception classes described above are abstract classes, and we used them in order to classify the concrete exceptions found during the modeling phase. We will also use abstract classes as an implementation artifice, in order to respect substituability. In the example Fig. 10, this is done making *ExcDamagedVol* specialize both *ExcDamaged* and *ExcGiveBackBookVol*. As another example, let us look at Fig. 14[6]. Suppose that the *Rectangle* class has a *setEdge* method, which can signal an *Ex-*

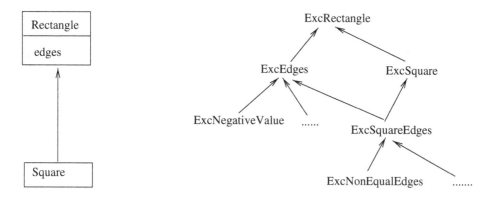

Fig. 14. A concrete case

cNegativeValue exception; suppose that the *setEdge* method redefined in *Square* can signal, in addition to that, an *ExcNonEqualEdges* exception. The two abstract classes *ExcEdge* and *ExcSquareEdge* found during the modeling phase allow us to respect substituability: every *setEdge* method will announce in its signature that it can signal *ExcEdge*.

When we want to implement this inheritance hierarchy in C++, there is no problem, because C++ allows multiple inheritance. The situation in Java is not as good; here we must use all the usual means in order to simulate multiple inheritance [13]: duplicating features and classes, using interfaces.

Refining the Exception Catching Level When an exception belongs to a hierarchy, a thrown instance of this exception can be caught either by a specific handler, especially written for it, or by a handler devised for one of its ancestor classes, whatever may its level be. The more detailed the hierarchy, the bigger the choice

---

[6] This example does not intend to answer the old question "must or must not *Square* be a subclass of *Rectangle*"; how could we give this answer context-free? It only shows how one can organize exceptions if one wishes *Square* to be a subclass of *Rectangle*.

of the exception catching level. In example Fig. 10, we can be interested either in all book exceptions, in which case we catch *ExcBook*, or only in exceptions associated with giving back a book, in which case we catch *ExcGiveBack*, etc.

Open Questions From the methodological point of view, we would like to have rules which help us to determine what kinds of exceptions we must seek for associating with a class: rules based on the nature of the class' features and associations (aggregation, symmetrical or dissymmetrical relation), rules based on the significance of the attributes (essential versus accidental), etc.
Other classifications exist, built along other criteria (e.g. the classic "fatal and recoverable exceptions", or `logic_error`, `runtime_error`, . . . as in C++ [4]). It would be interesting to combine the different points of view, in order to integrate them in the modeling.

To conclude, we think that the approach we propose has not yet been explored, and would be very helpful on designing exceptions. But a lot of fundamental work remains to be done, in order to define a methodology for the conception of exceptions, and an appropriate associated notation.

Acknowledgements. We would like to thank Christophe Dony, Roland Ducournau, and Thérèse Libourel for their comments and suggestions on previous versions of this paper.

References

[1] Rational Software Corporation. *UML v 1.1, Semantics*, september 1997. version 1.1 ad/97-08-04.
[2] G. Booch, J. Rumbaugh, and I. Jacobson. *The Unified Modeling Language User Guide*. Addison-Wesley, 1999.
[3] http://www.python.org/doc/essays/stdexceptions.html.
[4] B. Stroustrup. *The C++ Programming Language. Third Edition*. Addison-Wesley, 1998.
[5] K. Arnold, J. Gosling, and D. Holmes. *The Java Programming Language. Third Edition*. Addison-Wesley, 2000.
[6] D. Flanagan. *Java in a nutshell. Third Edition. Java 1.2*. O'Reilly, 1999.
[7] D. Flanagan. *Java in a nutshell. Second Edition. Java 1.1*. O'Reilly, 1997.
[8] S. Oaks and H. Wong. *Java Threads*. O'Reilly, 1997.
[9] *Taligent's Guide to Designing Programs. Copyright 1995*. Taligent, Inc.
[10] D. Meyer. *Eiffel: the language*. Prentice-Hall, 1992.
[11] C. Dony, J. Purchase, and R. Winder. Exception Handling in Object-Oriented systems: Report on ECOOP'91 Workshop W4, 1991.
[12] C. Dony. Exception Handling and Object-Oriented Programming: Towards a Synthesis. *ACM SIGPLAN Notices*, 25(10):322–330, october 1990. Proceedings of ECOOP-OOPSLA'90.
[13] J. Rumbaugh, M. Blaha, W. Premerlani, F. Eddy, and W. Lorensen. *Object-Oriented Modeling and Design*. Prentice Hall Inc. Englewood Cliffs, 1991.

[14] E. Gamma, R. Helm, R. Johnson, and J. Vlissides. *Design Patterns*. Addison-Wesley, 1994.

[15] T. Valkevych and S. Drossopoulou. Formalizing Java Exceptions, in ECOOP'2000 Workshop W2: Exception Handling in Object-Oriented systems. June 2000.

[16] J.L. Knudsen. Exception Handling versus Fault Tolerance, in ECOOP'2000 Workshop W2: Exception Handling in Object-Oriented systems. June 2000.

[17] A. Mikhailova and A. Romanovsky. Behaviour Preserving Evolution of Interface Exceptions, in ECOOP'2000 Workshop W2: Exception Handling in Object-Oriented systems. June 2000.

Supporting Evolution of Interface Exceptions

Anna Mikhailova[1] and Alexander Romanovsky[2]

[1] Department of Electronics & Computer Science, University of Southampton
Highfield, Southampton, SO17 1BJ, UK
`aam@ecs.soton.ac.uk`
[2] Department of Computing Science,
University of Newcastle upon Tyne
Newcastle upon Tyne, NE1 7RU, UK
`alexander.romanovsky@newcastle.ac.uk`

Abstract. Interface exceptions (explicitly declared exceptions that a method can propagate outside) are an inherent part of the interface describing the behaviour of a particular class of objects. Evolution of system behaviour is thus necessarily accompanied by and reflected in the evolution of interface exceptions. While the evolution of normal system behaviour is adequately supported by various language mechanisms, such as subtyping and inheritance, few contemporary object-oriented programming languages offer support for the evolution of interface exceptions. Some languages allow interface exceptions to be specialised and deleted while subtyping, but none of them provides adequate support for adding exceptions. In this paper we propose two complementary solutions to dealing with additional exceptions introduced during system evolution. To solve the problem of non-conforming interfaces resulting from the addition of new exceptions in a development step, the first proposal uses rescue handlers and the second one employs the forwarding technique.

1 Introduction

Organising interface exceptions into hierarchies and specialising them along with the specialisation of classes is in the spirit of the object-oriented paradigm. Few contemporary programming languages support a systematic hierarchical treatment of exceptions in an object-oriented style. We analyse what a more permissive object model supporting evolution of interface exceptions should be like, and propose an improved model supporting exception addition that can be incorporated into existing languages. Since in our model all exceptions that a method can signal (propagate) outside must be declared in its interface, addition of new exceptions involves adding a new declaration in the method interface.

When specialising a class into a subclass, it is often necessary to

- specialise interface exceptions to subtypes of the exceptions signalled by the superclass
- remove interface exceptions signalled by the superclass
- add new interface exceptions, in addition to those signalled by the superclass

A. Romanovsky et al. (Eds.): Exception Handling, LNCS 2022, pp. 94–110, 2001.

We study in detail these cases, focusing on the semantic implications that they cause in resulting programs. Our analysis of the existing (statically-typed) languages supporting an object-oriented style of exception handling, most notably Java [6], Arche [7], and Modula-3 [2], indicates that, at best, these languages permit specialising and deleting interface exceptions while subtyping, but none of them provides adequate support for adding exceptions.

We propose two type-safe solutions to the problem of non-conforming interfaces resulting from the addition of new exceptions in a development step. The first proposal is best suited for the top-down system development approach. The need for introducing a new interface exception may arise, for instance, because a new data structure can deliver new exceptional behaviour. This proposal is based on extending a language with a new construct, a rescue handler, which steps in to rescue the situation when no ordinary handlers are available. Our second proposal is best suited for the bottom-up approach to system development, within which we might want to match an existing class (e.g. from a class library) with an existing interface (e.g. provided by a framework). If the class has extra interface exceptions not signalled by the interface which the class matches otherwise, we propose to employ the forwarding technique, widely used in practical system development to solve interface mismatch problems.

2   Object-Oriented Exception Handling: The Object Model

Exceptions are abnormal events which can happen during the program execution. Most programming languages and systems provide special facilities and language mechanisms for handling exceptions in a disciplined way. More modern object-oriented languages support an object-oriented style of exception handling: they allow arranging exceptions into classes and structuring them into class hierarchies. Apart from delivering better structuring, clarity and conciseness of the resulting code, this approach also promotes genericity and polymorphism, characteristic of the object-oriented style of program development, in the treatment of exceptions.

Recognising the significant advantages of this approach, we also consider the object model where exceptions are class instances, and classes of exceptions are structured into hierarchies. Exceptions can be explicitly created by instantiating the corresponding exception classes and can be initialised using constructors with input parameters. Exceptions can also be created implicitly, when they are raised or signalled. In this case a default (parameterless) constructor is invoked to create an instance of an exception class.

A class, a method, or a block of code can be viewed as an *exception context* (also known as *scope*), so that developers can declare exceptions and associate handlers with such a context: when an exception is raised in an exception context, the control is transferred to the corresponding handler.

In our view, an important feature of an exception handling mechanism is its ability to differentiate between *internal exceptions* to be handled inside the context and *external exceptions* propagated from the context. These two kinds of exceptions are not clearly separated in many languages, although they obviously serve different purposes. The separation can be achieved under two conditions: contexts are program units that have interfaces (e.g. classes or methods), and the concept of *exception context nesting* is defined. Most of the existing exception handling mechanisms use *dynamic exception context*, such that the context is the method or the object being currently executed. Some mechanisms use *static exception contexts* based on the corresponding declaration.

The execution of the context can be completed either successfully or by propagating an (external) *interface exception*. The propagated interface exception is treated as an internal exception raised in the containing context. The simplest example of the dynamic nested context is nested procedure calls. In fact, this is the dominating approach to exception handling which suits well the client/server or remote procedure call paradigms.

In our model, methods are dynamic exception contexts. Each method can be dealing with a set of internal exceptions, each of which must have a corresponding handler associated with the method. Internal exceptions are *raised* in the method code and have to be handled inside the method. Each object type (interface) can have explicitly declared interface exceptions; all interface exceptions that a method can *signal* are to be declared in the method signature using a special signal clause. Interface exceptions are signalled by the method code or by handlers associated with it. Note that interface exceptions of the method called in another method are internal exceptions of the latter and have to be handled at its level. We follow the *termination model* of exception handling [5]. With the termination model, after an internal exception has been handled, the execution of the corresponding method is terminated and the control returns back to the caller.

An example presented in Fig. 1 illustrates the difference between internal exceptions handled by the object's methods and external (interface) exceptions signalled outside the object to be handled by object's clients. The class Bank represents banks working with accounts of type Account, and its subtypes CurrentAccount, and SavingsAccount. The method transfer of class Bank can be used to transfer a certain amount of money from one account to another. If the specified current account fromAccount doesn't have enough money, as signalled by its withdraw method, an attempt is made to withdraw this amount from a savings account. The method transfer has two interface exceptions: NotEnoughMoneyException and SavingsAccountUsedException. The former is signalled if there is not enough money to be transferred even on the savings account, and the latter is signalled to inform the caller about the fact that the savings account has been used (although the money has been successfully transferred). Internal exceptions NotEnoughMoneyException signalled by withdraw methods of fromAccount and sAccount are handled inside the method transfer.

Only interface exceptions can be propagated outside the class in our model. All possible violations of this rule must be either detected at compile time or must cause a predefined Failure exception to be propagated outside the class.

```
class Bank {
  ...
  public void transfer (CurrentAccount fromAccount, SavingsAccount sAccount,
                Account toAccount, int amount)
      signals NotEnoughMoneyException, SavingsAccountUsedException
  {
    try {
      fromAccount.withdraw(amount);
    }
    catch(NotEnoughMoneyException neme) {
      try {
        sAccount.withdraw(amount);
        toAccount.deposit(amount);
        signal new SavingsAccountUsedException();
      }
      catch (NotEnoughMoneyException neme) {
        signal new NotEnoughMoneyException();
      }
    }
    toAccount.deposit(amount);
  }
```

Fig. 1. Example of the difference between internal and interface exceptions

This exception is signalled in some other situations, for example, when it is impossible to leave the object in which an exception has occurred in a known consistent state corresponding to one of the interface exceptions.

For simplicity, we do not consider multiple inheritance.

3 Behaviour Refinement Requires Exception Evolution

3.1 Behaviour Evolution

The evolution of system behaviour is always performed as the evolution of system components. Changes of the component behaviour often cause changes of their interface. Very often the behaviour evolution results in increasing complexity of software, forcing system developers to modify the system structure, to handle this complexity. The most typical way of achieving this is by decomposing some components into several subcomponents. These subcomponents can either be hidden in a higher-level *wrapping* component which conforms to the interface of the original component, or they can themselves replace the initial component and be used by the original component's clients.

There are multiple ways in which the system behaviour can evolve. The most obvious are improving functionality of the components by replacing old fragments of the design, e.g. code, with new better ones (*refinement*), and adding new functionality (*extension*). Apart from these, there are also other forms of evolution that deserve attention as well: *deleting functionality* and *merging functionality*. These four forms of behaviour evolution cover the main possible directions in which system design can proceed.

Contemporary programming languages provide several language mechanisms supporting behaviour evolution. The principle mechanism supporting behaviour evolution in the context of object-oriented programming is *inheritance*. The classical view is to associate inheritance with *conceptual specialisation* in system modelling and design [9]. This form of inheritance, sometimes referred to as strict inheritance, unifies subclassing (*implementation inheritance*) with subtyping (*interface inheritance*), forcing code reuse and behaviour evolution to be necessarily accompanied by conceptual specialisation. Since these two processes are to a certain extent unrelated, this unification appears to be too restrictive for dealing with evolutionary development of complex systems. In particular, the addition of truly new properties requires re-constructing system parts from scratch [9].

To overcome these limitations, the newer object-oriented languages, like Java and Sather, separate interface inheritance responsible for conceptual specialisation, and implementation inheritance dealing with code reuse and behaviour evolution. This results in separate subtyping and subclassing hierarchies. This separation of concepts to a large extent facilitates system design and evolution, because more creative ways of abstraction modification can be explored while subclassing, without the need to maintain behavioural compatibility.

3.2   Conceptual Specialisation, Subtyping and Subclassing

Conceptual specialisation, sometime also referred to as *subtyping*, underlies the evolution and behaviour refinement of object-oriented software. Subtyping polymorphism can be used to substitute subtype objects for supertype objects dynamically, at run-time. This permits clients of supertype objects to benefit from conceptual specialisation by using more specialised subtype objects instead of more general supertype objects. For example, method transfer of Bank can take as argument toAccount an object of type CurrentAccount or SavingsAccount, both of which are subtypes of type Account which is the declared type of toAccount. Subtyping is usually denoted by <:, so that e.g. CurrentAccount <: Account, and we will follow this convention here as well.

To ensure that all client's requests for method calls on subtype objects can be responded to by supertype objects instead, subtyping requires syntactic conformance of objects' methods. The subtyping relation can be a simple extension, or can allow modification in a subtype of inherited method signatures so that the types of method input parameters become *contravariant* and the types of method output parameters become *covariant*. Contravariance means that subtyping on the types of method parameters is in the opposite direction from subtyping on the interfaces having these methods. Respectively, covariance means that subtyping on the types of method parameters is in the same direction as subtyping on the interfaces having these methods.

The intuitive meaning of contravariance and covariance of method parameters is that clients should be able to invoke methods on a subtype object, supplying it with input arguments and obtaining the results, the same way as they would invoke the corresponding methods on a supertype object. Then input supplied by a client should always be accepted by a subtype method and output produced by the latter should always be acceptable for the client. For more detailed information on covariance and contravariance we refer to [1].

Subclassing or implementation inheritance allows the developer to build new classes from existing ones incrementally, by inheriting some or all of their attributes and methods, overriding some attributes and methods, and adding extra methods.

In most object-oriented languages, such as Simula, Eiffel, and C++, subclassing forms a basis for subtype polymorphism, i.e. signatures of subclass methods automatically conform to those of superclass methods, and, syntactically, subclass instances can be substituted for superclass instances. As the mechanism of polymorphic substitutability is, to a great extent, independent of the mechanism of implementation reuse [3], languages like Java and Sather separate the subtyping and subclassing hierarchies.

For simplicity, we will consider here subclassing to be the basis for subtyping and will analyse how behaviour refinement of subclasses with respect to their superclasses influences evolution of exceptions. The same principles also apply to systems with separate subclassing and interface inheritance hierarchies, although in these systems subclassing is not necessarily accompanied by behaviour-preserving refinement and can just reflect a behaviour evolution.

3.3   Specialising Exceptions

Analysing the nature of interface exceptions, it is easy to see that like method output parameters, they are entities *returned* from a method. As such, like output parameters they are likely to have covariant nature. Indeed, if instead of signalling an exception of type ArrayException in a subtype SortedArray of Array, we will signal an exception SortedArrayException, clients using SortedArray object and expecting an exception of type ArrayException should be able to deal with its special case, SortedArrayException. Such covariant exception specialisation ensures that clients using a subtype object instead of a supertype object are never faced with unexpected method results, in this case exception occurrences.

As it is perfectly type-safe to covariantly redefine (specialise) interface exceptions, some languages actually permit this kind of redeclaration. The object-oriented language Modula-3 was one of the first to introduce some form of interface exception specialisation, although exceptions are not classes here. A procedure declaration includes a list of all exceptions that can be signalled. The language allows procedure redeclaration while exporting interfaces: all exceptions that a redeclared procedure can signal must be declared in the exported procedure declaration.

Method declaration in Java can contain the throws clause that has to include all checked exceptions that the method can signal. Java imposes the following

rule on the checked exceptions that method n overriding method m of the superclass can throw: for every exception class listed in the throws clause of n, either
the exception class or one of its superclasses must be listed in the throws clause
of m. For example, we can have

```
public interface Buffer {                    public interface InfiniteBuffer extends Buffer {
   void set (char) throws BufferError;           void set (char) throws InfiniteBufferError;
}                                            }
```

provided that InfiniteBufferError <: BufferError.

Naturally, this rule permits specialising one exception class in the throws
clause of the parent method to several of its subclasses in the overriding method.

A very similar approach is used for dealing with interface exceptions during
subtyping in the programming language Arche [7].

3.4   Removing Exceptions

Apart from specialising interface exceptions while subclassing, some existing
programming languages also permit removing them. For example, Java stipulates
the "Catch or Specify Requirement" which requires that a method either catches
an exception by providing an exception handler for that type of exception, or it
specifies that it can throw that exception. What this rule effectively permits is
removing in a subclass method an exception signalled by a parent method by
handling it internally. As example from [6] illustrates this situation:

```
public interface Buffer {
   char get() throws BufferEmpty, BufferError;
}public interface InfiniteBuffer extends Buffer {
   char get() throws BufferError;
}
```

It is interesting to note that removing interface exceptions, unlike removing
methods, does not restrict the functionality of a subtype. While method removal
can by no means be viewed as behaviour-preserving and type-safe, interface exception removing indicates that exceptional or erroneous behaviour is *reduced* in
a subtype, and as such can be viewed as behaviour refinement. Clearly, removing
interface exceptions in a subtype preserves type safety. Clients using a subtype
object instead of a supertype object will never be faced with an exception they
are not ready to handle, because fewer exceptions are signalled by the server
object. Being prepared to handle the same exceptions as before, the clients will
carry out the actual handling less often.

As demonstrated by these examples, the existing languages support covariant
redeclaration of interface exceptions and their removal. However, considering
general ways in which systems can evolve (Section 3.1), it is clear that these ways
of inheriting, redeclaring and removing interface exceptions are too restrictive
and should be relaxed to support other forms of behaviour evolution as well.

3.5   Exception Inheritance for Exception Evolution

Miller and Tripathi in [8] rightfully point out that the exception handling mechanisms in existing object-oriented languages are oriented towards implementation only and, as such, do not provide an adequate support for system development. We are interested in a mechanism supporting implementation development as well as system evolution. This kind of an exception handling mechanism will help to bridge the gap between different models used at various stages of the software life-cycle and to make the transition between different stages seamless.

First, we would like to identify the features that an exception handling mechanism supporting various forms of behaviour evolution should possess. For this, let us consider all the possibilities one might potentially like to exercise in re-declaring exceptions when developing a subclass. The existing languages allow specialising exceptions, as discussed above, and removing them. Both forms of exception evolution are useful but insufficient, because they cover only a part of the complete picture.

Exception merging is another form of exception evolution. It seems to be possible that at some step of class evolution it will be decided that several independent interface exceptions of a method have to be merged into one exception. This can happen if we find out that they are caused by similar reasons or that we do not want them to be different. For example, heap and stack are usually implemented in the same space but one grows from the bottom and the other one from the top. We may decide to merge the corresponding two exceptions into a single no_memory exception if they have to be treated in the same way. Although it may be possible to propose some specialised solutions supporting such functionality, for simplicity we consider that this problem can be solved by deleting exceptions and adding new ones.

3.6   New Functionality – New Exceptions

When specialising or extending classes, the existing approaches to dealing with interface exceptions at best permit to specialise and remove superclass interface exceptions in subclasses. However, when developing complex software, developers might be faced with the need to address system evolution requirements for which these interface exception changes are too restrictive.

Consider, for example, the setting illustrated in Fig. 2. Suppose that initially our design consists of classes Application and Document. An application works with a number of documents and can create new documents, open existing documents and close documents. The correspondingly named methods in class Application implement this functionality. A document provides methods that its clients, in particular the application using this document, can invoke to open, save, and close the document. For example, when an application needs to close a specified document, it checks whether the document has been saved since the last modification, saves it if it hasn't and closes the document.

Suppose now that we want one document to be viewed and edited in several windows. To achieve this, we employ the usual Observer Pattern [4], creating

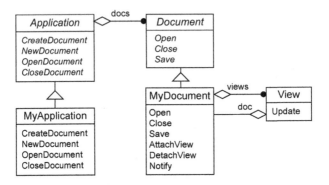

Fig. 2. Example of new functionality requiring new exceptions

new classes MyDocument and View, such that each MyDocument instance can be observed by a set of View instances. Views can be attached to and detached from a document using the correspondingly named methods of MyDocument. Whenever a document is changed in one of the views, it notifies each of its views about the change by broadcasting the method Update.

The problem arises when we are trying to implement MyDocument's Close method. When an attempt is made to close a document which is simultaneously modified is several windows, we would like to signal an exception MultipleView-CloseException. But as method Close of Document does not signal any exceptions, this redeclaration of its interface in MyDocument would be illegal in all the languages supporting only covariant interface exception redeclaration.

As demonstrated by this example, what we would like to have is more flexibility, enabling the kind of interface exception redeclaration when a subtype method can signal *completely new exceptions*. This observation is also made by Miller and Tripathi, who note in [8]: "For exceptions, new functionality may need new exceptions that are not subtypes of exceptions from the parent method". Further, the authors conclude that "[...] evolutionary program development suggests exception non-conformance".

Fortunately, this apparently desirable exception non-covariance (or "non-conformance" in terms of [8]) can be successfully dealt with, to circumvent type-theoretic problems. In the following section we present our proposal on how to deal with non-covariant interface exception redeclaration, without sacrificing the type safety provided by the existing exception handling mechanisms. In this manner, a more flexible, yet safe, exception handling mechanism can be built.

4   Adding New Interface Exceptions

We envision two closely related ways of dealing with new interface exceptions added in a subclass. The first approach is based on using *rescue handlers* –

default handlers attached to the class introducing new exceptions. The second approach employs the forwarding technique.

4.1   Using Rescue Handlers

The General Idea Consider a class C and its subclass C', which inherits methods of C, overriding some of them, and adds some new methods. Suppose that a method m of C signals an exception E and its counterpart in C' signals instead an exception D which is not a subtype of E. In addition, suppose that a new method n of C' signals an exception F.

As we know, clients of C might not be aware of the existence of C' and the handlers that these clients provide are only prepared to handle the exceptions explicitly declared in the interface of C. On the other hand, clients of C' which see the new exception signalled by m can provide a handler for this exception.

To deal with the new exceptions for which no handlers are available in the client code that invoked the methods signalling these exceptions, we define a default handler – the rescue handler. We chose to call this handler a rescue handler because it is used for the specific situation when clients do not know how to deal with new interface exceptions of their servers, being unaware of their existence, and the rescue handler steps in to rescue the situation. Clearly, this rescue handler should be attached to a server class in which the new exceptions are declared. Of course, it is easy to envision a scenario with which more than one method of a subclass signals the same non-covariant exception; if we have introduced a new data structure or some new functionality in C' then several of its methods might need to signal the exception D. In this case, a rescue handler for a new exception signalled by a particular method of a class should be associated with this method. This association of a rescue handler to a particular method rather than to the whole class might be necessary because rescue handling of an exception might require variations depending on the method signalling it. Syntactically, attaching a rescue handler to a particular method will amount to marking the rescued exception with the name of this method. When no ambiguity arises or when one kind of rescue behaviour is satisfactory for all methods signalling this exception, we provide a single rescue clause for each new exception at the class level. We illustrate rescue handlers at both the class level and the method level in Fig. 3. The rest of the discussion applies to both cases.

We view the rescue handler as an auxiliary code executed in the server context when the client does not have the handler for the interface exception signalled by the server. Rescue handlers can manipulate the server state, trying to recover it (possibly with some degradation) or can transfer it to a state corresponding to another server interface exception which will be signalled by the rescue handler.

An important point to note here is that this scenario is type-safe. The client calling a method will never be asked to handle an exception which it does not expect and for which it does not have a handler. The client only gets to handle those exceptions that are declared in the interface of its declared server. The new exceptions signalled by the server's subclass are handled by a rescue handler associated with the server's subclass itself. The task of the compiler is then to

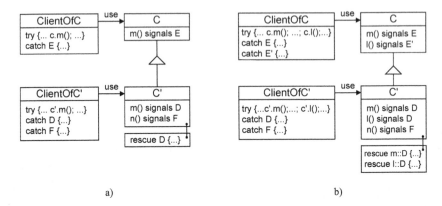

Fig. 3. Rescue handlers at class level (a) and at method level (b)

check that *every new exception of the subclass has an associated rescue handler attached to the subclass.*

Naturally, the client that is aware of the existence of a particular interface exception signalled by the server can deal with this exception in a more sensible and efficient manner, through defining a handler that supersedes the rescue handler.

Using this approach, we can now solve the problem in our example of applications and documents. We can allow MyDocument's Close method to signal the new MultipleViewCloseException, and define a rescue handler for it, attached to the class MyDocument. Such a rescue handler can, for example, close all views open on the document and then close the document itself. Then any Application instance invoking MyDocument's Close method will never be faced with MultipleViewCloseException unknown to it: the rescue handler will handle it and return control to Application.

Moreover, the clients of MyDocument, aware of the fact that the method Close of the latter can signal MultipleViewCloseException, can handle this exception in a more sensible manner, superseding the rescue handler provided by MyDocument. For example, MyApplication which works with MyDocument directly, rather than via subsumption through Document, can define a handler for MultipleViewCloseException that will pop-up a dialog inquiring the user whether he really wants to close the document along with all its views, or only wants to close specific views, leaving the document open in the other views.

Propagating an Exception Apart from providing some computations attempting to fix the problem, or simply returning the object into a consistent state, the rescue handler can also signal exceptions. Naturally, the exceptions that it can signal must be either subtypes of the exceptions signalled in the corresponding parent method, or they also can be the predefined Failure exceptions. More formally, for classes C and C' such that

```
class C {                          class C' extends C {
    void m() signals E₁,...,Eₙ {       void m() signals E'₁,...,E'ₖ,F₁,...,Fₘ {
        ...                                ...
    }                                  }
}                                  rescue F₁{...signal new H₁()...}
                                       ...
                                   rescue Fₘ{...signal new Hₘ()...}
                               }
```

where $E'_1,\ldots,E'_k$ are subtypes of some exceptions among $E_1,\ldots,E_n$ and $F_1,\ldots,F_m$ are new non-covariant exceptions, every H_j, for $1 \leq j \leq m$, must be a subtype of some E_i, for $1 \leq i \leq n$, or Failure:

$$(\forall j \mid 1 \leq j \leq m \cdot (\exists i \mid 1 \leq i \leq n \cdot H_j <: E_i) \vee H_j = \mathsf{Failure})$$

This rule extends to hierarchies of larger depth in an obvious manner, recursively: if a method m defined in a subclass C'' of C' signals an exception G which is non-covariant to either of $E'_1,\ldots,E'_k,F_1,\ldots,F_m$ then a rescue handler for this exception defined in C'' can only throw exceptions that are either subtypes of $E'_1,\ldots,E'_k,F_1,\ldots,F_m$ or Failure.

Implementation Details Let us consider now how our proposal can be implemented in practice; in particular, how the control is passed at runtime between client objects and supplier objects signalling new exceptions. Two general scenarios are of interest here:

1. The client is unaware of a new exception and the rescue handler is to be invoked
2. The client is aware of a new exception and provides its own handler, which is invoked superseding the rescue handler.

Suppose that we have a certain class NewSupplier extending some parent class Supplier and overriding a method m of the latter so that it signals a new (non-covariant) exception E.

```
class NewSupplier extends Supplier {
    void m() signals E {
        try {
            S₁;
            signal new E();
            S₂;
        }
        catch (−internal exceptions−) {−handle internal exceptions−}
    }
    ...
    rescue E {R_E}
}
```

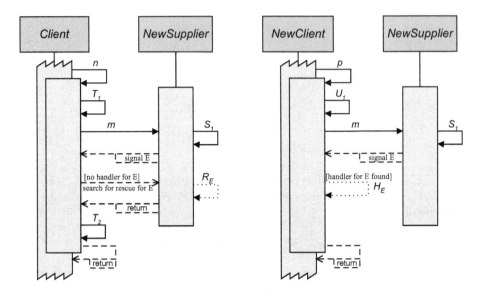

Fig. 4. Control flow for clients invoking a method signalling a new exception

Suppose also that we have two clients for NewSupplier, the one using it through subsumption and unaware of the new exception E (we will call it Client), and NewClient which knows that it uses NewSupplier and is prepared to deal with its new exception.

```
class Client {                class NewClient {
    void n() {                    void p() {
        try {                         try {
            T₁;                           U₁;
            s.m();                        s.m();
            T₂;                           U₂;
        }                             }
        catch B {H_B}                 catch D {H_D}
        catch C {H_C}                 catch E {H_E}
        ...                           ...
    }                             }
    ...                           ...
}                             }
```

We illustrate the control flow for both scenarios in Fig. 4, using sequence diagrams. As usual, the vertical dimension represents time and the horizontal dimension represents the actors involved in a collaboration; time proceeds down the page. Solid arrows denote method invocations and ordinary actions, like assignments and iterative statements; dashed arrows denote control passing between the actors involved; finely dashed arrows denote exception handler invocations.

As shown in this diagram, when the method n is invoked on Client, the first action to be performed is T_1. For simplicity, we have shown this action as the one performed on Client itself, but in reality it can be something more involved, like a sequence of method invocations. The invocation of m on NewSupplier results in transferring control to the latter, which executes S_1 and then can signal the exception E, which is new and unknown to Client. The control is passed to Client, which searches for a handler for E and, having not found one, returns the control back to NewSupplier. The latter searches for a rescue handler for E, and having found R_E executes it. Provided that R_E successfully fixes the problem, the control is returned back to Client which executes T_2 and returns control to the client which invoked method n. In case the rescue handler R_E itself signalled an exception, this exception is propagated to Client which reacts to this exception in the usual way, handling it or propagating it further. Recall that all exceptions signalled by R_E are required to be either covariant to one of the interface exceptions of Supplier's method m, or the predefined Failure exception.

Consider now the collaboration between NewClient and NewSupplier. NewClient is aware of the possibility that method m of NewSupplier signals E and is prepared to handle it. When E is indeed signalled, NewClient catches it and invokes the handler H_E. This handler supersedes the rescue handler provided by NewSupplier. It is interesting to note that, conceptually, the "ordinary" handler defined in the client overrides the rescue handler in the server, although they are located in different classes.

Strictly speaking, with (successful) rescue handling we deviate from the termination model of exception handling employed elsewhere in our model. The reason for this is that exception handling takes place in the server context rather than the client context. If the server itself has managed to correct the problem in the associated rescue handler, it terminates normally and returns control to the client. There is no need to terminate the client which can be left unaware of the exceptional situation that has been successfully resolved and just proceed normally.

As we already mentioned above, our solution to the problem of new exception introduction is type-safe. The type safety is imposed through requiring that a compiler verifies that every new exception of a subclass has an associated rescue handler attached to the subclass. To enforce this safety rule, we can always provide a default rescue handler signalling Failure.

Inheriting Rescue Handlers When subclassing a class providing rescue handlers for new exceptions, the rescue handlers are inherited and can be overridden. When no new rescue clause is provided in a subclass, the one from the parent method is inherited. To override a rescue clause for a particular exception, the subclass should simply provide a new rescue clause for this exception. There is no need to delete rescue clauses in a subclass, because even if we drop the interface exceptions for which rescue handlers were defined in a superclass, no harm is done if these handlers are inherited.

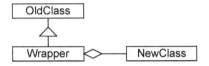

Fig. 5. Forwarding OldClass method calls to NewClass via Wrapper

An important special case of this rule is applied when a new exception is covariantly redefined in a subclass of a subclass signalling and rescuing the new exception. The designer of such a subsubclass may choose to either use the existing rescue handler for the corresponding superclass exception or to develop a new rescue handler. For example, if a subclass C' of C signals a new exception E and provides a rescue handler R_E for it, then a subclass C" of C' signalling instead a subtype E' of E can either inherit R_E or redefine it with R'_E that can be better suited to rescue E'. By default, when no new rescue clause is provided, the one from the parent method is inherited.

4.2   Forwarding to the Rescue

Using rescue handling to solve the problem of new interface exceptions is perfectly suitable for the top-down system development approach, when we face the need to introduce an interface exception in a development step. As discussed above, the need for introducing a new non-covariant interface exception may arise because a new data structure can deliver new exceptional behaviour.

However, rescue handling is of little help if we are to use a bottom-up approach to system development. With this approach, we might want to match an existing class (e.g., from a class library) to an existing interface (e.g., provided by a framework). It is quite likely to happen that the class has extra interface exceptions not signalled by the interface which the class matches otherwise.

To reiterate our example of applications and documents, suppose that the class MyDocument, described above, is supplied by a certain class library. Suppose also that we have an object-oriented framework containing an interface Document with methods Open, Close and Save. The class MyDocument almost exactly matches the interface Document, except for the MultipleViewCloseException signalled by its method Close.

Fortunately, architectural solutions that have proven their usefulness in solving closely related interface mismatch problems, literally speaking, come to the rescue in this situation as well. In particular, *forwarding* or the Wrapper Pattern [4], is an architectural solution that allows clients using instances of NewClass, which is an improved, more specialised version of some OldClass, but with a slightly mismatching interface, instead of instances of OldClass.

The idea behind forwarding is to introduce a subclass of OldClass, Wrapper, which aggregates an instance of NewClass and forwards OldClass method calls to NewClass through this instance. We illustrate this forwarding scheme in Fig. 5.

We can apply the same approach to solving the problem of mismatching interface exceptions, if we turn the new interface exceptions of NewClass into internal exceptions of Wrapper. The latter, having the same (or conforming) interface as OldClass, simply forwards all method calls to the corresponding methods of NewClass, catching and handling all NewClass's interface exceptions that cause the interface mismatch with OldClass. With this approach, clients of OldClass can effectively use NewClass, without being concerned that the latter signals an exception of which they are unaware.

In our example of applications and documents, we can solve the problem caused by mismatching interface exceptions in the class MyDocument as illustrated in Fig. 6. The class DocWrapper implements the interface Document by aggregating an instance of class MyDocument and forwarding all method calls to the corresponding methods of MyDocument. The method Close of DocWrapper is defined to forward the method call to MyDocument and catch the MultipleViewCloseException that the latter can signal.

As Wrapper classes are just ordinary classes, they can be extended and reused in the usual way.

The two approaches to handling new interface exceptions, the one employing rescue handlers and the one using the forwarding technique, nicely coexist, complementing each other. If a class provides rescue handlers for some of the interface exceptions signalled by its methods, and in addition the application using this class provides a wrapper class catching and handling these exceptions, then the wrapper's handler supersedes the rescue handler provided by the class.

5   Conclusions and Future Work

There is a significant gap between methods used for system modelling and design at the earlier phases of the system development life cycle and the methods

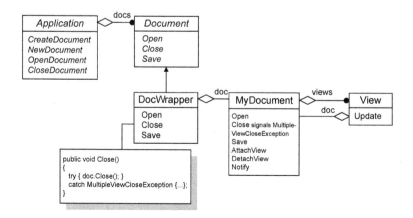

Fig. 6. Forwarding Document method calls to MyDocument via DocWrapper

and mechanisms supporting the implementation development. One of the reasons for this is a different view these methods and languages have on the way interface exceptions can evolve. In particular, none of the existing programming languages allows adding interface exceptions, which is vital for adding new functionality during system evolution. In this paper we have proposed two type-safe approaches which can be introduced into object-oriented languages to make it possible to add interface exceptions during subclassing. Our future research will focus on further development of these ideas. The intention is to apply these features in design and implementation of several case studies, to analyse possible implementations of these language mechanisms and their overheads, and to propose a formalism for reasoning about systems containing subclasses which have new exceptions and which employ our approaches for dealing with them.

Acknowledgements. We would like to thank Christophe Dony, Ricardo Jiménez-Peris, Jørgen Lindskov Knudsen, and Anand Tripathi for valuable comments and constructive criticism. Anna Mikhailova's research is supported by the European IST project MATISSE and Alexander Romanovsky's research by the European IST DSoS project.

References

1. M. Abadi and L. Cardelli. A Theory of Objects. Springer-Verlag, 1996.
2. L. Cardelli, J. Donahue, L. Glassman, M. Jordan, B. Kalsow, and G. Nelson. Modula-3 language definition. Technical Report 52, Digital Equipment Corporation, Systems Research Center, 1989.
3. W. R. Cook, W. L. Hill, and P. S. Canning. Inheritance is not subtyping. In Seventeenth Annual ACM Symposium on Principles of Programming Languages, pages 125–135, San Francisco, CA, Jan. 1990.
4. E. Gamma, R. Helm, R. Johnson, and J. Vlissides. Design Patterns: Elements of Reusable ObjectOriented Software. Addison-Wesley, 1995.
5. J. B. Goodenough. Exception handling: Issues and a proposed notation. Communications of the ACM, 18(12):683–696, Dec. 1975.
6. J. Gosling, B. Joy, and G. Steele. The Java Language Specification. Sun Microsystems, Mountain View, 1996.
7. V. Issarny. An exception handling mechanism for parallel object-oriented programming: towards the design of reusable, and robust distributed software. Journal of Object-Oriented Programming, 6(6):29–40, 1993.
8. R. Miller and A. Tripathi. Issues with exception handling in object-oriented systems. In M. Aksit and S. Matsuoka, editors, ECOOP '97 — Object-Oriented Programming 11th European Conference, Jyväskylä, Finland, volume 1241 of Lecture Notes in Computer Science, pages 85–103. Springer-Verlag, New York, NY, June 1997.
9. A. Taivalsaari. On the notion of inheritance. Comp. Surveys, 28(3):438–479, September 1996.

Concurrent Exception Handling

Valérie Issarny

INRIA, UR Rocquencourt
Domaine de Voluceau, BP 105, 78 153 Le Chesnay Cédex, FRANCE
{Valerie.Issarny}@inria.fr

Abstract. This paper discusses the cooperation exception handling model that comes along with a mechanism for multi-party interaction, in order to support the development of robust distributed applications running over a local area network. Lessons learnt from this work and its relation with today's common practice in the area of distributed computing are further considered.

1 Introduction

Since the appearance of distributed systems, fault tolerance and the possibility to use parallelism have been considered as two fundamental properties to be supported [17]. In that context, there has been a number of research work at the level of both programming languages and underlying operating systems to enforce those two properties. From the 80s to the early 90s, one popular approach was to offer a distributed programming language and associated distributed runtime system to be deployed over a local area network, with the language and possibly underlying system based on the object paradigm. The concern for enabling fault tolerance and exploiting parallelism has been addressed at both the language and system levels. At the system level, mechanisms for efficiently distributing units of work over the network as well as for enabling application-transparent fault tolerance have been proposed. At the language level, this has led researchers to introduce various concurrent languages where parallelism was either implicit or explicit, and mechanisms for specifying fault tolerance measures within applications (e.g., exception handling, transactions). This paper discusses one such work, focusing on the definition of programming language support enabling application-specific fault tolerance within distributed software systems [12].

Various design considerations come up when devising some new programming language support. Relevant criteria may be subjective and conflicting, and relate to issues as diverse as expressive power, performance at runtime of the resulting applications, ease of use, how application correctness gets promoted. All these factors were taken into account for the design of the fault tolerance mechanism that is discussed in this paper. However, the factor that has been the most influencing is the one that relates to promoting the semantics correctness of the developed applications. It follows that a rigorous definition of the proposed mechanism was to be provided. Accounting for the other factors led us to design

A. Romanovsky et al. (Eds.): Exception Handling, LNCS 2022, pp. 111–127, 2001.

an *exception handling* facility since it serves developing at low performance cost a number of application-specific fault tolerance techniques. Then, the mechanism may be complemented with more powerful but more costly means, supported by the underlying runtime system, if stronger dependability properties need be achieved (e.g., atomicity). When addressing fault tolerance capabilities, it is further essential to help the programmer to deal with redundancy [8] from the standpoint of both design diversity, and replication of computations and data. In the context of distributed systems where the effective use of the underlying architecture parallelism is beneficial, the above concern may be addressed through a mechanism for *multi-party interaction* [21], which enables specifying concurrent activities and cooperation among them. Specifically, we exploited here the notion of *multiprocedure* [1] that is the outcome of a generalizing approach to the integration of parallelism and procedures. Here too, our primary objective of offering language support promoting the development of correct programs has led to propose a rigorous definition of the mechanism selected for managing multi-party interactions.

This paper is organized as follows. Section 2 discusses the *cooperation exception handling model* that is the result of the aforementioned design considerations for enabling disciplined exception handling within distributed software systems. After providing an overview of the model, its integration within a simple language offering two mechanisms supporting respectively the model and the multiprocedure notion is sketched, and is followed by the axiomatic definition of the language. Section 3 briefly addresses practical usage of the proposed model associated with the multiprocedure notion, in an object-oriented language aimed at distributed computing over a local area network, giving an example of application embedding fault tolerance support. The work that is discussed in this paper is the outcome of a study undertaken in the late 80s where distributed computing was not as common as it is nowadays. Section 4 concludes the paper with the lessons learnt from this experience some ten years after. It further relates the proposal with today's common practice in the area of distributed computing, considering in particular the predominance of Java and C++ as programming languages and the ever growing acceptance of middleware platforms and component-based software development.

2   The Cooperation Exception Handling Model

This section gives an overview of the *cooperation model* of exception handling [11], which is aimed at an imperative concurrent programming style where concurrency is explicit. The model allows static as well as dynamic creation of processes. Assuming that processes are combined in blocks, the model allows these blocks being statically as well as dynamically nested. Finally, processes communicate by message passing. Clearly, many existing programming languages would satisfy some parts of the properties. However, the model is better exploited when integrated within a language offering a mechanism for multi-party interactions.

Addressing exception handling in the above framework is one of the distinctive features of the cooperation model. Most of the proposals introducing an exception handling mechanism targets a particular concurrent language. Furthermore, these mechanisms are often based on a model of exception handling designed for sequential languages, thus evicting concurrency aspects from the model. The following subsection gives the basic principles of the cooperation model. It is then followed by a presentation of a mechanism implementing the model within a simple block structured concurrent programming language enabling multi-party interactions; the resulting language is further formally defined in Subsection 2.3.

2.1   Base Definitions

The cooperation model of exception handling privileges simplicity over power. Therefore, it is firstly based on an extension of the termination model of sequential programming languages. Then, in a concurrent framework, the occurrence of an exception within a process may interfere with the behavior of other processes. For instance, consider two processes that synchronize at some point of their execution. If one of them terminates exceptionally before synchronizing, the other gets blocked, waiting for a communication with the terminated process. In order to avoid such a deadlock, the definition of the termination model is extended with the notion of *global exception handling*.

Global exception handling. Under the cooperation model, an exception whose occurrence prevents achievement of an expected synchronous communication leads to the exceptional termination of the process signaling the exception. Such an exceptional termination is expressed by signaling a *global exception*, which is by definition known from the other program processes. In general, a process P *catches* a global exception when it communicates synchronously with a process Q that terminates exceptionally by signaling the global exception. Finally, when a process catches a global exception, the handler of the exception is looked for within the process from the synchronization point, as in the sequential case. The introduction of global exceptions places requirements on process declaration: a process should declare the global exceptions it signals.

Concerted exception handling. When processes are components of a nested parallel operation, the exceptional termination of one of them leads to the exceptional termination of the parallel operation. The exception signaled by the operation should nonetheless be stated since embedded processes may concurrently signal distinct exceptions. As it has been advocated in [4], the occurrence of many exceptions may be indicative of an exceptional state dependent upon the composition of all the signaled exceptions. An exception resulting from such a composition is qualified as *concerted*. The computation of a concerted exception cannot be generally implicitly defined since it requires semantics knowledge about exceptions. Such a computation thus relies on a *resolution function*, which takes as input concurrent exceptions and returns the resulting concerted exception. In sequential programs, an exception handler is associated with a sequential command and has the same scope. This definition is extended to a parallel operation. Handlers associated with a parallel operation have the same degree of parallelism as the operation and handle the concerted exceptions that the operation signals. Declaration of such handlers can be easily achieved: it suffices to associate each handler component to the corresponding operation component.

Additional considerations. Static verification of syntactic as well as semantics correctness of programs places requirements on exception handling. *Propagation of exceptions* along the invoking chain should be *explicit*. The handler of any exception can then be statically determined. Any exception signaled by a block that can be dynamically nested should be declared in the block's header. Thus, for any exception, it can be checked that a corresponding handler is declared and that handler parameters are in accordance with exception ones. Practically, since there is possibly a large number of exceptions to be accounted for (e.g., given those that may be raised by the underlying system), *default exception handling* may be supported through the propagation of the default exception *failure* when an exception has no handler associated with it in the given context of occurrence.

2.2   A Language Supporting the Cooperation Model

This subsection illustrates the integration of the cooperation model within a simple block structured language, which further integrates the notion of multi-procedure for enabling multi-party interactions [1]. The body of a multiprocedure consists of a collection of blocks (or components) that are executed concurrently. Each component takes as input a subset of the multiprocedure formal parameters and returns a subset of the result. A component is bracketed by a (*begin, end*) pair and contains a set of local declarations as well as a sequence of commands. A multiprocedure is called in the same way as a procedure. Nonetheless, the execution is carried out differently: (*i*) a multi-context is created, (*ii*) parameters are made available to the multi-context, (*iii*) commands of the different components are executed in parallel, (*iv*) results are built out of each component contribution and made available to the caller, (*v*) the multi-context is destroyed. A multiprocedure may issue a *coordinated call*. This is a natural extension of the procedure call mechanism. The subset of the multiprocedure components joining together to call a multiprocedure are all synchronized. When the call is terminated, results -if any- are made available to all the components of the caller before their parallel activities are resumed. Naturally, the coordinated call for a single-blocked multiprocedure is the traditional procedure call. The relationship between calling multiprocedure blocks and called multiprocedure ones is a *many in many* nesting.

The syntax of the language is given in Figure 1; except the syntax related to multiprocedures, it is very close to the one introduced in [5]. The declaration

```
PROG     ::= prog N = RF MPDECL VDECL C
RF       ::= | resol r (handles EL, signals EL) = VDECL RC ; RF
MPDECL   ::= | mproc Mp(v F; vr F; r F) [EL]
                using r = MPBODY ; MPDECL
F        ::= | v : int , F
EL       ::= e(F) | e(F), EL
VDECL    ::= | var v : int; VDECL
MPBODY   ::= COMP | COMP || COMP
COMP     ::= (v F ; vr F ; r F) [EL] = VDECL; C
C        ::= | ▷ e(R) | S | PC | C; C
R        ::= | v, R
S        ::= v := E | if B then C else C fi | while B do C od | begin C end |
             Mp(va, vra, ra) with CL | Mp(va, vra, ra)
CL       ::= i | i, CL
PC       ::= [B : C] | { C } [HD]
HD       ::= EL : C | EL : C ; HD
```

Fig. 1. A language supporting the cooperation model

of a program (PROG) states the resolution functions, multiprocedures and variables, which are known in the program N. A resolution function (RF) implicitly takes as input an array, **exc**, of exceptions, with each exception belonging to the list after **handles**, and it returns one of the exceptions from the list after **signals**. A multiprocedure header lists value, value-result, result parameters; the list of exceptions (EL) it may signal; and the resolution function r to be called when at least one component signals a (global) exception. When a resolution function is invoked, the array **exc** gives the exceptions signaled by the signaling components of the calling multiprocedure, and the multiprocedure signals the exception returned by the resolution function. For instance, consider a multiprocedure m having 5 components, which uses a resolution function r to compute concerted exceptions. Assuming an execution of m such that components 2 and 4 signal global exceptions e and f respectively, the function r is invoked with $exc[2] = e$, $exc[4] = f$ and $exc[i] = null$ for remaining array elements, and the multiprocedure m signals the exception returned by r. If the *using* clause is not stated, then a default function[1] is invoked. For simplification reasons, only program variables of type integer are considered. A multiprocedure body (MP-BODY) embeds the parallel composition of a set of components. A component is made of a set of declarations and a command C. A component header lists the global exceptions (EL) signaled by the component. Component parameters state the multiprocedure parameters the component deals with. Two components of a multiprocedure cannot share value-result nor result parameters. It is further assumed that each variable that occurs in a component body is either locally

---

[1] The default concerted exception is *failure* if at least two exceptions are concurrently signaled and either the exceptions are distinct or one of them is parameterized. Otherwise, the default exception is the one being signaled.

declared or is a parameter (no global variables are allowed) and that multiprocedures are not recursive. Commands RC used in resolution function body are
those given in C plus a command enabling to test the value of exceptions. This
last command, not detailed here, is similar in essence to the type case command.
A command may be the empty command, the signal command ($\triangleright e$), a simple
command (S), a protected construct (PC) or may be composed sequentially from
other commands. The arguments of the signal command must be distinct and
declared variables. A simple command S is either an assignment, a conditional, a
loop, a block, a multiprocedure *cocall* (read *coordinated call*), or a multiprocedure
(single) call. The syntax for boolean expressions B is not detailed here, and it is
assumed that their evaluation does not lead to exceptions. Integer expressions
E are not detailed either; their evaluation may lead to exceptions overflow (*ovf*)
and underflow (*udf*). A multiprocedure coordinated call states the components
(CL) with which the caller wants to cooperate. Those components should belong
to the same multiprocedure instance. Component names are given by the place
of the component in the parallel composition declaration. It is assumed that the
actual arguments of multiprocedure calls are declared variables, all distinct and
that formal parameters of a multiprocedure are always rightly covered by the
arguments. When the call is coordinated, the formal parameters to be assigned
are explicitly stated by all the members of that call. Finally, coordinated calls of
the form "$m(actuals_1)$ *with* l_1, ..., $m(actuals_n)$ *with* l_n" are said to be *matching*
if for any i, $1 \leq i \leq n$, $l_i \cup \{i\}$ is equal to $l_j \cup \{j\}$ for all j, $1 \leq j \leq n$, and
if $\cup_{i=1}^{n} actuals_i$ matches formal parameters of m. With respect to the definition
of the cooperation model, a component that participates in a coordinated call
catches global exceptions if the components with which it wants to cooperate
terminate by signaling a global exception. In this case, a concerted exception is
evaluated and its handler is looked for within the catching component. There are
two kinds of protected constructs PC. One makes the invocation of a handler C
dependent upon the truth of a boolean expression B; the other associates one or
several handlers with a set of exceptional exit points of a command C. When the
body of a multiprocedure component is a command of the second kind, handlers
of HD are components of the handlers associated to the multiprocedure.

    For illustration, an example of a syntactically well-formed program piece is
provided in Figure 2. This gives the *sum_fac* multiprocedure computing the sum
of two factorials, where it is assumed that the multiprocedure is always invoked
with arguments whose value is positive. The *fact* and *sum* multiprocedures may
both signal the *ov* exception, which propagates the *ovf* exception that is signaled
by an expression evaluation. The resolution function *r_sum_fac* resolves exceptions concurrently signaled within *sum_fac* components. It returns *ov* whatever
the values of the input exceptions are[2]. Notice that the exception *ov* returned
by the resolution function *r_sum_fac* is not handled by the multiprocedure components but is directly propagated to the caller.

---

[2] This function actually corresponds to the default resolution function.

resol r_sum_fac(**handles** ov() ; **signals** ov()) = **begin** ▷ ov **end**
mproc fact(**v** x : **int**; **r** fx : **int**) [ov()] = *not detailed : fx = x!*
mproc sum(**v** x : **int**, y : **int** ; **r** s : **int**) [ov()] = *not detailed : s = x + y*
mproc sum_fac(**v** a : **int**, b : **int** ; **r** sf : **int**) [ov()] **using** r_sum_fac =
   (**v** a : **int** ; **r** sf : **int**) [ov()] =
      var f1 : **int**;
      begin
         {fact(a,f1)}[ov() : ▷ ov()]; {sum(x = f1, sf = s) **with** 2}[ov() : ▷ ov()]
      end ||
   (**v** b : **int**) [ov()] =
      var f2 : **int**;
      begin {fact(b,f2)}[ov() : ▷ ov()]; {sum(y = f2) **with** 1}[ov() : ▷ ov()] **end**

Fig. 2. A multiprocedure example

2.3   Axiomatic Semantics

This subsection addresses the rigorous definition of the programming language
discussed in the previous subsection. It presents the axioms and rules of inference
enabling to deduce properties of the programs written in the language. The
axiomatic definition of multiprocedures, in the absence of exceptions, directly
follows from [7]. A proof of pre- and post-assertions about a multiprocedure
is done in two stages: (1) separate proofs are constructed in isolation for each
multiprocedure component; and (2) the separate proofs are combined and shown
to cooperate.

   The axiomatic definition of individual multiprocedure components in the
presence of exception handling is based on the work of [5]. The advantage of this
approach is a clear separation between the validation of program properties in
the presence and in the absence of exceptions. A statement of the system is of the
form $p \{C\}$ x:q whose interpretation is *if C is invoked in a state in which p is true
and if C terminates at x, then q is true after C's execution*; x can be either *end* or
an exception label. When x is equal to end, the abbreviation $p \{C\}$ q is meant for
$p \{C\}$ *end:q*. A program P with k exit points is then termed *robust* if it terminates
at a declared exit point for any possible input state. The notion of correctness
for a one entry/multi-exit programs is a straightforward extension of that for one
entry/one exit programs. To specify the expected behavior of a program P, which
signals k exceptions, $(k + 1)$ pairs (r_i, s_i), $0 \leq i \leq k$ which give pre- and post-
assertions are needed. The pair (r_0, s_0) denotes the expected standard behavior
of P while pairs (r_j, s_j), $1 \leq j \leq k$ specify its expected exceptional behavior.
A program P is partially correct if the statement $r_i \{P\}$ x_i:s_i is verified for all
pairs.

   Figure 3 gives the most relevant proof rules that enable to prove partial
correctness of programs written in the target language; these subdivide into
the rules used at stage (1) for constructing separate proofs for multiprocedure
components, and the rules used at stage (2) for proving the properties of the

overall multiprocedure. For simplification reasons, it is assumed that exceptions are not parameterized.

A1 – Signal axiom

$$p \{ \triangleright e \} e : p$$

R1 – Sequential composition rule 1

$$\frac{p \{C_1\} \, q, \, q \Rightarrow r, \, r \{C_2\} \, x : s}{p \{C_1 \, ; \, C_2\} \, x : s}$$

R2 – Sequential composition rule 2

$$\frac{p \{C_1\} \, e : q}{p \{C_1 \, ; \, C_2\} \, e : q}$$

R3 – Protected construct rule 1

$$\frac{p \Rightarrow \neg B}{p \{[B : C]\} \, p}$$

R4 – Protected construct rule 2

$$\frac{p \Rightarrow B, \, p \{C\} \, x : q}{p \{[B : C]\} \, x : q}$$

R5 – Protected construct rule 3

$$\frac{p \{C\} \, q}{p \{\{ \, C \, \} \, [e_1 : C_1 \, ; \, ... \, ; \, e_n : C_n \,]\} \, q}$$

R6 – Protected construct rule 4

$$\frac{p \{C\} \, e_i : q, \, q \{ \, C_i \, \} \, x : r}{p \{\{ \, C \, \} \, [\mathcal{H} \,]\} \, x : r}$$

A2 – Coordinated call axiom

$$p \{ \, \mathcal{C} \, \} \, x : q$$

R7 – Coordinated call rule

$$\frac{p \Rightarrow pre(m), \, pre(m) \, \{ \, B_m \, \} \, x : post(m)}{p[a; b \, / \, x; y] \, \{ \, \mathcal{C}_m \, \} \, x : post'(m)}$$

R8 – Parallel composition rule 1

$$\frac{\text{proofs of } p_i \, \{ \, C_i \, \} \, x_i : q_i, \, i = 1, ..., n, \, \text{cooperate}}{\frac{(exc_1 = x_1 \wedge ... \wedge exc_n = x_n) \, \{ \, \mathcal{R} \, \} \, e_i : r}{q_1 \wedge ... \wedge q_n \wedge MI \, \{ \, C_{i_1} \, || \, ... \, || \, C_{i_n} \, \} \, y : q}}{p_1 \wedge ... \wedge p_n \wedge MI \, \{ \, [P_1 \, || \, ... \, || \, P_n] \, \} \, y : q}$$

R9 – Parallel composition rule 2

$$\frac{\begin{array}{c}\text{proofs of } p_i \, \{ \, C_i \, \} \, x_i : q_i, \, i = 1, ..., n, \, \text{cooperate}\\ exc_1 = x_1 \wedge ... \wedge exc_n = x_n \, \{ \, \mathcal{R} \, \} \, e : r\end{array}}{p' \, \{ \, [P_1 \, || \, ... \, || \, P_n] \, \} \, e : q'}$$

Fig. 3. Proof rules and axioms

Proving properties of a multiprocedure component. Proof rules for sequential commands that are not related to exception handling are quite trivial and hence not provided here (e.g., see [5] for detail). Axiom **A1** states that when an exception is signaled, the exception becomes the exit point of the enclosing block. Regarding sequential composition, when the first command of a sequential composition terminates normally, the sequential composition command inherits the exit point of the second (**R1**); when the first command of a sequential composition terminates exceptionally, the following commands are not executed and the whole sequential composition terminates exceptionally (**R2**). A command [B:C] terminates normally if the boolean expression B is evaluated to false or if B is evaluated to true and C terminates normally (**R3** and **R4**). The command can signal an exception if B is evaluated to true and C signals an exception (**R4**). Considering the command { C }[$e_1 : C_1$; ... ; $e_n : C_n$], either C terminates normally (**R5** with $\mathcal{H}$ being of the form: $e_1 : C_1$; ... ; $e_i : C_i$; ... ; $e_n : C_n$) or C signals an exception handled by the protected construct (explicit propagation of exceptions) (**R6**). Let now $\mathcal{C}$ denote any cocall command, axiom **A2** where p and q refer only to variables local to the component from which $\mathcal{C}$ is taken, implies that *any* post-assertion q and *any* exit point x can be deduced after a coordinated call. However, q and x cannot be arbitrary since they must pass the cooperation test at stage (2) of the proof. Using the axioms and rules introduced so far, rules given for other sequential commands in [5], and *consequence* rules also defined in [5], separate proofs for each components can then be established. This is presented, as usual, by *proof outlines* in which each sub-statement of a component is preceded and followed by corresponding assertions.

Proving properties of a multiprocedure. Once separated proofs have been constructed for the individual components of a multiprocedure, they get combined. With each proof of: $p \{P_1||...||P_n\} x{:}q$, a multiprocedure invariant *MI* and an appropriate *bracketing* are associated. The *MI* invariant expresses global information about a multiprocedure; it may refer to the formal parameters and local variables of all the components in the multiprocedure. The purpose of bracketing is to delimit the multiprocedure sections within which the multiprocedure invariant need not necessarily hold. Precisely, every component P_i is *bracketed* if the brackets '$\prec$' and '$\succ$' are interspersed in its text so that (*i*) for each program section $\prec$B$\succ$, B is of the form B_1 ; $\mathcal{C}$; B'_1 where B_1 and B'_1 do not contain any cocall commands, and (*ii*) all the cocall commands that are not discarded due to an exception signal, appear only within brackets as above.

Let $m(\boldsymbol{x}, \boldsymbol{y}, \boldsymbol{z}) :: B_m$ denote a multiprocedure m where: $\boldsymbol{x}, \boldsymbol{y}, \boldsymbol{z}$ denote the formal parameters $\boldsymbol{x}_1, ..., \boldsymbol{x}_{nc}$; $\boldsymbol{y}_1, ..., \boldsymbol{y}_{nc}$; $\boldsymbol{z}_1, ..., \boldsymbol{z}_{nc}$ of the multiprocedure components with nc being the number of components in the multiprocedure m; and B_m denotes the multiprocedure body ($||_{j=1}^{nc} B_j$). Assertions $pre_i(m) \{B_m\} x_i{:}post_i(m)$ can be associated with any given multiprocedure m where both $pre_i(m)$ and $post_i(m)$ are constructed by conjoining, respectively, the pre- and post-assertions of the various components with the invariant *MI* associated to the multiprocedure. The formal data parameters referred to by the predicates $pre(m)$ and $post(m)$ may only be $\boldsymbol{x}, \boldsymbol{y}$ and $\boldsymbol{y}, \boldsymbol{z}$ respectively. The predicates may also refer to constants and *free variables* to describe initial and final values.

Consider now a multiprocedure m and matching cocalls $\mathcal{C}_1^m, ..., \mathcal{C}_{npc}^m$. The cocall post-assertion is given by the multiprocedure assertion as specified by rule **R7** where:

- $\mathcal{C}_m$ denotes $||_{j=1}^{npc} \mathcal{C}_j^m(\boldsymbol{a}_{k_j}, \boldsymbol{b}_{k_j}, \boldsymbol{c}_{k_j})$,
- $\boldsymbol{a}, \boldsymbol{b}, \boldsymbol{c}$ denote $(\boldsymbol{a}_{k_1}, ..., \boldsymbol{a}_{k_{npc}})$, $(\boldsymbol{b}_{k_1}, ..., \boldsymbol{b}_{k_{npc}})$, $(\boldsymbol{c}_{k_1}, ..., \boldsymbol{c}_{k_{npc}})$, respectively,
- $post'(m)$ denotes $post(m)[\boldsymbol{b}; \boldsymbol{c} / \boldsymbol{y}; \boldsymbol{z}]$, and
- $p[\boldsymbol{u}/\boldsymbol{v}]$ denotes the assertion obtained from p by substituting (simultaneously) $\boldsymbol{u}$ for all free occurrences of $\boldsymbol{v}$.

Three other rules are used to prove the properties of a multiprocedure. One is applied when all the multiprocedure components terminate normally, the two others are when at least one of the components terminates exceptionally. The first rule is similar to the one of [7] and is not repeated. When one component terminates exceptionally, the resolution function, noted $\mathcal{R}$, is invoked. If a handler is associated to the multiprocedure for the returned concerted exception, the multiprocedure post-assertion is given by the handler assertion as specified by **R8**, provided that no variable free in *MI* is subject to change outside a bracketed section and that P_j's, $j = 1, ..., n$ are of the form: "$\{C_j\}[e_1:C_{1_j};....;e_i:C_{i_j};....;e_n:C_{n_j}]$". If the concerted exception is not handled by the multiprocedure, the exception is propagated to the caller as specified by **R9** where p' and q' denote $p_1 \wedge ... \wedge p_n \wedge MI$ and $q_1 \wedge ... \wedge q_n \wedge MI$ respectively, and provided that no variable free in *MI* is subject to change outside a bracketed section and that components do not declare a handler for e. Intuitively, proofs cooperate if each execution of a multiprocedure validates all the post-assertions of the cocall commands calling it. Let $\mathcal{E}_m$ denote the set of exceptions signaled by the multiprocedure m, $\mathcal{G}_i$ denote the set of global exceptions signaled by the ith component of m, and *with* denotes the set of components explicitly named as participants in matching coordinated calls. Further assume a given bracketing of a multiprocedure $[P_1 || ... || P_n]$ and a multiprocedure invariant *MI*. Bracketed sections $\prec B_1 \succ$, ..., $\prec B_{npc} \succ$ are *matching* if they contain matching coordinated calls $\mathcal{C}_1^m, ..., \mathcal{C}_{npc}^m$ to some multiprocedure m. The proofs $p_i \{P_i\} x_i:q_i$, $i = 1, ..., n$ are then said to *cooperate* if:

(i) the assertions used in the proofs $p_i \{P_i\} x_i:q_i$ have no free variables subject to change in P_j, for $i \neq j$;

(ii) the statement: "$(\wedge_{i=1}^{npc} pre(B_i) \wedge MI) \{ ||_{i=1}^{npc} B_i \} (\wedge_{i=1}^{npc} post(B_i) \wedge MI)$" holds for all matching bracketed sections $\prec B_1 \succ$, ..., $\prec B_{npc} \succ$ when:
   - $npc = |with|$,
   - the statement enclosing each B_i is of the form: "$pre(B_i) \{ B_i \} b : post(B_i)$", for all i, $i = 1, ..., npc$, where $b \in \{ end, \mathcal{E}_m \}$ (assuming the bracketed sections jointly call the multiprocedure m), and
   - the statement preceding each "$pre(B_i) \{ B_i \} b : post(B_i)$" is of the form: "$pre(C_i) \{ C_i \} end : post(C_i)$", for all i, $i = 1, ..., npc$;

(iii) given matching bracketed sections $\prec B_1 \succ$, ..., $\prec B_{npc} \succ$, the three following conditions hold when $|with| > npc$:
   - $\forall j : j \in with - \{1, ..., npc\}, a_j \in \mathcal{G}_j$,
   - $\wedge_{\forall j:j \in with-\{1,...,npc\}} exc_j = a_j \{ \mathcal{R} \} e : r$,
   - the statement enclosing each B_i is of the form: "$pre(B_i) \{ B_i \} e : post(B_i)$" and "$(pre(B_i) \wedge MI) \Rightarrow post(B_i)$", for all i, $i = 1, ..., npc$,

- the statement preceding each "$pre(B_i)$ { B_i } $b : post(B_i)$" is of the form: "$pre(C_i)$ { C_i } $end : post(C_i)$", for all i, $i = 1, ..., npc$;

In the definition of *cooperation*, points (i) and (ii) come from the corresponding definition given in [7] while point (iii) copes with global exception handling. Point (ii) is related to coordinated calls that actually lead to a multiprocedure execution. Point (iii) considers coordinated calls where at least one expected participant terminates by signaling a global exception. The following axiom and proof rules are needed to establish cooperation: coordinated call axiom, coordinated call rules, parameter substitution rule and variable substitution rule. The two last proof rules are given in [7]. Finally, to complete the proof system, the following rules from [7] are also needed: preservation rule, substitution rule, and the auxiliary variable rule. Due to the lack of space, we do not provide here an example of proof using the presented system; the interested reader is referred to [11].

3   Cooperation Exception Handling in an Object-Oriented Setting

From a practical point of view, the cooperation model of exception handling has been integrated within a concurrent object-oriented language, called Arche [3]. The language is aimed at distributed computing over a local area network and comes along with a dedicated distributed object-oriented runtime system [2]. One of the design considerations in the elaboration of Arche was to promote the development of robust distributed software, from the standpoint of both easing reasoning about the program behavior and providing support for fault tolerance. The former concern has led to the design of a strongly typed object-oriented language based on a simple concurrency model where objects are independent processes and synchronization within each object relies on the following: (1) any method call is synchronous and its acceptance by the invoked object is implicit; (2) mutual exclusion is enforced within the object by enabling the execution of a single method at a time; (3) conditional synchronization relies on a mechanism that is compatible with inheritance; and (4) objects may cooperate through a mechanism for multi-party interaction that is a special form of multiprocedure. This last mechanism is called *multimethod*, and consists in the invocation of a method on a group of objects. Arche further embeds an exception handling mechanism that implements the cooperation model presented in the previous section. The definition of the mechanim is not detailed since it is quite direct from the previous section. There are however two additional features in the exception handling mechanism of Arche. They lie in: (i) offering support for asynchronous exception handling due to the asynchronous creation of objects, and (ii) the definition of a subtyping relation over exceptions, which are defined as object types. The interested reader is referred to [13] for a detailed presentation of the mechanism. We give here an example taken from [13] that illustrates the use of Arche mechanisms (i.e., exception handling and multimethod) for developping robust distributed applications. The chosen application is the two phase commit protocol with which the reader is assumed to be familiar and whose detailed description may notably be found in [10].

Example: two phase commit protocol. Assume a distributed action, qualified as *recoverable*, that has established recovery points and that wants to commit its computation after having modified data located on different nodes. Nodes participating to the action are called *participants*. Each of these nodes is supposed to be able to commit and abort the part of the action it performed. Finally, a particular node, called *coordinator*, is assumed to be associated to the recoverable action. This last node can access all the action participants. The two phase commit protocol ensures that all the participants either commit or abort their participation to the recoverable action. Implementation of the coordinator and participants is given below where we do not adhere to the Arche syntax but rather uses one that is closer to common object-oriented languages, and hence easier to interpret. Regarding the creation of an object, it leads to the creation of a process, which initializes by running the constructor method and then waits for incoming calls that get selected for execution according to the embedded conditional and mutual exclusion synchronization. For the sake of brevity, we omit the specification of conditional synchronization in the following.

The definition of the *coordinator* class is given in Figure 4. Participants of the recoverable action are registered in the sequence variable p, which defines a group of objects on which multimethods can be invoked. The (virtual) *write_log* method aims at recording performed actions within a log and is thus specific to any recoverable action; the implementation of *write_log* is to be provided by subclasses of *coordinator*. The *add_part* method is straightforward; it appends the newly involved participant to the sequence p. Validation of the recoverable action is carried out through the *commit* method, which first logs the fact that the recoverable action is in the first phase of validation. The method then invokes the multimethod *vote* of p, i.e., *vote* is concurrently executed by each of the action participants. Due to some failure, none of the participants may be reachable. In this case, the *timeout* exception is signaled to the coordinator by the run-time system. A component of the *vote* multimethod may either terminate normally or signal *nok*. Signaling *nok* means that the participant wants to abort its participation to the action. Consider first that all the participants terminate normally, i.e., the action may commit. In this case, the second phase consists in logging validation and in calling the *commit* multimethod on p. This call is enclosed in an exception handling command because the *timeout* exception may still occur, e.g., due to failure of the underlying communication medium. Notice that if a subset of the multimethod's components is reachable, this causes concurrent signals of the *timeout* exception by the remaining components. According to the semantics of the underlying exception handling mechanism, a concerted exception is computed. However, there is no need for a resolution function here. Since the *timeout* exception is not parameterized, the default concerted exception will always be an instance of *timeout*. Consider now that at least one of the components of the *vote* multimethod signals *nok*. The resulting concerted exception is computed by means of the *res_vote* resolution function, which always signals *exc_vote* and discards participants that signal *nok*. It follows that the handler of *exc_vote* sends only the *recovery* message to the nodes that either did not reply to the coordinator or acknowledged for validation. Note that the implicit formal parameter of any resolution function is the sequence of exceptions *exc_seq*. Furthermore, the actual parameter of any resolution function contains as many elements as the signaling multimethod embeds components; the *exception* associated to a node that terminates normally (i.e., that expects to validate its participation) being of type *terminated*. Finally, for the sake of brevity, re-emission of messages has been omitted in the proposed algorithm even though the *timeout* exception may be signaled by multimethods called within handlers.

```
class coordinator {
    seq of participant p = <>;
    resolution res_vote handles nok signals exc_vote {
        int i = 0; seq of participant part = <>;
        while (i < exc_seq.length()) {
            exception case (exc_seq[i]) {
                nok: {skip}
                else {part.append(p[i])};};
            i := i + 1;
            };
        signal exc_vote(part);
        };
    void write_log(action a) {};
    void add_part(participant part) {p.append(part)};
    void commit() signals nok {
        boolean ok = false;
        // Phase 1
        try using res_vote { write_log(a_begin); p.vote (); write_log(a_valid);}
        catch(exc_vote e) {write_log(a_rec); e.part().recovery(); signal nok;}
        else {write_log(a_rec); p.recovery(); signal nok;};
        // Phase 2
        try {p.commit()}
        catch(timeout t) {p.commit()};
        };
}
```

Fig. 4. The *coordinator* class

The definition of the *participant* class is given in Figure 5. The *alarm_clock* object, instance of the predefined class *timer*, enables instances of class *participant* to be aware of delay expiration during the protocol first phase. The creation of *alarm_clock* within the initialization method (i.e., **new** *c_timer(self, delay)*) specifies the calling object, i.e., the enclosing participant, and the delay whose value is passed as argument when the instance of *participant* is created.

```
class participant {
    action my_action = a_begin;
    timer alarm_clock;
    void participant(int delay) {alarm_clock = new timer(self, delay)};
    void write_log(action a) {};
    void my_vote() signals nok { if my_action == a_rec {signal nok }};
    void alarm() { if my_action == a_begin {write_log(a_rec); my_action = a_rec};};
    void vote() signals nok {
        try {my_vote(); write_log(a_ok); my_action = a_ok;}
        catch(nok e) {write_log(a_rec); my_action = a_rec; signal e;}
        else {write_log(a_rec); my_action = a_rec; signal nok;}
    };
    void commit() {write_log(a_valid); my_action = a_valid;};
    void recovery(){ if my_action == a_ok {write_log(a_rec); my_action = a_rec};};
}
```

Fig. 5. The *participant* class

The provided example highlights most of the benefits of using the cooperation exception handling model in a distributed object-oriented setting. In addition to the ease of reasoning about program behavior brought by the rigorous definition of the cooperation model and related mechanisms, the distributed object-oriented setting enables the development of reusable robust distributed software. Considering the given example, provided classes may be reused to implement customized two phase commit protocols. They have to be at least specialized to define the implementation of *write_log* and *my_vote*, which are specific to the target distributed action. It is interesting to note that the exception *nok*, originally signaled by *my_vote* may be specialized to provide more information about the cause of action failure. In such a case, the *vote* method has not to be modified: the variable *e* declared in *nok*'s handler may be any exception whose type is a subtype of *nok*. On the other hand, the *commit* method of *coordinator* would have to be redefined; specific handling of the exception is strongly dependant upon the considered application.

In general, various experiments were undertaken to investigate whether the Arche language was appropriate to program robust and reusable distributed applications. This led to encouraging results. In addition to the example discussed above, an application based on the technique of N-version programming was developed. This last example also uses the exception handling and multimethod facilities. Summarizing the combined advantages of these facilities, the notion of multimethod provides a useful tool to simply express management of distributed data structures while the exception handling mechanism allows keeping these data consistent in the presence of failure.

4   Conclusions

The cooperation exception handling model that has been discussed in this paper built upon a number of earlier sound results. It extends the termination model for sequential programming since the model simplicity eases quite significantly reasoning about the behaviour of programs in the presence of exceptions. The work further built upon results in the area of proofs of both concurrent programs and programs with exception handling. In addition to being useful for providing the formal definition of the cooperation model, they proved to be quite influential for guiding the model definition. The contribution of the work presented in this paper, at the time it was introduced, lay in two aspects: (i) the proposal of a general concurrent exception handling model that could be integrated in different concurrent languages, and (ii) the introduction of a formal definition of an exception handling facility aimed at concurrent programming. Although the author has not been studying extensively recent bibliography in the area of concurrent exception handling, there seems to have been few related recent results. The author's view about this issue is that despite the advent of distributed computing, the development of concurrent programs remains a complex task. This then leads in practice to (i) promoting quite primitive languages from the perspective of the underlying concurrency model, and (ii) treating fault-tolerance support as secondary, where the latter mostly relies on the base termination exception handling model for sequential programming. However, it should also be recognized that demonstrating the actual benefit of advanced concurrent software fault tolerance means in general, and of the cooperation model in particular, would require experiments with a number of large real applications. This is rarely undertaken and at least this step was not extensively undertaken by the author.

Since the work discussed in this paper was introduced, distributed computing has evolved in a drastic way. From the standpoint of supporting programming languages, almost none of the concurrent languages that originated from results in the distributed system research field are used in practice although they certainly influenced how distributed systems are now developed. In addition to C++ that was already popular in the early 90s, the Java language appears as another major player. Regarding exception handling in a sequential setting, the mechanism that is offered in both C++ [9] and Java [16] adheres to the same model for sequential exception handling upon which our proposal was built, i.e., the termination model. From a concurrency point of view, concurrency is in general addressed through a simple model of threads, and exception handling is there dealt with by propagating of the exception along the thread, which may ultimately lead to the termination of the embedding concurrent application. On the other hand, no support for multi-party interactions is offered although it is our belief that such a facility is crucial for developing dependable systems as it serves as a sound base ground for dealing with redundancy. To the best of our knowledge, such a concern has led to few research efforts in the recent past. We identify mainly the proposal of the Coordinated Atomic action (CA action) notion [20,18], which addresses in an homogeneous way fault tolerance means for concurrent activities that either cooperate or compete, while our proposal focused solely on cooperating activities.

From the perspective of distributed (operating) system support, here too, almost none of the distributed systems that were proposed at the end of the 80s are in use today. The common practice is to rely on a middleware that offers a base distributed inter-process communication system (e.g., remote procedure call), which may be customized using a number of advanced services for distribution management (e.g., transaction, fault-tolerance) [6]. It is however fair to state that all the middleware platforms that are proposed build upon results from the distributed system research community. Considering fault tolerance in this context, it mostly relies on application-transparent means, which are implemented at the middleware level. However, middleware platforms deal in general with the occurrence of exceptions by enabling the propagation of exceptions among interacting processes, which may then handle the exceptions internally. Support for multi-party interactions is not addressed except through base multicast protocols but without accounting for exception handling. Relevant work in the area is the aforementioned CA action proposal whose usage for applications developed over a middleware platform is being investigated.

A quite recent approach to the development of distributed software systems relates to the component-based technology, which may be considered as a generalization of the middleware notion. A significant advantage of this approach is that it promotes software reuse, enabling the design and implementation of software systems out of COTS (Commercial Off The Shelf) components. This may be further assisted through the principled design of the system software architecture [19] as for instance illustrated in [14]. This is the author's belief that architecture-based development of complex software systems constitutes an effective solution towards enabling the development of robust distributed systems, while accounting for their various instances as allowed by the ongoing technological evolution (e.g., pervasive computing is foreseen as a significant future trend). The concern for dependability is further becoming more crucial than ever since it is no longer confined to the area of safety critical systems but applies to nearly all systems given the underlying business issues. In that context, we have started a study about providing application-specific fault tolerance means within systems developed using an architecture-based approach. This proposal focuses on the issue of exception handling [15] and the one relating to dealing with redundancy is still to be investigated.

Acknowledgments. The author would like to acknowledge Jean-Pierre Banâtre with whom the work on cooperation exception handling was elaborated.

References

1. J-P. Banâtre, M. Banâtre, and F. Ployette. The concept of multi-functions, a general structuring tool for distributed operating system. In *Proceedings of the Sixth Distributed Computing Systems Conference*, 1986.

2. M. Banâtre, Y. Belhamissi, V. Issarny, I. Puaut, and J-P. Routeau. Arche: A framework for parallel object-oriented programming above a distributed architecture. In *Proceedings of the Fourteenth IEEE International Conference on Distributed Computing Systems*, pages 510–517, 1994.

3. M. Benveniste and V. Issarny. Concurrent programming notations in the object-oriented language arche. Research Report 1822, INRIA, Rennes, France, 1992.

4. R. H. Campbell and B. Randell. Error recovery in asynchronous systems. *Transactions on Software Engineering*, SE-12(8):811–826, 1986.

5. F. Cristian. Correct and robust programs. *IEEE Transactions on Software Engineering*, SE-10(2):163–174, 1984.

6. W. Emmerich. *Engineering Distributed Objects*. J. Wiley & Sons, 2000.

7. N. Francez, B. Hailpern, and G. Taubenfeld. Script: A communication abstraction mechanism and its verification. *Science of Computer Programming*, 6:35–88, 1986.

8. F. Gartner. Fundamentals of fault tolerant distributed computing in asynchronous environments. *ACM Computing Surveys*, 31(1):1–26, 1999.

9. J. Gosling, B. Joy, and G. Steele. *The Java Language Specification*. Addison-Wesley, 1996.

10. J. Gray. *Notes on DataBase Operating Systems*, volume 60 of *Lecture Notes in Computer Science*. Springer Verlag, 1978.

11. V. Issarny. An exception handling model for parallel programming and its verification. In *Proceedings of the ACM SIGSOFT'91 Conference on Software for Critical Systems*, pages 92–100, 1991.

12. V. Issarny. *Un modèle pour le traitement des exceptions dans les programmes parallèles*. Thèse de doctorat, Université de Rennes I, Rennes, France, 1991.

13. V. Issarny. An exception handling mechanism for parallel object-oriented programming: Towards reusable, robust distributed software. *Journal of Object-Oriented Programming*, 6(6):29–39, 1993.

14. V. Issarny, C. Bidan, and T. Saridakis. .Achieving Middleware Customization in a Configuration-based Development Environment: Experience with the Aster Prototype. In *Proceedings of the Fourth International Conference on Configurable Distributed Systems*, pages 275-283, 1998.

15. V. Issarny and J-P. Banâtre. Architecture-based exception handling. In *Proceedings of the Thirty Fourth Hawaii International Conference on System Sciences*, 2001.

16. A. Koening and B. Stroustrup. Exception handling for C++. In *Proceedings of* USENIX *C++ Conference*, pages 149–176, 1990.

17. S. Mullender, editor. *Distributed Systems*. ACM Press, 1989.

18. B. Randell, A. Romanovsky, R. J. Stroud, J. Xu, and A. F. Zorzo. Coordinated Atomic Actions: from Concept to Implementation. Research Report TR 595, University of Newcastle upon Tyne, Newcastle upon Tyne, UK, 1997.

19. M. Shaw and D. Garlan. Software Architecture: Perspectives on an Emerging Disciplines. Prentice Hall, 1996

20. J. Xu, B. Randell, A. Romanovsky, C. M. F. Rubira, R. J. Stroud, and Z. Wu. Fault tolerance in concurrent object-oriented software through coordinated error recovery. In *Proceedings of the Twenty-Fifth IEEE International Symposium on Fault-Tolerant Computing*, pages 499–508, 1995.

21. Y-J. Young and S. Smolka. A comprehensive study of the complexity of multiparty interaction. *Journal of the ACM*, 43(1):75–115, 1996.

Exception Handling in Agent-Oriented Systems

Anand Tripathi and Robert Miller

Department of Computer Science
University of Minnesota, Minneapolis MN 55455

Abstract. Agent-oriented programming may be the next generation paradigm to try and tame the software complexity beast. Agents are active objects capable of autonomous behavior. Mobility can be one of the attributes of agents in open systems. A software system could be structured as a dynamic, and possibly evolving, ensemble of cooperating agents. However, there is very little in the literature on how to effectively handle exceptions in agent-oriented software systems. Agent-oriented systems have all the exception handling concerns of sequential and concurrent systems, as well as some new issues that arise due to mobility and security in open systems. This paper develops an exception handling model whose salient feature is the separation and encapsulation of exception handling for an agent environment in a special agent called a *guardian*. The model presented here builds upon the notions of events, exceptions, notifications, and commands in an agent ensemble, and presents a number of exception handling patterns that can be used by a guardian. The model presented here is being investigated in the context of the Ajanta mobile agent programming system.

1 Introduction

Agent-oriented software engineering represents the next step in the evolution of composition based development methods. Agents are a way to manage software complexity [9]. An agent is an encapsulated computing component that is situated in some environment, and that is capable of flexible, autonomous action in that environment in order to meet its design objectives [18]. An agent represents an active entity with an execution context together with a thread of execution and control. An agent-oriented system is intrinsically a concurrent system where the agents and their execution environments represent active entities. Such systems may be distributed when agents and environments are located at different nodes in a network.

The typical characteristics of an agent are that it is autonomous, mobile, cooperates with other agents, can learn, and can be reactive or proactive (deliberative) [13]. The most important characteristic of an agent is autonomy, which means that the agent is capable of determining its actions based on its current environment and execution context. A reactive agent executes actions only in response to requests from other agents or its environment, whereas a proactive (deliberative) agent can initiate actions spontaneously based on its own state

A. Romanovsky et al. (Eds.): Exception Handling, LNCS 2022, pp. 128–146, 2001.

and the state of its environment. Agents may be capable of learning based on their past execution to guide their future behavior. The ability of a group of agents to communicate with each other is important to realize systems that inherently rely on composition of active components. An agent that possesses the mobility attribute is able to migrate in a network, from one host environment to another. The main advantages of the mobile agent paradigm lie in its ability to move client code and computation to remote server resources, and in permitting increased asynchrony in client-server interactions [7].

Complex systems are generally managed with respect to three criteria [1]: decomposition, abstraction, and hierarchy or organization. Agents meet these three criteria by allowing a problem to be decomposed into a number of smaller, related sub-problems. Abstraction is supported by considering each of the sub-problems to be a sub-system (i.e., a subsystem becomes an agent). Agents, since they are autonomous, can reorganize themselves dynamically to better coordinate together to solve a problem. Agent-oriented software design appears promising for a large class of applications, particularly those in open distributed systems, such as distributed collaboration frameworks, enterprise workflow management systems, manufacturing systems, distributed simulations, and network monitoring and management systems.

In recent years there has been a surge of activities in the area of agent based software systems. The research activities in this area have focused on various different aspects of agent programming, such as agent communication languages, multi-agent planning and coordination protocols, and support for agent mobility using mobile code technology as well as the development of mobile agent programming platforms. Recently, a number of systems have emerged from research labs and commercial organizations to support mobile agent programming [17, 10]. A vast majority of these are based on the Java programming language; these systems are thus able to leverage the object-orientation features for abstraction, encapsulation, dynamic binding, inheritance, and reflection. Moreover, Java's support for code mobility and its security model facilitate designs of suitable mechanisms for mobile agent execution in open distributed systems. However, most of the current mobile agent programming systems do not address the problems related to exception handling in mobile agent applications.

There is very little in the literature concerning exception handling in agent-oriented systems. Without effective exception handling, it is doubtful that agent-oriented systems will be able to realize their full potential. Exception handling is even more challenging when agents are mobile in an open system, and where the interactions between agents and their environments may be ad hoc without any *a priori* plan. Moreover, mobility raises possibilities of exception conditions arising due to node/link failures. Security and protection mechanisms complicate this picture even further by introducing various unexpected failure conditions.

Often, exception handling in a program is the most complex, misunderstood, poorly documented, and least tested part of a software system [14]. This leads to the conclusion that exception handling has to be either simplified or taken out of the hands of the average programmer (i.e., something else does the more complex exception handling).

The agent programming system and its exception handling model presented here uses the latter approach by separating global level exception handling concerns from the application agents, and encapsulating them in special agents whose primary purpose is to monitor and control application agents with respect to exception conditions. Such specialized agents may use generic patterns for global exception handling. The exception handling model adopted in this work has four key components:

1. A special agent called a *guardian*, which acts as an exception handler for a set of agents in an application.
2. Exceptions are viewed as *internal* and *external* with respect to an agent. External exceptions propagate outside of an agent to its guardian.
3. Events, exceptions, notifications, and commands are used to communicate between a guardian and its monitored agents.
4. Exception handling patterns can be used by a guardian to handle commonly occurring situations in an agent ensemble.

The main feature of this system is support for encapsulation of global exception handling concerns in guardian agents of an application, thus separating them from the design of the application agents. This approach is similar to the one proposed in [11]. Moreover, a guardian can use exception handling patterns for commonly occurring conditions. This allows different patterns to be implemented by changing the guardian, without requiring changes to the application agents.

The next section elaborates the specific issues for exception handling in agent systems. Section 3 presents the proposed model based on the notion of guardians. Section 4 shows how this model relates to the well-known and widely used concepts and models for exception handling in sequential, concurrent, and distributed systems. In Section 5 we outline some simple patterns that can be used in designing a guardian to handle commonly occurring failure conditions in agent systems. The focus of Section 6 is on the integration of this model in the Ajanta agent programming system. We present here the specific programming primitives and protocols that are provided by the Ajanta system to support the guardian mechanism in mobile agent applications. Section 7 presents the conclusions and the future direction of this work.

2   Design Issues

Security and robustness are among the most important requirements of an agent programming environment. The main focus of this paper is on robustness and exception handling problems, therefore, we do not address here security related problems. However, one must note that a security violation would generally result in the signaling of an exception during an agent's execution.

An agent based application needs mechanisms to recover from errors that are encountered by its roaming agents at remote nodes. For recovery and debugging purposes, the error handling mechanisms should be able to examine the state of the agent to perform any recovery. Also, for debugging purposes an application developer also needs access to the state of a remote agent when its execution fails due to an error. In general, due to its autonomous nature and security concerns, a remote server may not be willing to continue hosting an agent that has encountered an exception. Moreover, it may not support access to the agent's state to a remote process trying to perform debugging or error recovery actions.

A recovery action by an application may require interrupting other agents that belong to the application and possibly altering the course of their execution. This requires mechanisms for remote control and interruption of mobile agents. Moreover, such control needs to be performed in a secure manner. Also, a user may sometimes require a high degree of confidence in executing an agent based application and may need mechanisms to remotely control its agents. Therefore, an ideal agent programming system should provide suitable mechanisms in which a user can monitor her roaming agents' status and control them remotely, irrespective of their current locations.

Typically an agent environment should be designed to cope with exceptions that generally arise in traditional software systems due to illegal operations, resources restrictions, or design faults. In the following discussion we focus on a broad characterization of only those additional classes of exceptions that are related to some of the unique characteristics of such environments.

Mobility exceptions: An agent, being autonomous, can make a migration request to roam in the network. There are a number of cases when a migration request could result in an exception. For example, an agent makes a request to migrate to a non-existing host, or the destination host refuses to accept the agent, or the communication link to a host has failed. A migration request may also fail due to security reasons if the verification of an agent's credentials fails at the destination host.

Security exceptions: An agent may not be granted permission to execute in some environment, or may not be given adequate resources to do its task. Typically a host would enforce restrictions on an agent's access to its resources such as files, network ports, and application objects. Moreover, it may impose a limit on usage of resources such as CPU and memory, or on the duration for which an agent can live in its environment. A security exception could also arise when an agent's state is found to be illegally modified or the verification of its credentials fails.

Communication exceptions: These arise when an agent tries to communicate with another agent. There could be various reasons for these exceptions. For example, the system fails to locate the receiver agent, or the receiver migrates just before the communication request arrives. Communication may also fail if the host environment raises a security exception because the agent is not allowed access to network resources.

Coordination exceptions: A typical situation of a coordination exception is the case when one agent fails to communicate with another agent by some specified time. This is the typical timeout exception. An example of a more complex exception is a deadlock condition in a group of cooperating agents. One needs mechanisms to detect this type of conditions and then signal an exception to the members in the group. Another example of a coordination exception is in the case of a barrier-join protocol when an agent fails to arrive at the barrier due to some fatal failure.

Configuration exceptions: These arise due to a misconfigured system. For example, appropriate privileges are not set for an agent to execute in an environment. Another example of misconfiguration is when an agent fails to load the code for the classes that it needs for its designated task. Most often, a configuration exception arises due to incorrect and inadequate privileges granted to an agent.

3   A Model for Exception Handling in Agent Systems

An *event* is the condition that causes a program's execution to be directed to a handler. An exception is an event that is caused by a program using a language construct (e.g., *throw*), or raised by the underlying virtual machine. Exceptions are synchronous in the sense that an explicit program statement must signal the exception. An exception only has meaning in the same thread that signaled the exception.

An *interrupt* is an event originating externally to an agent; i.e., it is not caused by the agent program executing an explicit statement. It is asynchronous in that the program has no knowledge when it will occur. An incoming message to a thread may cause an interrupt, with the interrupt handler being the message handler. An interrupt handler may signal an exception to the interrupted program, thus 'converting' an asynchronous event into a synchronous one.

A *notification* is a message sent from one agent to another. The notification itself is not an exception, but the message handler may signal an exception based on the information contained in the notification. A notification message can contain two types of information: *exception* or *command*. An *exception notification* is one that the sender does not know what the receiver will do with it. A *command notification* means the sender expects the receiver to execute the specified action (i.e., the sender is commanding the receiver to do some action).

Exceptions that are signaled in an agent are broadly classified into two categories: *internal* or *external*. An internal exception is one that is completely handled by the agent. The agent does not go outside itself to handle the exception. An external exception is one that is not fully handled by the agent. An external exception does not necessarily mean that the exception has no handler in the agent; it only means that the agent did not handle the exception completely within itself. In general, an internal exception is one that an agent expects and knows how to handle. External exceptions are ones that are unexpected or involve cooperation with other agents.

A *guardian* is an agent with a special relationship to other agents in an agent based application. It acts as a global exception handler and monitor for its application agents. As a global exception handler, it can 'handle' an agent's unhandled exceptions, as well as any external exceptions arising in an agent. As a monitor, it can deal with situations that involve coordination or cooperation between all the monitored agents. For example, if several monitored agents need to synchronize at a barrier, then without a guardian each agent would have to know all the other agents that are involved in the barrier. With a guardian, it is much simpler since the guardian is a centralized agent.

An agent is situated in an environment, and a distributed agent-based system may consist of multiple environments. An environment represents a host or a server process in the network. An agent may be mobile, i.e. capable of migrating from one environment to another. We view the execution environments also as agents that are generally stationary, i.e. they lack mobility. Thus, the interactions between an agent and its environment can be viewed in the same way as those between two agents.

Figure 1 illustrates a typical multi-agent application environment. This application consists of four agents and one guardian. An agent can notify and send an exception to its guardian. The guardian can issue various kinds of commands to its agents or it may query status of an agent by either directly communicating with it or its environment.

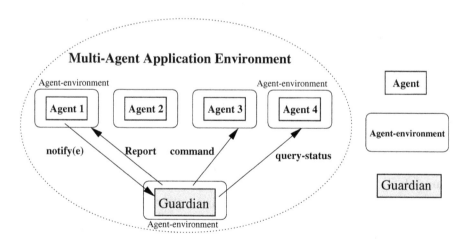

Fig. 1. A Multi-Agent Application Environment

Figure 2 shows the typical structure of exception code within an agent. On an exception, the agent first checks whether the exception could be handled locally. In case of an external exception, the agent communicates with the guardian. The guardian then returns an appropriate command, based on the condition. It may instruct the agent to either retry the operation, or terminate itself, or co-locate with the guardian and report to it for further recovery.

```
retryLabel: try {
    ...
}
catch (InternalException e) {
    ...
}
catch (ExternalException e) {
    command = notifyGuardian( e );
    if (command == RETRY) {
      goto retryLabel;
    } else
      if (command == TERMINATE) {
         throw terminateException;
      } else
         if (command == REPORT) {
            throw colocateException ( report(e) );
         }
}
```

Fig. 2. Example of internal and external exception handling by an agent

Mobility exceptions generally require selection of an alternate plan. It is possible to provide an agent with an itinerary, which includes internal exception handling actions to select an alternate plan for the agent [15]. If no such alternate plan is available, then the guardian should be asked to take a global action based on the state of the other agents in the application.

One of the goals of robust programming is for an agent to be able to recover from an error. Security exceptions are ones that an agent cannot handle itself, because there is nothing an agent can do to increase its authority to access the resource it was denied. A guardian can simplify this. It can possibly have higher security privileges, and so it could grant a failed agent some additional privileges and then restart it. This can all be done using external exceptions and commands.

Coordination exceptions typically require a global view of the situation to take any remedial actions. For this a guardian is well suited as it can communicate with other agents, and possibly alter their plans.

Another kind of exception is a configuration exception. It is signaled when the environment does not give to an agent access to all of the resources needed by it. It is a combination of security, resource allocation, and network exceptions. Here also a guardian could take necessary steps to correct the system configuration. Configuration exceptions cannot be handled by the agent that causes them. However, a guardian could be trusted and have special privileges. It could correct the configuration error, and restart the failed agent. Alternatively, a guardian could restart the failed agent on another node which the guardian feels has a higher probability of agent success.

When an agent communicates an exception to its guardian, the guardian may need to examine the state of the agent signaling the exception or the states of some other agents in the ensemble, including the environment agents. In some cases only the state of the signaling agent needs to be examined. For example, if an agent encounters a mobility exception, indicating a host being inaccessible due to communication failures, the guardian can possibly change its itinerary to pursue an alternate plan. In this case only the state of the agent is examined and changed by the guardian. If an agent encounters a security exception due to misconfiguration, the guardian may need to communicate with the agent's environment to set up the configuration correctly, for example to grant the agent some additional privileges. Consider the example of a pipelined execution of a set of agents. An agent may encounter a timeout exception if its upstream agent fails to deliver some data in time, or it encounters a communication exception if the downstream agent is inaccessible. In this case the guardian has to examine the status of the upstream or downstream agents by communicating with their environments.

From the above discussion we conclude that a guardian needs mechanisms to examine the state of the agent signaling an exception, and it may also need to determine the state of other agents in an ensemble by communicating with them or their environments. In some cases it may need to control the behavior of its monitored agents by terminating them or changing their execution plans.

4   Patterns of Exception Handling by a Guardian

Patterns are exception handling strategies or actions to be executed when certain abnormal events occur. An exception handling pattern is a policy that a guardian invokes. The agents monitored by a guardian may become involved in the pattern with the commands/notifications sent to them by the guardian. Some examples of patterns are restarting an agent that fails on a node, aborting concurrent search agents as soon as one agent satisfies the search, and terminating child agents if the parent agent terminates. A guardian can be designed using some commonly occurring patterns of exception handling. There are many possible patterns, and here are a few examples:

Barrier synchronization: This involves a group of agents cooperating in a barrier synchronization. Suppose that an agent in the group fails due to an unhandled exception. This agent will report to the guardian using the exception notification mechanism. The guardian can examine the failed agent's status, and after determining that it failed before joining a barrier, it can examine the status of the group's progress towards the barrier synchronization. The guardian can send a notification to the other participating agents to not wait for the failed agent, and send a command notification to them to either continue or abort.

Pipeline failures: A set of agents execute in a pipelined configuration. An agent receives some data from its upstream agent, and then passes it to its downstream agent after performing some processing. An agent may encounter an exception when the communication with its upstream neighbor times out or it is unable to reach the downstream agent. In this case, it sends a notification to the guardian, which could then check the status of the other agent and initiate a recovery action. For this it needs to query that agent's environment. The recovery action by the guardian may involve reconfiguring the pipeline or restarting a failed agent.

Primary-backup server recovery: A reliable service is implemented using a pair of agents, acting as a primary server and its backup. If the primary server fails, the guardian for this system can either try to repair and restart it, or it can send a command notification to the backup agent to take over as the primary and create a new backup.

Deadlock detection and recovery in an agent group: Assume that a set of agents are acquiring various global resources, and that all these agents have the same guardian. Whenever an agent tries to acquire such a resource, it notifies its guardian with an exception notification. The guardian's exception handler stores the information, and determines, based on information obtained from other agents, if the acquisition will result in deadlock. If so, the guardian can send a command notification to an agent to tell it to relinquish some of the resources. Similarly, if an agent times out in receiving some data from another agent, it can notify the guardian, which can then construct the global state to determine if deadlock has occurred. If so, it can then recall, terminate or restart some agents.

Recovery and restart of a failed agent: Before an agent completely terminates due to an error, it sends an exception notification to its guardian, and waits for a command from it. The command can be to either terminate, restart itself, or send back to the guardian all error information. The guardian may be able, with information from other agents, to restart the failed agent with proper parameters.

Configuration update: The environment an agent uses needs to be modified (e.g., user needs to be authorized to a resource). Generally, an agent would not have sufficient privileges to do that, but a trusted guardian could. If a guardian receives a security exception notification from an agent, the guardian may be able to correct the authorization problem by communicating with the agent's environment, and then restart or resume the agent.

Patterns further separate internal exception handling from external exception handling. A guardian takes much of the burden away from an application agent exception handler when dealing with external exceptions. The guardian determines the pattern. The guardian is doing the exception analysis and has a global view to try and determine the best course of action via the pattern. The agent just needs to respond to command notifications from its guardian.

Updating or adding new patterns is equivalent to updating a guardian. Regardless of the guardian's patterns, an agent does not handle any more exceptions. An internal exception is still an internal one, and an external exception is still an external one. Thus, updating a pattern does not require updating an agent.

However, what is critical relative to an agent is the set of command notifications that an agent is expected to respond to. The separation of guardian from agent exception handling works because the guardian does not necessarily need to know an agent's complete state. It just needs to know enough to determine a pattern, and assume that the command notification it sends to agents is faithfully followed.

The end effect is that changing a pattern is changing a guardian, while changing a command notification also changes an agent. If command notifications are carefully selected, a given agent may be able to adapt to a wide range of circumstances, dependent on the particular guardian chosen.

5   Relationship to Fundamental Models

It is important to examine here the relationship of exception handling in agent systems with the models for exception handling in sequential, concurrent, and parallel/distributed programs [5,3,8]. There are two reasons for this:

1. By showing the relationship of an agent to a thread, it implies that an agent will have similar exception handling problems as threads.
2. This also implies that any programming system that supports the various thread environments (sequential, concurrent, and distributed) with exception handling can also support the agent exception handling model presented here. In particular, we chose to implement an agent system (Ajanta) using Java, and so we should be able to illustrate agent system exception handling using Java constructs.

Agents have a direct analogy to sequential, concurrent, and distributed programs. A sequential program corresponds to a single-agent system situated in an environment represented by the host operating system. Concurrent threads are multiple agents that happen to share a common environment. Distributed programs are agents that have a fixed relationship (e.g., a client and server agents, or peers in an agent group) and are situated in different environments in a network.

Thus, agents have all the exception handling problems of sequential, concurrent, and distributed systems, as well as a few more. It will be useful to briefly summarize the significant exception handling problems in these three kinds of programming models. Though there are many problems in exception handling, we believe that they can be summarized as follows. Also note that there is a hierarchy: sequential exception handling problems are also in concurrent programs, and concurrent exception handling problems are also in distributed exception handling. Finally, the exceptions we are interested in are external exceptions. Internal exceptions are completely handled by an agent.

We first turn to the basic issues related to exception handling in sequential programs.

Exception propagation: This determines how to search for a valid handler. Dynamic propagation follows the call chain or registration of a handler, while static propagation follows the program structure (e.g., a class handler).

Unhandled exceptions: These arise when an exception is signaled in the program, but a valid handler for the exception is not found. How to deal with unhandled exceptions in a program is an important issue.

Program flow control model: An unhandled exception in a program block can cause the block to be either terminated, retried, or resumed into.

Conceptually, a guardian is similar to a static class handler, but it is dynamically associated with the agent object. An agent can pass an exception to its guardian when it encounters an external exception. It is possible to statically determine the exceptions that an agent would pass to its guardian because only external exceptions involve a guardian, and it is known statically which exceptions those are. In an agent's code, the handler search is first dynamic (handler associated with the stack invocation), followed by a static handler search (the guardian). The invoking of the guardian as an exception handler is similar to the notion in [4] of invoking a class handler if the current stack invocation does not have a handler. By binding a different guardian to an agent at runtime, one can change the recovery policies on external exceptions generated by the agent.

The advantages of a static handler [12] include a clearer separation of exception handling from the normal path, distinction between internal (local) and external (non-local) exceptions (relative to a guardian), no new additional language constructs are required, and there is always at least one handler for any exception (the guardian is also invoked for any exception not handled by an agent).

A guardian differs from other static handler approaches, such as those in [12, 2]. A guardian is dynamically bound to the agent, which is critical because it separates external exception handling from internal exception handling, and it allows a guardian to be outside the agent class (thus allowing a guardian to have a global view).

In an agent system, exception propagation includes an agent's guardian as a dynamic handler registration. The guardian is not in the call stack, nor is it necessarily part of the program. Due to the dynamic registration, the guardian can be invoked at any point along the propagation path, not necessarily after all the agent's handlers have been searched. This allows for the guardian to simulate any one of the exception models dynamically. For example, an agent's local handler sends an exception notification to the guardian. The guardian can send a command notification back indicating to terminate (the local handler re-throws the exception), resume (the local handler handles the exception), or retry (the local handler returns from the procedure it is in with a fail return code, allowing the invoker to call the procedure again).

In systems that support class handlers, using a guardian is straightforward. The class handler invokes a guardian's remote method on an external exception. In systems with dynamic propagation, a handler is first searched for in the current execution context (stack frame). The exception is propagated along the call chain until a handler is found. If the handler is part of an agent class method, and it is an external exception, then the handler can access the guardian, giving the appearance of a class handler.

Exception handling models in concurrent systems are required to address two important issues:

Asynchronous exceptions: When one thread signals an exception to another thread, the issue is when and how to deliver this exception to the target thread.

Exception resolution: determining which exception(s) a target thread receives if multiple exceptions are simultaneously sent to it from multiple threads. A special case of exception resolution is during synchronizing (or coordinating) concurrent threads, such as barrier synchronization or conversations [3].

It should be noted here that the model in [3] requires that all processes in a conversation participate in cooperative exception handling. In contrast, the model presented here does not necessarily require all agents in an application to participate in cooperative recovery through its guardian. However, it is possible for a guardian to require all its agents to be involved in a recovery action. Our model provides a framework to incorporate different policies for cooperative exception handling among agents.

Recall that in an agent system, concurrent threads are represented by agents, and that we are only dealing with external exceptions. An asynchronous exception has different meaning depending if the agent is a guardian or not. By definition, an agent cannot send an external asynchronous exception to any agent other than its guardian. A guardian can only receive external asynchronous exceptions (as notifications) from other agents. That is, a guardian does not have a guardian, so it cannot signal an asynchronous exception to itself (it would be a synchronous exception, and the guardian's handler would consider it to be an internal exception).

So, external asynchronous events received by an agent can only be commands. External asynchronous events received by a guardian can only be exceptions. This considerably simplifies the agent's asynchronous exception handling, because it does not have to determine what to do, just execute a command.

Exception resolution is similar. If multiple agents simultaneously and asynchronously raise external exceptions, they all must go to the guardian. The guardian, possibly using some pattern, determines the action to take and sends a command to the affected agents. Note that all these events use the exception mechanism, as explained earlier.

In an asynchronous system, in case of concurrently raised multiple exceptions, the primary concern is to resolve them, possibly by combining some exceptions, and to find a suitable handler for the resolved exception [3,19]. In a distributed environment, causal relationship among concurrent exceptions may be important in the resolution process. For that, one may need to consider global ordering and causality relationships between exception events signaled by distributed agents. For an agent ensemble in a distributed environment, a purely distributed solution for coordination and exception resolution may not be most efficient. For that reason the guardian can serve as a central coordinator for event ordering and exception resolution.

Recall that the guardian is on the agent's handler propagation path, and is invoked as the external handler for the agent's unhandled exceptions. The agent has not terminated yet. The guardian can have a debug interface that allows the programmer to query the agent through commands, or the guardian can automatically collect a set amount of data. Once again, the guardian can use a pattern to determine what to do.

Host crashes or communication link loss means an agent lost its guardian, or a guardian lost an agent. If an agent loses its guardian, then it should be delivered a notification that directs it to either bind to a new guardian, or terminate itself. Agents must be safe, meaning they cannot exist if there is no one (i.e., its guardian) controlling them. If a guardian loses an agent, then it receives an internal asynchronous exception. Depending on the pattern, the guardian may create a new agent to replace the lost one, or do nothing. With a guardian, it is not mandatory that other agents receive a notification that an agent was lost. If the guardian knows whether the agents were cooperating (e.g., performing a barrier synchronization) then agents receive notifications of a lost agent only as needed.

6   Exception Handling in the Ajanta System

We now describe the exception handling model that we have developed and integrated in the Ajanta mobile agent programming system. The mechanism designed for Ajanta implement the basic model that we have presented in Section 3. It is based on the notion of associating one or more guardian agents with an agent application. It also supports secure delivery of commands and notification events to agents. We refer to this framework as agent system exception handling because it deals only with external exceptions, which require global level decision-making for recovery.

Ajanta[1] [15] is a Java-based framework for programming *mobile agent* based applications on the Internet. Ajanta is implemented using the Java [6] language and its security mechanisms. It also makes use of several other facilities provided by Java, such as object serialization, reflection, and remote method invocation.

In Ajanta, the mobile agent implementation is based on the generic concept of a *mobile object*. Agents encapsulate code and execution context along with data; they execute in the environments provided by *Agent Servers* at different nodes in a network. An agent can be mobile, i.e., it can migrate from one agent server to another. Programming abstractions are provided to specify an agent's tasks and its migration path. The Ajanta system provides facilities to build customizable *agent servers* to host mobile agents, and a set of primitives for the creation and management of agents. Ajanta also provides a secure name service

---

[1] See http://www.cs.umn.edu/Ajanta for more documentation and information related to the availability of a public domain version of this system.

for location-independent naming of all global entities, such as the agents and the agent servers.

6.1   Agent Servers – Defining an Execution Environment for Agents

Security is an important requirement of an agent infrastructure. The base class called `AgentServer` provides the generic functionality to host agents, create a protected environment for their execution, transfer agents from one server to another using its Agent Transfer Protocol (ATP), and respond to various agent control functions. An application specific agent server is implemented by inheriting from the base `AgentServer` class. It can be easily customized for specific services by creating appropriate resources (objects) and making them available to the visiting agents through its `resourceRegistry`. A visiting agent can request access to a resource through this registry. The resource then constructs a suitably restricted proxy [16], based on its security policy, and gives the agent a reference to this proxy. The agent cannot access the resources directly, and the proxy object ensures that sensitive operations are disallowed and throws a security exception if the agent tries to execute any such operation. Ajanta ensures that the proxy class is loaded from a trusted codebase. Details of this proxy mechanism can be found in [15].

6.2   Structure of an Agent

The `Agent` class implements the generic functionality of a mobile agent. It defines the protocol for handling the arrival and departure events of an agent at a server. Each agent is bound to its host environment using which the agent can request various services from its current server. These services include obtaining access to local resources, registering itself as a resource, or requesting migration.

An agent can request migration to another server using the `go` primitive of its `host` environment to migrate to another server. The agent specifies the name of the server to which it wants to move to, and it also specifies the method to be executed at the destination server after migration. Ajanta system uses Java's reflection facility for specifying this. A method specification consists of a method name, the list of its formal parameter types, and the list of actual parameters to be passed to this method on execution at the destination server. Another primitive facilitates an agent to co-locate itself with some specified object. To co-locate with its guardian, the agent throws the `colocateException`, which is not handled by the agent. Because it becomes and 'unhandled' exception, it causes the agent to be automatically relocated in the guardian's environment.

We use Java's object serialization facility to implement agent mobility in Ajanta. Agents are simply serializable Java objects. Note however that object serialization only captures the data values in an object's state; it cannot capture the execution state of the thread (or threads) currently executing that object's methods. Thus, when the agent object is deserialized at the remote server, a new thread is assigned to execute a method specified in the migration request.

The concept of itineraries is built above the go primitive and is not an essential part of the basic agent structure. An agent can be created with an itinerary to visit different servers and perform some designated tasks at those servers [15]. In [15] we have discussed how an itinerary can be created from generic migration patterns, and how a pattern can perform some internal exception handling to select an alternate plan of execution.

The agent is usually created by an application program – we call this the *creator* of the agent. An agent's *owner* is the human user whom the agent represents. An agent carries with it a credentials object, which is signed by its owner. Its tampering can be detected. It contains the names of the agent, its owner and the creator. For exception handling and error recovery in a mobile agent application, the Ajanta programming model associates with an application a stationary *guardian* agent. An application creates and assigns to each of its agents a *guardian* agent. The name of its guardian is contained in an agent's credentials.

6.3   Guardians

When an agent arrives at a sever, the server creates a thread to execute the agent's public method specified in the transfer request. The creation of the server thread and its invocation of the agent's method is transparent to the programmer. The base **AgentServer** implements this facility; using Java reflection, this is designed to be a generic facility to allow execution of any types of agents. The agent method executed by the server thread can throw any of the exceptions, as indicated in the invoked method's signature. However, the server thread is generic in its structure. It can catch such exceptions, but cannot perform any meaningful recovery actions. To handle such situations, guardian model is adopted.

During its execution, an agent may encounter some exception conditions. Some of these may be handled within the agent's code. These are the internal exceptions. When an agent encounters an exception that is not handled by its code, there are two options available to the agent. One option is to continue to be situated in its current environment and remotely interact with the guardian. The second option is to co-locate with the guardian.

In the first option, while handling an exception, an agent can request the help of its guardian. It can do so by invoking the **notify** method of the guardian. Through the invocation of this method, the agent passes to the guardian the exception object. This invocation is authenticated for security, so the guardian knows the verified identity of the calling agent. After examining the exception condition, the guardian can return a directive to assist the agent in its further actions. It is the application programmer's task to define such directives.

In the second option, the agent is co-located with its guardian. If an exception is not handled by the agent, then such an exception is signaled to the server thread executing the agent's code. The server thread then transports the agent to its guardian with the appropriate *status* information, including the exception that caused the agent to fail. This migration is done using the co-location mechanism described above.

The guardian's location can be determined using the Ajanta name service. On co-location, the agent invokes the **report** method of the guardian object and passes to the guardian a reference to itself. The guardian can then examine the agent's state as described below.

Every agent contains an **AgentStatus** object, which is a vector containing the status of its execution at the hosts visited so far. The status of an agent's execution at the various servers visited by it is described by the **AgentStatus** object. This vector contains **NotificationRecord**s. These records show whether the status of the agent is okay. If not, it contains the exception encountered by the agent, together with the stack trace for the exception to help in debugging. A notification record with the appropriate exception object is added to the status vector by the current server when an agent is to be sent to its guardian for error recovery.

When the agent invokes the **report** method of its guardian, the guardian can inspect the agent's state, and if appropriate, modify it and re-launch the agent. The agent may be asked to restart its itinerary, or sent back to the host, where it encountered the exception, to resume its activities.

Structure of a guardian is an application developer's responsibility. This can be based on some of the patterns presented in the previous sections of this paper. Ajanta provides some additional mechanisms using which the guardian can perform application-wide recovery actions. For example, in an agent-based program consisting of a group of agents, the recovery action may require termination of some or all of the agents in a group. Should one of the members encounters a non-recoverable exception that affects the execution of the entire program, that member needs to be terminated. These mechanisms are described below.

6.4   Agent Monitoring and Control

For a guardian to perform global recovery and error handling in an ensemble of cooperating agents, Ajanta provides three commands – **recall**, **retract**, and **abort** – which the guardian can invoke on its agents to control their execution. It might be sometimes necessary to recall an agent back, because its owner/creator/guardian needs to modify its further course of execution to perform some error recovery actions. There are other situations where these primitives can be useful; for example, the creator of an application may decide to terminate or recall an agent because it has received results from another agent sent out to perform the same task. At times the owner might have lost control over the agent, and may even need help from the hosting server to ship the agent back. All these primitives are invoked on the server hosting the agent, which can be determined by querying the name service. For security reasons, all of these control primitives are executed only when invoked by the agent's owner, creator, or guardian.

The **recall** method of an agent server can be invoked through its RMI interface to recall an agent hosted at that server. The server sends the agent to its guardian after the agent has completed its execution at that server. There are two forms of this primitive. In the first form, the agent is directed to co-locate with its guardian and then execute the guardian's report method. Using the other form, the agent can be directed to co-locate with a specified target object, and then execute its report method.

The server hosting the agent first authenticates the invoker of the recall method. If the invoker is either the owner, creator, or guardian, then it sets some information in the agent's status object for it to migrate and report to the designated target object after it has completed its computation at the current server. This is done by the host server by calling the agent's `recallCommand` method. As a part of the system-defined *exit* protocol, every agent checks its status object for any pending recall. If a recall command is pending, the agent invokes the `co-locate` primitive to migrate to the target object's server. Once relocated there, the agent invokes the `report` method of the target object.

The `retract` primitive allows the caller to retract an agent back or send it to its guardian or another target object 'immediately'. The agent is interrupted in whatever action it may be performing at the current host and is directed to report to the target immediately. The `abort` primitive allows the caller to kill the agent immediately. This primitive is useful if, for example, an agent's creator feels that the agent needs to be terminated because of some fatal error. This primitive is also useful to terminate all agents of an aborted application.

7 Conclusions and Directions for Future Research

Agents represent another opportunity to create flexible programs. However, without robust exception handling, it is likely agent-oriented programming will be just as successful as past paradigms. The complexity of correct exception handling leads us to conclude that global exception handling with a global handler should be separated from application agents, and that generic patterns for common exception situations can be provided by a global handler.

This paper has proposed an agent-oriented exception handling model that has four components: a global exception handler through a special agent called a guardian; exceptions are either internal or external; the relationships between events, exceptions, notifications, and commands; and exception handling patterns.

The similarity between the basic exception handling problems in sequential, concurrent, and distributed programs and with agents has been discussed. Those problems are exception propagation, unhandled exceptions, and program flow control in sequential programs; asynchronous exceptions and exception resolution in concurrent and distributed programs. Agents also add new exception handling problems, due to mobility, security, and communication failures.

It has been shown how the use of a guardian as a global exception handler can simplify exception handling of these problems within the context of an external exception. Some example exception handling patterns which a guardian would invoke include barrier synchronization, primary-backup server recovery, deadlock detection and recovery in an agent group, recovery and restart of a failed agent, and configuration updates.

This paper's proposal is currently being designed into the Ajanta mobile agent system. Ajanta incorporates the guardian concept, but does not provide any patterns. Future work includes incorporating patterns in the Ajanta system, fault-tolerant guardians (e.g., a guardian has a guardian), mobile guardians, and support for agent groups to organize agent ensembles (the ensemble including a guardian).

Acknowledgments: This work was supported by National Science Foundation grants ANIR 9813703, EIA 9818338, and ITR 0082215.

References

1. BOOCH, G. *Object-Oriented Design with Applications.* Benjamin/Cummings Publishing Company, 1994.
2. BORGIDA, A. Exceptions in object-oriented languages. *SIGPLAN Notices 21*, 10 (October 1986).
3. CAMPBELL, R. H., AND RANDELL, B. Error Recovery in Asynchronous Systems. *IEEE Transactions on Software Engineering* (1986), 811–826.
4. DONY, C. Exception handling and object-oriented programming: towards a new synthesis. In *Proceedings of European Conference on Object Oriented Programming (ECOOP'90)* (October 1990), pp. 322–330.
5. GOODENOUGH, J. B. Exception Handling: Issues and Proposed Notations. *Communications of the ACM* (December 1975), 683–696.
6. GOSLING, J., JOY, B., AND STEELE, G. *The Java Language Specification.* Addison-Wesley, August 1996.
7. HARRISON, C. G., CHESS, D. M., AND KERSHENBAUM, A. Mobile Agents: Are they a good idea? Tech. rep., IBM Research Division, T.J.Watson Research Center, March 1995. Available at URL http://www.research.ibm.com/massdist/mobag.ps.
8. ISSARNY, V. An Exception-Handling Mechanism for Parallel Object-Oriented Programming: Toward Reusable, Robust Distributed Software. *Journal of Object Oriented Programming* (October 1993), 29–40.
9. JENNINGS, N. R. On agent-based software engineering. *Artificial Intelligence* (2000), 277–296.
10. KARNIK, N. M., AND TRIPATHI, A. R. Design Issues in Mobile Agent Programming Systems. *IEEE Concurrency* (July–September 1998), 52–61.
11. KLEIN, M., AND DELLAROCAS, C. Exception Handling in Agent Systems. In *Proc. of the ACM Conference on Autonomous Agents'99* (1999), pp. 62–68.
12. KNUDSEN, J. Better exception-handling in block-structured systems. *IEEE Software* (May 1987).
13. MORREALE, P. Mobile Software Agents. *IEEE Spectrum* (April 1998), 34–41.
14. PARNAS, D. L., VAN SCHOUWEN, J. A., AND PO, K. S. Evaluation of Safety-Critical Software. *Communcations of the ACM* (June 1990), 636–648.
15. TRIPATHI, A., KARNIK, N., VORA, M., AHMED, T., AND SINGH, R. Mobile Agent Programming in Ajanta. In *Proceedings of the 19th International Conference on Distributed Computing Systems* (May 1999).

16. TRIPATHI, A. R., AND KARNIK, N. M. Protected Resource Access for Mobile Agent-based Distributed Computing. In *Proceedings of the 1998 ICPP Workshop on Wireless Networks and Mobile Computing* (August 1998), IEEE Computer Society, pp. 144–153.

17. WONG, D., PACIOREK, N., AND MOORE, D. Java-based Mobile Agents. *Communications of the ACM 42*, 3 (March 1999), 92–102.

18. WOOLRIDGE, M. Agent-based Software Engineering. *IEE Proc Software Engineering* (1997), 26–37.

19. XU, J., ROMANOVSKY, A., AND RANDELL, B. Concurrent Exception Handling and Resolution in Distributed Object Systems. *IEEE Transactions on Parallel and Distributed Systems 11*, TPDS (November 2000), 1019–1032.

Action-Oriented Exception Handling in Cooperative and Competitive Concurrent Object-Oriented Systems

Alexander Romanovsky[1] and Jörg Kienzle[2]

[1]Department of Computing Science, University of Newcastle upon Tyne
Newcastle upon Tyne, NE1 7RU, UK
alexander.romanovsky@ncl.ac.uk

[2]Software Engineering Laboratory, Swiss Federal Institute of Technology
CH - 1015 Lausanne Ecublens, Switzerland
joerg.kienzle@epfl.ch

Abstract. The chief aim of this survey is to discuss exception handling models which have been developed for concurrent object systems. In conducting this discussion we rely on the following fundamental principles: exception handling should be associated with structuring techniques; concurrent systems require exception handling which is different from that used in sequential systems; concurrent systems are best structured out of (nested) actions; atomicity of actions is crucial for developing complex systems. In this survey we adhere to the well-known classification of concurrent systems, developed in the 70s by C.A.R. Hoare, J.J. Horning and B. Randell, into cooperative, competitive and disjoint ones. Competitive systems are structured using atomic transactions. Atomic actions are used for structuring cooperative systems. Complex systems in which components can compete and cooperate are structured using Coordinated Atomic actions. The focus of the survey is on outlining models and schemes which combine these action-based structuring approaches with exception handling. In conclusion we emphasise that exception handling models should be adequate to the system development paradigm and structuring approaches used.

1 Introduction

System structuring is employed to successfully deal with the growing complexity of modern computer systems. The need to cope with abnormal system behavior makes system design more complicated and, as experience shows, more error-prone. Exception handling was therefore introduced as a disciplined and structured way of handling abnormal system events [7]. It is usually a very important part of any general structuring technique used in system design as it adds new ways of concern separation which are vital for dealing with abnormal situations: it allows us to separate normal code from exception handlers during system design and structuring, introduces a dynamic separation of the execution of normal code and handlers, and provides two ways of returning the control flow after the execution of a system component. This clearly shows that exception handling mechanisms should rely on the way the system is structured and be an integral part of system design. Many researchers regard exception handling as a means for achieving system fault tolerance [5, 18], and we share this view. In this context exception raising follows error detection, exception handling equals to error recovery and units of system structuring are units of

A. Romanovsky et al. (Eds.): Exception Handling, LNCS 2022, pp. 147–164, 2001.
© Springer-Verlag Berlin Heidelberg 2001

exception handling and of recovery. Exception handling is used for incorporating application-specific fault tolerance.

Considerable effort has been devoted to developing exception handling models for sequential object-oriented systems, so a common understanding exists on many topics in the field. Many practical systems have been designed using these features. The situation is different in concurrent object-oriented systems. Although several schemes combining concurrency and exception handling have been proposed, research in this area is still scattered and most concurrent systems use sequential exception handling. It is our belief that this is not the way it should be as exception handling features should correspond to the programming feature used in system design. The choice of a way to introduce exception handling into such systems depends on the way concurrent systems are to be developed and structured because exception handling is a system design issue, and language features should assist in and impose proper design. Exception handling is tightly coupled with program structure and therefore the way in which the dynamic execution of concurrent systems is structured influences possible ways of introducing exception handling into such systems.

Several schemes have been proposed for introducing different units of system structuring into concurrent object-oriented systems, but only rarely do they incorporate exception handling features. And even when they do, they neither provide a general exception handling model nor fit in with the main principles of object-oriented programming properly. Although this is an area of very active research, there are still many unclear points and unsolved problems here. A general common understanding does not seem to exist. The purpose of this survey is to outline the existing approaches and to compare them, to discuss problems to which satisfactory solutions have yet to be found and to show likely directions of future research.

2   Concurrency and System Structuring

Many researchers view all object-oriented systems as inherently concurrent but this is justified only if object consistency is somehow guaranteed. In reality, concurrency adds a new dimension to system structure and design. Concurrent systems are extremely difficult to understand, design, analyse or modify. To do this successfully, we need concurrency features which would relate to the specific characteristics of both object-oriented systems and the applications to be designed.

2.1   Single Method Concurrency

Concurrency in object-oriented systems is usually provided at the level of separate method calls and objects (e.g. in integrated languages [30], which unify processes and objects by defining objects as active entities). This allows object consistency to be guaranteed and concurrency aspects of object behaviour to be addressed (see Fig. 1). In this case the units of system structure and behaviour are separate method calls and objects.

2.2   Competitive and Cooperative Systems

Complex object-oriented systems often need sophisticated and elaborate concurrency features which may go beyond the traditional concurrency control associated with separate method calls. The existing single method approaches do not scale because we deal with each single operation separately. There is a need for using units of system structuring which encapsulate complex behaviour and embrace groups of objects and of method calls. These units should represent dynamic system execution as opposed to the static declaration of objects inside objects. For example, it clearly makes no sense to declare all potential clients of a server in a bigger object. System understanding, verification and modification is facilitated if system execution is recursively structured of units encapsulating several method calls or/and objects.

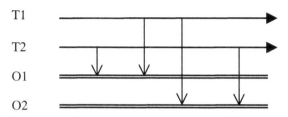

Fig. 1. Two threads T1 and T2 access objects O1 and O2 concurrently

Another concern which makes it necessary to extend the single-object view of system structuring is provision of fault-tolerance: in many situations one cannot guarantee that erroneous information is always contained inside an object. Without this strong assumption, we have to deal with very complex error containment domains consisting of several interconnected objects. For example, an error in a server can affect several client objects, so it will not be sufficient to recover only one of them (a client or the server). There are many applications which require such structuring units: banking systems, CSCW systems, complex workflows, control of modern production lines and cells, etc.

Various classifications of concurrent systems play an important role in identifying general approaches/techniques as they make it possible to concentrate on characteristics which are specific to different categories of systems and to develop methodologies and supports which make it easier to develop systems of different categories. To better understand additional considerations that we believe should be taken into account in addressing issues of system structuring, let us consider the classification of concurrent systems in [18] (which, in its turn, follows classifications in [10, 11]). Three categories are outlined here; they are independent (disjoint), competing and cooperating systems.

Competitive concurrency exists when two or more active components are designed separately, are not aware of each other, but use the same passive components. Programmers (would like to) live in an artificial world in which they do not have to care about other concurrent activities. They access objects as if they had them at their disposal. This concurrency is used, for example, when clients access a server; some of the mechanisms supporting it are the RPC and synchronisation constraints.

Cooperative concurrency exists when several components cooperate, i.e. do some job together and are aware of this. They can communicate by resource sharing or explicitly, but the important thing is that they are designed together so that they can cooperate to achieve their joint goal and use each other's help and results. Existing systems sometimes provide support for single one-to-one communications, a direct cooperation of equal partners: rendezvous, signals, message send/receive.

Many researchers rely on the concept of *atomicity* in developing structuring approaches to system design. Concurrent object-oriented systems (and systems in general) are easier to understand and to analyse (see, for example [2, 17]) if their execution is built out of atomic units encapsulating several objects and method calls, provided no information crosses the borders of such units. The ability to nest such units is vital for dealing with system complexity in a scalable way (we say that a unit is *nested* if it contains a subset of objects or/and method calls from the containing one). Providing fault tolerance is essentially facilitated in systems whose execution is structured out of such *atomic units* as these units confine erroneous information (see [28] for a detailed discussion).

2.3   Structuring Competitive Systems

Atomic transactions incorporating several object calls are the main approach to structuring competitive systems (Fig. 2). Atomicity, consistency, isolation and durability (ACID) are the fundamental properties of such units [8]. A transaction can end either by committing all updates made on the objects or by aborting them. The ACID transactions form the dynamic units of system execution and as such can be nested in many models and implementations. These transactions are oriented mainly towards tolerating hardware faults of different types: transient faults, node crashes, etc.

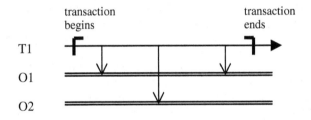

Fig. 2. Transaction incorporating several calls of several objects (O1 and O2)

This approach works well for database, client-server or simple bank systems but many applications nowadays require more sophisticated features. The original transaction concept has been further developed; in particular, additional concurrency at the caller side is often allowed.

The concept of a *multithreaded transaction* (MTT) has been used in different transactional models for quite a long time. Very typical examples are the CORBA transaction service [20] and Arjuna [21]. Several threads can perform operations on a set of transactional objects within an MTT (Fig. 3). One of them starts a transaction, then others learn its identity, using which they can access transactional objects within the MTT. If a thread commits or aborts, the transaction does the same. This model is quite general and flexible, it has been used in many industrial applications. However, it leaves the burden of a highly labour-consuming and error-prone coordination of threads inside an MTT to application programmers as it does not impose any discipline on what these threads can do (guaranteeing the ACID properties of server objects is of paramount concern here). For example, any thread can decide to leave the MTT without knowing whether it is committed or aborted. In this model threads do not actually join the transaction because the transaction support is not aware of the concurrency, and transactional objects do not guarantee mutual exclusion for threads of the same transaction. The thread exit from an MTT is not coordinated. Another problem with the MTT model is that programmers have to start and commit/abort transactions explicitly because transactional structure is separate from method/object structure.

Generally speaking, a very similar transactional model is provided by Enterprise JavaBeans architecture (EJB) [6]. EJB allows system developers to associate several client threads with the same transactional context. Unfortunately, this architecture supports only flat transactions (nesting is not allowed).

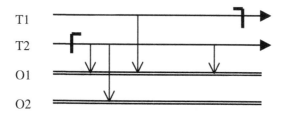

Fig. 3. CORBA multithreaded transactions

Applications built using the object-based language Argus [19] are composed of guardians, each of which provides an interface consisting of callable procedures called handlers. Handlers can fork concurrent threads which are joined when a handler is completed (see Fig. 4). Handler execution forms an atomic transaction; the execution of nested handler calls are performed as nested transactions.

The Argus approach has been very influential: Vinari/ML [9] and Transactional Drago [14] have similar computational models. Vinari/ML offers a transactional extension of SML which allows creating transactional versions of high-order functions; in this model new participants are explicitly forked by existing participants. Transactional Drago is an extension of Ada (it requires a pre-compiler and a special run-time support) which allows any program block to be declared and executed as an ACID transaction. Tasks declared inside this block are executed together with the block as additional transaction participants and they are to be completed before the transaction can end.

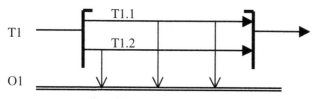

Fig. 4. Argus multithreaded transactions

A new model, called open multithreaded transactions (OMTT), has been recently proposed to allow developing systems with a richer concurrency than that of Argus yet keeping the transaction boundary on the caller (thread) side under control [15]. In the OMTT model multiple threads, called joined participants, can join a transaction, and any transaction participant can fork a thread which becomes a new transaction participant called a spawned participant (Fig. 5). The restriction is that if a participant has been created inside a transaction it has to be completed inside it. Note that such participants take part in the execution of the final commit/abort protocol. The OMTT can be nested: only participants of the containing transaction can join the nested one. Transactional support effectively consists of two parts: one guarantees the ACID properties of the objects called by transaction participants, the other coordinates transaction participants (transaction entry, exit, nesting). Transaction participants can see each other's updates of transactional objects but the entire transaction is isolated from the rest of the system. In some ways this scheme allows participants to (loosely) cooperate but the idea is that they do not depend on each other and have their own goals inside such a transaction.

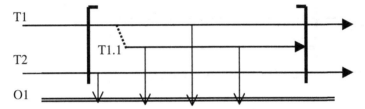

Fig. 5. Open multithreaded transactions

The concurrent object-oriented language Arche [13] allows dynamic grouping of objects. A group of N caller objects can synchronously call methods with the same names and signatures in a group of M server objects (e.g. objects of the same type); all these methods form a *multioperation*. Multioperation results are returned to all callers (Fig. 6). Some servers can synchronously call another multioperation. Arche relies on a competitive concurrency model (other multioperations compete for server objects) with a simple concurrency control based on mutual exclusion. Cooperation of servers executing a multioperation is not supported in the model, although a multioperation can issue a call to another multioperation which can only be performed jointly by all group components; this forms a basis for multioperation nesting. Arche does not use the full-fledged model of atomic transactions: multioperations are atomic only if the callees do not call external objects. This computation model has proved useful for implementing object replication and for employing diversely designed objects.

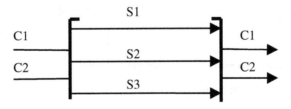

Fig. 6. Multioperation in Arche: callers C1 and C2 call a group objects S1, S2, and S3

2.4   Structuring Cooperative Systems

Many object-oriented systems provide features only for performing single acts of one-to-one cooperation. For a number of reasons, this is not sufficient when complex cooperative applications, such as complex CSCW systems or workflows, are to be developed. First of all, the approach should scale well to be useful for designing such systems in which more than two objects have to cooperate to achieve joint goals. Secondly, it should rely on structuring units which can be made atomic and nested (to cope with system complexity). Another concern is providing fault tolerance: we need such atomic units to keep under control erroneous information which can be smuggled between several objects (e.g. several clients of the same server). If we do not structure systems out of such units we encounter serious problems in defining the recovery region. This complex multi-participant cooperation should be a system design concern as we do not want to reason about it using single two-participant interactions (which can be done but can dramatically increase the responsibility of programmers and as such be error-prone).

The general concept of *atomic actions*, proposed in [4], answers all these concerns. Several participants (threads, processes, objects, etc.) enter an action and cooperate inside it to achieve joint goals (Fig. 7). They are designed to cooperate inside the action and are aware of this cooperation. These participants share work and explicitly exchange information in order to complete the action successfully. Atomic actions structure dynamic system behaviour. To guarantee action atomicity, no information is allowed to cross the action border. Actions can be nested (a subset of the participants of the containing action can join a nested action). Participants leave the action together when all of them have completed their job. If an error is detected inside an action all participants take part in a cooperative recovery. Atomic actions provide a sound framework for developing schemes intended for tolerating faults of different types: hardware faults, software design faults, transient faults, environmental faults, etc. The *conversation* scheme [23] was the first atomic action scheme proposed: it uses software diversity and participant rollback to tolerate design faults. A number of atomic action schemes incorporating different fault tolerance techniques have been developed since then for different languages: CSP, Concurrent Pascal, Ada, OCCAM, Java (with and without extensions); for distributed, multiprocessor and single computer settings; for different application requirements [24].

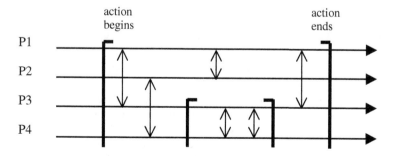

Fig. 7. Atomic actions: participants P1-P4 take part in the containing action, participants P3 and P4 in the nested action

There could be several structuring ways of incorporating atomic actions into object-oriented and object-based systems. The first approach is to introduce actions as classes or objects with methods representing participants, one each (as, for example, in the schemes [16, 32]). The computation model allows all participants to be active at the same time. The downside is that in this case we are losing the ability to treat participants as classes. Another approach is to view actions as sets of participant objects. For example, in scheme [26] a set of objects takes part in an atomic action by executing one method each; the action here is formed as a set of separate methods. Interfaces of participant objects have to be extended to allow their synchronisation on the action entry, exit and nesting. In both scenarios we need a special support to coordinate participant execution. These ideas allow us to make use of the many advantages of object-oriented programming while designing new object-oriented atomic action schemes (including their supports) and applying them.

2.5   Structuring Systems with Cooperative and Competitive Concurrency

Developers of the Coordinated Atomic action (CA action) concept [25, 33] realised that many realistic systems to be modelled/controlled by software have elements of both cooperation and competition and that it is important to allow them to be combined within one system. CA actions provide a framework for dealing with different kinds of concurrency and achieving fault tolerance by integrating and extending two complementary concepts - atomic actions [4] and atomic transactions [8]. Atomic actions are used to control cooperative concurrency and to implement coordinated error recovery whilst transactions are used to maintain the consistency of shared resources in the presence of failures and competitive concurrency (Fig. 8).

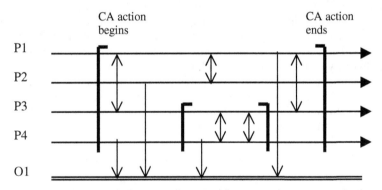

Fig. 8. CA atomic actions: action participants access transactional objects

Each CA action is designed as a stylised multi-entry procedure with roles which are activated by action participants cooperating within the CA action. Logically, the action starts when all roles have been activated and finishes when all of them reach the action end. CA actions can be nested. The state of the CA action is represented by a set of local and transactional objects. Transactional objects can be used concurrently by several CA actions in such a way that information cannot be smuggled among them and that any sequence of operations on these objects bracketed by the start and completion of the CA action has the ACID properties with respect to other sequences. The execution of a CA action looks like an atomic transaction for the outside world. Action participants explicitly cooperate (interact and coordinate their executions) through local objects (for example, those of message, mailbox or buffer classes). All participants are involved in recovery if an error is detected inside an action since conceptually it makes no difference which of them detects an error and the whole action represents the recovery region. Object-orientation plays an important role in the CA action concept and in developing different Java and Ada implementation schemes: concrete actions, action roles, local object and transactional objects are viewed as instances of classes.

3   Exception Handling

Exceptions are abnormal events which can happen during program execution. Many languages and systems provide special features for handling them in a disciplined way. These features allow programmers to *declare* exceptions and enable programmers to treat a program unit as the *exception context* and to associate exceptions and *exception handlers* with such context, so that when an exception is raised in this context, execution stops and a corresponding handler is searched for among the handlers (there are some models in which one can propagate an exception straight outside the context). In our opinion, the vital feature of any exception handling mechanism is its ability to differentiate between *internal exceptions* to be handled inside the context and the *external exceptions* which are propagated outside the context: these exceptions are not clearly separated in many languages although it is obvious that they are intended for different purposes.

This separation can be done provided the following conditions are met: contexts are associated with program units which have interfaces and the concept of *context nesting* is defined. Most existing exception handling mechanisms use dynamic exception context nesting in which case the execution of the context can be completed either successfully or by interface exception propagation - this exception is treated as an internal exception raised in the *containing context*. The simplest example of the dynamic nested context is nested procedure calls. Actually this is the dominating approach which suits the client/server or remote procedure call paradigms well and which is used in most systems and languages (e.g. in C++, Ada, Java, CLU).

External exceptions allow programmers to pass (in a disciplined, unified and structured fashion) different outcomes to the containing context. This can be used to inform it of the reasons for abnormal behaviour and of the state in which the context has been left, to pass partial results, etc. Another important issue which exception handling models have to address is defining the state in which the context is left when an external exception is propagated. Some systems provide an automatic support which guarantees the "all-or-nothing" semantics: if an exception is propagated outside, all modifications made inside the context are cancelled. Another possibility (which originates in the Inscape software development environment [22]) is to allow the context to be left in several states: an initial state (an abort exception is propagated); successfully committed state (if no exception is propagated outside); and several "partial" committed states, when the requested result cannot be achieved but partial (or degraded, alternative) results are still acceptable (external exceptions are propagated). It is clear that developing supports to provide such functionalities is a difficult task, this is why in many systems all responsibility of leaving the context in a known and consistent state rests entirely with application programmers.

The model of exception handing in object-oriented programming follows all fundamental principles of building such mechanisms. Exception handling is usually associated with either dynamic (method calls) or static (object/class declaration) system structuring: exception contexts are methods or classes, interface exceptions are declared in the type (often in method signatures). Unfortunately, in many concurrent object-oriented systems exception handling is, in essence, sequential as it is related to single classes or separate methods.

4   Single Method Exception Handling in Concurrent Systems

In many concurrent object-oriented systems (e.g., Java, Guide, Arche and Ada) exceptions are propagated through nested (and, sometimes, remote) method calls and exception contexts are either separate methods or objects. These systems provide features for guaranteeing object consistency when several clients issue concurrent calls. This is a very important issue but in our opinion this type of exception handling is not sufficient for many reasons. If only mechanisms of this type are employed exception handling is effectively separated from concurrent programming. Moreover, such mechanisms rely on a very simplistic view of concurrent system structuring and of handling abnormal events in such systems. Some researchers (e.g. [3]) argue that special features for involving several concurrent objects in exception handling are so difficult to develop and use that object-oriented system developers should use only sequential exception handling. Thus, an essential but a most difficult feature to provide is random interruption of a thread when an exception is raised in another thread. We believe that this misunderstanding is due to the fact that exception handling issues are being considered separately from those of system structuring, which is clearly wrong for many reasons: first, exception contexts are (should be viewed as) units of system structuring; secondly, dynamic system structure is defined by exception context nesting and, thirdly, interface exceptions have to be part of structuring units.

In our opinion, there are no reasons why exception handling should have to be sequential in concurrent systems. Concurrency clearly adds a new dimension to system design and execution. And exception handling should keep up with this new feature. Moreover, concurrent exception handling should be associated with the way a concurrent system is structured in the same manner in which this works for sequential systems. We consider such support for exception handling in concurrent programming vital for dealing with the complexity of concurrent systems. Ideally, exception contexts (i.e. structuring units) should encapsulate complex behaviour consisting of several operations on several objects.

There have been some attempts to address this problem. For example, the Oz language [31] allows associating a handler with a thread. This handler is initiated before the thread is terminated, which can be used for handling any exceptions raised in any threads as well as for those propagated out of the outmost context in the thread. Language Facile (an extension of SML) [29] allows us to declare the same exception in several processes; when this exception is raised in any of them, the execution of all processes which declared this exception is interrupted and handlers are called (the process terminates if it has not a handler for this exception). Another example is Ada, in which an exception propagated out of the accept body during rendezvous is signalled in the context of the caller and of the callee containing the accept body.

A more sophisticated example is an extension of the concurrent object-oriented language ABCL/1 by a concurrent exception handling mechanism [12]. This extension relies on the ABCL/1 computational model, within which method calls are viewed as message transmissions between concurrent objects, and methods as operations initialised by accepting the corresponding messages. Exceptions are treated here as signals that can be transmitted between objects. Any method call can be accompanied by a special tag indicating the reply destination: the tag is the name of the object which will receive the method results (the reply). The exception context is a block of statements or a method body. In the extended ABCL/1 a new notion of *complaint* is introduced. It is similar to the notion of reply but intended for informing another object (complaint destination) of any unexpected things occurring during object (method) execution. Complaints (a type of failure exceptions) can be of four kinds: unaccepted messages, time-outs, system-defined (predefined) and user-defined complaints. Complaint destination can be declared in each object, which changes the direction of exception propagation from methods (objects).

Language $\mathcal{E}_{CSP}$ is another interesting attempt to introduce exception handling into concurrent systems [1]. In this language, if a process cannot continue its normal execution because of an exception, it signals a global exception so that any process which will be communicating with this process in the course of its normal execution will get an exception raised in its context.

Unfortunately, the schemes above neither relate exception handling to structuring concurrent systems, nor scale well. They do not provide any support for leaving the exception context in a known consistent state. Usually all responsibility for transferring information about exceptions among several processes and their coordinated handling is left with programmers.

5 Action-Oriented Exception Handling

Structuring complex concurrent systems using atomic actions offers us a straightforward choice of exception contexts. (By atomic actions we mean all types of atomic units of structuring system behaviours discussed above in Section 2: atomic transactions, atomic actions, CA actions.) Treating such units as contexts seems the most beneficial way because these atomic units have clearly defined borders, can be nested and no information can cross the unit border. It is important that this approach is compatible with the way we structure sequential systems for exception handling, which is based on nested method calls. The general exception handling model can easily be applied here to allow internal exceptions and corresponding handlers to be associated with such structuring unit. Actions can have interfaces enriched by external exceptions which the unit can propagate into the containing exception context (i.e. into the containing structuring unit). Atomicity of actions (i.e. of exception contexts) is vital for dealing with abnormal events (i.e. exceptions) as it guarantees the containment of all (potentially erroneous) information which should be involved in exception handling and recovery. Clearly, the atomicity of action execution has a general importance for all phases of system development: it facilitates reasoning about the system, system understanding, verification and development, tolerating faults of different types, etc. In addition, it guarantees the most beneficial way of information and behaviour encapsulation, when no intermediate results can be seen from the outside and the execution of units is indivisible. This is why we believe that exception handling in concurrent systems should be action-oriented.

There is an important question which should be addressed while developing support for such atomic units. There is a lot of evidence indicating that it is very likely that multiple exceptions are raised at the same time in a concurrent (and, in particular, distributed) system [27, 35]. These complex situations have to be correctly resolved, and atomic actions give a simple and well-structured way of dealing with them. First of all, concurrent exceptions raised in concurrent (sibling) actions are handled separately. To deal with exceptions raised inside an atomic action, paper [4] proposes the concept of *exception tree* which includes all exceptions associated with this action and imposes a partial order on them in such a way that a higher exception in the tree has a handler which is capable of handling any lower-level exception or any combination of them. The idea is to handle the *resolved* exception which corresponds to the tree node that is higher than nodes of all concurrent exceptions raised in the action. Recently this approach has been further developed to allow action exceptions to be ordered by a resolution graph and to provide an improved decentralised resolution algorithm [35].

Generally speaking, atomicity of actions means that the intermediate results of action execution are not seen from the outside; we will adhere to this understanding in the following discussion of different action schemes. Some of these schemes allow partial (but consistent) action results to be achieved and the system to be moved in a new consistent state when an exception is propagated outside this action; others subscribe to the idea that if any exception is signalled outside an action, the "nothing" semantics should be provided.

5.1   Exception Handling in Competitive Systems

The designers of transactional systems often do not incorporate exception handling but use return error codes instead. There are many problems with this approach. Firstly, the use of return codes has always been described as a canonical example of bad practice caused by the absence of the exception handling mechanism [7]. Secondly, even if the core language has exception handling, it is completely separated from transactions and, as a result, application exception handling (including the exception context, exception propagation, etc.) is separated from the transactional structure. The CORBA transaction service [20] (Fig. 3) is a typical example of this: it offers a very sophisticated MTT model but programmers can use only sequential exceptions (e.g. those of C++ or Java): any exception raised in an MTT transaction can cross its border unnoticed, each MTT participant deals with its exceptions separately, the MTT transaction is not the exception context, one cannot define or handle exceptions at the transaction level. Actually, the transaction border is not clearly defined in this model as participant threads are not coordinated in any way.

It is symptomatic that the designers of EJB [6] have made a serious efforts to combine exception handling with transactions. This model allows us to develop a system in which any exception signalled by a transactional object can affect the execution of the whole transaction. For example, one can mark the transaction for abort, re-raise the same or another exception, try to recover the situation and continue the transaction, abort the transaction and re-raise the same exception, etc. However, it is clear that MTTs are not full-fledged exception contexts because multiple participants are not coordinated (e.g. they are not informed when the transaction is aborted) and because such transactions cannot be nested.

The most general approach to incorporating exception handling into competitive systems is to allow each transaction to have internal exceptions with handlers inside and external exceptions described in the transaction interface. Generally speaking, interface exceptions are to be propagated to the containing transaction. It is important to be able to associate some external exceptions with the abort outcome; when other exceptions are signalled, the state of all objects involved should be known and committed. The problem here is to introduce transactional exception handling into the object-oriented context and to avoid having different exception mechanisms for sequential and concurrent programming (i.c. for individual threads and for transactions) within the same system.

Argus [19] (Fig. 4) provides a very powerful extension of sequential object-oriented exception handling. Methods (called handlers in this model) are atomic transactions which have external exceptions declared in their interfaces. Threads can be forked inside, allowing very rich computations to be performed concurrently. Unlike the CORBA MTT, all Argus threads have to be synchronised and joined when the transaction commits or aborts. An interface exception is propagated to a single-threaded caller when any thread inside the transaction signals it. Any thread may decide to signal an exception with or without transaction abort, which makes it possible to commit partial results and to associate different results with different exceptional outcomes. Internal thread exceptions have to be dealt with separately by individual threads as the system does not provide any coordination for dealing with such exceptions (which suits the competitive nature of this model well). Argus offers a special construct for handling interface exceptions rather than making it possible for the containing transaction to deal with them explicitly at its level.

The exception handling model of Vinari/ML [9] is in many ways similar to that of Argus but it does not differentiate between external and internal exceptions: it is not possible to declare external exceptions in transactional functions; a transaction is always aborted if any exception is propagated outside the transactional function; if there is no local thread-level handler for an exception, it gets propagated outside the transaction.

Transactional Drago [14], unlike Argus and Vinari/ML, resolves concurrent exceptions raised by several participating threads before signalling a resolved exception outside the transaction. In this model, external exceptions cannot be declared in the transaction interface, and any exception which is not handled by a thread locally aborts the transaction and gets propagated outside it.

The OMTT model clearly separates internal and external exceptions. Each participant has to have handlers for all of its local exceptions. If it cannot handle it, it has to explicitly signal an external exception which always causes the transaction abort. External exceptions propagated by a joined participant are raised in the containing context of the caller thread. There is a predefined exception Abort_Transaction which can be signalled by spawned participants if they decide to abort the transaction. This exception is propagated to the callers of all joined participants if they do not signal their external exceptions concurrently.

In Arche (Fig. 6) each multifunction member represents an isolated exception context and as such can signal an external exception. When all members have completed their execution, a resolution function is applied, and the resolved exception is propagated to all caller contexts (unless an appropriate action is taken by programmers). This approach can clearly leave member objects in inconsistent states.

5.2   Exception Handling in Cooperative Systems

Exception handling in cooperative systems can be quite naturally incorporated into the atomic action framework [4, 35]. A set of internal and external exceptions is associated here with each action, and these exceptions are clearly separated. The model is recursive, and all external exceptions of an action are viewed as internal ones of the containing action (Fig. 7). Each object participating in the action has a set of handlers for all internal exceptions. In this approach, action participants cooperate not only when they execute program functions (i.e. during normal activity) but also when they handle abnormal events. This is mainly due to the fact that when an atomic action is executed, an error can spread to all participants, and the system can be returned into a consistent state only if all participants are involved in handling. This is why, when an exception is raised in any participant, appropriate handlers are initiated in all of them. An action can be completed either by signalling an interface exception into the context of the containing action or normally (without internal exceptions being raised or after a successful cooperative handling of such exceptions). Concurrent internal exceptions are resolved using a resolution graph, so that handlers for the resolved exception are called in all participants (see Fig. 9).

Even though several object-oriented schemes incorporating this kind of exception handling have already been proposed (several of them will be mentioned in Section 5.3 as this research has been mainly conducted in the context of developing the CA action concept), there are still some theoretical and practical problems to be addressed. It is not clear, for example, how to make an ordinary object also capable of performing, when required, the functions of an action participant: the computational models and object interfaces are very different for these two entities. There are still unclear points as to how properly combine sequential exception handling and atomic action exception handling in order to allow compatibility. The problems of inheriting and refining action and role classes or types have not yet been addressed (let alone the refinement of action exceptions, exception handlers, etc.).

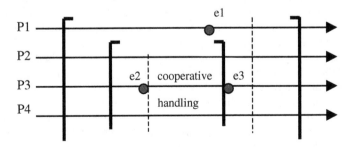

Fig. 9. Exception handling in cooperative systems: internal exception e2 is in the nested action (in participant P3); after an attempt to handle it cooperatively (by P3 and P4) interface

exception e3 is propagated to the containing context. Another exception, e1, is raised concurrently in this context, and these two exceptions have to be resolved before cooperative handling starts at the level of this action

5.3   Exception Handling in Systems with Cooperative and Competitive Concurrency

Conceptually, exception handling in CA actions [25] (Fig. 8) is very similar to that in atomic actions [4]: all action participants are involved in cooperative handling of any internal exception, internal exceptions raised concurrently are resolved, external exceptions are explicitly propagated by action participants, etc. (Fig. 9). The main extension is an explicit dealing with local and transactional objects [35].

The CA action interface can contain one or more abort exceptions, a predefined failure exception and a number of exceptions corresponding to partial (committed and consistent) results which the action can provide. In the latter case it uses external exceptions to inform the containing action of the fact that it has not been able to produce a complete required result and, indirectly, of the state in which objects have been left and of the partial results produced. When an abort interface exception is signalled, the CA action is aborted: all local objects are destroyed (although, to improve performance, they can be simply re-initialised if software diversity or retry are used for recovery) and all modifications of transactional objects are cancelled. A failure interface exception is signalled by the support when some serious problems are encountered; for example, the support cannot abort or commit the states of transactional objects. When an interface exception corresponding to a partial result is signalled outside an action, the state of all transactional objects is committed before raising this exception in the containing context. In all these cases signalling an interface exception means that the responsibility for dealing with such abnormal event is passed to a higher level in the system structure. The identity of the exception (with, possibly, some output parameters) and the associated post-conditions provide this level with all information it might need about the reasons for the exception and the current system state.

There has been considerable experimental research on developing object-oriented CA action schemes in Java and Ada and on applying CA actions to developing realistic case studies: a series of Production Cell case studies, including a fault tolerant one [34] and a real time one; a distributed internet Gamma computation; an auction system and a subsystem of a railway control system which deals with train control and coordination in the vicinity of a station. This research has produced first ever field results on applying exception resolution: elaborate resolution graphs have been built for a system controlling a complex industrial application with high reliability and safety requirements [34].

6   Conclusions

The purpose of this survey is to analyse the exception handling models used in concurrent (mainly object-oriented) languages and systems. Development of exception handling features is tremendously complicated by the fact that exception handling is a crosscutting issue which affects all other techniques and mechanisms used in system development as any of them can encounter abnormalities of different types and has to deal with them properly. Poorly developed models can undermine the basic purpose of exception handling, which is concerned with dealing with abnormalities in a disciplined and uniform way throughout the whole system (design and execution). In this survey we wanted to demonstrate the main trends in developing exception handling models for complex concurrent systems and to compare the existing models using some fundamental ideas we believe in as the criteria:

- exception handling should reflect the way systems and their execution are structured
- exception handling is the most general mechanism for achieving system fault tolerance
- concurrent systems should be structured in a way which is different from that of structuring sequential systems
- (nested) actions containing the execution of several objects should serve as (nested) exception contexts
- atomicity of structuring unit execution is crucial for both fighting system complexity and providing system fault tolerance

In conclusion, we would like to emphasise that advanced exception handling models to be employed in concurrent object-oriented systems should relate to

- the development paradigm adhered to (e.g. object-orientation)
- the main implementation features (e.g. information and behaviour encapsulation, typing, inheritance, concurrency, distribution)
- the type of concurrency (competitive, cooperative, disjoint)
- the system development (design) techniques used
- the way systems are structured (objects, classes, actions, modules)
- the application-specific characteristics of the system to be designed

Acknowledgments: Alexander Romanovsky has been supported by the EC IST RTD Project on Dependable Systems of Systems (DSoS). Jörg Kienzle has been partially supported by the Swiss National Science Foundation project FN 2000- 057187.99/1.

References

[1] Banatre, J.P., Issarny, V.: Exception Handling in Communication Sequential Processes. Technical Report 660, INRIA-Rennes, IRISA (1992)

[2] Best, E.: Semantics of Sequential and Parallel Programs. Prentice Hall. London New York (1996)

[3] Buhr, P.A., Mok, W.Y.R.: Advanced Exception Handling Mechanisms. IEEE Transactions on Software Engineering, **SE-26**, 9 (2000)

[4] Campbell, R.H., Randell, B.: Error Recovery in Asynchronous Systems. IEEE Transactions on Software Engineering, **SE-12**, 8 (1986) 811-826

[5] Cristian, F.: Exception Handling and Tolerance of Software Faults. In Lyu, M.R. (ed.): Software Fault Tolerance. Wiley (1994) 81-108

[6] Enterprise JavaBeans. Specification, v.1.1, Sun Microsystems, Inc. (1999)

[7] Goodenough, J.B.: Exception Handling, Issues and a Proposed Notation. Communications of ACM, **18**, 12 (1975) 683-696

[8] Gray, J.N., Reuter, A.: Transaction Processing: Concepts and Techniques. Morgan Kaufmann, San Mateo, California (1993)

[9]   Haines, N., Kindred, D., Morrisett, J.G., Nettles, A.M., Wing, J.M.: Composing First-Class Transactions. ACM Transactions on Programming Languages and Systems, **16**, 6 (1994) 1719-1736

[10]   Hoare, C.A.R.: Parallel Programming: an Axiomatic Approach. In Goos, G., Harmanis, J. (eds.): Language Hierarchies and Interfaces. Lecture Notes in Computer Science, Vol. 46. Springer-Verlag, Berlin Heidelberg New York (1976) 11-42

[11]   Horning, J.J., Randell, B.: Process Structuring. Computing Surveys, **5** (1974) 69-74

[12]   Ichisugi, Y., Yonezawa. A.: Exception Handling and Real Time Features in Object-Oriented Concurrent Language. In Yonezawa, A., Ito, T. (eds.): Concurrency: Theory, Language, and Architecture. Lecture Notes in Computer Science, Vol. 491. Springer-Verlag, Berlin Heidelberg New York (1991) 92-109

[13]   Issarny, V.: An Exception Handling Mechanism for Parallel Object-Oriented Programming: Towards Reusable, Robust Distributed Software. Journal of Object-Oriented Programming, **6**, 6 (1993) 29-40

[14]   Jimenez-Peris, R., Patino-Martinez, M., Arevalo, S.: TransLib: An Ada 95 Object Oriented Framework for Building Transactional Applications. Computer Systems: Science & Engineering Journal, **15**, 1 (2000) 113-125

[15]   Kienzle, J., Romanovsky, A.: Combining Tasking and Transactions: Open Multithreaded Transactions. Presented at the 10th Int. Real-Time Ada Workshop, Avila, Spain (2000) (to be published in AdaLetters, 2000)

[16]   Kim, K.H.: Approaches to Mehcanization of the Conversation Sccheme Based on Monitors. IEEE Transactions on Software Engineering, **SE-8**, 3 (1982) 189-197

[17]   Kurki-Suonio, R., Mikkonen, T.: Liberating object-oriented modeling from programming-level abstractions. In Bosch, J., Mitchell, S. (eds): Object-Oriented Technology: ECOOP'97 Workshop Reader, Lecture Notes in Computer Science, Vol. 1357. Springer-Verlag, Berlin Heidelberg New York (1998) 195-199

[18]   Lee, P.A., Anderson, T.: Fault Tolerance: Principles and Practice (1990)

[19]   Liskov, B.: Distributed Programming in Argus. Communications of the ACM, **31**, 3 (1988) 300-312

[20]   Object Management Group Object Transaction Service. Draft 4. OMG. OMG Document (1996)

[21]   Parrington, G.D., Shrivastava, S.K., Wheater, S.M., Little, M.C.: The Design and Implementation of Arjuna. USENIX Computing Systems Journal, **8**, 3 (1995) 255-308

[22]   Perry, D.E.: The Inscape Environment. In Proc. of the 11th International Conf. On Software Engineering. Pennsylvania (1989) 2-11

[23]   Randell, B.: System Structure for Software Fault Tolerance. IEEE Transactions on Software Engineering, **SE-1**, 6 (1975) 220-232

[24]   Randell, B., Romanovsky, A., Rubira, C., Stroud, R., Wu, Z., Xu, J.: From Recovery Blocks to Coordinated Atomic Actions. In Randell, B., Laprie, J.-C., Kopetz H., Littlewood, B. (eds.): Predictably Dependable Computer Systems. Springer-Verlag, Berlin Heidelberg New York (1995) 87-101

[25]   Randell, B., Romanovsky, A., Stroud, R.J., Xu, J., Zorzo, A.F.: Coordinated Atomic Actions: from Concept to Implementation. Computing Dept., University of Newcastle upon Tyne. Technical Report 595 (1997)

[26]   Romanovsky, A.: Conversations of Objects. Computer Languages, 21, 3/4 (1995) 147-163

[27]   Romanovsky, A., Xu, J., Randell, B.: Exception Handling and Resolution in Distributed Object-Oriented Systems, in Proc. of the 16th International Conference on Distributed Computing Systems, Hong Kong (1996) 545-552

[28]   Romanovsky, A.: On Structuring Cooperative and Competitive Concurrent Systems. Computer Journal, **42**, 8 (1999) 627-637

[29] Thomsen, B., Leth, L., Prasad, S., Kuo, T.-S., Kramer, A., Knabe, F., Giacalone, A.: Facile Antigua Release - Programming Guide. TR ECRC-93-20, ECRC GmbH, Germany (1993) http://www.ecrc.de/research/projects/facile/report/report.html

[30] Tripathi, A., Van Oosten, J., Miller, R.: Object-Oriented Concurrent Programming Languages and Systems. Journal of Object-Oriented Programming, **12**, 7 (1999) 22-29

[31] Van Roy, P., Haridi, S., Brand, P., Smolka, G., Mehl, M., Scheidhauer, R.: Mobile Objects in Distributed Oz. ACM Transactions on Programming Languages and Systems, **19**, 5 (1997) 804-851

[32] Wellings, A.J., Burns, A.: Implementing Atomic Actions in Ada 95. IEEE Transactions on Software Engineering, **SE-23**, 2 (1997) 107-123

[33] Xu, J., Randell, B., Romanovsky, A., Rubira, C., Stroud, R., Wu, Z.: Fault tolerance in concurrent object-oriented software through coordinated error recovery, in Proc. of the 25th International Symp. on Fault-Tolerant Computing. Pasadena, California (1995) 499-509

[34] Xu, J., Randell, B., Romanovsky, A., Stroud, R. J., Zorzo, A. F., Canver, E., von Henke, F.: Rigorous Development of a Safety-Critical System Based on Coordinated Atomic Actions, in Proc. of the 29th International Symp. on Fault-Tolerant Computing, Madison, (1999) 68-75

[35] Xu, J., Romanovsky, A., Randell, B.: Concurrent Exception Handling and Resolution in Distributed Object Systems. IEEE Transactions on Parallel and Distributed Systems. **TPDS-11**, 11 (2000) 1019-1032

Exception Handling and Resolution for Transactional Object Groups*

Marta Patiño-Martínez[1], Ricardo Jiménez-Peris[1], and Sergio Arévalo[2]

[1] School of Computer Science
Technical University of Madrid (UPM)
28660 Boadilla del Monte, Madrid, Spain
{mpatino,rjimenez}@fi.upm.es
[2] Escuela de Ciencias Experimentales
Rey Juan Carlos University
28933 Móstoles, Madrid, Spain
s.arevalo@escet.urjc.es

Abstract. With the advent of new distributed applications like on-line auctions and e-commerce, the reliability requirements are becoming tighter and tighter. These applications require a combination of data consistency, robustness, high availability and performance. However, there is no single mechanism providing these features. Data consistency is preserved using transactions. Robustness can be obtained by foreseeing and handling exceptions. Objects groups can help in increasing the availability and performance of an application. In order to attain the growing demand of higher levels of reliability it is necessary to integrate these mechanisms with a consistent semantics. This article addresses this topic and studies the role of exceptions in this context.

1 Introduction

With the increasing importance of new distributed applications such as on-line auctions and e-commerce, stronger reliability guarantees are required. These applications need availability, data consistency and high throughput. Traditional reliability techniques by themselves, like transactions or group communication, only provide a subset of these properties. With the integration of these techniques is possible to satisfy the surging need for higher levels of reliability.

Group communication [2,10] is one of the basic building blocks to build reliable distributed systems. Although, group communication primitives were proposed in the context of groups of processes, they have been integrated with the object oriented paradigm [15,17,8,16] resulting in what has been named object groups.

A *group of objects* is a set of distributed objects that share the same interface and behave as a single logical object. Clients interact with object groups as with

---

* This work was partially supported by the Spanish Research Council, CICYT, under grant TIC94-C02-01 and the Madrid Regional Research Council (*CAM*), contract number CAM-07T/0012/1998.

A. Romanovsky et al. (Eds.): Exception Handling, LNCS 2022, pp. 165–180, 2001.

regular objects. Transparently to the client, invocations are multicast to all group members. Object groups have traditionally been used to increase either system availability or performance. If all the group objects are exact replicas, object failures can be masked. On the other hand, distributing a method execution among the group objects can increase performance.

Transactions [6] provide data consistency in the presence of failures and concurrent accesses. Transaction properties have become crucial for building reliable applications. Their use has spreaded from databases to a more general setting, namely distributed systems. The importance of transactions has been recognized in the CORBA object transactional service (OTS) [19], Java transaction service (JTS) [26], and Enterprise Java Beans [25] standards. But, also several general purpose programming languages and libraries have incorporated them, such as Avalon [4] and Arjuna [24].

Our research has been motivated by the need to provide a consistent integration of these mechanisms. In our proposal, clients can enclose a set of group invocations within a transaction to preserve their atomicity. Object group methods can be executed as transactions. In this way, object consistency is guaranteed in the presence of failures and concurrent accesses.

In this context the semantics of exceptions need to be precisely defined. Exception handling plays a key role in our approach. First, the abort of a transaction is notified by means of an exception. Second, exceptions have been integrated in the context of transactions acting on groups of objects, providing forward (exception handling) and backward (transactions) recovery to guarantee data consistency. As the nature of object groups is concurrent several exceptions can be raised concurrently. Concurrent exception resolution is provided to notify the abortion of the corresponding transaction with a single and meaningful exception.

This article concentrates on two main issues. First, it is discussed how forward and backward recovery provided by exceptions and transactions, respectively, have been integrated. And second, it is shown how to deal with concurrent exceptions within the context of transactional groups.

The rest of the article is organized as follows. Next section describes the features of transactional object groups. Section 3 discusses exception handling in this framework. Section 4 proposes linguistic support for our exception model. Implementation issues of this exception model are presented in Section 5. Finally, we compare our proposal with related work and present our conclusions.

2   Transactional Object Groups

2.1   Object Groups

An object group can be considered a distributed implementation of a class. Members (objects) of an object group share the same interface (the one of the class) and can be located at different sites of a network. Method invocations are reliably multicast to all the group members. Reliable multicast messages are delivered to all the group members or none of them. This property helps to keep the consistency among group members, as all of them will process the same method invocations. Multicast is also virtually synchronous [1], that is, membership (view) changes are delivered at the same logical instant at all the members. This means that the members that transit from one view to the next one have processed the same set of method invocations before the view change. Therefore, the programming of reliable object groups is simplified.

We distinguish two kinds of object groups based on their functionality: replicated and cooperative object groups.

Replicated object groups (replicated groups to abbreviate) provide hardware fault-tolerance. They implement active replication. That is, all the objects process each method invocation. In a replicated group all the objects are exact replicas. They have the same state and deterministic code.

Objects of a replicated group behave as a state machine [23]. Method invocations are reliable multicast and also total ordered [10] to guarantee that behavior. Total order means that all the members of a group receive method invocations in the same order. All group members start from the same state and process the same method invocations in the same order. This feature together with the restriction of not allowing concurrency within methods ensures the determinism of replicated groups [12]. If each object of a group is placed at a different site, the group can tolerate up to $k - 1$ site failures, being k the number of objects in the group. Therefore, the distribution and replication of objects is used to increase the availability of a logical object. For instance, let?s consider a name service that maps services to servers in a distributed system (e.g., CORBA). This service is critical in the sense that when it is not available, clients cannot contact the servers as they cannot find out their location, and the system blocks. Replicating the name server object prevents this situation, providing the required availability.

Replication is transparent both in front of clients and servers. Clients of a replicated group invoke group methods as if the object were non-replicated. Since all the group members have the same state and code, they will produce the same answers, therefore a single answer is returned to group clients (Fig. 1.b). Replicated groups can invoke other objects. That is, they can act as clients. When a replicated group invokes another object (replicated or not), duplicated requests must be avoided. In our approach only one method invocation takes place (Fig. 1.c) to preserve the single object behavior of the group. Answers are returned to all group members. To our knowledge only *GroupIO* [7], a group communication library, implements such a behavior.

On the other hand, in a *cooperative object group* (or cooperative group) distribution is used to increase the throughput of the system. The state of an object is distributed among the group members and thus, method invocations are executed in parallel, decreasing latency. Hence, the state of the objects of a cooperative group can be different. Even method implementation can be different. For instance, a cooperative group can represent a bank and each member can represent a branch of a bank. In this case, the state of the objects is different.

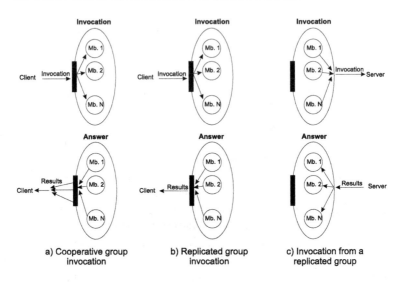

Fig. 1. Interaction with object groups

The group can provide an operation to pay the interest to each bank account at the end of the month. That operation will be performed in parallel by all the group objects.

During the execution of a method in a cooperative group, each object of the group can create new threads to execute concurrently that method. This feature allows taking advantage of the multiprocessing capabilities of the underlying system. Thus, two levels of concurrency can be used to execute a method invocation in a cooperative group, the inherent parallelism provided by object distribution and local multithreading at each object.

Cooperative groups also behave as a single logical object in front of clients and servers. Since the state and the code can be different, each object can return a different result. The final result is composed at the client site before delivering it to the client application (Fig. 1.a). For instance, a method computing the total balance of a set of accounts will compose the results adding all the object results.

Unlike replicated objects, objects of a cooperative group are aware of each other and they can communicate among them. For instance, a cooperative group can store the agendas of the staff of a company, where each group member holds a department agenda. An agenda contains information about the schedule of an employee. The group can provide a service to set meetings among members of several departments in a given period of time. When this service is invoked, group objects communicate among them to notify the availability of the members of their departments to find a common free slot to set the meeting.

2.2   Transactions

Transactions [6] are used to preserve data consistency in the presence of failures and concurrent accesses. A transaction either finishes successfully (commits) or fails (aborts). A transaction provides the so-called ACID properties. *Atomicity* ensures that a transaction is completely executed (it commits) or the result is as it were not executed (it aborts). If a transaction aborts, the atomicity property ensures that the state is restored to a *previous* (consistent) one. Hence, transaction atomicity provides backward recovery. *Isolation* or serializability guarantees that the result of concurrent transactions is equivalent to a serial execution of them. *Durability* ensures that the effect of committed transactions is not lost even in the advent of failures.

Transactions can be nested [18]. Nested transactions or subtransactions can be executed concurrently, but isolated from each other. They cannot communicate among them due to the isolation property. No concurrency is allowed in the traditional nested transaction model apart from concurrent subtransactions. If a subtransaction aborts only that subtransaction is undone, the parent transaction does not abort. Therefore, subtransactions also allow confining failures within a transaction. However, if a transaction aborts, all its subtransactions will abort to preserve the atomicity of the parent transaction. We propose a more general model, *group transactions* [20], where a transaction can have several concurrent threads, either local or distributed. Those threads can communicate among them and share data as they belong to the same transaction.

2.3   Transactional Object Group Services

If a client interacts with several groups and the atomicity of the whole interaction must be preserved, multicast by itself does not help. The reliability property of multicast is concerned with a single message (method invocation). To keep the atomicity of several group invocations, a *super-group* [22] can be created. This super-group contains all the groups the client will contact. However, this solution is very expensive. Creating groups dynamically takes some time and the groups' programming gets more complicated. Messages must be decomposed to know which part belongs to which group of the super-group. Additionally, this approach does not deal with recovery (needed in case of aborts or failures) nor with concurrency control (needed for concurrent clients). A simpler approach is to enclose the whole interaction within a transaction. The transaction automatically guarantees the atomicity property.

Transactional object groups provide atomic services. Clients must interact with transactional object groups within a transaction. Methods of a transactional group are executed as subtransactions, which are run by all the group objects. A subtransaction corresponding to a method invocation on an object group is a *distributed transaction* that has as many distributed threads as there are objects in the group.

Subtransactions on replicated groups are highly available. They survive site failures without aborting. A subtransaction (method invocation) in a replicated group will commit as far as there is an available member. This contrasts with the traditional approach where the failure of a single replica aborts all ongoing transactions [9].

When a transaction (method invocation) is executed in a replicated group, it just has a thread per object to enforce the determinism of the group. However, this restriction does not apply to cooperative groups. Each object of a cooperative group can create new threads on behalf of the (sub)transaction the object is running. The lifetime of those threads does not expand beyond the method execution. As the objects of a cooperative group work to achieve a common goal, it is required that all the group members finish successfully to commit a transaction. That is, a subtransaction in a cooperative group will commit, if all its threads finish successfully, otherwise it will abort.

3   Exceptions in Transactional Object Groups

3.1   Exceptions and Transaction Aborts

The operation domain is decomposed into *standard* and *exceptional domains* [3]. An operation invoked within its standard domain terminates successfully. On the other hand, an operation invoked within its exceptional domain leads to an exception *raising*, if the situation is detected. If the exception was foreseen, an *exception handler* can fix the situation and bring the system to a new consistent state (forward recovery), that is, the exception is *handled*. Exception handlers are attached to *exception contexts*, i.e., regions where exceptions are treated uniformly. Nested operation invocations yield to (dynamic) exception context nesting. An unhandled exception in an exception context causes its termination and it is *propagated* to the outer exception context.

We propose to use exceptions within transactions to attain forward recovery. In this way we integrate backward and forward recovery provided by transactions and exceptions, respectively. In the advent of foreseen errors a new consistent state within a transaction (Fig. 2) can be obtained (those that the transaction programmer has considered), preventing the transaction abort.

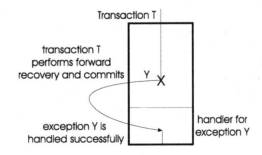

Fig. 2. Exception handling within a transaction

Unfortunately, every exception (error) cannot be foreseen nor every exception can be handled. In our proposal, transactions act as firewalls for unhandled exceptions applying automatically backward recovery (transaction abort) when an unhandled exception is propagated outside the transaction boundary (Fig. 3).

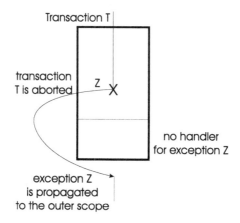

Fig. 3. Exception propagation outside a transaction

As exceptions are used to notify abnormal situations, any exception that is propagated outside the scope of a transaction causes its abort. If the transaction had been able to handle the exception internally, it would mean that forward recovery was successfully applied within the transaction. However, if the error could not be handled, backward recovery (undoing the transaction) is automatically performed. If the transaction commits, no exception is raised.

Fig. 4 shows how forward and backward recovery are combined. Subtransaction $T1.1$ raises an exception (Y). The exception is not handled in $T1.1$ and therefore, it is propagated to the enclosing scope $(T1)$. As a consequence, $T1.1$ aborts (backward recovery). Thread $th0$ handles the exception (forward recovery) and transaction $T1$ continues.

We propose the use of exceptions to notify transaction aborts. Since transaction programmers can define their own exceptions, using exceptions to notify aborts provides more information about the cause of an abort than the traditional abort statement. This integration can be seen as the identification of transaction commit with the standard domain and transaction abort with the exceptional domain of a transaction.

3.2   Concurrent Exceptions

In our model, client transactions can be multithreaded to increase performance. Due to multithreading, two or more exceptions can be raised concurrently. In

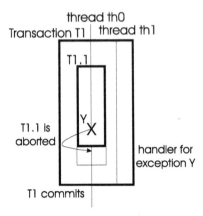

Fig. 4. Combined forward and backward recovery

this case, the transaction is aborted, as it happens with a single-threaded transaction, and an exception is propagated to notify the abort. However, when there are concurrent exceptions, it is necessary to perform exception resolution (*local resolution*) to choose a single exception to notify the transaction abort. This situation is depicted in Fig. 5.

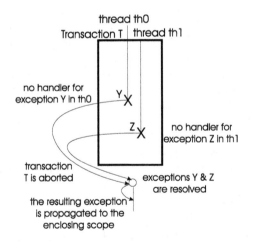

Fig. 5. Concurrent exceptions and exception resolution

A similar scenario can happen during the execution of a group method. An object group method is executed concurrently by all the group members. If multiple exceptions are raised, a single exception should be propagated to the outer scope, in this case, the scope where the method was invoked. Hence, a mechanism for *distributed exception resolution* is also needed. We call it distributed exception resolution, since it is performed among the distributed objects of a group. Two cases must be considered: resolution in replicated groups and in cooperative ones.

Replicated object groups behave deterministically. If a group object raises an exception, all of them should raise the same exception. However, there are some situations where the determinism of a replicated group is no longer respected. For instance, when group members are writing to a file and one of the members cannot write because of a local disk failure. If a member of a replicated group raises an exception that the rest of the members do not raise, it is considered faulty and removed from the group. Generalizing, a voting process is used for distributed exception resolution in replicated groups, and those members that are not in the majority are considered faulty and are removed from the group. If no majority it is obtained, the abort_error exception is raised provoking the transaction abort. Handling concurrent exceptions in this way avoids state divergence among the replicas.

In a cooperative group, each object can raise a different exception during the execution of a method. What it is more, as each object can create local threads during the execution of a method, concurrent exceptions can be raised even within a single object. Concurrent exceptions raised within an object (local exceptions) are more related among them that those exceptions raised at different objects (distributed exceptions). It is our opinion that it is more adequate to apply exception resolution in two stages instead of a single global one, as it is usual.

The first level is a *local exception resolution* performed among the threads of a method at a given object. This resolution can be different for each object of a group. As a result of this resolution, each object will yield at most one exception. If two or more objects of a group raise exceptions, distributed resolution is applied. This resolution constitutes the second level. Distributed exception resolution takes the exception raised by each group member (if any) and returns a single exception. Observe that each object will propagate at most one exception. If more than one exception is raised in an object, local exception resolution will return a single exception. Therefore, only an exception is propagated at each object. These two levels of exception resolution in cooperative object groups yield to a *hierarchical exception resolution*.

The situation is depicted in Fig. 6. A method has been invoked in the group. The group is executing the method. The three objects of the group (*obj.1, obj.2* and *obj.3*) have two threads. At object *obj.*1, thread *th1* raises the exception Y and thread *th11* raises Z. None of the exceptions is handled in its corresponding thread. Object *obj.*1 applies local exception resolution. As a result, transaction T finishes at *obj.1* raising exception W. At *obj.2* a single exception is unhandled (X). Therefore, no local resolution is applied. Transaction T finishes at *obj.2* raising exception X. *obj.3* finishes transaction T succesfully. As two objects have finished the transaction raising an exception, distributed exception resolution is applied among the exceptions (W and X) raised by the group objects. The exception resulting from this resolution (A) is propagated to the client to notify the abort of transaction T.

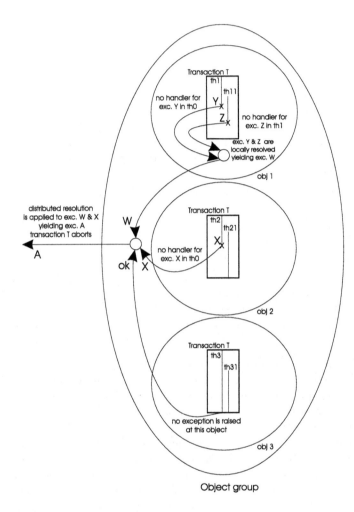

Fig. 6. Local and distributed exception resolution

4   Linguistic Support

The mechanisms previously described have been included in an Ada 95 extension, *Transactional Drago* [21]. Ada 95 is a programming language that provides objects, concurrency and exception handling, therefore, the extension of the language is quite natural. Although, in this section we refer to Ada, the same linguistic mechanisms can be easily applied to any programming language that provides objects, concurrency/distribution and exceptions, for instance, Java. The runtime of Transactional Drago is provided by TransLib [13] an object oriented library that can be used in combination with Ada.

Our proposal consists of introducing two new constructs: the *transactional block*, and *transactional object groups*. A transactional block allows to initiate a transaction (or transactional scope). Transactional blocks have a similar syntax to the Ada block statement. A keyword is used to distinguish a regular block statement from a transactional one. As block statements can have attached exception handlers, no new instruction is needed to handle aborts (since they are propagated as exceptions). Nesting of transactional blocks is used to implement nested transactions. Data items declared within a transactional block are subject to concurrency control (they are atomic) and can also be persistent. In order to ease the programmer task, concurrency control is implicitly set in Transactional Drago. In particular, read/write locking is used.

Ada tasks are used to create local threads where they are allowed (transactional blocks and methods of cooperative groups). If tasks are declared within a method of a cooperative object, they will be local threads of the associated transaction. A method (and a transactional block) cannot terminate until all its threads terminate, as happens with the regular block statement in Ada.

The Ada exception model is based on the termination model [5]. In this model when an exception is raised, the scope where the exception is raised terminates. Scopes in Ada are subprograms, task bodies, block statements, ... Unhandled exceptions are propagated from one scope to the enclosing one until they are successfully handled or they reach the outermost scope, which can be either the main program or a task. An unhandled exception in the main program causes its termination with a run-time error, whilst in a task, it causes the task termination. We have modified the behavior of unhandled exceptions in tasks when they belong to a transaction. Instead of losing the exception, the Transactional Drago runtime handles it to prevent its loss and enforce the semantics presented above.

Transactional object groups are provided, extending the Ada distributed systems annex by introducing a new kind of partition (Ada unit of distribution) corresponding to an object group. There is a peculiarity about cooperative object groups. In these groups there is a single class specification, but there might be multiple implementations (up to one per object of the group). Replicated object groups have a single implementation and only the number of replicas needs to be defined in this case.

In Ada there is no resolution of concurrent exceptions. In Transactional Drago exception resolution clauses are provided to associate resolution functions for concurrent exceptions either to a transactional block or to a cooperative object group method. These functions take two exceptions as arguments and return the resulting exception[1]. If n exceptions are concurrently raised within a transaction, the resolution function will be called $n-1$ times by the runtime system to obtain the final exception.

---

[1] In fact, as exceptions cannot be passed as arguments in Ada 95, exception identities are used for this purpose.

5   Implementation

The main implementation issue in the integration of transactional object groups and exceptions is how to combine exception handling and resolution with transaction termination protocols (commit and abort). Termination of traditional single-threaded transactions is trivially determined. A transaction finishes when its code executes the last statement of a transaction, which determines the outcome of the transaction. It finishes successfully, if a commit was executed. Otherwise, it aborts. However, the termination of a multithreaded transaction is not that easy. First, it is necessary to find out *when* it terminates. And second, it must be determined *how* it terminates, that is, whether it commits or aborts. If the transaction aborts, an exception must be choosen. In order to achieve this task, we have combined three different algorithms: commit protocol, abort protocol, and exception resolution algorithm into one. We have called it *hierarchical termination algorithm*.

First, let's discuss the behavior of the protocol in the case of a non-distributed (client) multithreaded transaction. Initially, a thread (the main thread) starts a transaction. Once the transaction has started, this thread may spawn additional threads (secondary threads) that will also work on behalf of the transaction. Unlike in the traditional single-threaded model, it is necessary to perform a termination protocol where the main thread waits for the outcomes of all the transaction threads. If the transaction aborts (due to the exceptional termination of one or more threads), the termination protocol will apply the resolution function to obtain a unique exception. Then, it will abort the transaction and propagate the resulting exception to the enclosing exception context. If the transaction commits, the appropriate actions will be taken to make the results permanent.

Method invocations of object groups are performed as subtransactions. If the group is cooperative, these subtransactions might have two levels of concurrency. At the first level there is a thread at each group object that executes a method invocation. Those threads are distributed. The second level (is optional, and only available in cooperative groups) corresponds to local threads created in an object method. The termination algorithm is performed in two stages corresponding to the two concurrency levels. First, each object waits for the outcome of its local threads. It produces a successful outcome or an exception. In case of concurrent exceptions, the local resolution function is applied. Then, the caller acts as coordinator of the distributed termination. It waits for the outcome of each of the objects. Again, the final outcome is commit if all the objects finished successfully. In case of an abort, the exception propagated is chosen applying the distributed resolution function to the exceptions propagated by the distributed objects (that can be the result of a local resolution).

Transactions in replicated object groups also need a termination protocol. The caller plays the role of coordinator and waits for the results of all the group members. The majority decides the outcome of the transaction. If the outcome is abort, the exception raised by the majority is propagated to the caller. The objects not included in the majority are removed from the group. If the outcome is commit, no exception is propagated. If no majority is reached, the transaction aborts propagating the `abort_error` exception to the caller.

6   Related Work

There have been few attempts to integrate transactions and exceptions in the literature. One of the first ones was Argus [14], a distributed transactional programming language. Its approach is an orthogonal integration where transactions can commit or abort, independently of how they terminate (normally or exceptionally). In our opinion this implies some dangers. In particular, committing a transaction that terminates exceptionally is quite dangerous. An exception indicates that an operation has been called in its exceptional domain and hence, that the postcondition is not guaranteed. Therefore, if the transaction commits, a state that might be inconsistent is being made permanent.

[27] presents an approach for integrating coordinated atomic actions and exceptions. This work deals with a different context where processes join explicitly on-going atomic actions at different moments to cooperate within them. These processes are autonomous entities (for instance, different devices of a manufacturing system) that at some points cooperate to perform a particular action. For this reason, when an exception is raised within a coordinated atomic action, the exception is propagated to all the participants in the action.

Although, this approach is quite indicated for autonomous (active) entities, it is not applicable to a transactional system, where servers are passive entities that only perform work on behalf of clients. In particular, existing threads cannot join on-going transactions. In our approach, threads are created when an object group method is called. Those threads terminate with the method. Exceptions raised by any of these threads are not propagated to other group members. Resolution is applied and the result is propagated to the enclosing scope.

Arche [11] is a parallel object-oriented programming language. In this language a notion of object groups is provided. An object group is defined as a sequence of objects. The signature of a group operation (or multi-operation) results from converting each parameter from the original class (the base class of the group) into a sequence of parameters of the original type. This object group definition is targeted to the explicit parallelization of algorithms, and strongly contrasts with the one provided in our approach, where distribution is hidden behind the object group, and thus, it is transparent to the client of the group. This definition also differs in that it does not provide any fault-tolerance. Object group invocations are unreliably multicast to the group members. In our approach reliable multicast and transactions provide fault-tolerant atomic services.

Arche also provides exception handling. Exceptions are defined as objects to allow their extension/redefinition in subclasses. Two kinds of exceptions are defined: global and concerted. When a member of a group raises a global exception, the exception is propagated to all the group members if they try to synchronize with the signaler of the global exception. Concerted exceptions are used in synchronous multi-party communication. Exception resolution (possibly, user-defined) takes place for this kind of exceptions. If during cooperation, one or more members of a group raise an exception, a concerted exception is then locally computed and raised within each of the members.

Concerted exceptions have some similarities with concurrent exceptions in our approach. In both cases, exception resolution takes place and can be user-defined. However, resolution functions take different forms. In Arche, resolution functions take as parameter a sequence of raised exceptions, whilst in our approach, a binary resolution function is used. Arche's approach is more flexible, but it is also more complex for the programmer as it is necessary to iterate through the sequence of exceptions. Our approach is less flexible in this aspect, but it is much simpler from the programmer viewpoint, as the code of the resolution function only deals with two exceptions. Additionally, the iteration through the sequence of exceptions is performed by the underlying system for the sake of reliability. Additionally, in Arche there is a single level of resolution, while in our approach, there are two levels due to the nature of cooperative groups. Another difference between Arche and the approach we have presented comes from differences in the host languages. Arche uses an object oriented exception model, while our proposal uses the Ada exception model, that is not object-oriented, and extends it to deal with object groups.

There are several proposals for implementing distributed object groups [15, 17,8,16], but none of them deals with the semantics of exceptions.

7   Conclusions

All the concepts we have used in the article, namely transactions, exceptions, multithreading, and object groups, are implemented in modern object-oriented languages and systems. The importance of transactions as a mechanism to program reliable distributed systems has been recognized in current standards. Examples of this are CORBA object transaction service (OTS) [19], Java transaction service (JTS) [26], or the transactional support of Enterprise Java Beans [25]. Exceptions are already part of current object-oriented languages, like C++ and Java, and systems, e.g., CORBA. Multithreading has been around for more than a decade and it is supported by Java and CORBA, and by all modern operating systems. Object groups are becoming increasingly important and there several research efforts in this direction. However, a consistent integration of all of them has not been addressed to our knowledge in any language or system. The work presented in this article addresses how to integrate these existing mechanisms in a consistent way.

In this article we have presented a new use of exceptions in the context of transactional object groups. This approach is novel in that integrates backward and forward recovery provided by transactions and exceptions. This allows the use of forward recovery within a transaction.

The second contribution is a proposal of semantics for exceptions raised by object groups. Two cases have been considered depending on the group functionality. In replicated groups, the implicit exception resolution is used to avoid divergence of replicas' state. In cooperative groups exception resolution is user defined. Additionally, this semantics have also been integrated in the context of transactions. It has been proposed how to integrate the commit and abort protocols of transactions with exception resolution in a single algorithm. Thus, no additional cost is paid for exception resolution.

We believe that transactional object groups will play an important role in simplifying the programming of future reliable distributed systems, and therefore, a clear semantics for exceptions should be provided for these kinds of systems.

References

1. K. P. Birman and R. Van Renesse. *Reliable Distributed Computing with Isis Toolkit.* IEEE Computer Society Press, Los Alamitos, CA, 1993.
2. K.P. Birman. *Building Secure and Reliable Network Applications.* Prentice Hall, NJ, 1996.
3. F. Cristian. Exception Handling and Software Fault Tolerance. *ACM Transactions on Computer Systems*, C-31(6):531–540, June 1982.
4. J. L. Eppinger, L. B. Mummert, and A. Z. Spector, editors. *Camelot and Avalon: A Distributed Transaction Facility.* Morgan Kaufmann Publishers, San Mateo, CA, 1991.
5. J. B. Goodenough. Exception Handling: Issues and a Proposed Notation. *Communications of the ACM*, pages 683–696, 1975.
6. J. Gray and A. Reuter. *Transaction Processing: Concepts and Techniques.* Morgan Kaufmann Publishers, San Mateo, CA, 1993.
7. F. Guerra, J. Miranda, Á. Álvarez, and S. Arévalo. An Ada Library to Program Fault-Tolerant Distributed Applications. In K. Hardy and J. Briggs, editors, *Proc. of Int. Conf. on Reliable Software Technologies*, volume LNCS 1251, pages 230–243, London, United Kingdom, June 1997. Springer.
8. R. Guerraoui, P. Felber, B. Garbinato, and K. R. Mazouni. System support for object groups. In *ACM Conference on Object-Oriented Programming Systems, Languages and Applications (OOPSLA'98)*, October 1998.
9. R. Guerraoui, R. Oliveira, and A. Schiper. Atomic Updates of Replicated Objects. In *Proc. of the Second European Dependable Computing Conf. (EDCC'96)*, volume LNCS 1150, Taormina (Italy), October 1996. Springer Verlag.
10. V. Hadzilacos and S. Toueg. Fault-Tolerant Broadcasts and Related Problems. In S. Mullender, editor, *Distributed Systems*, pages 97–145. Addison Wesley, Reading, MA, 1993.
11. V. Issarny. An exception-handling mechanism for parallel object-oriented programming: Toward reusable, robust distributed software. *Journal Object-Oriented Programming*, 6(6):29–40, October 1993.
12. R. Jiménez Peris, M. Patiño Martínez, and S. Arévalo. Deterministic Scheduling for Transactional Multithreaded Replicas. In *Proc. of the Int. Symp. on Reliable Distributed Systems (SRDS)*, pages 164–173, Nürnberg, Germany, October 2000. IEEE Computer Society Press.
13. R. Jiménez Peris, M. Patiño Martínez, S. Arévalo, and F.J. Ballesteros. TransLib: An Ada 95 Object Oriented Framework for Building Dependable Applications.

Int. Journal of Computer Systems: Science & Engineering, 15(1):113–125, January 2000.

14. B. Liskov. Distributed Programming in Argus. *Communications of the ACM*, 31(3):300–312, March 1988.

15. S. Maffeis. Adding Group Communication and Fault-Tolerance to CORBA. In *Proc. of 1995 USENIX Conf. on Object-Oriented Technologies*, June 1995.

16. G. Morgan, S.K. Shrivastava, P.D. Ezhilchelvan, and M.C. Little. Design and Implementation of a CORBA Fault-tolerant Object Group Service. In *Proc. of the Second IFIP WG 6.1 International Working Conference on Distributed Applications and Interoperable Systems, DAIS'99*, June 1999.

17. L. E. Moser, P. M. Melliar-Smith, P. Narasimhan, L. Tewksbury, and V. Kalogeraki. The Eternal System: An Architecture for Enterprise Applications. In *International Enterprise Distributed Object Computing Conference*, pages 214–222, September 1999.

18. J. E. B. Moss. *Nested Transactions: An Approach to Reliable Distributed Computing*. MIT Press, Cambridge, MA, 1985.

19. OMG. *CORBA services: Common Object Services Specification*. OMG.

20. M. Patiño Martínez, R. Jiménez Peris, and S. Arévalo. Integrating Groups and Transactions: A Fault-Tolerant Extension of Ada. In L. Asplund, editor, *Proc. of Int. Conf. on Reliable Software Technologies*, volume LNCS 1411, pages 78–89, Uppsala, Sweden, June 1998. Springer.

21. M. Patiño Martínez, R. Jiménez Peris, and S. Arévalo. Synchronizing Group Transactions with Rendezvous in a Distributed Ada Environment. In *Proc. of ACM Symp. on Applied Computing*, pages 2–9, Atlanta, Georgia, February 1998. ACM Press.

22. A. Schiper and M. Raynal. From Group Communication to Transactions in Distributed Systems. *Communications of the ACM*, 39(4):84–87, April 1996.

23. F. B. Schneider. Implementing Fault-Tolerant Services Using the State Machine Approach: A Tutorial. *ACM Computing Surveys*, 22(4):299–319, 1990.

24. S. K. Shrivastava. Lessons Learned from Building and Using the Arjuna Distributed Programming System. In K.P. Birman, F. Mattern, and A. Schiper, editors, *Theory and Practice in Distributed Systems*, volume LNCS 938, pages 17–32. Springer, 1995.

25. Sun. *Enterprise JavaBeans*. http://java.sun.com/products/ejb/index.html.

26. Sun. *Java Transaction Service*. http://java.sun.com/products/jts/.

27. J. Xu, A. Romanovsky, and B. Randell. Coordinated Exception Handling in Distributed Object Systems: from Model to System Implementation. In *Proc. of Int. Conference on Distributed Computing Systems, ICDCS-18*, May 1998.

Experiences with Error Handling in Critical Systems

Charles Howell[1] and Gary Vecellio[1]

[1] The MITRE Corporation, 1820 Dolley Madison Boulevard, McLean, Virginia, 22102,
USA
{Howell, Vecellio}@mitre.org

Abstract. Over the past several years, we have analyzed the error-handling
designs of a variety of critical applications and have discovered serious defects
even in well-tested and mature systems. In this paper, we will describe specific
recurring patterns of error handling defects we have observed in critical
systems. It seems clear that the design, implementation, and testing of error
handling are often not given adequate attention and resources.

1 Introduction

Software is often used in critical applications where the consequences of failure are
potentially enormous. At the same time, the complexity of individual applications and
the interactions among "systems of systems" is growing, making it essential that
critical software is robust.

Over the past several years, we have analyzed the error-handling designs of a
variety of critical applications and have discovered serious defects even in well-tested
and mature systems. The systems we have analyzed cover a broad range of domains,
languages, sizes, and criticality. They include two air traffic control systems, a flight
control system, torpedo safety interlocks, a metropolitan electrical power distribution
control system, a combat control system, a command and control display framework,
and a submarine ship control system. Sizes range from a few thousand source lines of
code to well over 350,000 SLOC. Languages include MC6800 assembler, Java, Ada
83, and C++.

In the following sections, we will describe specific recurring patterns of error
handling defects we have observed in real systems. The fact that we have found these
defects – sometimes potentially critical – in the error handling portions of a broad
range of critical systems is a strong demonstration of the continuing issues that need
to be addressed. It seems clear that the design, implementation, and testing of error
handling are often not given adequate attention and resources.

2 Patterns

This section addresses specific error-prone exception handling patterns. It presents a
collection of patterns that we have observed in various real-world applications. The
patterns range from simple syntactic constructs to complicated dynamic calling

A. Romanovsky et al. (Eds.): Exception Handling, LNCS 2022, pp. 181–188, 2001.

structures. Identifying instances of some of these patterns requires propagation analysis and language specific analysis.

2.1 Unanticipated Propagation

This pattern relates to the propagation of an exception to section of client code that is not prepared to handle the exception. An example of this pattern is when an exception propagates up the call stack until it causes a program (or thread) to abort execution. Typically, the only handling of the exception occurs by the runtime system that usually prints a diagnostic message to the stand output when the program terminates. Conversely, in the languages and runtime systems we have examined, thread termination is silent. Either case is rarely the desired behavior in safety, mission, or business critical applications.

The technical cause of this pattern is related to the use of programming languages that do not require or enforce the specification of exception propagation information in module interfaces (e.g., Ada 83). That is, propagation can not be unanticipated if the exceptions propagating to a client are specified in the server interface. The Java programming language is an example of one approach to this issue. Java enforces propagation information for certain, but not all, types of exceptions. The Java language designers understood the importance of unanticipated propagation, but they also understood the design and development costs associated with interfaces and logic to deal with exceptions that represent potentially unrecoverable errors (the Java language calls this type of exception RuntimeException).

That said, our experience has been that it is usually the case that designers favor some form of graceful shutdown, or at least the generation of better diagnostic messages. For example, it may be desirable to have a few firewalls where propagating exceptions are caught and appropriate a restart or graceful shutdown is performed. It is rarely the case that unconstrained propagation of an exception to an outer scope is the desired design strategy.

2.2 Invalid Termination of Propagation

This pattern relates to the termination of propagation (catching the exception) without returning the system to an appropriate state or otherwise taking some other appropriate action. This pattern is a frequent cause of subtle bugs in systems we have examined. One of the patterns we have repeatedly seen is a handler with just some sort of print statement to let the programmer know that an exception has occurred. After the stack trace is printed program execution will continue assuming that the events were handled correctly. We euphemistically coined the phrase "novocaine effect" to describe this pattern because the system may be in a corrupted state, but externally appears to be functionally correctly. We have seen this pattern all too often in critical systems. Not explicitly taking corrective action to deal with the exception may be the right choice, but more often the appropriate action is to propagate it up the call chain, restore state to some default setting, or attempt an alternate computation. The following code fragment (slightly sanitized) is from a mission critical system.

```java
for (int i = 0; i < listenerList.size(); i++) {
  try {
    ChartObjectListener listener =
      (ChartObjectListener) listenerList.elementAt(i);
    switch(event.getType()) {
      case EventManager.OBJECT_DOWN_EVENT:
        listener.objectDown(event);
        break;
      case EventManager.OBJECT_UP_EVENT:
        listener.objectUp(event);
        break;
      case EventManager.OBJECT_BOX_EVENT:
        listener.objectBox(event);
        break;
      case EventManager.OBJECT_DESELECT_EVENT:
        listener.objectDeselect(event);
        break;
    }
  } catch (Exception e) {
    e.printStackTrace();
  }
}
```

After the stack trace is printed (no doubt puzzling the system operator if they see it at all), the loop is exited normally. Program execution will continue on with the assumption that the events were handled correctly. Obviously, printing a message does nothing to alter the program's erroneous state. The consequences of this erroneous assumption are not clear, but are almost certainly not what the implementor intended.

The treatment of method or function parameters is a particularly subtle cause of problems in error handling we have observed in code when exception propagation is terminated, and deserves special attention. These patterns relate to exception handlers that catch exceptions, but do not properly set the associated method or module's parameters. In some programming languages such as Ada 83, modules may have multiple parameters potentially modified by a called procedure. In Ada 83 these are referred to as "out" or "in out" parameters. When an exception handler does not propagate an exception, care should be take to set (or reset) the values of all "out" or "in out" parameters either to a meaningful intended value or to some distinguished value that denotes an error condition. If the handler does not set the values for these parameters, the calling subprogram may attempt to use these values erroneously, lacking any indication of the occurrence of an exception.

The following sample is typical of a pattern we have often seen in Ada 83 programs we have analyzed.

```ada
with Text_IO;
procedure Blah ( Param1 : out Type1;
                 Param2 : in out Type2 ) is
begin
  <sequence of statements>
exception
  when Exception1 => raise;
```

```
when others => Text_IO.Put_Line ("Problem in Blah");
end Blah;
```

If the others handler in the example above is executed, callers of procedure Blah will have no indication that a problem occurred, yet the values could be in an indeterminate state.

2.3 Anonymous Exceptions

This pattern relates to the exceptions that propagate out of their name scope. Unless the strategy to handle exceptions is to gracefully shutdown the system, it is usually necessary to name an exception to perform specific processing. Anonymous exceptions can not be named, and therefore, can not be processed in an exception specific manner. Exceptions are generally statically declared in a declarative region, and their scope (visibility) is the same as that region, while exceptions dynamically propagate arbitrarily up a call sequence, including out of the exception's name scope. When an exception is anonymous it can only be caught with an exception independent handler (e.g., a handler like catch (Throwable e) {}). Languages that model exceptions as objects (e.g., Java) somewhat mitigate this problem. While the exception still can't be named, an object can carry enough information to allow it to be processed.

Consider the following Java fragments:

```
package mypackage;
class MyPackagedException extends Exception { }

public class UnnamedExceptionProp {
  public void method1 () throws Exception {
    throw new MyPackagedException();// Line #6
  }
}

package mypackage2;
import mypackage.*;
public class UnnamedExceptionMain {
  public static void main (String args[]) {
    UnnamedExceptionProp u = new UnnamedExceptionProp();
    try {
      u.method1(); // Line #7
    } catch (Exception e) {
        e.printStackTrace();
    }
  }
}
```

If the class Exception in the catch clause is replaced with the class MyPackagedException the compiler will complain about no visibility of the declaration. The routines above produce the following output when executed (the line numbers .java:6 and .java:7 are indicated in the source code above):

```
java UnnamedExceptionMain
mypackage.MyPackagedException
 at mypackage.UnnamedExceptionProp.method1
                          (UnnamedExceptionProp.java:6)
 at UnnamedExceptionMain.main(UnnamedExceptionMain.java:7)
```

Our experience indicates that anonymous executions are a particular problem with software reuse or common code. This occurs because it is necessary to have a scope that includes the newly developed and the reused or common code. This is difficult to accomplish without up front planning and design.

2.4 Mapping Exceptions

This pattern relates to the mapping the information conveyed by exceptions into other mechanisms like error codes. This typically occurs when applications are developed using multiple programming languages with different exception handling capabilities (e.g., C and Java). At different locations in a program (e.g., where different languages interface, at message passing interfaces, at the operating system interface) there is often a mapping between the use of return codes and the throwing of exceptions. This is typically a mapping of specific return code values to specific exceptions. A common mistake we have observed in implementing this is strategy is to fail to completely cover the range of return code values. The fact that this is such a frequent problem in systems we have reviewed is an illustration of the inadequate testing of error handling paths and conditions. An example only slightly sanitized from a safety critical system illustrates this issue.

We have an Ada 83 function that interfaces with assembler routines. These assembler routines will pass back a return code indicating success or failure:

```
function Start_Radar return INTEGER;
pragma interface (ASSEMBLY, Start_Radar);

Return_Code : INTEGER;
. . .
Return_Code := Start_Radar;
if Return_Code /= 0 then
  Raise_On_Class (Return_Code);
end if;
```

The procedure Raise_On_Class is a simple utility to map return codes to Ada 83 exceptions:

```
procedure Raise_On_Class
  (Class : INTEGER)  is
begin
  case Class is
    when  1 => raise Status_Error;
    when  2 => raise Mode_Error;
    when  3 => raise Name_Error;
    when  4 => raise Use_Error;
```

```
    when   5 => raise Device_Error;
    when   6 => raise End_Error;
    when   7 => raise Data_Error;
    when   8 => raise Layout_Error;
    when  -1 => raise System_Error;
    when others => null;
  end case;
```

The implementation of Raise_on_Class is crucial. In this implementation, any unexpected return codes will be ignored by the procedure, and the rest of the system will proceed as if no error occurred. In this case we proposed a slight change to the utility which addressed this problem:

```
procedure Raise_On_Class
   (Class : INTEGER)   is
begin
  case Class is
          when  0 => null;
    when   1 => raise Status_Error;
    when   2 => raise Mode_Error;
    when   3 => raise Name_Error;
    when   4 => raise Use_Error;
    when   5 => raise Device_Error;
    when   6 => raise End_Error;
    when   7 => raise Data_Error;
    when   8 => raise Layout_Error;
    when  -1 => raise System_Error;
    when others => raise Unknown_Error;
  end case;
end Raise_On_Class;
```

This also prevents success from being incorrectly reported if additional error codes are added during maintenance.

2.5 Propagation from Within Handlers

It is ironic, but a common oversight in exception handling code is to overlook the possibility of an exception being thrown while performing exception handling. Code in the exception-handling portion of a routine can throw exceptions just as readily as any other code, yet the need to plan for this is often ignored. For example, in a Java program, code in the catch clause of a try block can throw exceptions just as readily as any other code, yet the use of nested try blocks (to handle these subsequent exceptions) is often ignored. This is a simple design oversight that we have seen in multiple systems and in multiple programming languages. A simple Ada 83 example, sanitized from an Air Traffic Control system, illustrates the pattern. Consider a procedure that performs some processing and may detect an error. This is reported by raising an exception. The exception handler for the procedure will handle the exception, log the occurrence to a journal file, and reraise the exception to notify the calling procedure of the error.

```
procedure Some_Procedure is
begin
...
-- An Error_in_Logic is detected
raise Error_in_Logic;
...
exception
  when Error_in_Logic =>
    Logging_Procedure;
    raise;
end Some_Procedure;
```

Logging_Procedure may raise its own exceptions, however, and this eventuality is not considered in the exception handler for Some_Procedure.

```
procedure Logging_Procedure is
begin
  Text_IO.Open (...);
  ...
  -- Text_IO calls may raise Mode_Error, Status_Error, etc.
  -- mapping the original exception into an IO_Exception
  Text_IO.Close (...);
end Logging_Procedure;
```

In this case the result could be that the intended propagation of Error_In_Logic to the callers of Some_Procedure is replaced with the propagation of a Text_IO exception, leading to unknown results. Not considering exception handling in exception handling code appears to be a common design oversight.

3 Summary and Conclusion

Our experiences suggest that error handling requirements, design, and testing really are not given adequate attention during the development of even critical systems. The results of this inadequate attention include subtle problems that can be difficult to resolve during system integration, additional rework, and even latent defects that can be catastrophic.

In looking back on a wide range of problems with error handling in multiple programs implemented using multiple languages, two recurring themes struck us. The first is that very little of the testing we have seen explicitly exercises the error handling portions of the systems. More attention to error handling in general seems needed, particularly for critical systems, but the resources allocated to testing error handling seem to be particularly inadequate. This is compounded by the technical challenges in exercising error handling, which will often require fault injection and contriving unusual system states. The second recurring broad problem is the confusion between debugging and error handling. We have seen a great deal of error handling code that in fact is simply debugging support (e.g., printing stack traces or announcing the failure of a specific assertion is a specific portion of source code). These actions may be helpful to the developer or maintenance programmer in debugging, but are not at all useful in recovering from a detected error or shutting down gracefully.

The failure to pay adequate attention to error handling in critical systems seems very likely to be one contributor to the widespread fragility of software as noted the President's Information Technology Advisory Committee:

Software is the new physical infrastructure of the information age. It is fundamental to economic success, scientific and technical research, and national security. The Nation needs robust systems, but the software our systems depend on is fragile. Software fragility is its tendency not to work properly - or at all - for long enough periods of time or in the presence of uncontrollable environmental variation. Fragility is manifested as unreliability, lack of security, performance lapses, errors, and difficulty in upgrading.

[President's Information Technology Advisory Committee, February 24, 1999, http://www.ccic.gov/ac/report]

Implementing robust error handling in complex software systems will always present substantial challenges; no one remedy or "silver bullet" can address all of them. However, by placing a priority on the software's error-handling behavior, and enforcing this priority through all phases of software development, the level of robustness can be increased considerably. Significant cost drivers (e.g., software rework and extended software integration times) can be reduced. To ensure that sufficient attention is being paid to software error handling, developers should focus on the establishment of well-defined processes in three areas: (1) analyzing error-handling requirements during the development of the software requirements definition; (2) adopting a software error-handling policy and enforcing its use by all software developers during design and implementation; and (3) testing the error-handling aspects of the software and demonstrating that the software is robust.

Perhaps the clearest summary of our observations after analyzing a wide variety of error handling implementations in a range of critical systems is from Douglas Adams in Mostly Harmless, Book 5 of the Hitch Hiker's Guide to the Galaxy trilogy, Heinemann, London , 1992:

"The major difference between a thing that might go wrong and a thing that cannot possibly go wrong is that when a thing that cannot possibly go wrong goes wrong it usually turns out to be impossible to get at or repair."

References

1. Baldonado, M., Chang, C.-C.K., Gravano, L., Paepcke, A.: The Stanford Digital Library Metadata Architecture. Int. J. Digit. Libr. 1 (1997) 108–121
2. Bruce, K.B., Cardelli, L., Pierce, B.C.: Comparing Object Encodings. In: Abadi, M., Ito, T. (eds.): Theoretical Aspects of Computer Software. Lecture Notes in Computer Science, Vol. 1281. Springer-Verlag, Berlin Heidelberg New York (1997) 415–438
3. van Leeuwen, J. (ed.): Computer Science Today. Recent Trends and Developments. Lecture Notes in Computer Science, Vol. 1000. Springer-Verlag, Berlin Heidelberg New York (1995)
4. Michalewicz, Z.: Genetic Algorithms + Data Structures = Evolution Programs. 3rd edn. Springer-Verlag, Berlin Heidelberg New York (1996)

An Architectural-Based Reflective Approach to Incorporating Exception Handling into Dependable Software

Alessandro F. Garcia[1] and Cecília M. F. Rubira[2]

[1] Computer Science Department, PUC-Rio, Brazil,
afgarcia@inf.puc-rio.br,
WWW home page: http://www.inf.puc-rio.br/~afgarcia
[2] Institute of Computing, University of Campinas (UNICAMP), Brazil,
cmrubira@ic.unicamp.br,
WWW home page: http://www.ic.unicamp.br/~cmrubira

Abstract. Modern object-oriented software is inherently complex and has to cope with an increasing number of exceptional conditions to meet the system's dependability requirements. In this context, the goal of our work is twofold: (i) to present an exception handling model which is suitable for developing dependable object-oriented software, and (ii) to provide a systematic approach to incorporating exception handling during the design stage, that is, from the architectural design stage to the detailed design stage. The proposed approach employs the computational reflection concept to achieve a clear and transparent separation of concerns between the application's functionality and the exception handling facilities. This separation minimizes the complexity caused by the handling of abnormal behavior and facilitates the task of building dependable software with better readability, maintainability and reusability.

1 Introduction

Modern object-oriented software is inherently complex and has to cope with an increasing number of exceptional conditions to meet the system's dependability requirements [12,23]. Dependable object-oriented software detects errors caused by residual faults and employs exception handling measures to restore normal computation. The incorporation of exceptional behavior into software systems usually increases, rather than decreases, their complexity and, consequently, it makes more difficult the task of building high-quality applications. The perceived unreliability of existing object-oriented systems is often attributed to a poor software design related to exception handling [23]. Moreover, software developers usually postpone the exception handling aspects to the implementation stage [10]. In addition, exception handling is in general introduced into the application in an 'ad hoc' way [10,14], leading to software systems that are difficult to understand, maintain and reuse. As a consequence, exception handling activities should be incorporated into object-oriented systems in a disciplined and structured manner during the different development phases (analysis, design and

A. Romanovsky et al. (Eds.): Exception Handling, LNCS 2022, pp. 189–206, 2001.

implementation) in order to maintain under control the complexity caused by the handling of exceptional situations. In this work, we focus on the provision of exception handling during the design stage.

In this context, the goal of our work is twofold: (i) to present an exception handling model which is suitable for developing dependable object-oriented software, and (ii) to provide a systematic approach to incorporating exception handling during the design stage, more especifically, from the architectural design stage to the detailed design stage (Figure 1). The proposed exception handling model identifies suitable design choices for building dependable object-oriented applications, and presents guidelines for exception handling issues that should be followed throughout the application's design. This approach consists of three stages: the *architectural design stage*, the *architecture refinement stage*, and the *detailed design stage*. The *architectural design stage* presents a software architecture for building dependable applications. The proposed architecture defines the fundamental components to deal with the different exception handling aspects, namely, exceptions, handlers and the exception handling strategy. Moreover, it provides earlier the context in which more detailed design decisions related to exception handling can be made afterwards during detailed design and implementation stages. Since complex software systems are often concurrent, the proposed architecture also provides a generic infrastructure which supports uniformly both concurrent and sequential exception handling. The *architecture refinement stage* applies the computational reflection concept [18] to the fundamental components defined previously in order to achieve a transparent separation of concerns between the application's functionality and the exception handling facilities. The *detailed design stage* presents a set of design patterns which are used to refine the fundamental components; the detailed design of each component is described by means of a specific design pattern. These patterns follow the computational reflection notion and describe solutions which are independent of programming language or exception handling mechanism.

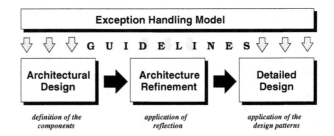

Fig. 1. Exception Handling During the Design Stage

The remainder of this text is organized as follows. Section 2 introduces the terminology and problems related to sequential and concurrent exception handling. Section 3 presents object-oriented techniques for design reuse and software structuring used in this work and Section 4 describes our exception handling model. Section 5 shows the proposed software architecture for exceptional handling and Section 6 details this architecture. Section 7 presents a set of design patterns for exception handling applied to the architecture. Section 8 discusses some implementation issues. Section 9 gives a brief comparison with related work. Finally, Section 10 summarizes our conclusions and suggests directions for future work.

2 Exception Handling

Exception Handling in Sequential Systems. Dependable software developers usually refer to errors as exceptions because they are expected to occur rarely during a system's normal activity [7]. These exceptions should be specified internally to the system and an instance of an exception raised at run-time is termed an *exception occurrence*. Extra-information about an exception occurrence, such as its name, description, location, and severity, is usually necessary for handling it [15]. This extra-information is passed either explicitly by the application component that has raised the exception, or implicitly by an exception handling service.

Dependable applications need to incorporate exception handling activities in order to behave suitably in a great number of exceptional situations. Exception handling activities are structured by a set of *exception handlers* (or simply *handlers*) [16]. A handler may be valid for one or more exceptions. Handlers are attached to a particular region of normal code called a *protected region*. Each protected region can have a set of attached handlers, and one of them is invoked when a corresponding exception is raised. Handlers can be attached to *blocks of statements, methods, objects, classes*, or *exception classes* [3,4,8,9,15,21]. Handlers attached to exception classes are usually called *default handlers*. They are often the most general handlers, and must be valid in any part of the program.

An exception handling strategy should be followed after an exception occurrence is detected. In general, the *normal control flow* of the computation is deviated to the *exceptional control flow*. The deviation of the control flow is followed by the search for a suitable handler to deal with the exception occurrence. The handler search is performed according to a search algorithm. When a handler is found, it is invoked and the computation is returned to its normal control flow. The returning point where the normal flow continues also depends on the chosen model for the continuation: the *termination* model, or the *resumption* model. In the termination model, execution continues from the point at which the exception was handled. In the resumption model, the execution has the capability to resume the internal activity of the component after the point at which the exception was raised.

Exception Handling in Concurrent Systems. In this work, cooperative activities of a dependable concurrent object-oriented system are structured as a set of atomic actions. We refer to these activities as *concurrent cooperative actions* (or simply *actions*). An action provides a mechanism for performing a group of methods on a collection of objects concurrently. The interface of an action includes its participants and methods (and their respective objects) that are manipulated by the participants. In order to perform an action, a group of threads should execute each participant in the action concurrently (one thread per participant). Threads participating in an action cooperate within the scope of the action by executing methods on objects, and exchange information only among those which are participants of that action. Threads cooperate and communicate with each other by means of *shared objects*. Participants may enter the action asynchronously but they have to exit the action synchronously to guarantee that no information is smuggled to or from the action.

Exceptions can be raised by participants during an action. Some of them can be handled internally by a local handler attached to the participant that raised that exception. We refer to these exceptions as *local exceptions*. Traditional exception handling strategies usually address this kind of exception. If an exception occurrence is not handled internally by a participant, then it should be handled cooperatively by all action participants. We refer to this kind of exception as *cooperating exception*, for which, a new concurrent exception handling strategy is required. A set of cooperating exceptions is associated with each action. Each participant has a set of handlers for (all or part of) these exceptions. Participants are synchronized and probably different handlers for the same exception have to be invoked in the different participants [6]. These handlers are executed concurrently, and cooperate in handling the exception in a coordinated way.

Moreover, various cooperating exceptions may be raised concurrently while action participants are cooperating. So, an algorithm for *exception resolution* is necessary in order to decide which cooperating exception will be notified to all participants of the action. The work in [6] describes a model for exception resolution called *exception tree*, which includes an exception hierarchy. When several cooperating exceptions are raised concurrently, the resolved exception is the root of the smallest subtree containing all raised exceptions. Cooperating exceptions can be of two different kinds in the exception tree: *simple exceptions*, or *structured exceptions*. Simple exceptions are leafs of the tree and correspond to cooperating exceptions which are raised one at a time. Structured exceptions are non-leaf nodes and correspond to two or more exceptions being raised concurrently. An exception tree should be specified for each action of the application.

3   Software Reuse and Structuring Techniques

Software Architecture and Patterns. A system's software architecture is a high-level description of the system's organization in terms of *components* and their interrelationships [22]. To each component is assigned a set of responsibilities. The components must interact with each other using pre-described rules, and must fulfill their responsibilities to other components as imposed by the architecture. Each component conforms to and provides the realization of a set of *interfaces*, which make available services implemented by the component. Software patterns are important vehicles for constructing high-quality architectures.

Patterns are abstracted from recurring experiences rather than invented, and exist at different levels of abstraction. *Architectural patterns* define the basic structure of an architecture and of systems which implement that architecture [5]; *design patterns* are more problem-oriented than architectural patterns, and are applied in later design stages. Usually the selection of a design pattern is influenced by the architectural patterns that were previously chosen. Design patterns can refine general components of an architecture, providing detailed design solutions. In this work, components of the proposed architecture are refined by a set of design patterns which follows the overall structure of the *Reflection* architectural pattern [5]. The reflection pattern is based on the concept of computational reflection and meta-level architectures.

Meta-Level Architectures. Computational reflection [18] is defined as the ability of observing and manipulating the computational behavior of a system through a process called *reification*. This technique allows a system to maintain information about itself (*meta-information*) and use this information to change its behavior. It defines a *meta-level architecture* that is composed of at least two dimensions: (i) a *base level*, and (ii) a *meta-level*. A *meta-object protocol* (*MOP*) establishes an interface among the base-level and the meta-level components. A MOP provides a high-level interface to the programming language implementation in order to reveal the program information normally hidden by the compiler and/or run-time environment. As a consequence, programmers can develop language extensions, and adapt component behavior or even make changes to the systems more transparently.

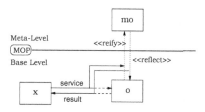

Fig. 2. A Meta-Level Architecture

The extensions of the behavior of base-level objects can be implemented at the meta-level. Reflection can be used to intercept and modify the implementation of operations in the object model. For the purpose of illustration, suppose that for each base-level object o there exists a corresponding meta-object mo that represents the behavioral and structural aspects of o (Figure 2). If an object x sends a message service to an object o, the meta-object mo intercepts the message service, *reifies* the base-level computation and takes over the execution; later mo returns (or *reflects*) the response to x. From the view point of x, computational reflection is transparent: x sends a service request to o, and receives a response with no knowledge that the message has been intercepted and redirected to the meta-level.

4   An OO Exception Handling Model

The exception handling model that we have applied in this work was primarily designed to facilitate the development of reliable and reusable software components [13]. In this section, we present the main features of our model which establishes the guidelines that should be followed during the architecutre refinement and detailed design stages (Figure 1). In the literature, one can find several exception handling models (such as [3,4,8,9,21]) that follow many of the guidelines presented here. However, none of them encompass all the good points at the same time. A recent study [15] has shown that existing models are still far from the ideal exception handling model for developing dependable object-oriented systems. So our exception handling model synthesizes the good qualities of existing systems in order to provide a simple and effective model which is more appropriate for developing dependable object-oriented software.

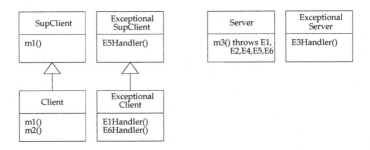

Fig. 3. Normal and Exceptional Class Hierarchies [13]

Guideline 1. Separation between Normal and Exceptional Activities.
The explicit separation between normal and exceptional behaviors is a main concern when using exception handling techniques. This design choice improves several system's quality aspects, such as readability, maintainability, and reusability. We propose that developers should structure their applications by creating a set of *normal classes* which implement the normal activities of software components, and a set of *exceptional classes* which implement the abnormal ones (Figure 3). In Figure 3, methods of the exceptional class ExceptionalSupClient are handlers for the exceptions that should be treated within methods of the class SupClient. The exceptional classes ExceptionalSupClient and ExceptionalClient are organized hierarchically so that the resulting hierarchy is orthogonal to the normal class hierarchy (SupClient and Client). Exceptional class hierarchies allow exceptional subclasses to inherit handlers from their superclasses.

Guideline 2. Representation of Exceptions as Objects. Different types of exceptions are organized hierarchically as classes. The class Exception is the root of this hierarchy. Various exception handling mechanisms also adopt this approach, such as [3,4,8,9]. The class CooperatingException extends the class

Exception and allows the definition of exceptions that may be raised by cooperative actions needing coordinated recovery (Section 2). Exceptional responses that may be signaled by a method must be described in its signature (Figure 3).

Guideline 3. Multi-Level Attachment of Handlers. Designers should organize their systems by attaching handlers to different levels of protected regions such as classes, objects, methods and so on. Firstly, handlers may be associated to exceptions themselves. Secondly, they may be also associated to a class. In this case, an exceptional class should be created. In addition, object handlers may also be defined. To implement handlers associated to individual objects, a new exceptional class must be created. This new class contains methods that implement the object handlers for the exceptions that should be treated in any method of the object.

Guideline 4. Explicit Propagation of Exceptions. Despite gains in programming simplicity, the use of automatic propagation of exceptions remains fault-prone because they are the least well documented and tested parts of an interface [8]. The adoption of explicit propagation of exceptions has a number of benefits [17,25]: (i) the handling of signaled exceptions is limited to the immediate caller; (ii) if a signaled exception is not handled in the caller, then the predefined exception failure is further propagated; (iii) the exception still may be resignaled explicitly within a handler to a higher-level component.

Guideline 5. Termination Model. The rationale of the termination model is simpler and more suitable for the construction of dependable systems [7]. The resumption model is more flexible, but more difficult to be used correctly.

5   The Architectural Design Stage

If an architecture that includes design policies for error/exception handling is chosen from the outset, a proper use of exception handling throughout the development of the system can be obtained. We propose a generic software architecture that integrates sequential and concurrent exception handling [14] (Figure 4). Applications that adopt this architecture to handle their exceptions can reuse the exception handling facilities provided by the architecture's components.

The Architectural Components and their Responsibilities. The architecture has four components: (i) the *Exception* component, (ii) the *Handler* component, (iii) the *Exception Handling Strategy* component, and (iv) the *Concurrent Exception Handling Action* component. Table 1 summarizes the components and their responsibilities. The responsibilities are classified in two groups: (i) *application-dependent* responsibilities (ADR), and (ii) *application-independent* responsibilities (AIR). Application-dependent responsibilities are directly related to the application's functionality and include, for instance, facilities for specification of exceptions and handlers, raising of application exceptions, and specification of concurrent cooperative actions. Application-independent responsibilities include, for instance, facilities for extra-information management, handler invocation, deviation of control flow, handler search, participant synchronization and exception resolution. These responsibilities are related to management activities of exception handling. The architecture's components interact with each other as prescribed by the architecture in order to fulfill their application-independent responsibilities

Table 1. Components' Responsibilities [14].

#	Component	Responsibilities
1	Exception	Specification and raising of local and cooperating exceptions (ADR)
		Management of extra-information (AIR)
2	Handler	Specification of handlers (ADR)
		Invocation of handlers (AIR)
3	Exception Handling Strategy	Search of handlers (AIR)
		Deviation of the control flow (AIR)
4	Concurrent Exception Handling Action	Specification of concurrent cooperative actions (ADR)
		Synchronization and exception resolution (AIR)

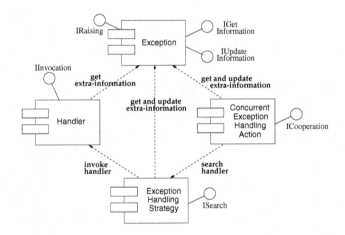

Fig. 4. A Software Architecture for Exception Handling [14]

Relationships between Components. Figure 4 depicts the components and their interrelationships. The *Exception* component works as an extra-information holder, keeping information about application exceptions which are used by the other components. They interact with the *Exception* component in order to get and update information about exception occurrences. The *Exception Handling Strategy* component implements services related to the general strategy for exception handling. Its responsibilities are the deviation of control flow and the search for handlers. This component plays a central role in the architecture and interacts with all other components. It interacts with the *Exception* component to get extra-information about an exception occurrence while searching for its corresponding handler. After a handler is found, it asks the *Handler* component to invoke the exception handler. The *Exception Handling Strategy* component also interacts with the *Concurrent Exception Handling Action* component. The latter uses the services provided by the former in order to carry out the strategy for concurrent exception handling. For example, when cooperating exceptions are raised during an action, the exception resolution is accomplished by the *Concurrent Exception Handling Action* component, and then the *Exception Handling Strategy* component is responsible for locating the different handlers for the resolved exception. In this work, the strategy for concurrent exception handling extends the atomic action paradigm described previously in Section 2.

Interfaces of the Components. The interfaces are used either by the architecture's components themselves, or else by the application while using the exception handling services. Figure 4 illustrates the architecture's components and their interfaces. The interfaces are categorized in two groups: (i) *private* interfaces, or (ii) *public* interfaces. Private interfaces define the services that are only visible by the components of the architecture. Public interfaces define the services that are visible by both the application and architecture. The *Exception* component implements three public interfaces: (i) the interface IRaising, (ii) the interface IGetInformation, and (iii) the interface IUpdateInformation. The interface IRaising allows the application to raise exceptions by invoking the method raise. The interface IGetInformation allows the application and other architecture's components to obtain extra-information about the exception occurrences. Finally, the interface IUpdateInformation allows its clients to update extra-information about exceptions. The *Handler* component implements the private interface IInvocation. This interface allows the *Exception Handling Strategy* component to invoke a handler when the appropriate handler has been found. The *Exception Handling Strategy* component conforms to the private interface ISearch that provides the *Concurrent Exception Handling Action* component with the service for handler search. The *Concurrent Exception Handling Action* component implements the public interface ICooperation which is acessible by the application to create concurrent cooperative actions.

6   The Architecture Refinement Stage

Separation of Concerns. As stated previously, software designers should tailor the components of the architecture in order to add the functionality related to specific applications. Note that each architectural component includes application's functionality and also management activities for exception handling. In order to obtain a clear separation of concerns between the application's functionality and the exception handling services, the architecture and their components incorporate a meta-level architecture, following the overall structure of the

Reflection pattern (Section 3). Figure 5 presents the proposed meta-level architecture which is composed of two dimensions: the base level, and the meta-level. The architecture's base level encompasses the application-dependent elements, such as exceptions, handlers, normal activities, and concurrent cooperative actions. The architecture's meta-level consists of meta-objects which perform the management activities for exception handling.

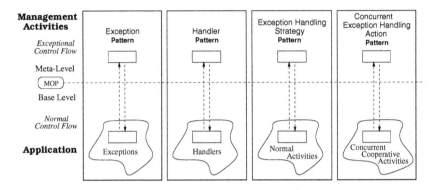

Fig. 5. The Architecture Refinement [14]

Transparency. The *Reflection* pattern also captures the benefit of transparency provided by computational reflection. For the purposes of this work, object states, results and invocations of methods of the application (base-level) are intercepted and reified by the MOP, and potentially checked and altered by the meta-objects (meta-level) in order to carry out the management activities for exception handling. For instance, results of methods are checked transparently by the meta-objects to verify if such methods have raised any exception. MOP intercepts at run-time the exceptional results and deviates the normal control flow of the base-level application to the exceptional one at the meta-level. When the management activities are concluded, MOP returns the computation to the application's normal flow. Therefore, the meta-objects execute their management activities transparently from the viewpoint of the base-level.

7   The Detailed Design Stage

After application designers reuse the architecture (Section 5) and refine its components (Section 6), some questions arise in this context, such as: (i) how to specify simple and cooperating exceptions and to handle them uniformly, (ii) how to specify handlers, (iii) how to perform the synchronization of action participants and other management activities in a way that is transparent to the application, and (iv) how to apply the guidelines suggested in Section 4. In this work, design patterns are proposed in order to refine the general components of our architecture. However, we would like to emphasize that it is possible to apply the design patterns for exception handling in the absence of reflection. In such a case, the benefits of transparency are lost. Due to space limitations, in this work, we discuss only the reflective version of the design patterns. The work [14] describes our patterns in more detail.

7.1   The *Exception* Pattern

Context. Fault-tolerant software designers should be able to specify local and cooperating exceptions in their applications. These exceptions may be raised at run-time during the application's normal activity. Extra-information is required by the application in order to handle an exception occurrence.

Problem. The software architecture should support the definition and raising of local and cooperating exceptions. Moreover, a flexible and reusable software architecture is required to make the exception specification easier and to separate concerns between application exceptions and extra-information management. Several *forces* are associated with this design problem: (i) local and cooperating exceptions should be defined uniformly, (ii) software developers should be able to construct exception trees easily, and (iii) the exception occurrence itself should carry the extra-information necessary for its handling.

Solution. Use the *Reflection* architectural pattern in order to separate classes responsible for managing extra-information (meta-level) from the ones used to specify application exceptions (base level). Different types of exceptions are organized hierarchically as classes which are termed *exception classes* (*Guideline 2*). Exception trees are defined by using the *Composite* design pattern [11]. Exception occurrences are base-level objects created at run-time when an exception is raised, and are termed *exception objects*. Meta-objects are associated transparently with exception objects for keeping extra-information about the exception occurrences. Extra-information is reified as meta-objects which keep meta-information collected at run-time about the corresponding exception occurrence. Meta-objects alter transparently the state of the exception objects in order to make this information available for the application. As a result, the exception object keeps extra-information necessary for its handling.

Consequences. The *Exception* Pattern offers the following benefits:

- *Uniformity.* Both local and cooperating exceptions are uniformly defined as exception classes.
- *Simplicity.* Exception trees are easily defined. Application developers define exception trees without writing an exception resolution procedure for each concurrent cooperative action of the application.
- *Reusability and Extensibility.* The representation of local and cooperating exceptions as classes promotes the reusability and extensibility of the exception classes.
- *Readability and Maintainability.* Applications whose exceptions are represented as objects are easier to understand and maintain than applications where exceptions are mere symbols (numbers or strings) [12].

- *Easy incorporation of default handlers.* Since exceptions are represented as classes, default handlers can be defined as methods on exception classes.

7.2   The *Handler* Pattern

Context. Fault-tolerant software designers need to specify handlers for local and cooperating exceptions that are expected to occur during the normal activity of their applications. A handler is invoked when a corresponding exception is raised.

Problem. The infra-structure of the software architecture should be organized in order to allow application developers to define the exception handlers in a way that separates them from the application's normal activity. In addition, this infra-structure should promote the separation between the application components containing the exception handlers and the architectural components responsible for invoking the eligible handler. The following *forces* shape this solution: (i) exception handlers for local and cooperating exceptions should be defined in an uniform manner, and (ii) the software architecture should include multi-level attachment of handlers (*Guideline 3*).

Solution. Use the *Reflection* architectural pattern in order to separate the class responsible for invoking handlers (meta-level) from the classes used to specify the application handlers (base level). The base-level defines the *exceptional classes*, i.e., the application classes that implement the handlers for local and cooperating exceptions (*Guideline 1*). Exceptional classes can contain method, object and class handlers. The *normal classes* are located at the base-level and implement the application's normal activities (see Section 7.3). The meta-level consist of meta-objects which are associated with exceptional classes, and are responsible for invoking the exception handlers transparently.

Consequences. *Handler* Pattern has the following consequences:

- *Uniformity.* Handlers for both local and cooperating exceptions are defined uniformly as methods on exceptional classes.
- *Readability and Maintainability.* This pattern provides explicit separation between normal and error-handling activities, which in turn promotes readability and maintainability.
- *Flexibility.* The multi-level attachment of handlers allows developers to attach handlers to the respective levels of classes, objects and methods.
- *Reusability.* Exceptional class hierarchies allow exceptional subclasses to inherit handlers from their superclasses and, consequently, they allow exceptional code reuse.
- *Lack of Static Checking.* A possible disadvantage of this pattern is that it may not be easy to check statically if handlers have been defined for all specified exceptions.

7.3   The *Exception Handling Strategy* Pattern

Context. Exception occurrences can be detected during execution of a protected region of the application's normal activity. The normal control flow is deviated to the exceptional one and an appropriate handler is searched.

Problem. The software architecture should be organized in a disciplined manner: the components responsible for the deviation of the normal control flow and for the handler search should perform their management activities in a nonintrusive way to the application. The following *forces* arise when dealing with such a problem: (i) exceptions should be propagated explicitly (*Guideline 4*), (ii) the chosen model for continuation of the control flow should be termination since it is more suitable for developing fault-tolerant systems.

Solution. Use the *Reflection* architectural pattern in order to separate classes responsible for the management activities (meta-level) from the ones that implement the normal activities of the application (base level). The base-level defines the application's logic where *normal classes* implement the normal activities. The meta-level consists of meta-objects which search transparently for the exception handlers. Meta-objects are associated with instances of the normal classes, and maintain meta-information concerning the protected regions defined at the base-level. A protected region can be a method, an object, and a class. The MOP is responsible for intercepting method results and switching normal control flow to exceptional one when exceptions are detected, by transferring control to the meta-level. With the available meta-information, meta-objects find the handler that should be executed when an exception occurrence is detected in a given protected region. When the execution of the handlers is concluded successfully, the MOP returns control flow to the application's normal computation according to the termination model. Meta-objects are responsible for controlling the explicit propagation of exceptions (*Guideline 4*).

Consequences. *Exception Handling Strategy* Pattern has the following consequences:

- *Transparency.* The meta-level objects bind transparently the normal activity and corresponding handlers without requiring programmers to use new features to specify protected regions.
- *Readability and Maintainability.* The normal code is not amalgamated with the exceptional code. As a consequence, both normal and exceptional code are easier to read and maintain.
- *Compatibility.* The *Exception Handling Strategy* pattern can be used together with an exception handling strategy implemented in the underlying programming language, and they can complement each other.

7.4   The *Concurrent Exception Handling Action* Pattern

Context. Fault-tolerant software designers should be able to specify concurrent cooperative actions. These actions must be controlled at run-time and their participants have to exit the action synchronously. During the execution of an action, a number of cooperating exceptions can be raised. As a consequence, a service of exception resolution is necessary to determine the cooperating exception which is to be handled by all participants of the action.

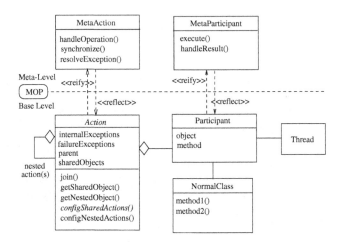

Fig. 6. *Concurrent Exception Handling Action* pattern class diagram [14]

Problem. The software architecture should support the definition of actions. Moreover, a disciplined approach is required in order to separate concerns and minimize dependencies between the application actions and the strategy for concurrent exception handling (i.e. the management mechanisms for synchronization and exception resolution). Some *forces* are associated with this design problem: (i) the definition of actions should be done in a structured manner to avoid an increase in the software's complexity, and (ii) the strategy for concurrent exception handling should be a consistent extension of the general strategy for exception handling.

Solution. Use the *Reflection* architectural pattern for segregating classes responsible for the management mechanisms (meta-level) from the classes which must be derived for defining the concurrent cooperative actions of the application (base-level)(Figure 6). The base-level provides developers with classes for creating the concurrent cooperative actions of their applications; the definition of nested actions is also supported in order to control the system's complexity and allow better organization of both normal and error handling activities of the enclosing action. The MOP itself intercepts and reifies invocations of methods and their results. The meta-level implements the management mechanisms based on reified invocations and results, and on the available meta-information. So, meta-objects are responsible for synchronizing the action participants and perform the exception resolution process.

Consequences. Using this pattern has the following consequences:

- *Uniformity.* The strategy for concurrent exception handling is a consistent extension of the general strategy for exception handling.
- *Transparency and Simplicity.* Management mechanisms for exception handling are performed transparently to the application. Application programmers focus their attention on the identification of concurrent actions.
- *Complexity Control.* This pattern allows programmers to define nested actions.
- *Readability, Reusability and Maintainability.* The application code is not intermingled with invocations of methods responsible for synchronization and exception resolution. As a consequence, it improves readability, which in turn improves reusability and maintainability.

8   Architecture Usage and Implementation

The exception handling model and patterns proposed in this paper have been developed based on our study of a number of exception handling proposals [12, 15], and on our extensive work implementing fault-tolerant object-oriented systems [13,14]. Since our exception handling approach is independent of programming language or exception handling mechanism, a wide range of robust applications developers can employ it. A prototype of our exception handling system was built using the Java programming language, without any changes to the language itself by means of a meta-object protocol called *Guaraná* [20], a flexible MOP developed at the Institute of Computing, UNICAMP, Brazil.

We have been used our exception handling software architecture to implement some experiments such as the *Station Case Study* [2]. This case study is a subsystem of the railway control system that deals with train control and coordination in the vicinity of a station. Trains transport passengers from a source to a destination station. Stations usually have several platforms on which trains can stop (no more than one train on each platform at a time). Trains can execute some join cooperative concurrent action when they stop at the same station together; for example, passengers can change trains during this stop to make their journey faster. We assume that errors caused by faults (for example, a train do not stop) are detected and fault tolerance measures employed to restore normal computation. Sensors check whether trains stopped at this station, and whether they leave the station after the cooperative action has finished. We have used the *Concurrent Exception Handling Action* pattern to design the Station action (and its nested actions) that coordinates the execution of an activity concerned with cooperation between two trains calling at a particular station. In addition, we use the *Handler* pattern to structure the ExceptionalTrain class which implements handlers for the exceptions that can be raised by Station action participants, and the *Exception* pattern to define simple and concurrent (structured) exceptions.

9   Related Work

Dealing with several exceptional conditions at different phases of system development has been recognized as a serious problem which has not received enough attention [1,10]. In fact, related work in this area has been scarce, and most of it associates exception handling only with objects, making no attempt in considering exception handling within software development lifecycle [10]. More recent work which deals with *obstacles* in a goal-driven approach for requirements engineering has provided systematic techniques for identifying failure behaviors in requirements specifications [24]. The work in [10] presents an approach which emphasizes the separation of treatments of requirements-related, design-related, and implementation-related exceptions during the software lifecycle, by specifying the exceptions and their handlers in the context where faults are identified.

10   Conclusions and Ongoing Work

This paper presented a software architecture meant to be simple enough to enable the use of exception handling techniques in the development of dependable software. A software system's quality requirements are largely permitted or restrained by its architecture; so if an appropriate architecture that supports exception handling is chosen since the outset of the design phase, a proper use of exception handling techniques throughout the software development can be obtained. This software architecture: (i) defines the fundamental components related to exception handling, (ii) integrates uniformly both sequential and concurrent exception handling, (iii) is independent of programming language or exception handling mechanism, and (iv) its use can minimize the complexity caused by handling abnormal behavior. We proposed the use of computational reflection to refine the architecture's components, and provide a clear separation of concerns between the exception handling services and the application's functionality. Specific applications can then reuse the exception handling facilities provided by the architectural components, allowing developers focus their attention on the application-dependent functionality. We also introduced a set of exception handling patterns which can be used to simplify the task of creating exception handling mechanisms in order to provide forward error recovery.

The proposed software architecture has the potential to bring exception handling to complex software systems of several sectors, such as manufacturing, communications, defense, transportation, and aerospace, due to its simplicity and ease of implementation. Moreover, our approach allows that a new different exception mechanism be incorporated into a system when the exception mechanism provided by the target language is not suitable for the developer's purposes (we applied this idea with the Java language as described in Section 8). We are also actively investigating the employment of our approach to provide exception handling service for component-based software systems.

Acknowledgments. This work has been supported by CNPq/Brazil under grant No. 141457/2000-7 for Alessandro, and grant No. 351592/97-0 for Cecília. She is also supported by the FINEP "Advanced Information Systems" Project (PRONEX-SAI-7697102200).

References

1. Avizienis, A.: Toward Systematic Design of Fault-Tolerant Systems. Computer 30(4):51–58 (1997)
2. Beder, D., Romanovsky, A., Randel, A., Snow, C., Stroud, R.: An Application of Fault Tolerance Patterns and Coordinated Atomic Actions to a Problem in Railway Scheduling. ACM Operating System Review, 34(4):21–31 (2000)
3. Borgida, A.: Language Features for Flexible Handling of Exceptions in Information Systems. ACM Transactions on Database Systems, 10(4):565–603 (1985)
4. Borgida, A.: Exceptions in Object-Oriented Languages. ACM Sigplan Notices, 21(10):107–119 (1986)
5. Buschmann, F., Meunier, R., Rohnert, H., Sommerlad, P., Stal, M.: A System of Patterns: Patterns-Oriented Software. John Wiley & Sons, (1996)
6. Campbell, R., Randell, B.: Error Recovery in Asynchronous Systems. IEEE Transactions on Software Engineering, 12(8):811-826 (1986)
7. Cristian, F.: Exception Handling and Software Fault Tolerance. IEEE Transactions on Computers, C-31(6):531–540, (1982)
8. Cui, Q., Gannon, J.: Data-Oriented Exception Handling. IEEE Transactions on Software Engineering, 18(5):393–401, (1992)
9. Dony, C.: Exception Handling and Object-Oriented Programming: Towards a Synthesis. ACM Sigplan Notices, 25(10): 322-330, (1990)
10. de Lemos, R., Romanovsky, A.: Exception Handling in the Software Lifecycle. Int. Journal of Computer Systems Science and Engineering, (Accepted in 2000)
11. Gamma, E., Helm, R., Johnson, R., Vlissides, J.: Design Patterns - Elements of Reusable Object-Oriented Software. Addison Wesley Publishing Company, (1995)
12. Garcia, A.: Exception Handling in Concurrent Object-Oriented Software. Master's thesis, Institute of Computing, University of Campinas, Brazil, March (2000)
13. Garcia, A., Beder, D., Rubira, C.: An Exception Handling Mechanism for Developing Dependable Object-Oriented Software Based on a Meta-Level Approach. Proceedings of the 10th IEEE ISSRE, USA, November (1999), 52–61
14. Garcia, A., Beder, D., Rubira, C.: An Exception Handling Software Architecture for Developing Fault-Tolerant Software. Proceedings of the 5th IEEE HASE, USA, November (2000), 311–320
15. Garcia, A., Rubira, C., Romanovsky, A., Xu, J.: A Comparative Study of Exception Handling Mechanisms for Building Dependable Object-Oriented Software. Technical Report CS-TR-714, Comput. Dept., Univ. of Newcastle upon Tyne, (2000)
16. Goodenough, J.: Exception Handling: Issues and a Proposed Notation. Communications of the ACM, 18(12): 683–696, (1975)
17. Liskov, B., Snyder, A.: Exception Handling in CLU. IEEE Transactions on Software Engineering, 5(6):546–558, (1979)
18. Maes, P.: Concepts and Experiments in Computacional Reflection. ACM SIGPLAN Notices, 22(12):147–155, (1987)
19. Moon, D., Weinreb, D.: Signalling and Handling Conditions. LISP Machine Manual, 4th Edition, MIT Artif. Intelligence Lab, Cambridge, Massachussets, (1983)
20. Oliva, A., Buzato, L.: Composition of Meta-Objects in Guaraná. Proceedings of the Workshop on Reflective Programming in C++ and Java, OOPSLA'98, Vancouver, Canada, (1998), 86–90
21. Pitman, K.: Error/Condition Handling. Contribution to WG16, revision 18, Proposals for ISO-LISP. AFNOR, ISO/IEC JTC1/SC 22/WG 16N15, (1988)

22. Shaw, M. and Garlan, D.: Software Architecture - Perspectives on an Emerging Discipline. Prentice Hall, (1996)
23. Sommervile, I.: Software Engineering. Fifth Edition, Addison-Wesley, (1995)
24. van Lamsweerde, A., Letier, E.: Handling Obstacles in Goal-Oriented Requirements Engineering. IEEE Trans. on Software Engineering, 26(10):978–1005, (2000)
25. Yemini, S., Berry, D.: A Modular Verifiable Exception Handling Mechanism. ACM Transactions on Programming Languages and Systems, 7(2):214–243, (1985)

Adapting C++ Exception Handling to an Extended COM Exception Model

Bjørn Egil Hansen[1] and Henrik Fredholm [2]

[1] DNV AS, DNV Software Factory, Veritasveien 1,
1322 Høvik, Norway
Bjorn.Egil.Hansen@dnv.com
[2] Computas AS, Vollsveien 9, P.O.Box 482,
1327 Lysaker, Norway
hf@computas.no

Abstract: This paper describes how correctness and robustness of component-based systems can be improved by categorising exceptions by component state and cause, and handling them accordingly. Further, it is shown how this model is supported in C++ in a COM-based environment, also simplifying the code for exception detection, signalling, and handling.

1   Introduction

The reliability of a software system is to a high degree determined by the reliability of the software components comprising the system [4]. For a software component to be reliable it must be robust and able recover various exceptions or failures that may arise at run-time. Code for exception detection, handling, and signalling often amounts to a substantial portion of the code. This is especially the case in a multi-language environment, mixing different exception models, and requiring transformation between different exception representations.

To allow flexible system configuration and system evolution, e.g. making changes to a component, replacing a component with another, or adding new components, each of the components should have minimum dependency on the other components. Loose coupling between components is also important with respect to exception handling and the mechanisms used. As argued in [2], a termination mechanism mixes well with the information hiding principles underlying data abstraction, and consequently also component based systems. The focus should be on the local transition, on the exceptions that may arise during a state transition and on maintaining a consistent local state of the component. It is the responsibility of the developer of the component to detect, handle, and signal exceptions based on the state of the component, the arguments of the call, and the results from lower-level components.

In software development projects there are always conflicts between different requirements, and the development team has to make trade-offs between time-to-market, functional requirements, and non-functional requirements, like reliability. The resources used on reliability are often scarce, hence it is important to concentrate the

A. Romanovsky et al. (Eds.): Exception Handling, LNCS 2022, pp. 207–216, 2001 effort on those exception situations that contribute to the overall reliability of the system. Whenever reliability is sacrificed for other requirements, the failure situations should be clearly distinguishable from correct behaviour and easily traceable in the code. If the system reliability turns out to be unacceptable it should be possible to increase the overall reliability by improving individual components of the system, i.e. taking control over more of the failure situations.

This paper is based on work done in the BRIX team in DNV IT Solutions. The main purpose of this group is to provide the various application development teams with common solutions to software technical needs. Most BRIX solutions are based on Microsoft's COM technology and C++ as implementation language.

In section 2 the differences between C++ exception handling and COM exception handling are briefly outlined. Section 3 describes the BRIX language independent exception model, which is based on the COM exception model. In section 4 we present how the BRIX exception model is supported at C++ level. Finally, in section 5 we draw some conclusions.

2   COM Exception Handling in C++

COM supports signalling of exceptions [1], but the mechanisms used are different from the throw and catch in C++ [3]. To signal an exception in COM, three different mechanisms are used in combination:

- By convention all interface methods on a COM objects should return a status (an HRESULT), indicating success or exception/failure of the method invocation.
- To pass extra information to the client, COM provides two API functions:
  SetErrorInfo: Used by the COM object (signaller) to pass an exception object containing the extra information to the client.
  GetErrorInfo: Used by the client to obtain the exception object.
- In addition, the COM object must implement the ISupportErrorInfo interface to indicate which interfaces support exceptions. This interface should be used by the client to determine whether or not the result of the GetErrorInfo is reliable.

This obviously increases the burden on a C++ programmer. When implementing a COM object in C++, the programmer must be careful to catch all C++ exceptions and convert them into HRESULTs, possibly augmented with extra information in an exception object.

To detect and handle exceptions from a COM object in a C++ client, the result of each COM-call must be checked specifically by looking at the returned HRESULT. In a naïve implementation of a C++ client this will typically result in an unreadable mix of HRESULT checking of the COM calls and catching of C++ exceptions of internal C++ calls.

There is also a mismatch in the exception models of COM and C++. While we in C++ may specialise exceptions in hierarchies, COM overloads the HRESULT. Thus, the meaning of an HRESULT code very likely will be different for different methods, and the code should not propagate unmodified up through the call stack.

When programming in Visual Basic or Java (on Microsoft's Java VM), the conversion between native exceptions and the HRESULT and the COM exception information object is done automatically by the respective run-time systems. Thus, in these environments the COM exception representation and signalling mechanism are integrated with native exception mechanisms, giving a more transparent programming model. In section 4 we will see how the BRIX Exception System contributes to integration with the C++ exception mechanisms.

3   BRIX Exception Model

A component-based system is comprised of components accessing each other through interfaces. An interface may be defined specifically for a concrete implementation, complete both with respect to standard and exceptional behaviour. However, in COM it is common to have general interfaces allowing a variety of implementations. For a specific implementation there may be resource constraints not anticipated on the specification level, resulting in exceptions outside the specified exceptions.

To achieve flexible configuration and system evolution the BRIX Exception System provides the component developer with mechanisms for detection, handling, and signalling of specified exceptions, as well as mechanisms for detection and signalling of unspecified exceptions. To facilitate this, when focusing on the state transition within one component, we categorise exceptions/failures according to two orthogonal criteria:

- State of the lower-level component after the exception/failure has occurred:
  - *Controlled exception*: The component is in the same consistent state as before the method call.
  - *Uncontrolled exception*: The component is in an undefined and possibly inconsistent state. This corresponds to the notion of failure exceptions in [2].
- Cause of the exception:
  - *Operational exception*: The cause of the exception is outside the control of the component, typically when allocating resources (e.g., memory, files, or network connections) or validating input.
  - *Implementation exception*: The cause of the exception is due to faults in program code.

In table 1 we discuss the four categories of possible exceptional situations, and propose a recommended action and an alternative action as a guide to where to concentrate the exception handling effort.

In the table we see that controlled operational exceptions are the only cases where explicit exception handling is recommended to increase the overall robustness of the system. Using the default BRIX exception mechanisms in this case will lower the robustness of the system, as the exception is transformed to an uncontrolled exception when propagated and most likely will cause the system to abort.

Table 1. Exception categories in the BRIX Exception model. We assume having a higher-level component A calling a method on component B, being our focus, and B calls a method on lower-level component C

	Operational	Implementation
Controlled	*Controlled Operational Exception*: The cause is an operational exception in the lower-level component C. C has recovered to the same state as before the call.	*Controlled Implementation Exception*: The lower-level component C has rejected the call because of a precondition violation, i.e. the exception is caused either by improper use by component B, too strict implementation of the precondition validation, or incomplete interface specification. C has recovered to the same state as before the call.
	Recommended action: If it is a specified exception, mask the exception if possible. Otherwise, recover state and signal a Controlled Operational Exception to higher level component A.	*Recommended action*: Use default mechanism that signals an Uncontrolled Implementation Exception to the higher-level component A. Fix bug at appropriate level.
	Alternative action: Use default mechanism that signals an Uncontrolled Operational Exception to the higher-level component A.	*Alternative action*: If the cause is an incomplete specification or a too strict precondition implementation in C, and neither of these can be changed, component B should be rewritten to avoid the problem.
Uncontrolled	*Uncontrolled Operational Failure*: The failure is due to an operational exception in the lower-level component C which C was not prepared to handle, and C has not been able to recover to a consistent state.	*Uncontrolled Implementation Failure*: The failure is due to an unanticipated exception occurrence in the lower-level component C, resulting in a possibly inconsistent state, invalidating the invariant or post-condition.
	Recommended action: Use default mechanism that signals an Uncontrolled Operational Exception to the higher-level component A. Make C more robust by taking control of the exception.	*Recommended action*: Use default mechanism that signals an Uncontrolled Implementation Exception to the higher-level component A. Fix fault in C.
	Alternative action: If component C cannot be changed, component B or high-level component A should be rewritten to avoid the problem, or more run-time resources should be made available to avoid the problem	*Alternative action*: If component C cannot be changed, component B or high-level component A should be rewritten to avoid the problem.

For the other cases it is generally difficult and time-consuming to handle them in way that increases the robustness of the system. Instead it is recommended to use the default mechanisms to signal an uncontrolled exception to the higher-level component. The cause of the failure should be fixed off-line if required to achieve long term robustness.

Our goal is not to write totally correct programs, but to write partially correct programs [2], that is, programs that either produce the specified result (normal or exceptional) or a confined failure (unspecified exceptions) with respect to a complete specification. Partially correct programs are safe, in the sense that there are no unanticipated inputs (incomplete specification) and no unconfined failures (apparently correct results but actually erroneous with respect to specification). Thus, they will either produce the specified results or obvious failures.

A component may contain implementation faults. The BRIX Exception System contributes to the fault tolerance of the system by distinguishing between uncontrolled and controlled failures. Uncontrolled failures should result in abortion, while controlled failures may be tolerated, because the system is still in a well-defined state.

4   BRIX Support for C++ Exception Handling in COM

The exception handling code itself may be a significant source of errors. It is difficult to test and should be kept as simple as possible. In the following we will show how the BRIX exception mechanisms support detection, handling, and signalling of exceptions according to the categorisation of exceptions in the previous section, in a programming environment as described in section 2.

4.1   Handling C++ Exceptions

Given the specification of a factorial function in example 1, we will start with a naïve implementation and gradually make it more robust and correct. The examples below are based on [2].

Example 1: Specification of factorial. If a pre-condition is not met, the generic E_BX_PRECONDITION should be returned

```
// Calculates factorial of n and assigns the result to
// *pf
// Pre-conditions:
//    n >= 0
//    pf != NULL
// Exceptions:
//    E_OVERFLOW - if n! > max int
HRESULT Fact(int n, int* pf);
```

Firstly, to prevent C++ exceptions from propagating out of the component, two macros are used to enclose the code establishing default try and catch blocks. The macros take care of converting from C++ exceptions to HRESULT. Any exceptions not detected in the program code will be caught and signalled as an uncontrolled implementation exception. Example 2 shows an initial implementation for computing factorials. With respect to the specification in example 1 this implementation may result in either a) an unconfined failure for values of $n<0$ by returning 1 (erroneous result), b) a confined failure if $n!$ is larger than the maximum int value, or c) a confined failure if pf = NULL. Both the confined failures will be returned as uncontrolled implementation exceptions.

Example 2: Initial implementation encapsulating potential C++ exceptions by use of the BX_ENTER_COM and BX_RETURN_COM macros

```
HRESULT Calc::Fact(int n, int* pf)
{
    BX_ENTER_COM(Calc,Fact)

    int k=0,m=1;
    while (k<n) { k++; m*=k; }
    *pf = m;

    BX_RETURN_COM
}
```

We can increase the correctness and robustness of the implementation from example 2 by detecting and signalling a) and c) properly. There is no support for automatic checking of pre-conditions like in Eiffel [5]. However, this can be coded explicitly, as shown in example 3. A pre-condition failure results in a controlled implementation exception; hence, we have eliminated a) and c) and made the program partially correct and more robust.

Example 3: Eliminating failures a) and c) by using the BX_PRECOND macro to check that the input is valid. If the check fails an E_BX_PRECONDITION exception will be signalled, i.e. returned in the HRESULT

```
HRESULT Calc::Fact(int n, int* pf)
{
    BX_ENTER_COM(Calc,Fact)
    BX_PRECOND(n>=0)
    BX_PRECOND(pf!=NULL)
    ...
```

According to the specification E_OVERFLOW should be returned if $n!$ is too large. To take control over this situation we must add explicit detection and handling of the overflow. Example 4 illustrates this, where we have a try-catch block to detect the overflow. In the catch block we use bxhr which is defined by BX_ENTER_COM. This is an instance of BxHResult, which offers a range of functionality for detecting, signalling and handling exceptions. In this example RaiseError throws an exception containing the specified HRESULT value. This exception is caught by BX_RETURN_COM and the E_OVERFLOW is returned to the client. Thus, we have made the code more correct by handling this exception as specified. Also, we have contributed to the overall robustness of the system by eliminating an uncontrolled exception.

Example 4: Controlled overflow as specified

```
...
try
{
   int k=0,m=1;
   while (k<n) { k++; m*=k; }
   *pf = m;
}
catch(...)
{
   bxhr.RaiseError(E_OVERFLOW,...);
}
...
```

In the examples above we have seen how exceptions are detected and signalled using different mechanisms, e.g. precondition checking, explicit raising of exception, and by use of default detection and signalling. All is resulting in a corresponding HRESULT being returned to the client.

4.2   Handling COM Exceptions

In the examples below we will show how to detect, handle and propagate exceptions from lower-level COM components.

To detect, handle, and signal exceptions from a COM component, various mechanisms can be used resulting in different degrees of robustness. BxHResult redefines some of the assignment operators to provide short hand notation for detection and signalling of exceptions. In example 5 we have a class to represent a vector of 10 ints and defining a method to compute the factorial of each of the values and store them in the same vector. Using the |= operator we say that any exceptions returned from the method on the lower-level component will result in propagation of an uncontrolled exception from this component, whether or not the exception was controlled at the lower level. The |= operator propagates the exception by throwing a corresponding C++ exception which is caught by BX_RETURN_COM. If the Fact method in example 5 returns an exception, we may have an intermediate state where some values have been changed to their factorials where as others are unchanged, i.e. the component will be left in an undefined and erroneous state.

Example 5: Propagating an uncontrolled exception by use of the |= operator when not being able to recover to initial well-defined state

```
class Vector
{
   int v[10];
   HRESULT Factorials();
   ...
}
```

```
HRESULT Vector:: Factorials ()
{
    BX_ENTER_COM(Vector, Factorials)

    for (int i=0; i<10; i++)
        bxhr|=pCalc->Fact(v[i],&v[i]);

    BX_RETURN_COM
}
```

To avoid the uncontrolled exception in example 5 we must be able to recover the initial state in case of exceptions. Example 6 shows how this can be done in this simple case by keeping the new values in a temporary array until all the calculations have been done successfully. Thus, if the Fact method signals an exception, our state is still consistent and we should just signal a controlled exception to our caller. This is done by using the &= operator instead of the |= operator, which will transform any controlled exceptions to controlled implementation exceptions. However, if the Fact method signals an uncontrolled exception, as in example 2 and 3, an uncontrolled implementation exception will be signalled from this component. By focusing on the local transition and on keeping a local consistent state, we reduce the number of uncontrolled exception propagating through the system and the likelihood of abortions.

Example 6: Propagating a controlled exception by use of the &= operator

```
HRESULT Vector:: Factorials ()
{
    BX_ENTER_COM(Vector, Factorials)

    int u[10];
    for (int i=0; i<10; i++)
        bxhr&=pCalc->Fact(v[i],&u[i]);

    for (i=0; i<10; i++)
        v[i] = u[i];

    BX_RETURN_COM
}
```

Further, assume that the Factorials specification also states that an E_OVERFLOW exception should be signalled in case of overflows. With respect to this specification, the implementation in example 6 is partially correct and will result in a confined failure in case of overflow. In cases where the state is still consistent and the specified exceptions from the method on lower-level component is the same as for this method, we can use another operator %= to signal the same exception to the higher-level component, as illustrated in example 7. Hence, the implementation will be correct with respect to the overflow exception. However, the %= operator compromises correctness by introducing possible unconfined failures due to overloading of the HRESULT, and its use is not encouraged.

Example 7: Direct propagation of exception from lower-level component using the %= operator

```
. . .
int u[10];
for (int i=0; i<10; i++)
{
    bxhr%=pCalc->Fact(v[i],&u[i]);
}
. . .
```

Examples 5 to 7 show compact detection and signalling of uncontrolled, controlled, and specified exceptions using the redefined operators |=, &=, and %=, respectively, and how we gradually can increase the robustness and correctness of the system by making the local transitions more robust and correct.

In other situations it might be required that the exceptions are masked or at least handled more specifically. Example 8 shows one way this can be done using the redefined ^= operator. Instead of throwing an exception, the results from the call will be kept in bxhr for subsequent handling of the exception. In the case of a time-out, the exception is recovered and the call is retried once. If this fails the exception is propagated using the &= operator. If the first exception was not a time-out exception, the same exception is signalled to the caller. Exceptions can also be handled in the normal C++ way by enclosing a sequence of statements with a try and catch block.

Example 8: Masking/handling exceptions by using the ^= operator

```
. . .
bxhr ^= pSrv->Submit(data);
if (bxhr==E_TIMEOUT)
{  // Retry once
    bxhr.ErrorRecovered();
    bxhr &= pSrv->Submit(data);
}
else if (bxhr!=S_OK)
    bxhr.RaiseError(...);
. . .
```

Other features of the BRIX exception system which have not been emphasised here include checking of intermediate and final states by use of assertions and post-conditions, possibly resulting in uncontrolled implementation failures. Also there is rich support for logging of exceptional events, which may serve various purposes:

simplifies debugging of the system both during development and operation, supports operator/end-user in identifying possible lack of resources (causing operational exceptions).

5   Conclusion

The BRIX Exception System contributes to correctness and robustness in several ways:

- By distinguishing controlled and uncontrolled exceptions, we believe to achieve fault-tolerance both with respect to specification and implementation faults. Also we reduce the number of unconfined failures by having an explicit notion of and support for uncontrolled exceptions. Hence, it will be easier to achieve partial correctness [2].
- By taking control over more failure situations at the component level, we may increase the overall robustness of a system by upgrading or replacing individual components.
- By focusing on the local state and transition, providing a programmed exception handling style using pre/post-conditions and assertions for state validation and mechanisms for tight control of the results from lower-level components. Contrary to [5] all pre/post condition validation has to be done explicitly. However, when handling complex states and transitions, expressing pre/post-condition may be difficult resulting in possible unconfined failures [2], and intermediate checks may be preferable.
- By virtually forcing the developer to decide on the local implications of exceptions occurring for each line of code. Also the BRIX exceptions mechanisms make it simple to implement those decisions by providing default propagation mechanisms and overloaded operators for exception checking.

Acknowledgement. Many thanks to Are F. Tjønn and Johannes Hermanrud who supported both the development and the writing of this paper. Thanks also to Daniel Vatier and Egil P. Andersen for reviewing the paper and to rest of the BRIX team for providing an inspiring working environment.

References

1. Box, D.: Essential COM. Addison Wesley (1998)
2. Cristian, F.: Exception Handling and Tolerance of Software Faults. Chapter 4 in: Lyu, M. (ed.): Software Fault Tolerance. Wiley (1995) 81-107
3. Ellis, M. A., Stroustrup, B.: The Annotated C++ Reference Manual. Addison Wesley (1990)
4. Krishnamurthy, S., Mathur, A.P.: On the Estimation of Reliability of a Software System Using Reliabilities of its Components. 8th Int. Sym. on Software Reliability Engineering (ISSRE '97), November 2-5, 1997 Albuquerque, US
5. Meyer, B.: Object-Oriented Software Construction. Prentice Hall (1988)

Portable Implementation of Continuation Operators in Imperative Languages by Exception Handling

Tatsurou Sekiguchi[1,2], Takahiro Sakamoto[1], and Akinori Yonezawa[1]

[1] Department of Information Science, Faculty of Science, University of Tokyo
[2] PRESTO, Japan Science and Technology Corporation
{cocoa, takas, yonezawa}@is.s.u-tokyo.ac.jp

Abstract. This paper describes a scheme of manipulating (partial) continuations in imperative languages such as Java and C++ in a portable manner, where the *portability* means that this scheme does not depend on structure of the native stack frame nor implementation of virtual machines and runtime systems. Exception handling plays a significant role in this scheme to reduce overheads. The scheme is based on program transformation, but in contrast to CPS transformation, our scheme preserves the call graph of the original program. This scheme has two important applications: *transparent migration* in mobile computation and *checkpointing* in a highly reliable system. The former technology enables running computations to move to a remote computer, while the latter one enables running computations to be saved into storages.

1   Introduction

A situation often occurs that execution states of a running program have to be encoded into a data structure. Checkpointing [6] is a technique that improves reliability of a system by saving execution states of a running program periodically. In the context of mobile computation [2], there is a form of computation migration called *transparent migration* [13] or *strong mobility* [4], which means that the entire execution state of a running program including the call stack and (part of) the heap image are preserved on migration. During a transparent migration process, the execution states of a program are saved into a data structure, the data structure is transmitted to a destination host over the network, and finally execution states are reconstructed at that host from the data structure.

It is not difficult to capture and recover the call stack when a program language has call/cc (call with current continuation) primitive. Even in imperative languages, the capability of storing execution states including the call stack has often been implemented by compiler support and/or by runtime support. EmacsLisp, SmallTalk and some implementation of Standard ML (SML/NJ) have a primitive that dumps the execution image into a local disk.

This paper reports a completely different approach based on program transformation. This scheme is portable in the sense that it does not depend on

A. Romanovsky et al. (Eds.): Exception Handling, LNCS 2022, pp. 217–233, 2001.

structure of native stack frames nor implementation of virtual machines and runtime systems. An existing system therefore does not need to be extended to capture and restore execution states. This scheme has been developed mainly through the study on implementation of transparent migration on Java because Java allows Java programs to manipulate stack frames only in a restricted form. Exception handling plays a significant role in this scheme to reduce overheads.

The rest of this paper is organized as follows. Sect. 2 introduces operators manipulating continuations to clarify what is implemented by the scheme described in this paper. Sect. 3 describes how continuation operators are implemented by using an exception handling mechanism. Sect. 4 shows several applications. Sect. 5 discusses difficulties and limitations in the technique. In Sect. 6, we compare our technique with related work. Sect. 7 summarizes this work.

2   Partial Continuations

This section introduces a simple calculus of control [14] that was devised through development of SML/NJ. This calculus provides two *tagged* operators for manipulating partial continuations, which are almost analogous to Danvy's **shift** and **reset** [5], and Felleisen's $\mathcal{F}$ and **prompt** [9]. Our program transformation scheme essentially implements those operators for partial continuations in imperative languages.

This calculus is an extension of a call-by-value lambda calculus, and its semantics is defined in the style of structured operational semantics. A polymorphic type system is provided for the calculus. In this paper, however, we focus only on its operators for partial continuations. The syntax of these operators are defined as follows:

> cupto p as x in e capturing the functional continuation
> set p in e delimiting the effect of cupto

where p, e and x are metavariables that denote a *prompt*, an *expression* and a *variable*, respectively. [1] A prompt is a special constant, which is actually a tag that determines which **set** and **cupto** expressions are matched. The **cupto** operator captures the functional continuation up to the innermost **set** expression with the same prompt. The captured continuation is bound to variable x, and expression e is evaluated with this extended environment. The **set** expression delimits the effect of capturing a continuation. The outer context of the **set** operator is thus not captured. In contrast, **call/cc** (call with current continuation) operator in Scheme always captures the full continuation.

The evaluation rule is defined formally as follows:

$$\text{set } p \text{ in } E[\text{cupto } p \text{ as } x \text{ in } e] \longrightarrow (\lambda x.e)(\lambda y.E[y])$$

where E is an evaluation context in which the hole is not in the scope of a **set** expression with prompt p, and y is a fresh variable. An evaluation context [10] is

---

[1] Strictly speaking, there is a slight difference from the original operators. The set of valid expressions are restricted for our convenience.

an expression with a single special constant called *hole*. The position of the hole in an evaluation context is syntactically defined so that it designates the expression to be evaluated next, i.e. the redex of the evaluation context. We denote by $E[e]$ the result of replacing the hole in E with e, which implies that e is the redex of expression $E[e]$. In this evaluation rule, E represents the continuation of cupto expression up to the set expression. The continuation becomes $\lambda y.E[y]$ by the eta conversion. In the righthand side, e will be evaluated with an environment where the continuation is bound to x.

Various control operators can be implemented by composing these primitive control operators. Ref. [14] provides examples of implementation of call/cc, exception handling, and coroutines.

The notion of partial continuations was partly implemented in early programming languages such as PL/I and Mesa [17], where execution can restart at the instruction following the one that raised an exception when the exception is captured by an exception handler. In addition, a model of exception handling is proposed [8] in which resumption contexts are first class objects and are modifiable. Our scheme can be used to implement such an exception handling mechanism on imperative languages in a portable manner.

3   Emulating Continuations

This section describes how the control operators in Sect. 2 are implemented in imperative languages such as C++ and Java. Our scheme of implementation does not need to manipulate stack frames, but the overheads are quite low due to exception handling mechanism. Our scheme is based on program transformation. In contrast to the CPS transformation, however, a code transformed by our scheme preserves the original call graph (although additional method invocations are inserted to maintain continuation operation). A CPS transformed program easily overflows the call stack if the base language is a typical imperative language. In this section, we suppose the target language to be Java bytecode because it is suitable for explaining the idea of our program transformation. Java virtual machine forbids a stack manipulation by Java bytecode itself because of concern for security. A program in Java bytecode cannot inspect nor modify stack frames. These facts obviously show that the scheme is portable and widely applicable to various imperative languages.

The transformer takes a program in an imperative language with the continuation operators as input, and produces an equivalent program in the base language. Moreover, the transformation is on per-method basis, i.e. from a method in the source program, a method and a class are created. This created class represents the execution states of the method. A program is transformed so that it explicitly manages its execution states. A captured continuation is a standard data structure in the base language, which implies that one can save and modify it, moreover, it is transmittable to a remote host. Though the transformation is implemented by using an exception handling mechanism, it does not prevent use of exception handling in a source program.

The transformation consists of two different sub-transformations: one for saving execution states and a resumption point, and one for restoring execution states. The transformation for saving execution states is described in Sect. 3.3, while the one for restoring is described in Sect. 3.4. Actually, the effects of two transformations are mingled in a transformed code.

Since a program is transformed and additional fragments are inserted to the original program, it incurs slowdown of *ordinary* execution (note that the part *not* relating to continuation operation also slows down). In addition, our scheme changes method signatures. An extra parameter is inserted to each method to pass a state object (this will be explained in Sect. 3.4).

```
public class Fib {
    public static void fib( int v1 ) {
        if ( v1 <= 1 )
            return 1;
        else {
            int v2 = fib (v1 - 2);
            return v2 + fib (v1 - 1);
        }
    }
}
```

Fig. 1. A pseudo code of Fibonacci function.

We use Fibonacci function in Fig. 1 to illustrate the transformation throughout this section. For readability, we use a Java-like pseudo code to denote a program, but in reality it consists of Java bytecodes.

3.1   Bytecode Analysis

To transform a bytecode program, we need information on a set of all *valid* frame variables (a kind of registers) and entries in the operand stack for each program point. A variable or an entry is valid if a value on it is available for every possible control flow. Types of frame variables and entries in the operand stack are also necessary. In addition, a transformed code must pass a Java bytecode verifier if the original code passes it. To obtain such necessary information on bytecode, bytecode analysis must be performed before transformation.

Our bytecode transformer requires exactly the same information as that for bytecode verification [15]. We had adopted type systems for Java bytecode verification to keep information on bytecode. Our transformer transforms bytecode programs based on this information. We use the type system of Stata and Abadi [22,23], and that of Freund and Mitchell [11]. Stata's type system provides information on types of frame variables and the operand stack. In addition, bytecode subroutines can be described. On the other hand, Freund's type system focuses on uninitialized values, that are fresh objects whose constructors are not invoked yet. An uninitialized value exists only for a brief period in ordinary execution since a constructor of an object is always invoked as soon as it is created, but it can be a source of type system violation [11].

If a bytecode is well-typed in their type systems, it tells that the bytecode program is verifiable. The type reconstruction problem is to find an appropriate type judgment for a given program (method). It is actually a verification algorithm itself. We have implemented a type reconstruction algorithm for the type systems although we had to extend them to the full set of Java bytecode except bytecode subroutine facility. As will be mentioned in Sect. 5, it is difficult to transform a bytecode subroutine into an efficient code. Bytecode subroutines are not supported in our current implementation.

```
public class ST_Fib_fib extends StateObject {
    public int      EntryPoint;
    public int[]    ArrayI;
    public long[]   ArrayL;
    public float[]  ArrayF;
    public double[] ArrayD;
    public Object[] ArrayA;

    public void     Resume() {
        Fib.fib( this, 0 );
    }
}
```

Fig. 2. A state class.

3.2 State Class

Our transformation algorithm defines a state class for each method. An execution state of a method is stored into an instance of the state class. Fig. 2 shows an example of a state class, where EntryPoint designates a resumption point, and variables of array types keep frame variable values and operand stack values. In addition, special values that manage state capture and restoration are also stored into those arrays. These special values include the state object for the current method, the state object for the caller of the current method, and a special exception that notifies migration. The size of each array is determined statically when a method is analyzed. Every state class is a subclass of a common super class (StateObject). Every state class has method Resume, which resumes the execution stored in a state object. This will be explained in Sect. 3.4.

3.3 Capturing a Continuation

Capturing a continuation consists of the following operations:

1. Saving all frame variable values and operand stack values in a method,
2. Saving a resumption point information in a method, and
3. Repeating the above for each method.

These operations essentially yield a logical copy of the stack. In case of the Java bytecode language, frame variables include all parameters of a method, and a resumption point is actually a program counter. In case of C++ and Java source-to-source transformation, operand stack values are not saved. Instead, temporary variables are introduced. When we have to save an execution state of a *partially* evaluated expression, that expression is split so that intermediate values can be saved. Consider the following piece of code:

```
x = foo() + bar();
```

To save the result of foo, the above expression is split in advance as follows:

```
tmp = foo();
x = tmp + bar();
```

The transformation algorithm inserts the following code fragments to a method:

- An exception handler for each method invocation. An occurrence of state capturing is notified by a special exception. The exception handler is responsible for saving an execution state. The program counter to be saved is known since an exception handler is unique for each resumption point. The set of valid frame variables and their types are found by the bytecode analysis described in Sect. 3.1.
- Instructions for saving valid entries on the operand stack into frame variables. Entries on the operand stack are defined to be discarded when an exception is thrown, which means that their values cannot be fetched from an exception handler. The basic idea for saving values on the operand stack is to make their copies in frame variables before the contents of entries on the operand stack are set. The valid entries on the operand stack are also found by the bytecode analysis. This care is needed only in case of Java bytecode.

When a continuation is captured by invoking a cupto operator, a special exception is thrown. If a method captures the exception, the method stores its execution state in a newly created state object defined for each method, and then it propagates the exception to the caller of the method. This process is repeated until the exception reaches a set operator with the same prompt.

Fig. 3 shows a result of transforming the method in Fig. 1 for state capturing. An exception handler that captures exception Notify is inserted for each method invocation. In the exception handlers, a resumption point and local variables are saved into a created state object. Since variable v2 is undefined at the first recursive invocation of method fib, The value of v2 is not saved in the first exception handler. The state object is stored in the exception object by e.append (s). Finally, the exception is re-thrown.

```
public static void fib( int v1 ) throws Notify {
    if ( v1 <= 1 )
        return 1;
    else {
        int v2;
        try {
            v2 = fib (v1 - 2);
        } catch ( Notify e ) {
            ST_Fib_fib s = new ST_Fib_fib();
            s.EntryPoint = 1;
            s.v1 = v1;
            e.append (s);
            throw e;
        }
        try {
            return v2 + fib (v1 - 1);
        } catch ( Notify e ) {
            ST_Fib_fib s = new ST_Fib_fib();
            s.EntryPoint = 2;
            s.v1 = v1;
            s.v2 = v2;
            e.append (s);
            throw e;
        }
    }
}
```

Fig. 3. A pseudo code transformed for state capturing.

3.4   Invoking a Continuation

Invoking a continuation consists of the following operations:

1. Restoring all frame variable values and operand stack values in a method,
2. Transferring the control to the resumption point in a method,
3. Reconstructing dynamic extents of active exception handlers, and
4. Reconstructing the call stack.

The execution states of a method are reconstructed from a state object. The call stack is reconstructed by calling the methods in the order in which they were invoked. Each method is transformed in advance so that it can restore its execution state from a state object. When a method is called with a state object as an extra parameter, it restores all the values of frame variables and the operand stack, and then it continues execution from the resumption point. When the extra parameter for a method is null, it indicates ordinary execution.

The transformation algorithm inserts the following code fragments to a method:

– Instructions that put a state object as an extra parameter for a method invocation instruction.
– Instructions, at the head of the method, that restore all valid frame variables and all valid entries on the operand stack. When the execution state of a method is restored, a state object is passed to the method as an extra parameter. The inserted code restores all valid frame variables and all entries on the operand stack at the resumption point. After restoring the frame variables and entries on the operand stack, the control is transferred to the resumption point.

```
public static void fib( StateObject s, int v1 ) {
    int v2;
    ST_Fib_fib c = null;
    if ( s != null ) {
        c = (ST_Fib_fib)s.callee;
        switch (s.EntryPoint) {
            case 1:   v1 = c.v1;
                      goto l1;
            default:  v1 = c.v1;
                      v2 = c.v2;
                      goto l2;
        }
    }
    if ( v1 <= 1 )
        return 1;
    else {
     l1:
        v2 = fib( c, v1 - 2 );
        c = null;
     l2:
        return v2 + fib( c, v1 - 1 );
    }
}
```

Fig. 4. A pseudo code transformed for state restoration.

Fig. 4 shows a result of transforming the method in Fig. 1 for state restoration. A parameter is added to pass a state object. When the extra parameter is null, the original body of the method is executed. Otherwise, the execution state is reconstructed from the state object. Variable c holds the state object of this method. It has a valid value only during state restoration. All the local variable values are restored from the state object, and then the control is transferred to the resumption point. Remember that this is actually a Java bytecode. We can therefore use goto instructions. A transformer for C++ can also use goto instructions. A source code transformer for Java uses another technique for control transfer [19]. Note that the scope of an exception handler is automatically recovered because restoring the execution state of a callee method is done by invoking the callee. This implies that the instruction that resumes the callee is the same instruction that invokes the callee in ordinary execution, which takes place in the scope of an exception handler.

Now we can see how `Resume` method in Fig. 2 resumes the execution. The first parameter (`this`) is a state object itself, and the second parameter is dummy since it is not used.

```
public interface Receiver {
       public void Receive( StateObject s ) throws Exception;
}
```

Fig. 5. An interface that receives a captured continuation.

3.5 The cupto and set Operators

Now we can explain how the operators manipulating partial continuations in Sect. 2 are implemented by using the techniques just shown. As mentioned in Sect. 3.3, we use a special exception (`Notify`) to notify the occurrence of state capturing. We define a subclass of class `Notify` for each occurrence of a prompt in the operators for continuations. A prompt corresponds to a subclass of class `Notify`.

Since Java does not have a way to extend an environment, we modify the semantics of the `cupto` operator so that it fits in Java. The abstract syntax of the `cupto` operator is as follows:

$$\text{cupto } p \text{ as } x \text{ in } e$$

When the above expression is evaluated, the functional continuation up to the innermost `set` expression with the same prompt is captured and bound to variable x. Then expression e is evaluated in the extended environment. Instead, we restrict the form of e to an object that implements interface `Receiver` in Fig. 5. The interface has method `Receive`, which takes an instance of a state class. When a continuation is captured, it is passed to e by invoking method `Receive` with the continuation. Variable x is thus not used. In sum, the new operator looks like:

$$\text{cupto } p \text{ in } o$$

where o denotes an object that implements interface `Receiver`.

This operator is implemented just as follows:

```
throw new p(o);
```

where p is a class name that corresponds to prompt p, and o is a variable that refers to object o. Object o is stored in the exception object in a constructor of p. This statement initiates the state capture process by throwing exception p.

On the other hand, the set operator, set p in e, is translated as follows:

```
try {
    e
} catch ( p x ) {
    Receiver r = x.getReceiver();
    StateObject s = x.getStateObject();
    r.Receive (s);
}
```

The receiver object and all the state objects are stored in the exception object. Method getStateObject returns the bottom of all state objects.

Finally, invoking a continuation is achieved by calling method Resume (shown in Fig. 2) in a state object.

3.6   Experimental Results

This section reports performance results on our implementation of program transformers. We measured execution efficiency, code size growth, and elapsed time of program transformation.

Table 1. Comparison in execution efficiency.

	elapsed time (ms)					
		with JIT			without JIT	
program	original	JavaGo	JavaGoX	original	JavaGo	JavaGoX
fib(30)	111	263 (+137%)	173 (+56%)	870	2553 (+193%)	1516 (+74%)
qsort(400000)	214	279 (+30%)	248 (+16%)	2072	2856 (+38%)	2597 (+25%)
nqueen(12)	1523	2348 (+54%)	1731 (+14%)	30473	36470 (+20%)	30843 (+1.2%)
_201_compress	33685	61629 (+83%)	40610 (+21%)	365661	713936 (+95%)	433439 (+19%)

(JDK 1.2.2, Intel Celeron(TM) Processor 500MHz)

	elapsed time (sec)	
program	original	transformed
fib(40)	40.0	36.1 (−10%)
qsort(4000)	36.4	37.0 (+2%)
multimat	14.0	15.2 (+9%)
bintree	3.4	3.9 (+15%)

(egcs-2.91.66, UltraSPARC Processor 168MHz)

Execution Efficiency of Transformed Programs Three kinds of code are evaluated: the original program, that transformed at source code level, and that transformed at bytecode level. The elapsed times of transformed programs were measured and compared. We use three transformers: JavaGo [19] as a Java source code transformer, JavaGoX [18] as a Java bytecode transformer, and a source code transformer for C++. The purpose of this experiment is to identify the overheads induced by inserted code fragments to the original programs. Captured continuations are thus not invoked during the execution of benchmark programs. The results are shown in Table 1 where _201_compress is a benchmark program included in SpecJVM98, multimat is an integer matrix multiply whose size is 200 × 200, and bintree is an application that inserts a random integer into a binary tree 100000 times.

Most part of the overheads in Java applications is due to the code fragments for saving the operand stack at resumption points. The overheads of the Fibonacci method is rather high because the method does almost nothing but invokes the method itself recursively. When the body of a method are so small, the relative overheads of inserted code fragments tend to be high. In this experiment, the overheads induced by our bytecode transformation are always less than those induced by JavaGo. For quick sort and N-queen programs, the overheads were approximately 15% of the original programs when the applications were executed with just-in-time compilation.

Our scheme works with C++ better than Java. The overheads due to source code transformation are less than those of Java bytecode transformation.

Table 2. Comparison in bytecode size.

	bytecode size (in bytes)		
program	original	JavaGo	JavaGoX
fib	276	884 (3.2 times)	891 (3.2 times)
qsort	383	1177 (3.1 times)	1253 (3.3 times)
nqueen	393	1146 (2.9 times)	976 (2.5 times)
_201_compress	13895	22029 (1.6 times)	18171 (1.3 times)

Growth in Bytecode Size of Transformed Programs The growth in bytecode size due to program transformations is shown in Table 2. The growth rates for these programs are approximately three times. We think that these results would be the worst case because the relative overheads of inserted code fragments tend to be high when an original method is small. Actually, growth rate falls down in a large application (_201_compress).

The size of bytecode produced by the bytecode transformer is very similar to the size of bytecode produced in the source code transformation. But their characteristics are quite different each other. In case of JavaGo, the size of transformed bytecode is proportional to square of the deepest depth of loops. In contrast, the size of bytecode transformed at bytecode level is proportional to the number of resumption points and valid values.

Table 3. Elapsed time for analysis and transformation.

	elapsed time per method (ms)	
program	analysis	transformation
fib	235	79
qsort	285	81
nqueen	267	80
_201_compress	150	59

Elapsed Time of Program Transformation The elapsed time for analysis and transformation of the bytecode transformer is shown in Table 3. In every case, analysis takes more time than transformation. However, the total elapsed time is short. We believe that these figures show our bytecode transformer is practical enough. The elapsed time for _201_compress is obviously shorter than those of the other applications. The reason is that _201_compress has many methods. The other applications are quite small one. They have only one or a few methods. In case of _201_compress, the memory cache can work effectively.

4   Application

We point out that our scheme for continuation manipulation based on program transformation finds at least two applications.

4.1   Mobile Computation

Mobile computation is a promising programming paradigm for network-oriented applications where running computations roam over the network. Various kinds of applications are proposed such as electric commerce, auction, automatic information retrieval, workflow management and automatic installation.

To move a program execution to a remote host, the execution states of a thread must be saved and be restored. It is, however, difficult for a Java program to manipulate the stack because the Java security policy forbids it. Two different approaches have been proposed for realizing transparent thread migration in Java: virtual machine extension [21] and program transformation schemes [1,12,18,19,26]. Migration is called *transparent* [13] or *strong* [4] if a program execution is resumed at a destination site with exactly the same execution state as that of the migration time. The relationship between partial continuation and transparent thread migration was first pointed out by Watanabe [28]. In the program transformation schemes, a thread migration is accomplished by three steps:

- The execution states of a target thread are saved into a machine-independent data structure at the departure site. The thread terminates itself when the migration succeeds.

- The data structure representing the execution states of a target thread is transmitted through the network to the destination site.
- A new thread is created at the destination. Equivalent execution states of the target thread are reconstructed for the new thread.

The above entire process can be implemented by using only standard mechanisms of Java.

4.2   Checkpointing

Checkpointing [6] is a technique that makes a system more reliable by saving its execution states into a local disk periodically. When a system fails for some reason, the system states can be recovered from the last saved system image. A source code transformer for portable checkpointing is developed [24,25]. The idea is analogous to the case of mobile computation. Instead of sending encoded execution states to a remote computer, they are saved into a local disk.

5   Limitations

This section discusses the limitations of our scheme due to program transformation and Java proper problems.

5.1   Limitations due to Program Transformation

To save a continuation, all methods associated to the continuation must be transformed in advance. This implies that if the call stack includes stack frames of non-transformed methods, that part of the execution states cannot be saved. This situation often occurs in a program using graphical user interface since it often needs callback methods. Callback methods are invoked by a runtime system.

In our program transformation scheme, a continuation can be captured by the thread that will execute the continuation. A thread cannot make another thread capture a continuation in an efficient manner. This strongly restricts a way programs migrate in mobile computation. When a program execution that involves multiple threads is migrated to a remote host, we want a thread to move the other threads. But an efficient way of moving a set of threads by a particular thread has not been clear. In other words, subjective move [3] can be implemented in the way described in this paper, but objective move cannot be.

When a continuation is invoked, stack frames are reconstructed from state objects. This implies that values on the stack can be on different addresses from the original addresses when they were captured. When an object is allocated on the stack in C++, special care must be taken. For instance, the programmer should not derefer the address of that object since it changes when a continuation is invoked. Ramkumar gives a partial solution for this problem [25].

5.2   Java Proper Problems

It is difficult to save the state of bytecode subroutines in an efficient way since a return address of a bytecode subroutine cannot be saved into an object under the restriction of a Java bytecode verifier.

It is difficult to save the execution states in a class initializer because the programmer cannot call a class initializer. It is invoked by a runtime system when a class is loaded.

Locking is lost when a continuation is captured though locking is correctly recovered after state restoration. When a lock is acquired by a synchronized statement or a synchronized method, it will be released by an exception notifying state capturing.

6   Related Work

Implementation technique of partial continuations based on program transformation was studied to implement a Prolog system on the C language [16]. The notion of partial continuations is useful to implement the cut and delay primitives in Prolog: the former causes *backtracking* and the latter *freezes* computation of the proof of a goal until a particular variable is instantiated. Recently, the implementation technique has received much attention again and been developed through the study on implementation of transparent migration on Java. Java allows Java programs to manipulate stack frames only in a restricted form. Program transformation is known as the only way by which transparent migration is accomplished without extending virtual machines. The relationship between partial continuation and transparent thread migration was pointed out by Watanabe [28] and Sekiguchi [20]. Fünfrocken [12] pointed out that an exception handling mechanism could be used for notifying occurrence of state capturing with low costs. He developed a scheme of transparent migration for standard Java, but his scheme had difficulties in resumption of control in a compound statement. These difficulties were eliminated based on the idea of unfolding [1,19]. All these schemes were based on source code level transformation. Then a scheme based on bytecode transformation was devised [18,27].

The technique has been also developed for C and C++. Arachne threads system [7] is a distributed system in which a thread can be migrated to a remote host. It is also based on source-to-source transformation, but the overheads on normal execution in the system are more than 100% since every access to a local variable always incurs memory access. Porch [24] is a source code transformer for checkpointing. It shares a large part of our scheme, but it does not use exception handling to roll back the call stack since it is for the C language. Taga [26] developed a thread migration scheme based on source code transformation. It also exploits the exception handling mechanism to roll back the call stack.

The overheads due to the program transformation described in this paper can be reduced by the technique by Abe [1] and Taga [26]. The code fragments inserted for state restoration are needed only when execution states are reconstructed. When a method is transformed, their scheme generates two versions:

one is fully transformed and the other is transformed only for state capturing. In ordinary execution, only the latter methods are used.

7 Summary

We have shown a scheme by which operators for partial continuations can be implemented on imperative languages such as C++ and Java. It implies that continuation operators such as `call/cc` can be implemented on C++ and Java. This scheme is so portable that it does not need the knowledge of native stack frames nor runtime systems. It is based on program transformation, yet overheads on execution performance are quite low due to an exception handling mechanism. We have actually implemented transformers for Java [18,19] and C++ [26], and several benchmark measurements are reported in Sect. 3.6.

The study on this technique is not completed yet as we show several limitations in Sect. 5. Further work is needed to eliminate those limitations.

References

1. Hirotake Abe, Yuuji Ichisugi, and Kazuhiko Kato. An Implementation Scheme of Mobile Threads with a Source Code Translation Technique in Java. In *Proceedings of Summer United Workshops on Parallel, Distributed and Cooperative Processing*, July 1999. (in Japanese).
2. Luca Cardelli. Mobile Computation. In *Mobile Object System: Towards the Programmable Internet*, volume 1222 of *Lecture Notes in Computer Science*, pages 3–6. Springer-Verlag, April 1997.
3. Luca Cardelli and Andrew D. Gordon. Mobile Ambients. In Maurice Nivat, editor, *First International Conference on Foundations of Software Science and Computational Structures*, volume 1378 of *Lecture Notes in Computer Science*, pages 140–155. Springer-Verlag, 1998.
4. Gianpaolo Cugola, Carlo Ghezzi, Gian Pietro Picco, and Giovanni Vigna. Analyzing Mobile Code Languages. In *Mobile Object System: Towards the Programmable Internet*, volume 1222 of *Lecture Notes in Computer Science*, pages 93–109, April 1996.
5. Olivier Danvy and Andrzej Filinski. Abstracting Control. In *Proceedings of the 1990 ACM Conference on Lisp and Functional Programming*, pages 151–160, 1990.
6. Geert Deconinck, Johan Vounckx, Rudi Cuyvers, and Rudy Lauwereins. Survey of Checkpointing and Rollback Techniques. Technical report, ESAT-ACCA Laboratory, Katholieke Universiteit Leuven, Belgium, June 1993. O3.1.8 and O3.1.12.
7. Bozhidar Dimitrov and Vernon Rego. Arachne: A Portable Threads System Supporting Migrant Threads on Heterogeneous Network Farms. In *Proceedings of IEEE Parallel and Distributed Systems*, volume 9(5), pages 459–469, 1998.
8. Christophe Dony. Improving Exception Handling with Object-Oriented Programming. In *Proceedings of the 14th IEEE computer software and application conference COMPSAC'90*, pages 36–42, November 1990.
9. Matthias Felleisen. The Theory and Practice of First-Class Prompts. In *Conference Record of the Fifteenth Annual ACM Symposium on Principles of Programming Languages*, pages 180–190, 1988.

10. Matthias Felleisen, Daniel P. Friedman, Eugene Kohlbecker, and Bruce Duba. A Syntactic Theory of Sequential Control. In *Theoretical Computer Science*, volume 52, pages 205–237, 1987.

11. S.N. Freund and J.C. Mitchell. A Type System for Object Initialization in the Java Bytecode Language. *ACM Transaction on Programming Languages and Systems*, 21(6):1196–1250, November 1999.

12. Stefan Fünfrocken. Transparent Migration of Java-Based Mobile Agents. In *MA'98 Mobile Agents*, volume 1477 of *Lecture Notes in Computer Science*, pages 26–37. Springer-Verlag, 1998.

13. Robert S. Gray. Agent Tcl: A Transportable Agent System. In *Proceedings of the CIKM Workshop on Intelligent Information Agents, Fourth International Conference on Information and Knowledge Management*, 1995.

14. Carl A. Gunter, Didier Rémy, and Jon G. Riecke. A Generalization of Exceptions and Control in ML-like Languages. In *Conference Record of FPCA'95 SIGPLAN-SIGARCH-WG2.8 Conference on Functional Programming Languages and Computer Architecture*, pages 12–23, June 1995.

15. Tim Lindholm and Frank Yellin. *The Java Virtual Machine Specification Second Edition*. Addison-Wesley, 1999.

16. Vincenzo Loia and Michel Quaggetto. High-level Management of Computation History for the Design and Implementation of a Prolog System. *Software – Practice and Experience*, 23(2):119–150, February 1993.

17. J. G. Mitchell and W. Maybury. *Mesa language manual*. Xerox PARC, April 1979. CSL-79-3.

18. Takahiro Sakamoto, Tatsurou Sekiguchi, and Akinori Yonezawa. Bytecode Transformation for Portable Thread Migration in Java. In *Proceedings of the Joint Symposium on Agent Systems and Applications / Mobile Agents (ASA/MA)*, pages 16–28, September 2000.

19. Tatsurou Sekiguchi, Hidehiko Masuhara, and Akinori Yonezawa. A Simple Extension of Java Language for Controllable Transparent Migration and its Portable Implementation. In *Coordination Languages and Models*, volume 1594 of *Lecture Notes in Computer Science*, pages 211–226. Springer-Verlag, April 1999.

20. Tatsurou Sekiguchi and Akinori Yonezawa. A Calculus with Code Mobility. In H. Bowman and J. Derrick, editors, *Proceedings of Second IFIP International Conference on Formal Methods for Open Object-based Distributed Systems*, pages 21–36. Chapman & Hall, 1997.

21. Kazuyuki Shudo. Thread Migration on Java Environment. Master's thesis, University of Waseda, 1997.

22. Raymie Stata and Martín Abadi. A Type System for Java Bytecode Subroutines. SRC Research Report 158, Digital Systems Research Center, June 1998.

23. Raymie Stata and Martín Abadi. A Type System for Java Bytecode Subroutines. In *Conference Record of POPL'98: 25th ACM SIGPLAN-SIGACT Symposium on Principles of Programming Languages*, pages 149–160, 1998.

24. Volker Strumpen and Balkrishna Ramkumar. Portable Checkpointing and Recovery in Heterogeneous Environments. Technical report, University of Iowa, 1996. TR-96.6.1.

25. Volker Strumpen and Balkrishna Ramkumar. Portable Checkpointing for Heterogeneous Architectures. In *Fault-Tolerant Parallel and Distributed Systems*, chapter 4, pages 73–92. Kluwer Academic Press, 1998.

26. Nayuta Taga, Tatsurou Sekiguchi, and Akinori Yonezawa. An Extension of C++ that Supports Thread Migration with Little Loss of Normal Execution Efficiency.

In *Proceedings of Summer United Workshops on Parallel, Distributed and Cooperative Processing*, July 1999. (in Japanese).

27. Eddy Truyen, Bert Robben, Bart Vanhaute, Tim Coninx, Wouter Joosen, and Pieere Verbaeten. Portable Support for Transparent Thread Migration in Java. In *Proceedings of the Joint Symposium on Agent Systems and Applications / Mobile Agents (ASA/MA)*, pages 29–43, September 2000.

28. Takuo Watanabe. Mobile Code Description using Partial Continuations: Definition and Operational Semantics. In *Proceedings of WOOC'97*, 1997.

Exception Handling in Object-Oriented Databases

Elisa Bertino[1], Giovanna Guerrini[2], and Isabella Merlo[1]

[1] Dipartimento di Scienze dell'Informazione
Università degli Studi di Milano
Via Comelico 39/41 - I20135 Milano, Italy
{bertino,merloisa}@dsi.unimi.it
[2] Dipartimento di Informatica e Scienze dell'Informazione
Università di Genova
Via Dodecaneso 35 - I16146 Genova, Italy
guerrini@disi.unige.it

Abstract. Exceptions in database systems can be used for two different purposes: to store data not conforming to the description provided
by the database schema, that is, exceptional data; and to handle exceptional situations during processing, that is, the usual execution exceptions of programming languages. In this paper we survey approaches to
both kinds of exceptions in OODBMSs, we discuss some uses of exceptions peculiar to databases, and relate exceptions with triggers, a typical
database functionality.

1   Introduction

The object-oriented paradigm played and is still playing a crucial role in over-
coming the well known problem of impedance mismatch between databases and
programming languages [5]. A relevant feature of (object-oriented) programming
languages is represented by *exception* mechanisms, which represent a powerful
mechanism for handling error or anomalous situations.

Exceptions can be used in databases according to two different perspectives:
execution exceptions and data exceptions. Execution exceptions are the classical
exceptions of programming languages. Their support in a database context requires a proper integration with the *transaction* mechanism typical of DBMSs.
Operations on the database are executed in atomic units that are either successfully terminated (*committed*) or, in case any problems occur, not executed
at all (*aborted*). Data exceptions, by contrast, refer to the possibility of storing
exceptional data, that is, data that do not fully conform to the general structure
of data described by the database schema. Support for exceptional data clearly
enhances the flexibility of the database system, but it also introduces some additional problems, some of which can be managed through the use of execution
exceptions.

A typical database notion that is obviously related to exceptions is moreover
the notion of *integrity constraint*. An integrity constraint is a property that

A. Romanovsky et al. (Eds.): Exception Handling, LNCS 2022, pp. 234–250, 2001.

data must satisfy in order to be a faithful representation of the application domain, thus to ensure data quality. Integrity constraints are usually expressed in a declarative way, e.g. through logical formulas. An integrity constraint violation is a particular kind of error condition, and thus one of the most obvious cases of execution exception. Apart from integrity constraint handling, some additional applications of execution exceptions have been proposed in the literature, mainly to facilitate data and schema evolution, thus, again, to enhance the flexibility of the system. Since moreover one of the most relevant functionalities achieved through *triggers* in the database context is integrity constraint enforcement, the notions of triggers and exceptions seem to be potentially related. They have however not been compared yet, nor the relationships between them clarified. All these issues will be considered in the paper.

The remainder of the paper is organized as follows. In the remainder of this section we recall some basic notions on exception handling and the Java/C++ exception handling mechanisms we refer to in what follows. Section 2 discusses data exceptions, whereas Section 3 deals with the support for execution exceptions offered by the object database standard ODMG. Sections 4 and 5 illustrates the use of execution exceptions to handle integrity constraints and to ease and control database evolution. Finally, Section 6 compares the notion of trigger with that of exception and Section 7 concludes the paper.

1.1   Exception Handling

Exception handling [16] is an approach to programming to deal with anomalous and error situations. The goal is to make systems more reliable by providing a framework for implementing software fault tolerance. An exception is thus a condition that prevents the continuation of the current method or scope. When an exceptional condition arises, processing cannot continue because the information necessary to deal with it is not available in the current context. Thus, the approach is to jump out of the current context and to relegate the problem to a higher context. This is what happens when an exception is thrown.

According to the exception handling terminology, a *context* is a section of code associated with a particular exception handler. This handler is activated if an exception is raised in the context. Java and C++ allow exception context specification in a *try block*: `try { ... }`. Arbitrary exception handlers can be attached to a try block and are identified by the `catch` keyword. A raised exception is an *exception object*, which is caught by a handler declared to handle exception objects of that object type. Since an exception is raised by an exception object, that object can carry specific information about the raised exception. This guarantees type-safe transmission of arbitrary amounts of information from a raised exception to a handler. If an exception has been raised, it is possible that no local handler is declared for this particular code segment. In this case one should look for handlers up the chain of invokers at run-time (*exception propagation*). If an unhandled exception reaches the outmost scope in a program, it is caught by a special system-declared handler, which usually aborts the program and issues an error message. Exceptions are raised and reraised with the `throw` keyword.

A *try* block may have several `catch` clauses. When an exception is thrown, each `catch` clause is examined in turn, to see whether the type of the exception object is assignable to the type declared in the `catch`. When an assignable `catch` clause is found, its block is executed and the following `catch` clauses are disregarded.

There are two main methods to handle the control flow after an exception occurs. *Termination semantics* continues execution after the context handling the exception, whereas *resumption semantics* continues the execution at the very point the exception occurred. Thus, in termination (which is what Java and C++ support) you assume that the error is so critical that there is no way to get back where the exception occurred, whereas in resumption the exception handler is expected to do something to rectify the situation.

2   Data Exceptions

Database systems rely on the uniformity that is imposed by a typed universe in order to achieve high performance. The notion of *schema*, providing a description of the structure of data to be stored in the database, is crucial for effective storage and retrieval. This requirement, however, contrasts with the need of flexibility arising in most application domains. This need can be seen as the need of storing *exceptional data*, that is, data not conforming to the general rules expressed by the schema. Because the requirement for exceptional data is quite strong in many database applications, several proposals to handle exceptional data have been formulated.

The first proposal is by Borgida [9]. In [9] he takes the view that the various constraints imposed in a database schema (both type constraints and integrity constraints) are normal conditions, and provides a **resume** statement to allow violations to such constraints to persist. Data considered to be the cause of a violation are marked in order to allow users of the database to "navigate" around it. Execution exceptions are then used to react when constraints are violated, and to detect and react when exceptional facts are accessed. To achieve this, the exceptional nature of certain data is marked by the presence of objects in a particular class, and these same objects are raised as exceptions when the exceptional data are retrieved. Moreover, by adopting a resumption model of exceptions, the actual exceptional value is returned. This approach allows one to handle objects with multi-valued attributes and new attributes, as well as exceptional instances, that is, objects declared as instances of a class though their structures do no to conform to that of the class. The notion of exceptional data (one which raises an exception when accessed) can also be used to deal with null values, estimates, and measurements.

Two features of the exception handling mechanism are crucial for this approach: the ability to define new exception types, and to organize them in a taxonomy; the ability to provide alternative actions depending on the context. To solve the problem of being unable to anticipate all exceptional situations at the time programs are written, the technique of allowing "on-line" handling of exceptions is proposed. This allows users to provide minor variations of existing transactions. Finally, the proposed mechanism still imposes some restrictions on constraint violations, allowing constraints to be suspended only in a controlled way. Moreover, the notion of *excuse*, that records who, why, and when violates the constraint, is introduced.

The idea, elaborated further in [11], that it is not possible to anticipate all possible states of the world during schema design has thus lead to the idea that classes should be able to have as instances *exceptional individuals* that do not satisfy all the constraints stated in the class definition. The proposed solution essentially provides for the special treatment of these individuals through run-time exception handling and, for efficiency, relies on the rarity of exceptional occurrences. In [10] situations are considered where entire collections of objects can be anticipated to be "exceptional", thus belonging to subclasses that partially contradict the superclass they inherit from. This notion is referred to as *non-strict inheritance*, and such class hierarchies are referred to as *class hierarchies with contradictions*. The idea of allowing integrity constraints not to hold for particular (exceptional) instances and subclasses is also investigated by Vlahavas and Bassiliades [21], where they talk of constraints with exceptions, distinguishing among constraint contradiction, constraint subsumption, constraint cancelation, constraint overriding, and instance exception.

The notion of *exceptional instance* has also been introduced in the O_2 object database system [15]. In O_2, due to the semantics of types, a tuple value can have extra attributes. For instance, given a class Monument the "Eiffel tower" object can have a state which also contains an attribute height, that is not an attribute of general monuments, since it does not appear in the type associated with the class Monument. Methods associated with the class Monument will not deal with this extra attribute; however, the standard operators available on tuple values will handle it. Exceptional attributes are allowed for any tuple object or value, named or not. One can also associate specific methods with named objects. These methods are used to characterize the exceptional behavior of an object. One can also override an existing method in the class of the object with an exceptional method.

Finally, the problem of dealing with exceptional data, that is, with data not conforming to a fixed schema, has also been dealt with in the context of semi-structured data [1,8]. In that context, where more flexibility is crucial, either the notion of a schema is completely eliminated, or the notion of conformance to a schema is weakened. In [8], for instance, the notion of class membership is weakened in the one of *weak membership*, which leads to an approximate typing or classification, since heuristic techniques are exploited to assign these exceptional data to the most similar class in the schema.

3   Execution Exceptions in ODMG

Execution exceptions have been incorporated in object-oriented DBMS by following the general principle of a seamless integration between the programming language and the database system. This means that the exception handling model of the language is extended to the DBMS. This has some obvious motivations: the programmer is not forced to know two different exception handling models, whose interactions in the same application would be difficult to understand and to manage. The interactions between exception handling and the transactional mechanism need, however, to be considered. Typically, moreover, a DBMS distinguishes between exceptions raised by a programmer of a database application (*developer exceptions*) and exceptions raised by the DBMS itself (*database exceptions*).

In this section we first briefly discuss the interactions between exception and transaction handling. We then present the general notions of the ODMG standard exception model.

3.1 Exceptions and Transactions

One of the differences between an exception handling facility for a programming language and a database system is that the database exception handler must support a mechanism to deal with active transactions when an exception occurs. This mechanism requires a tight coupling between transactions and the exception handler. Exception handling mechanisms for OODBMSs must in particular provide mechanisms to abort the active transaction if an exception has been raised.

The relationship between the exception model and transactions has been considered in the context of OpenOODB [18]. They point out that if dynamic transactions are supported, it is not possible to attach an exception handler to a transaction. There are two independent scopes: the static domain of the exception handler and the dynamic scope of the transaction. Consider the following situation:

```
try{
    db.beginT()
    ⋮
    }
catch (...){
    handle exception and abort the active transaction
    }
db.commitT();
```

If an exception occurs in the try block, the exception handler aborts the transaction and resumes normal execution after exception handler context. This causes an error, since the first statement after the try block tries to commit the transaction which the handler has just aborted. The programmer is thus responsible to ensure that the scope of a transaction does not intersect with the scope of the exception handler context.

3.2   Exceptions in ODMG

The ODMG [12] exception model is a superset of the Java/C++ exception model. Both support the termination model, exception propagation, and parameter passing in an exception object. The ODMG model additionally requires a mechanism to abort the active transaction if an exception has been raised.

In the ODMG data model a type specification includes the exceptions that can be raised by its operations. Each operation signature lists the names of any exceptions (error conditions) the operation can raise. In particular, each operation signature definition can include a raise clause, followed by a parenthesized list of exception names. Exception names appearing in operation signatures are defined through the exception clause in interface and class declarations, that allow one to specify an exception name optionally followed by a list of type, name pairs.

Example 1. [12] The interface Student, belonging to a university database, illustrates how exceptions are declared in ODMG ODL.

```
interface Student{
 exception UnsatisfiedPrerequisites;
 exception SectionFull;
 exception CourseFull;
 exception NotRegisteredForThatCourse;
 exception NotRegisteredInSection;
 boolean register_for_course (in Course course,in Section section)
   raises (UnsatisfiedPrerequisites, SectionFull, CourseFull);
 void drop_course(in Course c)
   raises (NotRegisteredForThatCourse);
 short transfer (in Section oldsection, in Section newsection)
   raises (SectionFull, NotRegisteredInSection);

interface Scope{
  exception DuplicateName{}
  exception NameNotFound{string reason;}
  exception InvalidType{string reason;}
  Structure add_structure(in string name, in list<Member> fields)
    raises (DuplicateName, InvalidType)
}
```

The ODMG exception model is the following. ODMG supports dynamically nested exception handlers, using a termination model of exception handling. Operations can raise exceptions, and exceptions can communicate exception results. Mappings for exceptions are defined by each language binding. When an exception is raised, information on the cause of the exception is passed back to the exception handler as properties of the exception. Control is as follows:

– The programmer declares an exception handler within a context C to handle exceptions of type T.

- An operation within a contained context C' may "raise" an exception of type T.
- The exception is "caught" by the most immediately containing context that has an exception handler. The call stack is automatically unwound by the runtime system out to the level of the handler. Memory is freed for all objects allocated in intervening stack frames. All the transactions that begun within a nested context, that is, unwound by the runtime system in the process of searching up the stack for an exception handler, are aborted.
- When control reaches the handler, the handler may either decide that it can handle the exception or pass it on (reraise it) to a containing handler.

An exception handler that declares itself capable of handling exceptions of type T will also handle exceptions of any subtype of T. A programmer who requires more specific control over exceptions of a specific subtype of T may declare a handler for this more specific subtype within a contained context.

4   Exceptions to Handle Integrity Constraints

Integrity constraints are declarative specifications of properties that must be satisfied by any database instance. In OODBMSs, constraints are typically used to restrict the admissible extent of a class, to impose restrictions on the state of individual objects, or to specify general laws that must be obeyed by sets of objects possibly belonging to different classes.

Integrity maintenance in object-oriented database systems has so far received limited attention. Most mechanisms for constraint enforcement support very limited forms of constraints. Among the most common types of constraints let us mention referential integrity, ensuring the existence of each referenced object, and the exclusiveness and dependency constraints associated with composite objects [6]. Support provided by OODBMSs for handling integrity constraints usually consists of either forbidding or rolling back the operations that violate constraints. However, this "everything or nothing" approach is not very flexible and causes high run-time overhead for consistency checking and rollback. Moreover, it leaves the burden of writing consistent transactions to the user. A more flexible approach to enforcement is to extend the system with capabilities for checking whether constraints have been invalidated by a transaction and repairing integrity violations, for instance by performing compensating actions.

Two main approaches have been proposed to ensure that the database satisfies its constraints after certain actions. The first one relies on the use of triggers (cf. Section 6) for integrity enforcement. Indeed, integrity constraints can be expressed by triggers, activated by any event likely to violate the constraint. The condition of the trigger tests for the actual occurrence of violations; if a violation is detected, then the action of the trigger either issues a rollback command or performs database manipulations for repairing constraint violations. The second approach is based on modifying methods in accordance to the specified integrity constraints. Under this approach, integrity maintenance is obtained by appropriate method modifications. Different proposals, however, modify methods in different ways. In the proposal of Schewe et al. [23], given some arbitrary methods and some constraints, a new set of methods is built, performing the "same" actions, but without violating the constraints. This approach handles a limited set of constraints. By contrast, in the proposal [17], for each update method an adorned version is created that checks the constraints of the class to which the method refers. Each method call is replaced with a call to the adorned version. Constraint checks are translated into preconditions on the actual data manipulation. Designers are allowed to define corrective actions upon expected constraint invalidation. This may result in several adorned method versions.

Recently, some proposals [2,14] have emerged to model integrity constraints as *persistent assertions*. Assertions [20] are conditional annotations that describe objects and method properties. Assertions annotate a class definition with preconditions, postconditions, and invariants. Any assertion violation is reported through an exception. Persistent assertions allow one to capture both code and data consistency, thus achieving an even stronger integration between the programming language and the database view. Persistent assertions are used to ensure the integrity of persistent data. In particular, in the NightCap system [14], assertions, derived from constraints expressed in UML's Object Constraint Language, are integrated in the PJama platform [4].

Example 2. The following are examples of persistent assertions, expressed in OCLJ [14], referring to the database schema of Example 1.

```
context Student inv UniqueCardNb:
  Student.allInstances().forAll(Student s1, s2 \ s1 != s2 ==>
                                     s1.cardNb != s2.cardNb)
context void Student.register(Section s, Course c)
  pre: c.hasSection().includes(s)
  pre: ! takes.includes(s)
  pre: c.openForRegistration()
  post: takes.includes(s)
  post: takes.size == takes.size@pre+1
  post: classes.includes(c)
```

In order to use assertions as integrity constraints, thus enforcing the consistency of persistent data, the assertion mechanism must be enhanced in the following way:

- the assertion runtime must be modified so that assertions might be checked on persistent instances;
- the assertion mechanism must handle object inconsistencies, by providing a way to declare and trigger repair actions.

Assertions are integrated inside classes, so that assertions will persist with classes. From a software engineering viewpoint, the violation of an assertion is a correctness error and the exception raised by the violation should not be caught. Taking the point of view of persistent data, stored data must be preserved, and if

possible eventually corrected whenever an error is detected. A repair mechanism
should be provided for inconsistent objects. In the NightCap approach assertions do not include repair actions, but inconsistency handlers are provided. These
handlers are associated with a specific scope (assertion, method, class, etc.) so
that repair methods can be called after an assertion failure.

Different inconsistency handlers are provided according to their scope (whole
store, class, method, ...). An inconsistency handler mainly consists of a method
`repair(Object o, Exception e)`, whose body contains the actions to repair
the object `o`, and `e` is the exception that has been raised. When an assertion
evaluation fails, the assertion runtime calls the most specialized inconsistency
handler (if any), which calls the repair method. After this call, the assertion
clause that was violated is checked again. If it fails again, the assertion runtime
might either call a more general inconsistency handler or raise an appropriate
exception to abort the transaction. To avoid composition problems, only the
most specialized inconsistency handler is activated in any scope.

When a method is called on an object, first the preconditions are checked.
Postconditions and invariants are checked at the end of the method body; postconditions are evaluated before invariants. As an assertion violation without
repair leads to a raised exception, this exception leads to the abort of the implicit
transaction that occurs between stabilization of the store. Using this exception-
based approach, the evaluation scheme of assertions will be able to be adapted
to systems providing more sophisticated transaction facilities than PJama.

The POET OODBMS [25] also provides a notion of constraint, and a corresponding `constraintViolation` exception, that, if thrown, causes the active
transaction to abort. However, POET does not provide any declarative language for expressing constraints. Rather, it supports a `Constraints` interface;
classes that implement `Constraints` must define and implement the three methods `postRead()`, `preWrite()`, and `preDelete()`. As their names imply, they
are automatically called after an object of the class is read into memory and
before the object is written to or deleted from the database. `preRead()` is an initialization method, whereas `preWrite()` and `preDelete` are clean-up methods.
Method `preWrite()` is very useful for data integrity checks. One may throw a
`constraintViolation` exception from the `preWrite()` and `preDelete()` constraint method implementations. As said, this exception causes the abort of the
active transaction.

5   Exceptions as a Support for Evolution

Another important use of execution exceptions in OODBMSs is related to the
potential they offer to support evolution. In the database context, since data
must survive for a long time, the ability to handle evolution is crucial. We recall,
moreover, that the notion of schema is central in the database context, thus
the support for evolution must not prevent one from taking advantage of the
schema. Two different forms of evolution can be considered, and for both of

them the use of execution exceptions has been proposed: *object migration* and *schema evolution*. In what follows we consider each of them in turn.

5.1   Object Migration

For long-lived systems such as databases, a given object will evolve over time. While state evolution (i.e., changes in the object property values) does not pose problems, type evolution, that is, the ability for an object to *migrate* to a class different from the one where it has been created, is more problematic.

This kind of evolution is frequent in application domains. Consider indeed an object that is currently a **Person**. As time passes, it can naturally become an instance of class **Student** and later an instance of class **Professor**. An important aspect of object migration is that it allows an object to modify its features, attributes and methods, while retaining its identity. This kind of evolution, however, is not supported by many systems, because of implementation and consistency problems. Consistency problems, in particular, arise when an object O, which is a member of a class C, is referred by an object O' as the value of an attribute A, whose domain is C; in such case, the migration of O to a superclass of C violates the integrity constraint established by specifying the domain for A. In other words, object O', after the migration of O, will have as value for attribute A an object which is not a member (neither direct nor indirect) of the class domain of A. The situation is similar to the one where the explicit deletion of a referred object is requested. Migration upward in the class hierarchy, indeed, can be seen as a "partial deletion" of the object.

Before discussing possible solutions to the consistency problems caused by migrations, let us recall that in object-oriented database systems there are two basic deletion policies. Under the first one, referred to as *explicit deletion view*, an object deletion statement is made available at user level.[1] By using such a command, object deletions are explicitly requested by users. Under the second policy, referred to as *garbage collection view*, users can only delete references from an object to another one. An object is then deleted (by the system) when it is no longer referred by any other object. In object systems with explicit deletion, there is the problem of dangling pointers, due to objects containing references to deleted objects. To avoid dangling references, Zdonik [26] proposes to keep a *tombstone object* in place of the deleted object. This solution overcomes the problem of dangling references, since each reference is either to the original object, or to its tombstone object. Each method following references from an object to other ones must handle the exceptions generated by the fact that the object no longer exists (and its tombstone is found, instead).

The problem of upward migrations is similar. If an object O migrates from a class C to a class C', with C subclass of C', an object can exist with a reference to O as an object of class C. The class modification is performed directly on the object and causes a change in the object state, namely, the deletion of specific

---

[1] Here and in what follows, the term user should be intended in the broader meaning of an actual user or an application.

attributes defined in the classes from which the object has migrated. If there are other objects referring to object O as a member of C, they must be notified that O is no longer a member of C. The problem is similar to that of deletion discussed above and a similar approach can be used. A tombstone can for example be placed in the object to denote that this object used to be a member of class C, but that now the attributes related to C have been deleted. Whenever a method tries to access the object's attributes specific to C, it must handle the exception denoting that those attributes are no longer available.

5.2   Schema Evolution

A typical situation in object-oriented databases is that also the schema must evolve in order to accommodate evolutions of the application needs. In many application domains is indeed impossible or unwanted to anticipate all possible states of the world when the schema is designed. When the schema evolves, a possible approach is to *convert* all instances of an evolved class so that they become consistent with the new version of the class. Of course this poses efficiency problems, and it requires converting all existing application programs to be consistent with the new interface. In [24] Skarra and Zdonik face the problem of preserving *type change transparency*, that is, not to convert the instances, and to keep old programs working on instances of new versions of a class, allowing new programs to work on old versions of a class. The solution involves the use of a version control mechanism and a set of exception handlers associated with the versions of a class. In this scheme, as a class evolves, new versions of that class are created. The old versions are not removed. Each object is connected to the class object under which it has been created. When a new version of a class is added, the designer must also add code fragments to other class versions to handle the cases for which there is a conflict between the old version and the new version.

The handlers effectively expand the behavior defined by each version so that instances of different versions may be used interchangeably by programs. The handlers added to each version correspond to behavior not defined by that version but defined by other versions of the class. Thus, when a class C is changed a new version C_i is created. The new version C_i carries handlers for any behavior that is not defined locally, but is defined by some other version of the type C_j. Moreover, handlers may be required by former versions of the type for behavior uniquely defined by the new version.

The behavior defined by a class consists of properties, operations, and constraints, where a single constraint may be on the domains of one or more properties or operation parameters. Exceptions occur when a property or operation referenced by a program is *undefined* for an object by its class version or when a constraint is violated with an *unknown* value supplied by a program or returned by an object. Handlers are added to a version for each *undefined* property or operation and for each *unknown* domain value that is defined in another version of the class. Handlers are classified as either *prehandlers* or *posthandlers*. A prehandler is executed when the definition of a property or operation referenced by the program cannot be found for the object or when the program has sent an *unknown* value to the object for a property or as an operation parameter. A posthandler is executed when the action within within the object has completed and the object is about to return a value *unknown* to the program. Handlers can perform arbitrary functions, but frequently they provide a mapping from one domain value to another.

An alternative use of execution exceptions related to schema evolution is proposed by Amiel et al. [3], where the focus is on schema consistency in schema evolution. An object-oriented database schema, indeed, must satisfy a number of rules to be consistent. These rules are sufficient conditions that guarantee that no type error can occur during the execution of a method code. The problem is that some schema updates may violate the consistency rules. The starting assumption of that work is that exceptions to schema consistency rules should be supported to facilitate schema evolution. However, they should be controlled in order to avoid type safety problems. They propose a tool that processes every method source code and determines whether a statement is unsafe, that is, may result in a run-time type error. If a statement has been detected unsafe, the tool automatically inserts a "check" clause around every unsafe statement in the source code; and let the user provide exception handling code. The tool can also automatically generate some default exception handling code. The user-defined exception handling code, if provided, is however type-checked by the tool. In particular, they introduce different kinds of exception (return exceptions, argument exceptions, disallowed signatures, and illegal substitutions) corresponding to the possible violations of the schema behavioral consistency rules.

6 Exceptions and Triggers

An important functionality provided by current relational and object-relational DBMSs is represented by *triggers*. This typical database functionality has no direct counterpart in object-oriented programming languages, and though trigger usefulness has been recognized also in the object-oriented context and a considerable amount of research has been carried out in the area of active object-oriented databases (see Section 6.1), triggers are not supported in current commercial OODBMSs. Aim of this section is thus to investigate whether and how the two notions can be related, and if the support of exceptions can offer any help or insight towards the introduction of triggers in OODBMSs. In the following, we provide an overview of triggers, then we compare the two mechanisms, and finally we conclude by discussing some open issues.

6.1   Triggers: Basic Notions

A trigger is a syntactical construct to define the reaction of the system. Triggers are usually specified by means of the *event-condition-action* (ECA) paradigm. Systems supporting triggers are called *active databases*. Active databases enable important applications, such as alerting users that a given event has occurred, reacting to events by means of suitable actions, and controlling the invocation of operations and procedures. Examples of functions that can be effectively performed by active database systems are integrity constraint enforcement, monitoring, authorization, statistics gathering and view handling. In the last ten years, there has been a growing interest in extending object-oriented database systems with triggers. Both Widom and Ceri [13] and Paton [22], besides describing the main concepts and features of active databases, provide a comprehensive overview of existing proposals and systems.

In an active rule, the *event* specifies what causes the rule to be triggered. Relevant triggering events can be internal events related to database operations (for example object creations and deletions), temporal events, external (that is, raised by the application), and user-defined events. In addition, in some systems it is possible to specify whether a rule must be triggered before or after its triggering event. Triggering events may also be *composite*, that is, combinations of other events. Useful operators for combining events are logical operators, such as conjunction, disjunction, negation, and sequences. Finally, we recall that in some approaches events are managed as objects.

In an active rule, the *condition* specifies an additional condition to be checked once the rule is triggered and before the action is executed. Conditions are predicates over the database state. In the most common approach, the condition is expressed as a query returning data, that are then passed to the rule action. Moreover, some systems allow triggers to refer to past database states. In an active rule, the *action* is executed when the rule is triggered and its condition is true. Possible actions include database operations and calls to application procedures. Several active database rule languages allow sequences of actions to be specified in rules.

Various systems differ not only with respect to the supported rule language, but also in terms of rule execution semantics. First of all, active database rule executions can be either *instance-oriented* or *set-oriented*. With an instance-oriented execution, a rule is executed once for each database "instance" triggering the rule and satisfying the rule condition. By contrast, rule execution is set-oriented if a rule is executed once for all database instances triggering the rule and satisfying the rule condition. Most of the systems support an instance-oriented rule execution.

The most straightforward approach to *rule processing granularity* is to evaluate a triggered rule condition and to execute its action within the same transaction in which the triggering event occurs, at the soonest rule processing point. However, for some applications it may be useful to delay the evaluation of a triggered rule condition or the execution of its action until the end of the transaction; or it may be useful to evaluate a triggered rule condition or execute its action in a separate transaction. These possibilities result in the notion of *coupling modes* [19]. One coupling mode can specify the transactional relationship between a rule triggering event and the evaluation of its condition, while another coupling mode can specify the transactional relationship between a rule condition evaluation and the execution of its action. Possible coupling modes are: *immediate* (takes place immediately following, within the same transaction), *deferred* (takes place at the commit point of the current transaction), *decoupled* (takes place in a separate transaction).

Another difference among existing systems is whether rule definitions are attached to classes (*targeted rules*). Attaching rule definitions to classes enhances modularization and allows an efficient detection of relevant events while there are sometimes useful rules triggered by events spanning sets of objects possibly from different classes (*untargeted rules*).

Another notion that is also extremely relevant for active rule semantics is that of *priority*. The execution semantics for active rules sometimes requires that one rule is selected from a set of eligible rules. For this reason, an active database rule language may include a mechanism for specifying rule priorities.

Finally, an important aspect when introducing triggers in object-oriented databases concerns trigger inheritance and overriding. Since inheritance is one of the most significant features of the object-oriented paradigm this is a fundamental problem to deal with. In spite of that, the influence of inheritance on triggers has not been deeply investigated in existing object-oriented database systems. Under some proposals triggers are always inherited and can never be overridden nor refined. Problems concerning trigger inheritance and overriding have been investigated in [7].

6.2 Comparison

In this section we identify some differences between the behavior that can be achieved through the specification of a trigger and the specification of a try block handling an exception. Of course, the trigger would react to a simple implicit event (explicit events[2] or composite events do not seem to have a counterpart in the exception mechanism). The first obvious difference that emerges is that triggers are not explicitly activated. Rather, the occurrence of the monitored event autonomously causes the triggering of the rule (this is the reason to call it *active* rule), whereas exceptions must be explicitly thrown and caught. In addition to that we can identify several other differences:

- A given event (independently of where it occurs) always triggers the same rules; by contrast, an exception can be handled in different ways depending on where it is caught. Exceptions have been indeed originally conceived as a mean to notify the caller of the fact that an exceptional situation has occurred (typically error situations), the reaction to the receipt of this information is thus highly dependent on the context.
- The action of the trigger is executed in addition to what the triggering transaction is doing, except than in two cases: instead-of triggers (whose action is executed instead of the triggering operation) and triggers whose action is a `rollback` (by effect of which the whole triggering transaction is undone). By contrast, under the termination approach, the body of a try

---

[2] Examples of explicit events are the temporal ones.

statement is executed only until an exception is thrown; when an exception is thrown, the remainder of the block is not executed and we pass to execute the catch clauses of the block.

- The occurrence of an event triggers all the rules monitoring that event. This means that an active system must handle problems related to rule priorities, how to choose a rule from the set of triggered rules, recursive and non-terminating behavior, etc. By contrast, exceptions are always caught by a single catch clause; if several catch clauses of a try block match with a thrown exception, only the block corresponding to the first catch clause is executed.
- Exceptions are characterized by a very fine "processing granularity", that is, the reaction to the throwing of an exception is super-immediate. By contrast, as we have discussed in Section 6.1, the processing granularity of triggers can be rather coarse (due to a lot of reasons).
- For what concerns inheritance, triggers and exceptions present deep differences. Usually triggers are not overridden in subclasses and full trigger inheritance is supported. In addition, new triggers can be defined in subclasses. By contrast, when a method is overridden in a subclass, only the exceptions that have been specified in the method in the superclass or a specialization of them can be thrown.

Thus, in some sense, triggers seem more high-level and more declarative constructs. Moreover, with the use of exceptions the risk of "spreading" the semantics of data, which can be expressed through a single trigger, seems more inherent. By contrast, the exception mechanism is more powerful in that it allows to express different reactions to the same situation.

Finally, another important difference we would like to point out is related to static analysis. While each method declares the exceptions it can throw, and correctness of these declarations is checked statically, the relationships among triggers are not explicitly declared and it is not trivial to deduce them. A lot of research effort has indeed been devoted to the development of static analysis techniques for sets of triggers.

7   Conclusions

In the paper we have briefly surveyed the notion of exception from a (object) database perspective. Both data and execution exceptions have been discussed, and the notion of execution exception has been related to classical "error-handling " mechanisms typical of the database context. Though we have not discussed at all implementation issues, some information on how an exception handling mechanism for OpenOODB has been realized can be found in [18].

References

1. S. Abiteboul. Querying Semi-Structured Data. In F. Afrati and P. Kolaitis, editors, *Proc. of the Sixth Int'l Conf. on Database Theory*, volume 1186 of *Lecture Notes in Computer Science*, pages 1–18. Springer, 1997.

2. S. Alagić, J. Solorzano, and D. Gitchell. Orthogonal to the Java Imperative. In E. Jul, editor, *Proc. Thelfth European Conference on Object-Oriented Programming*, Lecture Notes in Computer Science, pages 212–233, 1998.

3. E. Amiel, M. Bellosta, E. Dujardin, and E. Simon. Type-safe Relaxing of Schema Consistency Rules for Flexible Modeling in OODBMS. *VLDB Journal*, 5(2):133–155, 1996.

4. M. Atkinson and M. Jordan. Providing Orthogonal Persistence for Java. In E. Jul, editor, *Proc. Thelfth European Conference on Object-Oriented Programming*, number 1445 in Lecture Notes in Computer Science, pages 383–395, 1998.

5. F. Bancilhon. Object-Oriented Database Systems. In *Proc. of the Seventh ACM SIGACT-SIGMOD-SIGART Symposium on Principles of Database Systems*, 1988.

6. E. Bertino and G. Guerrini. Extending the ODMG Object Model with Composite Objects. In *Proc. Thirteenth Int'l Conf. on Object-Oriented Programming: Systems, Languages, and Applications*, pages 259–270, 1998.

7. E. Bertino, G. Guerrini, and I. Merlo. Trigger Inheritance and Overriding in Active Object Database Systems. *IEEE Transactions on Knowledge and Data Engineering*, 12(4):588–608, 2000.

8. E. Bertino, G. Guerrini, I. Merlo, and M. Mesiti. An Approach to Classify Semi-structured Objects. In *Proc. Thirteenth European Conference on Object-Oriented Programming*, number 1628 in Lecture Notes in Computer Science, pages 416–440, 1999.

9. A. Borgida. Language Features for Flexible Handling of Exceptions in Information Systems. *ACM Transactions on Database Systems*, 10(4):565–603, 1985.

10. A. Borgida. Modeling Class Hierarchies with Contradictions. In *Proc. of the ACM SIGMOD Int'l Conf. on Management of Data*, pages 434–443, 1988.

11. A. Borgida and K. Williamson. Accommodating Exceptions in Databases, and Refining the Schema by Learning from Them. In *Proc. Eleventh Int'l Conf. on Very Large Data Bases*, pages 72–81, 1985.

12. R. Cattel, D. Barry, M. Berler, J. Eastman, D. Jordan, C. Russel, O. Schadow, T. Stanienda, and F. Velez. *The Object Database Standard: ODMG 3.0*. Morgan-Kaufmann, 1999.

13. S. Ceri and J. Widom. *Active Database Systems - Triggers and Rules for Advanced Database Processing*. Morgan-Kaufmann, 1996.

14. P. Collet and G. Vignola. Towards a consistent viewpoint on consistency for persistent applications. In *Proc. ECOOP'2000 Workshop on Objects and Databases*, To appear as Lecture Notes in Computer Science, 2000.

15. O. Deux et al. The Story of O_2. *IEEE Transactions on Knowledge and Data Engineering*, 2(1):91–108, 1990.

16. J. Goodenough. Exception Handling: Issues and a Proposed Notation. *Communications of the ACM*, 18(12):683–696, 1975.

17. P. Grefen, R. de By, and P. Apers. Integrity Control in Advanced Database Systems. *IEEE Data Engineering Bulletin, Special Issue on Database Constraint Management*, 17(2):9–13, June 1994.

18. H. Kienle and P. Fortier. Exception-Handling Extension for an Object-oriented DBMS. In *Proc. of the International Database Engineering and Application Symposium*, pages 138–143, 1997.

19. D. McCarthy and U. Dayal. The Architecture of an Active Data Base Management System. In *Proc. of the ACM SIGMOD Int'l Conf. on Management of Data*, pages 215–223, 1989.

20. B. Meier. *Object Oriented Software Construction*. Prenctice Hall, 1988.

21. I. Vlahavas and N. Bassiliades. Modelling Constraints with Exceptions in Object-Oriented Databases. In P. Loucopoulos, editor, *Proc. Thirteenth Int'l Conf. on the Entity-Relationship Approach*, number 881 in Lecture Notes in Computer Science, pages 189–204, 1994.
22. N. Paton. *Active Rules in Database Systems*. Springer-Verlag, 1999.
23. K.-D. Schewe, B. Thalheim, J. Schmidt, and I. Wetzel. Integrity Enforcement in Object-Oriented Databases. In U. Lipeck and B. Thalheim, editors, *Proc. Fourth International Workshop on Foundations of Models and Languages for Data and Objects - Modelling Database Dynamics*, Workshops in Computer Science, pages 174–195, 1992.
24. A. Skarra and S. Zdonik. Type Evolution in an Object-Oriented Database. In B. Shriver and P. Wegner, editors, *Research Directions in Object-Oriented Programming*, pages 393–415. MIT, 1987.
25. POET SOftware. POET Java^{TM} Programmer's Guide (POET 6.0), 1999.
26. S. Zdonik. Object-Oriented Type Evolution. In F. Bancilhon and P. Buneman, editors, *Advances in Database Programming Languages*, pages 277–288. Addison-Wesley, 1990.

Error Handling in Process Support Systems

Fabio Casati[1] and Gianpaolo Cugola[2]

[1] Hewlett-Packard Laboratories,
1501 Page Mill Road, 1U-4, Palo Alto, CA, 94304, USA.
casati@hpl.hp.com
[2] Politecnico di Milano
Dipartimento di Elettronica e Informazione,
Via Ponzio 34/5, I-20133 Milan, Italy.
cugola@elet.polimi.it

Abstract. Process Support Systems (PSSs) are software systems supporting the modeling, enactment, monitoring, and analysis of business processes. Process automation technology can be fully exploited when predictable and repetitive processes are executed. Unfortunately, many processes are faced with the need of managing exceptional situations that may occur during their execution, and possibly even more exceptions and failures can occur when the process execution is supported by a PSS. Exceptional situations may be caused by system (hardware or software) failures, or may by related to the semantics of the business process.

In this paper we introduce a taxonomy of failures and exceptions and discuss the effect that they can have on a PSS and on its ability to support business processes. Then, we present the main approaches that commercial PSSs and research prototypes offer in order to capture and react to exceptional situations, and we show which classes of failure or exception can be managed by each approach.

1 Introduction

Mature business organizations are characterized by a high level of standardization in the set of activities carried out by their employees to pursue the organization's business mission (i.e., their *business processes*). This is true in particular for companies engaged in e-business activities, where business processes are executed in very high volumes and are automated for the most part. More human-oriented, flexible and dynamic organizations follow looser, adaptive process, but some notion of company-wide process still exists.

The quality of the business process affects the quality of the products and services delivered by the organization. As a consequence, in the last decades a lot of effort has been put in identifying techniques and methodologies to increase business process quality (and hence to provide better services at lower operating costs). In the area of information technology this efforts lead to the development of two different classes of tools: *Workflow Management Systems* (WfMSs) [1, 2] and *Process-centered Software Engineering Environments* (PSEEs) [3,4,5].

A. Romanovsky et al. (Eds.): Exception Handling, LNCS 2022, pp. 251–270, 2001.
© Springer-Verlag Berlin Heidelberg 2001

WfMSs are oriented to supporting generic business processes, while PSEEs have been specially conceived to support software development processes.

It is interesting to observe that, even if they were developed by different communities (WfMSs by people originally working in the area of Information Systems and Databases, while PSEEs by people working in the area of Software Engineering) modern WfMSs and PSEEs share more commonalities than differences. In particular, they are affected by similar problems that initially limited their adoption. As a consequence, in this paper we will not distinguish among the two classes of tools (this is becoming a common approach in the last few years) and we will refer to both of them with the common term of *Process Support Systems* (PSSs).

PSSs support business organizations in modeling, automating, monitoring, and measuring their business process. Usually, a PSS provides a *Process Description Language* (PDL), used to develop a model of the business process. This model may be used to consolidate the process knowledge, to support process assessment, measurement, and refinement, to communicate the business rules within the organization, and, most importantly, to *automate* (i.e., *enact*) and *monitor* business process executions. During process model enactment, the PSS uses the rules and constraints expressed in the model to automate the activities that can be carried out without the intervention of human agents, and to guide and support people in carrying out the activities that require their intervention. Furthermore, PSSs offer tools to monitor and analyze process executions, in order to detect inefficiencies and hence improve the process.

Process coordination and automation technologies are becoming widespread in both e-businesses as well as in traditional enterprises, due to the need of reducing operating costs and performing high-quality services. While current PSS technology does contribute to achieving these objectives, it still lacks the flexibility and robustness needed to adapt to the rapidly evolving business and IT environment and to handle exceptional events that may occur during process enactment [6,7,8]. Exceptional events may range from failures in the underlying infrastructure to unforeseen changes in the external environment that require a deviation from the planned course of actions.

In this paper we classify exceptional events that may occur during process model enactment, we analyze the problems that these events may generate, and we describe the possible approaches to efficiently handle them, possibly with minimal or no human intervention.

2   Some Preliminary Definitions

As noted in Section 1, in the last decades two different communities have worked to similar problem developing different tools (i.e., WFMSs and PSEEs), but also a different terminology[1]. In this section we give some preliminary definitions

---

[1] This is demonstrated by the considerable time that the two authors, coming from these different communities, have spent in order to synchronize concepts and terminology

of the terms we will use in the remainder of the paper. We also give a quick overview of the basic architecture of a PSS.

Process Description Language (PDL). Each PSS provides a *Process Description Language* (PDL), used to develop a model of the business process.

Process model. It is a static description of the expected business process expressed in a PDL[2]. A process model is typically composed of *activities* (or *tasks*), that represent work items to be executed by a human or automated *resource*. In addition, the process model include the description of the execution dependencies among activities.

Observe that some PDLs allow process engineers to describe the expected process together with the activities to be pursued to cope with undesired (but foreseen) events. As an example some PDLs provide explicit linguistic constructs for exception handling (see Section 4 for further details on this topic). Here we use the name "process model" to indicate the model of the expected business process, without considering any undesired event.

Process Support System (PSS). It is a software application that supports the specification, automation, and monitoring of business processes. Typical examples of PSSs are Workflow Management Systems and Process-centered Software Engineering Environments.

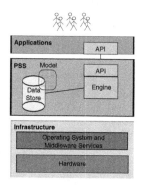

Fig. 1. The run-time architecture of a typical PSS.

A typical PSS (see Figure 1) is composed of an *engine*, which enacts a *process model* by scheduling activities and assigning them to the appropriate human or automated resource. A *Data Store* holds process definition and execution data as well as a description of the process resources. Usually, the data store is implemented by taking advantage of a DBMS, but PSSs exist that use the standard file system as their data store. Through an Application Programming Interface (API) the engine is able of controlling the execution of

---

[2] People working in the area of WFMSs often use the term *workflow schema*.

external applications, including the graphical user interface of the PSS itself. All these components run on top of a certain operating system and middleware, which provides advanced communication services to let the different components communicate and synchronize.

Observe that real PSSs have a much more complex architecture, including other components like process definition and monitoring tools, worklist managers, and so on. Sometimes they provide a distributed engine, or they use several DBMS distributed over a LAN to implement the data store. Since similar details are not relevant for the remainder of the paper they have not been included in Figure 1.

Actual process. It is the actual business process as it is performed in the real world. At each time instant, it may be described by the history of the activities that were performed to carry out the business process from the time it was started. It is a dynamic entity (i.e., it changes each time a new action is performed).

Observed process. During process model enactment, a PSS has a partial view of the actual process. The PSS, in fact, is only aware of the actions that the users perform under its control. All other actions are invisible to the PSS. This partial view of the actual process owned by the PSS is called the "observed process". At each time instant, it may be described by a history of the activities that the users performed under the PSS control to carry out the business process from the time it was started. It is the result of the enactment. Like the actual process, it is a dynamic entity.

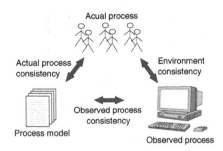

Fig. 2. The consistency relations among process model, actual process, and observed process.

Figure 2 shows the consistency relations that joins process model, actual process, and observed process when the process proceeds as expected. The actual process is consistent with the process model, i.e., it proceeds as described in the process model, without violating any of the constraints described there. Similarly, the observed process is consistent with the actual process. This means that the PSS has a correct view of the actual process. Finally, the observed process is consistent with the process model, which means that the PSS is enacting the process model and it is not violating any of the constraints stated in the model. As discussed in the following section, this ideal situation is not easy to achieve and maintain.

3   Undesired Events and Their Possible Effects

Business processes can be composed of many complex activities that need to be managed and synchronized, thus composing a very complex workflow that involves human and automated resources for a long time.

It is very common that during process execution something undesired happens. It may be something related to the underlying system, like a crash of a server, or a network fault; it may be something related to the PSS, like a crash in one of the applications invoked by the PSS to execute some process step; or it may be something related to the process itself, like a unforeseen situation that need to be managed before process could proceed. In all these cases the PSS must offer the right mechanisms to face the undesired event and to overcome it. Here we first classify the possible *undesired events*. Next, we show the techniques that can be leveraged to handle the different kinds of undesired events.

3.1   A Classification of Undesired Events

As a first initial classification it is useful to distinguish between *failures* and *exceptions*.

- Failures are system or network errors that originate from the PSS, from the applications invoked by the PSS, or from the underlying infrastructure on top of which the PSS is built and executed. As an example, they can be failures of the hardware that runs the PSS, crashes in the data store, or crashes of one of the applications controlled by the PSS engine. Failures affect the information system that supports the process.
- Exceptions are unexpected situations that are not part of the normal behavior of the process, and that require a deviation from the process model to be managed[3].

  Every time an event not captured by the process model occurs, we say that an exception has occurred. As an example, in some circumstances it may be necessary to change the order of execution of some activities, or to violate some timing constraints, or to let a unauthorized user perform a critical task because the person that was assigned to that task is not available.

---

[3] Observe that, as mentioned in Section 2, in this paper we do not consider the part of the process definition that copes with undesired (but foreseen) events as being part of the process model

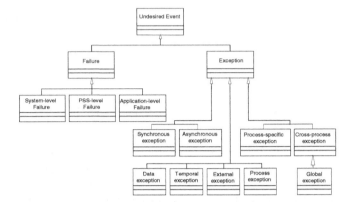

Fig. 3. A classification of undesired events.

A Taxonomy of Failures Depending on the layer of the PSS that originate the problem (see Figure 1), we distinguish among *infrastructure-level, PSS-level,* and *application-level* failures.

- Infrastructure-level failures originate from the hardware or from the operating system and middleware on top of which the PSS runs. Examples of this kind of failures are disk crashes, network faults, and operating system errors.
- PSS-level failures originate from the PSS. In particular, they may affect the PSS engine, the PSS data store, or the process model enacted by the PSS. Typical examples of this kind of failures are data store failures, or deadlocks, crashes of the PSS engine, or errors in the process model (e.g., a bug in the way an application is invoked or controlled through the engine API).
- Application-level failures affect the applications that run under control of the PSS to execute process steps. As an example, it may happen that an application invoked by the PSS engine crashes or it is not able, due to a bug, to save the results of the work the user has accomplished.

A Taxonomy of Exceptions Our analysis identified three main characteristics of exceptions, that have to be considered in understanding how they can be modeled: the *synchronicity,* the *scope,* and the *origin.*

Synchronicity. Exceptions may be *synchronous* or *asynchronous* with respect to the progression of the process. Synchronous exceptions occur at the start or completion of tasks and processes, while asynchronous ones may occur at any time during process execution. For instance, the output data of a task may return an unexpected null value. An example of asynchronous exception is instead the cancellation of an interview in a candidate interview process, which may happen at any time during the execution, and not only at the start or completion of a task. Synchronous exceptions can further be characterized by their localization: *localized* exceptions may be only caused by the execution of one (or few) tasks, while *sparse* exceptions may be caused by the execution of several tasks in a process, and therefore may occur at several stages during the execution of the process. For instance, a data constraint violation exception is localized if only one task may modify those data, and sparse otherwise.

Scope. Exceptions may be *process-specific*, i.e. they may be related to one specific process instance, or they may be *cross-process*, i.e. they may be related to and affect several process instances. Interview cancellations and deadline expirations are examples of process-specific exceptions. Instead, a hiring freeze would be cross-process, since it would affect every running instances of the *candidate interview* process. Exceptions can span over process boundaries both in their detection and in their recovery:

- *detection*: the occurrence of the exceptional situation may depend on the state of several instances, such as when a customer rents two or more cars in overlapping periods.
- *recovery*: managing the exceptional situation may require actions in several process instances, such as in the car rental example discussed above.

A distinguished kind of cross-process exception is represented by *global* exceptions, i.e. anomalous, generic situations that may possibly affect every process, and for which the reactions may be defined at the PSS level. The unavailability of a resource is an example of a global exception. The appropriate reaction may be defined at the global (PSS) level and possibly refined for specific processes if different policies need to be adopted.

Origin. Exceptions may be classified according to what generates them:

Data exceptions are raised by modifications to process relevant data. For instance, a modification to the trip's cost may cause an overdraft on the customer's account.

Temporal exceptions are raised at the occurrence of a given timestamp (e.g. a deadline for a task), periodically (e.g. every night at 7pm), or as a defined interval has elapsed since a reference event (e.g., 20 minutes after a fire alarm).

External exceptions are explicitly notified to the process engine by humans or external applications. An email by the candidate requesting the cancellation of the interview is an example of external exception.

Process exceptions are raised by state changes in a process instance or task execution. For instance, the firing of an already active task may be perceived as an exceptional situation.

Figure 3 summarizes through a UML model [9] the resulting classification of undesired events.

3.2   Possible Effects of Undesired Events

Typically, the effect of an unmanaged failure or exception is an action that breaks the consistency relationships shown in Figure 2. This often leads to the impossibility of continuing executing the business process under the control of the PSS.

To better clarify the possible effects of undesired events not adequately managed by the PSS, we introduce two new terms: we call *deviation* an action in the actual process that breaks one of the consistency relationships of Figure 2 and *inconsistency* the resulting state. Depending on the relationship broken we distinguish among (see Figure 4):

Actual process deviation. It is an action performed in the actual process that is not described in the process model or that violates some of the constraints expressed in the process model. Actual process deviations break the consistency relation between the actual process and the process model leading to an *actual process inconsistency.*

Observed process deviation. It is an action performed by the PSS that is not reflected in the process model. Observed process deviations break the consistency relation between the observed process and the process model, leading to an *observed process inconsistency.*

Environment deviation. [4] It is an action performed in the actual process or in the PSS that breaks the consistency relation between the actual process and the observed process. It typically occurs when someone performs an action that is relevant for the business process out of the PSS control. It leads to an *environment inconsistency.*

Observe that an environment inconsistency is definitely something to avoid. When an environment inconsistency occurs, the PSS has an incorrect or incomplete view of the actual process and, consequently, it cannot correctly support the actual process anymore.

Usually, actual process deviations are the result of an exception. To cope with an exception, in fact, the actual process must deviate from the process model, thus leading to an actual process deviation[5]. Moreover, since in general PSSs cannot deviate from the process model (i.e., observed process deviations are not possible), the effect of an actual process deviation is often an environment deviation. To avoid similar situations, it may be necessary for the PSS to deviate from the process model (i.e., to perform an observed process deviation), to continue mirroring the actual process even in presence of an actual process deviation. Model-relaxing approaches (see Section 4.2) can be adopted to pursue this goal.

4   Recovery Approaches

The ability to adequately manage undesired events without disruptions to the running business processes is crucial for modern PSSs that support mission-

---

[4] The name "environment deviation" follows from the common habit of calling "environment" the sum of the actual process plus the PSS supporting it [10].

[5] We observe again that we assume that the process model only includes the description of the normal behavior of a process. Mechanisms to specify exception handling behaviors as part of the process model will be introduced later in the paper.

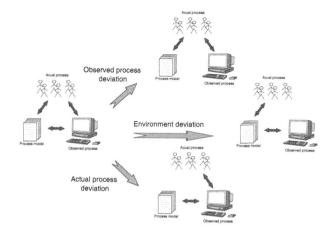

Fig. 4. Deviations and inconsistencies.

critical operations. Consequently, to be successful in the market, a PSS has to offer a set of mechanisms to react to the different classes of undesired events identified in Section 3.

In principle, different *recovery approaches* may be followed to react to failures and exceptions. We identify three possible classes of approaches, depending on the layer that implements them (see Figure 1): *infrastructure-level, PSS-level,* and *application-level* approaches. For its relevance, we also consider a fourth class of approaches that we call *process-model-level.* The next sections analyzes the different approaches.

4.1   Infrastructure and Application-Level Approaches

While exceptions are directly related to the existence of a PSS and can be adequately managed only by the PSS, failures (and particularly infrastructure and application-level failures) can be managed through general approaches involving the infrastructure and the application levels only.

Infrastructure and application-level approaches to failure handling have in fact been developed in several different contexts and most of them become mature years before the first PSS was developed. They include mechanisms like hardware redundancy to reduce the impact of hardware crashes, advanced network protocols and middleware mechanisms to cope with network faults, or software redundancy (e.g., using replicated servers) to cope with application failures.

While these mechanisms are designed to react either to infrastructure-level or to application-level failures, they provide little help to handle PSS-level failures and exceptions. In fact, these require a knowledge of the process model in order to be properly captured and managed.

Since this paper focuses on PSSs, analyzing these generic failure handling techniques in details is out of the scope of this work. Instead, in the following we focus on PSS and process-model-level approaches, described next.

4.2   PSS-Level Approaches

The PSS has a direct visibility of the process model and is responsible for scheduling tasks and for launching and managing applications, so it can provide powerful approaches to handle both failures and exceptions.

PSS-Level Failure-Handling Approaches. PSSs may implement mechanisms to cope with both infrastructure-level and application-level failures. As an example, the PSS may offer mechanisms to handle failures of the data store or of the middleware layer. Even PSS failures can be managed at the PSS level, by offering mechanisms to restore the last consistent state reached before the failure when the PSS is restarted (typically, this is obtained by taking advantage of a DBMS used to permanently store the PSS state).

In general, failure management at the PSS level implies the use of a combination of "undoing" and "redoing". As an example, network failures are often managed by retrying the communication until a success is reached, while to manage an application failure it is often necessary to undo the operations made by the activity that called the failed application, before trying to redo the entire activity. Similar approaches are adopted by a few research prototypes like SPADE [11,12,13], whose elementary tasks are implemented as transactions in the object-oriented DBMS that stores process instance data, thus allowing the engine to roll-back any task affected by a failure. A similar approach is adopted by Apel [14,15].

The main problem with undoing and redoing in PSSs is that often the tasks that have to be undone and redone are very complex. They could have side effects that cannot be undone and they could involve activities that cannot be controlled by the PSS (e.g., manual tasks). In other word, undoing and redoing require a knowledge of the application domain that the PSS alone cannot have. This motivations induced researchers and practitioners to introduce process-model-level approaches, which involve process modelers in modeling the recovery process together with the standard process.

PSS-Level Exception-Handling Approaches. In Section 3 exceptions have been defined as unexpected events that were not planned in the process model. Exceptions usually result in actual process deviations that, if not adequately managed, may result in environment deviations.

Current PSSs adopt two different approaches to cope with the need of deviating from the process model to react to exceptions: either they provide mechanisms to change the process model on-the-fly (*model-changing approaches*), or they provide mechanisms to explicitly deviate from the model without the need of modifying it (*model-relaxing approaches*).

With the first approach the model is changed before the deviation occurs so neither an actual process deviation, nor a PSS deviation is required to face the exceptional event. With the second approach the PSS adopts some kind of "relaxed" interpretation of the model to continue mirroring the actual process even in presence of an actual process deviation. In practice, the PSS reacts to an actual process deviation by performing a PSS deviation, thus avoiding an environment deviation. Figure 5 compares the two approaches.

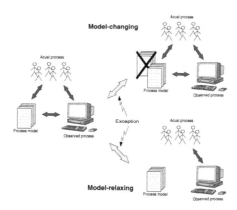

Fig. 5. PSS-level exception-handling approaches.

Model-Changing Approaches. In general, we may distinguish between:

– *Ad-hoc changes*, which are modifications applied to a single running process instance, which do not involve a change in the process model itself.
– *Bulk changes*, which refer instead to modifications of the process model collectively applied to a subset (or to all) the running instances of a process.

For instance, assume that a new agreement between Italy and the US requires Italian tourists traveling to the US to previously request and obtain a visa from the US consulate. If the travel reservation process (Figure 6-a) has not yet been modified according to the new law, then its execution does not lead to the successful completion of the business process.

Indeed, since the new law will affect several running instances (in principle all the running instances plus all the instances that will start in the future), a bulk approach is required. The travel reservation process model should be modified as described in Figure 6-b, where all travel reservations for Italian citizens traveling to the US will include a task for requesting the visa to the US consulate. Moreover, the process modeler has to choose how to manage currently running process model instances. In fact, although the modified process model of Figure 6-b can correctly support all new reservations, it may not be suited for completing the processing of reservations which are in progress. Intuitively,

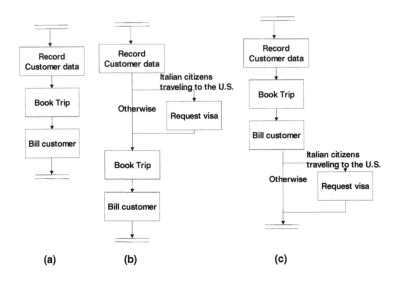

Fig. 6. The Travel Reservation Process. (a): initial version; (b): modified version; (c): ad-hoc version for managing instances that cannot be migrated to the correct version

all instances that are not concerned with Italian citizens going to the US or that are in their early stages (i.e., where task "record customer data" has not been completed yet) can *migrate* to follow the modified process definition shown in Figure 6-b. The other instances will have to be handled in an ad-hoc way, for instance by migrating to the process model shown in Figure 6-c, that still allows to achieve the goals of the process, although it is not the most appropriate and efficient way to execute it. In the context of PSS exceptions, *migrating* a process instance from a process definition (schema) S_1 to a schema S_2 means that the process engine will now schedule and assign tasks based on S_2 [16].

This and similar issues affecting bulk changes have been addressed by several research papers, such as [16,17,18,19,20,21,11,22]. Many of these approaches are based on the use of *migration rules*, to specify the future behavior of running instances once an exception has been detected. A migration rule identifies a subset of the running instances of a given process and specifies the schema to which instances in this subset should be migrated. For instance, in *eFlow* [23], rules have the form IF <condition> THEN MIGRATE TO <model>. The condition is boolean expression that identifies a subset of the running instances, while <model> denotes the destination schema. An example of migration rule is: IF (task_state(Book_Trip)=not_started) THEN MIGRATE TO "New_travel_req". The set of rules must define a partition over the set of running instances, so that each instance is migrated to at most one schema. Instances that do not satisfy any rule condition are not migrated.

This idea of explicitly stating the rules to migrate process model instances with an ad-hoc language has been further extended with process-model approaches (see Section 4.3), which leverages reflective PDLs to allow process modelers to define, as part of the process model itself, when and how the model should be changed during its execution.

Ad-hoc changes could be seen as a particular kind of bulk changes, where only one instance is migrated. For instance, InConcert [24] allows the process responsible to manually reassign a task to a different resource or to start the execution of an arbitrary task in the flow.

A different approach is taken by Endeavors [25], a distributed, extensible PSS infrastructure, which allows the object-oriented definition and specialization of activities, artifacts, and resources associated with a software development process. In Endeavors, process models can be changed very easily even by standard users. These model changes affect the currently running instance and they may affect all the new instances, also. The easiness through which process models can be changed is presented as the main mechanism both to cope with unforeseen situations and to solve the problem of which running instance should be affected by a new process model. Since ad-hoc changes can be easily performed they can be used to migrate any running instance as required, while new instances will automatically use one of the modified process models as decided by the process modelers at launch time.

Model-Relaxing Approaches. The key idea behind model relaxing approaches is to allow the PSS to explicitly deviate from the process model to cope with unforeseen situations. PSSs adopting this approach provide flexible mechanisms for process model enactment that allows users to perform process tasks even if they violate some of the constraints stated in the model. As an example, in Sentinel [26] tasks are characterized by a set of preconditions that implicitly determine their ordering. Users are allowed to invoke a task even if one of its preconditions is not satisfied and the PSS is able to track this event and to mark the data items that could be possibly affected by this deviation, thus supporting users to analyze the effects of PSS deviations, if necessary.

A similar approach is adopted by Prosyt [6], while [27] and [28] present a goal-oriented language: PEACE, which formalizes parts of a process model using an autoepistemic logic, thus allowing users' beliefs to be modeled, and allowing the PSS to reason about the differences between the user beliefs and the actual process. A PEACE process model may describe a wide range of process states and transitions and the right transition may be chosen based on the actual beliefs of the PSS with respect to the actual process.

Model relaxing approaches are best suited to cope with unforeseen events that require an immediate answer by the system and that is most likely that will not occur again in the future. In similar situations, ad-hoc process model changing approaches could be adopted also, but they require much more effort in order to change the model as required. In fact, model changing is a time consuming activity that requires the intervention of the process modeler. It is not reasonable to change the model each time some minor, unexpected event happens. In this situations, model relaxing approaches show all their power.

4.3   Process-Model-Level Approaches

The key idea behind process-model-level approaches is to involve process modelers, who have a precise knowledge of the application domain, in failure and exception handling. PSSs adopting these approaches give process modelers the chance to specify, as part of the process model, either the actions for undoing process tasks, or the actions to perform in case of failures and exceptions, or even the actions for modifying the process model itself when necessary.

In the first case, the weakness of standard PSS-level approaches to failure handling described in Section 4.2 are addressed by giving process programmers the ability of explicitly modeling application specific techniques for undoing or redoing critical tasks. In the second case, process modelers specify directly what to do when a undesired event occurs. In this case we talk of *expected exceptions* to refer to the set of predictable deviations from the normal behavior of the process whose handling has been explicitly coded has part of the model itself. This kind of undesired events are typically detected by the system and possibly managed with no human intervention. The need for the third approach comes from the consideration that traditional model-changing approaches do not offer a way to choose in an process-specific way the kind of allowed changes and the way these changes have to be applied.

Transactional Approaches As mentioned in Section 4.2, the main weakness of standard PSS-level approaches to failure handling is the difficulty of undoing complex business tasks without a precise knowledge of the process semantics. For instance, actions such as "send a letter" cannot be undone by restoring a previous database state. This problem can be managed by transactional approaches.

Transactional process models allow the definition of *regions* in the process model that should be executed atomically. At the request of the process responsible (or depending on the failure codes returned by task executions) the execution of the region can be aborted and rolled back to its entry point. Process execution can then be resumed by retrying the same path or by following an alternative route. Rollback of process regions is typically performed by executing a *compensating task* for each completed task, in the reverse order of their forward execution. A compensating task is an activity that semantically undoes the effect of another task. For instance, a task that reserves a car is compensated by a task that involves calling the car rental company to cancel the reservation. A similar model is for instance supported by *ConTracts* [29]. Several other PSSs implements similar approaches to failure handling. This section reviews the most relevant ones.

WAMO [30,7], WIDE [8], TREX [31], and Crew [32] extend the above approaches by providing more flexibility in the backward compensation/forward execution process: they allow the definition, for each task, of the point to which execution should be rolled back in case of failure and the specification of whether execution should be re-started or aborted from there; furthermore, based on the task properties or on predicates defined over process data, a task involved in a partial rollback and forward recovery may or may not be compensated or re-executed.

Commercial systems do not typically provide this kind of functionality. However, the Exotica project [33,34] has developed a tool that provides process designers of IBM FlowMark (an earlier version of MQ Workflow [35]) with an extended process definition language, allowing the implementation of advanced transaction models such as sagas and flexible transactions. Specifications in the extended model are then translated into FDL (FlowMark Definition Language) by properly inserting additional "compensating" paths after each task, to be conditionally executed upon a task failure (captured by means of the task return code).

Transactional approaches are effective in handling synchronous exceptions. However, they lack the required flexibility for handling generic exceptional situations. In addition, they are restricted in the class of allowed reactions, since they basically only allow a partial or total process rollback: in many exceptional situations, rolling back a process instance is not the appropriate reaction, and it is an extreme and expensive solutions in terms of lost work. Finally, current approaches can only capture process and data events.

Approaches Based on Explicitly Modeling Exceptions. These approaches allow process designers to explicitly model how to capture and react to *predictable* deviations from the normal behavior of the process. By explicitly modeling them, these exceptional behaviors can be managed by the PSS without the need for human intervention. There are two main sub-categories in this approach: one is based on *event nodes*, while the other is based on *Event-Condition-Action rules*.

Event Node Approaches. In the event node approach, the process meta-model includes a particular kind of node, often called *event node* (or event step), which is able to capture asynchronous events and to activate the successor node when the event is detected. There are many variations of this approach, depending on the types of events that can be captured and on how they can affect the process in which the task is defined. *Staffware* [36] and *eFlow* [23] are examples of PSSs that use this approach.

Event nodes can typically capture several types of events (for instance, in the case of *eFlow* they can capture all four kinds of originating events defined in Section 3.1), they can specify filter over (exceptional) events of interest, and they can capture event parameters into process variables. Hence, they are capable of *capturing* the exception. In the event node approach, the reaction is performed by activating a path in the process flow (the path connected in output from the event node). For instance, a node capturing candidate withdrawals in a candidate hiring process is an example of exception handling achieved through event nodes. However, as mentioned in the taxonomy of exception, this is not the only way an exception can be handled: in fact, an exception often requires a partial or global rollback of the process instance, or the notification of the problem to a selected user. In addition, process instances may have to be suspended in order to properly handle the exception. Hence, in order to be fully effective, the event node approach requires the PSS to provide specialized tasks that enable the specification of these kinds of behaviors.

A limitation of the event node approach is that every exception requires the definition of an event node (that captures the exceptional situation) and of the tasks that perform the corrective actions. Hence, when many exceptions need to be managed, the process model may become very complex. Consider for instance exceptions related to deadline expirations. If deadlines need to be specified for each node (as it often happens), then the process model becomes unmanageable. In general, event nodes are effective in managing all types of exceptions except cross-process and global ones. In fact, they can capture synchronous and asynchronous events; however, they must be specified within a process model (it is not possible in current PSSs to define "global" event nodes).

Rule-Based approaches. A few commercial systems and research prototypes (e.g., COSA [37], InConcert [24], WIDE [8] and ADOME-WfMS [38]) provide a rule-based language for the specification of exceptional behaviors. Rules typically take the form of event-action or event-condition-action statements, where the event defines when the rule should be activated, the condition (if present) verifies that the occurred event actually corresponds to an exception that must be managed, while the action handles the exception, by invoking the primitives provided by the rule language.

In order to exemplify these concepts, we now show how exceptional behaviors are specified by means of rules in the WIDE PSS (the other systems follow a similar or simplified model). The WIDE process definition language includes a rule language for defining expected exceptions, called *Chimera-Exc* [8]. In Chimera-Exc rules, triggering events belong to one of the four classes mentioned above (data, temporal, external, or process); the condition is a predicate over process data whose evaluation determines whether the action part should be executed or not, and may in addition return some bindings, passed to the action part in order to target the reaction over specific objects; finally, the actions can send notifications to selected resources, start, suspend or terminate the execution of tasks and process instances, reassign tasks to different resources, or rollback process instances. For example, the rule *negativeBalance* shown below is activated as the value of variable *balance* is modified in an *accountMgmt* process, and notifies a process responsible if the resulting balance is negative.

```
define trigger negativeBalance for accountMgmt
  events      modify(accountMgmt.balance)
  condition   accountMgmt(A), A.balance<0,
              occurred (modify(accountMgmt.balance), A),
  actions     notify (A.responsible, "Overdraft for customer" +
                    A.customerName)
end
```

With the rule-based approach, exception handling strategies can be defined at different levels of abstraction. For instance, a process definition language could allow rules to be defined at the task, process, or PSS level. Rules associated to a given task are triggerable only when the task is active; rules associated with a given process are triggerable when the instance is active, while global rules are always active. This kind of structuring allows the definition of exception handling strategies at the global level, valid for all processes and tasks. Exceptional behaviors can then be overridden (or integrated) at the local level. In general, many variations of the rule-based approach are possible, depending on the expressive power of the event, condition, and action language, and on the rule invocation and execution semantics.

In general, the rule-based approach is very powerful. It can handle both synchronous and asynchronous events, it can manage global and local exceptions, it can capture different kinds of originating events, and can handle localized as well as sparse exceptions. Its drawback lies in the intrinsic complexity of the rule language: in fact, it is yet another formalism that is needed to fully specify the process behavior, and its semantic is very subtle, so that it is easy to generate unforeseen and undesired behaviors.

Approaches Based on Explicit Modeling of the Meta Process The main weakness of generic model-changing approaches is their lack of flexibility and the impossibility of accurately controlling the expressive power of model changing. In general, the kind of changes allowed to a process model and the way these changes have to be applied and deployed are process-specific and cannot be specified one for all. *Reflective PDLs* solve this problem.

Generally speaking, reflective languages give programmers the ability of specifying how programs have to be changed at run-time. In process programming this means adding to the PDL some special constructs that allow process modelers to specify when and how the model have to be changed. We say that process programmers are able of specifying the *meta-process* as part of the process itself [21].

Several PSS adopt a reflective language. SPADE adopts a PDL called SLANG [39], which is based on Petri-Nets. SLANG allows both running process model instances and the process model itself to be treated as process data items that may be modified by the PSS in the way specified by the running process model. Similarly, OASIS [22] provides an object-oriented, reflective framework for the definition, customization, and evolution of software process meta-models and of the software process models that are their instances. In developing this framework, the authors started from the consideration that every process modeling approach relies on some specific set of abstractions that define a process meta-model. They observed that the ability to provide a uniform model of both the process model and the process meta-model is essential to capture complex processes and to manage the customization and evolution of process models and their meta-models.

5 Conclusions

In this paper we have discussed the problem of managing failures and exceptions in business processes. We have presented a taxonomy that classifies the different kinds of exceptional situations that may occur during PSS-supported process executions, and we have shown approaches that enable their handling, possibly with minimal or no human intervention. Exception handling techniques have been mostly developed in the academia, and are recently starting to be included in commercial PSSs that support mission-critical applications. In particular, they are increasingly needed and leveraged in e-business applications.

We expect that many of the techniques presented in this paper will be applied to the area of *e-services*, and specifically to e-service composition. Frameworks and platforms for developing and managing (composite) e-services will be the next battleground for large software vendors such as Sun, Microsoft, IBM, BEA, and HP. Indeed, the adaptation of PSS technology to support the robust and reliable composition of e-services is often named as one of the main opportunity for such vendors in order to achieve competitive advantage. The ability of automatically handling failures and exceptions will be paramount in this area, due to need of supporting high volume, low cost, and zero latency service delivery.

References

1. D. Georgakopoulos, H. Hornick, and A. Sheth, "An overview of workflow management: from process modeling to workflow automation infrastructure," *Distributed and Parallel Databases*, vol. 3, 1995.
2. H. Stark and L. Lachal, *Ovum Evaluates: Workflow*. Ovum ltd., September 1995.
3. A. Finkelstein, J. Kramer, and B. Nuseibeh, eds., *Software Process Modelling and Technology*. Research Studies Press Limited (J. Wiley), 1994.
4. A. Fuggetta and C. Ghezzi, "State of the art and open issues in process-centered software engineering environments," *Journal of Systems & Software*, vol. 26, July 1994.
5. V. Ambriola, R. Conradi, and A. Fuggetta, "Assessing process-centered environments," *ACM Transactions on Software Engineering and Methodology*, vol. 6, July 1997.
6. G. Cugola, "Tolerating deviations in process support systems via flexible enactment of process models," *IEEE Transactions on Software Engineering*, vol. 24, November 1998.
7. J. Eder and W. Liebhart, "Contributions to exception handling in workflow management," in *Proceedings of the EDBT Workshop on Workflow Management Systems*, (Valencia, Spain), Mar. 1998.
8. P. Grefen, B. Pernici, and G. Sanchez, *Database Support for Workflow Management: the WIDE Project*. Kluwer Academic Publishers, 1999.
9. J. Rumbaugh, I. Jacobson, and G. Booch, *The Unified Modeling Language Reference Manual*. Addison Wesley, 1999.
10. G. Cugola, E. Di Nitto, A. Fuggetta, and C. Ghezzi, "A framework for formalizing inconsistencies in human-centered systems," *ACM Transactions On Software Engineering and Methodology (TOSEM)*, vol. 5, July 1996.

11. S. Bandinelli, A. Fuggetta, C. Ghezzi, and L. Lavazza, "SPADE: an environment for Software Process Analysis, Design, and Enactment," in *Software Process Modelling and Technology* (A. Finkelstein, J. Kramer, and B. Nuseibeh, eds.), Research Studies Press Limited (J. Wiley), 1994.

12. S. Bandinelli, A. Fuggetta, C. Ghezzi, and S. Grigolli, "Process Enactment in SPADE," in *Proceedings of the Second European Workshop on Software Process Technology*, (Trondheim (Norway)), Springer-Verlag, September 1992.

13. S. Bandinelli, M. Braga, A. Fuggetta, and L. Lavazza, "The architecture of the SPADE-1 process-centered SEE," in *Proceedings of the 3rd European Workshop on Software Process Technology*, LNCS 772, (Villard de Lans (Grenoble), France), February 1994.

14. S. Dami, J. Estublier, and M. Amiour, "Apel: a graphical yet executable formalism for process modeling," in *Process Technology* (E. Di Nitto and A. Fuggetta, eds.), Kluwer Academic Publishers, January 1998.

15. J. Estublier, P. Y. Cunin, and N. Belkhatir, "Architectures for process support system interoperability," in *5th International COnference on Software Process*, (Chicago, Illinois, USA), pp. 137–147, June 1998.

16. F. Casati, S. Ceri, B. Pernici, and G. Pozzi, "Workflow Evolution," *Data and Knowledge Engineering*, vol. 24, pp. 211–238, Jan. 1998.

17. F. Casati, *Models, Semantics, and Formal Methods for the Design of Workflows and Their Exceptions*. PhD thesis, Politecnico di Milano - Dipartimento di Elettronica e Informazione, Milano, Italy, Dec. 1998.

18. S. Ellis, K. Keddara, and G. Rozenberg, "Dynamic change within workflow systems," in *Proceedings of the ACM Conference on Organizational Computing Systems (COOCS '95)*, (Milpitas, California), 1995.

19. C. Liu, M. Orlowska, and H. Li, "Automating handover in dynamic workflow environments," in *Proceedings of the 10th International Conference on Advanced Information Systems Engineering CAiSE'98*, (Pisa, Italy), June 1998.

20. M. Reichert and P. Dadam, "ADEPT$_{flex}$ - supporting dynamic changes of workflows without losing control," *Journal of Intelligent Information Systems*, vol. 10, pp. 93–129, Mar. 1998.

21. S. Bandinelli, A. Fuggetta, and C. Ghezzi, "Process model evolution in the SPADE environment," *IEEE Transactions on Software Engineering*, vol. 19, December 1993.

22. P. Jamart and A. van Lamsweerde, "A reflective approach to process model customization, enactment, and evolution," in *Proceedings of the Third International Conference on the Software Process (ICSP3)*, (Reston, Virginia), pp. 21–32, IEEE Computer Society Press, October, 10-11 1994.

23. F. Casati, L. Jin, S. Ilnicki, and M. Shan, "eflow: an open, flexible, and configurable system for service composition," in *Proceedings of the Workshop on E-Commerce and Web Information Systems*, (Milpitas, CA, USA), June 2000.

24. R. Marshak, "InConcert workflow," Tech. Rep. 20,3, Workflow Computing Report, Patricia Seybold Group, 1997.

25. G. A. Bolcer and R. N. Taylor, "Endeavors: A process system integration infrastructure," in *Proceedings of the Fourth International Conference on Software Process (ICSP4)*, (Brighton, UK), December 2-6 1996.

26. G. Cugola, E. Di Nitto, C. Ghezzi, and M. Mantione, "How to deal with deviations during process model enactment," in *Proceedings of the 17th International Conference on Software Engineering*, (Seattle (Washington - USA)), April 1995.

27. S. Arbaoui and F. Oquendo, "Peace: Goal-oriented logic-based formalism for process modelling," in *Software Process Modelling and Technology* (A. Finkelstein, J. Kramer, and B. Nuseibeh, eds.), Research Studies Press, J. Wiley, 1994.

28. S. Arbaoui and F. Oquendo, "Managing inconsistencies between process enactment and process performance states," in *Proceedings of the 8th International Software Process Workshop*, (Wadern (Germany)), March 1993.

29. A. Reuter, K. Schneider, and F. Schwenkreis, "Contracts revisited," in *Advanced Transaction Models and Architectures* (S. Jajodia and L. Kerschberg, eds.), New York: Kluwer Academic Publishers, 1997.

30. J. Eder and W. Liebhart, "The Workflow Activity Model WAMO," in *Proceedings of the 3rd International Conference on Cooperative Information Systems (CoopIs'95)*, (Wien, Austria), May 1995.

31. R. van Stiphout, T. D. Meijler, A. Aerts, D. Hammer, and R. le Comte, "TREX: Workflow transaction by means of exceptions," in *Proceedings of the EDBT Workshop on Workflow Management Systems*, (Valencia, Spain), Mar. 1998.

32. M. Kamath and K. Ramamritham, "Failure handling and coordinated execution of concurrent workflows," in *Proceedings of the 14th International Conference on Data Engineering(ICDE'98)*, (Orlando, FL, USA), Feb. 1998.

33. G. Alonso, M. Kamath, D. Agrawal, A. E. Abbadi, R. Gunthor, and C. Mohan, "Failure handling in large scale workflow management systems," Tech. Rep. RJ9913, IBM Almaden Research Center, Nov. 1994.

34. G. Alonso, D. Agrawal, A. E. Abbadi, M. Kamath, R. Gunthor, and C. Mohan, "Advanced transaction model in workflow context," in *Proceedings of the 12th International Conference on Data Engineering(ICDE'96)*, (New Orleans, LA, USA), Feb. 1996.

35. IBM, *MQ Series Workflow - Concepts and Architectures*, 1998.

36. Staffware Corporation, *Staffware Global - Staffware for Intranet based Workflow Automation*, 1997. Available at http://www.staffware.com/home/whitepapers/data/globalwp.htm.

37. Baan Company N.V. - COSA Soultions, *COSA Reference Manual*, 1998.

38. D. Chiu, K. Karlapalem, and Q. Li, "Exception handling with workflow evolution in "adome-wfms": a taxonomy and resolution techniques," in *Proceedings of the First Workshop on Adaptive Workflow Systems*, (Seattle, Washington, USA), Nov. 1998. Available at http://ccs.mit.edu/klein/cscw98/paper06.

39. S. Bandinelli, E. Di Nitto, and A. Fuggetta, "Supporting cooperation in the spade-1 environment," *IEEE Transactions on Software Engineering*, vol. 22, December 1996.

ADOME-WFMS: Towards Cooperative Handling of Workflow Exceptions

Dickson K.W. Chiu[1], Qing Li[2] and Kamalakar Karlapalem[3]

[1]Dickson Computer Systems, 7A Victory Avenue, 4th floor, Homantin,
Kowloon, Hong Kong
kwchiu@dickson-computer.com
[2]Department of Computer Science, City University of Hong Kong,
Tat Chee Avenue, Kowloon, Hong Kong
csqli@cityu.edu.hk
[3]Department of Computer Science, University of Science and Technology,
Clear Water Bay, Kowloon, Hong Kong
kamal@cs.ust.hk

Abstract. Exception handling in workflow management systems (WFMSs) is a very important problem since it is not possible to specify all possible outcomes and alternatives. Effective reuse of existing exception handlers can greatly help in dealing with workflow exceptions. On the other hand, cooperative support for user-driven resolution of unexpected exceptions and workflow evolution at run-time is vital for an adaptive WFMS. We have developed ADOME-WFMS via a meta-modeling approach as a comprehensive framework in which the problem of workflow exception handling can be adequately addressed. In this chapter, we present an overview of exception handling in ADOME-WFMS with procedures for supporting the following: reuse of exception handlers, thorough and automated resolution of expected exceptions, effective management of Problem Solving Agents, cooperative exception handling, user-driven computer supported resolution of unexpected exceptions, and workflow evolution.

1 Introduction

Workflow management system technology, though recent, has been regarded as one of the main types of advanced information systems. It is perceived that workflow technology not only requires the support for complex data model functionality, but also flexibility for dynamically modifying the workflow specifications, especially in cases of exception handling. Because of unanticipated possibilities, special cases, changes in requirement and operation environment, exceptions may occur frequently during the execution of a business process. An exception is an event (i.e., something that happens), which deviates from normal behavior or may prevent forward progress of a workflow. Upon unexpected exceptions, a comprehensive WFMS should support

A. Romanovsky et al. (Eds.): Exception Handling, LNCS 2022, pp. 271-288, 2001.

cooperative exception handling, i.e., provide assistance for the users to reallocate resources (data / object update) or to amend the workflow, such as adding alternatives (*workflow evolution*). Further, frequent occurrences of similar exceptions have to be incorporated into workflow specifications as *expected exceptions*. Such workflow evolution can help avoid unnecessary exceptions by eliminating error-prone activities, adding alternatives, or by enhancing the operation environment. This can lead to a WFMS that supports workflow adaptation through exceptions.

In contrast with traditional software systems, workflows usually evolve more frequently, making reuse a vital issue. Reuse of workflow definitions and exception handlers are very important for the smooth operation of a flexible WFMS. Support for workflow evolution at run-time is vital for an adaptive WFMS. There have been a few WFMSs designed to address these two problems (viz. reuse issues and workflow evolution) effectively and adequately. However, none of them promotes a meta-modeling supported, exception-centric WFMS. As such, we can have a simple but expressive core data dictionary (meta-schema), with extensive reuse opportunities.

An effective user interface is vital to the execution of the above features. We choose to use a web-based user interface because workflows and agents tend to be widely distributed, even involving other organizations across the Internet. The Internet supports mobile clients with electronic mail and notifying services such as „I Seek You" (ICQ), and they can access the WFMS with a web-browser. Direct message passing between clients and remote data sharing can be facilitated. On the other hand, web-based tools are a prevailing technology that has a wide range of utilities and off-the-shelf applications, supporting wide ranges of hardware and software platforms at a relatively low-cost.

We use an integrated, event-driven approach for execution, coordination, and exception handling in our WFMS. Events (such as database events / exceptions, or external inputs) trigger the WFMS Execution Manager to start an activity. The WFMS Execution Manager uses events to trigger execution of tasks, while finished tasks will inform the Execution Manager with events to proceed executing subsequent tasks. Upon an exception, exception events will trigger the WFMS Exception Manager to take control of resolutions.

In this regard, we have developed ADOME-WFMS, based on an Advanced Object Modeling Environment (ADOME [31]), with a novel exception centric approach. The key features are as follows: (i) effective coordination of Problem Solving Agents (PSAs) and an object-oriented capability-based approach to match tasks and agents; (ii) automatic resolution of expected exceptions and exception driven workflow recovery; (iii) dynamic binding of exception handlers to activities with scoping, and to classes, objects and roles; (iv) addition, deletion and modification of exception handlers at run-time through workflow evolution support; (v) specifying and reusing exception handlers upon unexpected exceptions and cooperative exception handling; and (vi) application of workflow evolution and workflow recovery in exception handling. Thus, adding a web-based user interface allows ADOME-WFMS to effectively support distribution of PSA and workflow execution even with a centralized control design.

In this chapter, we present an overview of flexible workflow enactment and online workflow evolution in an advanced object environment (an active OODBMS with role and dynamic schema support), with reference to ADOME-WFMS. More details regarding classification of exceptions and handlers, and modeling aspects for ADOME-WFMS are given in [11]. In addition, ADOME-WFMS exception driven workflow recovery has been presented in [17].

The rest of our chapter is organized as follows. Section 2 presents a meta-modeling approach to activity modeling, which facilitates reuse and workflow evolution. Section 3 presents the architecture of ADOME-WFMS with web-based PSA coordination and general mechanisms. Section 4 discusses how ADOME-WFMS handles expected exceptions and provide facilities towards cooperative exception handling with support for workflow evolution. Section 5 compares related work. Finally, we conclude the article with our plans for further research in Section 6.

2   Flexible Activity Meta-modeling in ADOME-WFMS

The activity model of ADOME-WFMS is in accordance with the WfMC standard [36]. Fig. 1 illustrates a requisition workflow, which is used as an example in the rest of the article. The requisition workflow is composed of the sub-activities „purchase request", „procurement", „payment arrangement" and task „receive and check goods". If the purchase order is on cash-on-delivery (COD) terms, the order of execution is „payment arrangement" and then „received and check goods". Otherwise, if the purchase order is on credit terms, the order is „receive and check goods" first and then „payment arrangement" upon payment due. This decision is represented with an OR-split and OR-join. The „purchase request" and „payment arrangement" sub-activities are further composed of other tasks, like „get product information", „fill in PR form", etc., as illustrated.

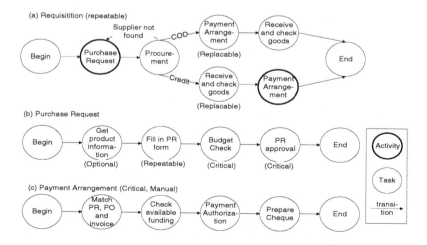

Fig. 1. Example Workflow of Requisition Procedure

2.1   Exception Centric View of a WFMS

After discussing why exception handling is important, we present an exception centric view of ADOME-WFMS. Fig. 2 shows main entities of a WFMS with their inter-relationships. Under an object-oriented approach, all these entities (including events and exceptions) are modeled as first-class objects.

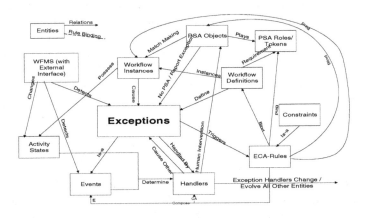

Fig. 2. Exception Centric View of a WFMS

The *WFMS* defines, manages and executes workflow definitions. It contains inter-faces to the external world and manages all entities in the system. It can detect various workflow exceptions. It can interface with PSAs and capture external exceptions. *Workflow (Activity) Definitions* specify workflow types and the requirements for their execution, together with any relevant expected exceptions. Workflow definitions can contain sub-workflow definitions in a composition hierarchy. An atomic sub-workflow (i.e. a leaf node of a composition hierarchy) is called a task. Users specify transitions among sub-activities (siblings in the activity composition hierarchy) to represent the possible execution paths. *Workflow (Activity) Instances* are run-time instantiations of workflow definition classes to be enacted. They possess activity states and can cause various exceptions. Workflow instances can contain sub-workflow and task instances according to their definition in the composition hierarchy. *Activity states* capture the status and progress of execution of activities. The state of an activity includes the data objects related to the activity, execution state and other house-keeping information for the activity.

PSA Objects are agents that can enact a task. Each PSA object can play various roles and possess tokens. The *Match Maker* of the WFMS assigns PSA Objects to workflow instances for execution based on role/token matching. (Lack of a suitable PSA is a typical workflow exception.) While carrying out the task, the PSA may report exceptions, and handle exceptions through human intervention. Human PSA objects can also participate in cooperative exception handling with the help of the

Human Intervention Manager (cf. Sect. 4.3). *PSA roles / tokens* are possessed by PSA objects. On the other hand, PSA roles /tokens specify the agent requirement of enacting a task. A *token* embodies certain capabilities of a PSA to execute certain functions / procedures /tasks, e.g., programming, database-administration, Japanese-speaking, while a *role* represents a set of responsibilities, which usually correspond to a job-function in an organization, e.g., project-leader, project-member, programmer, analyst, etc. A token can be a composite token, which is equivalent to a set of simple tokens, i.e., the composite token inherits all the capabilities of the simple tokens. The higher levels of the inheritance hierarchy have highly complex tokens that correspond to the capabilities of PSA-roles. Thus, capability-tokens and roles form a unified multiple-inheritance hierarchy (as explained in [14]).

Events are something that happens and are interesting to the system itself or to user applications. There is an *Event Detector* component in the active OODBMS for detecting data-driven events. Moreover, the WFMS core logic is able to detect workflow events related to workflow semantics. The external interface of the WFMS can detect external events. An event occurrence triggers appropriate handler(s) according to the relevant ECA-rule specifications. *Exceptions* are events that deviate from normal execution behavior. Different exceptions of the same type (e.g., deadline expiration) can occur anywhere in an activity and at any time. Thus, the active capability of the underlining OODBMS provides a good support for the specification of exceptions and the handlers in the form of ECA-rules.

ECA-rules (Event-Condition-Action rules, as explained in Sect. 4.2) specify the action to be taken upon the event if the condition part is true. They are bound to most other objects and classes of the WFMS, such as, workflow definitions, workflow instances, PSA objects, and roles/tokens. In order to share the ECA-rules in a controlled manner, we propose that a rule is applicable to a target object only after binding them. Note that constraints are expressed in ECA-rules. *Constraints* are used to maintain integrity and consistency. Activities violating constraints will cause exceptions.

Handlers are allowed to be sub-activities/tasks that can resolve exceptions. Thus, they need PSAs (human and/or software) for processing. Exception types and activity states are the most important factors for exception resolution. An exception handler is specified for resolving different types of exceptions. The exception handler can then change various entities at the instance or schema level in order to resolve the exception. However, the exception handler may possibly cause further exceptions, and the problem of cascaded exception must be addressed (cf. [17]).

2.2 ADOME-WFMS Meta-modeling: Some Prominent Aspects

Many of the earlier WFMSs [19] were built on top of traditional database technologies (e.g., relational databases). They fall short in facilitating / offering flexibility of modeling, ease of implementation, and/or in handling dynamic run-time requirements. Advanced features — objects, rules, roles, active capability and the flexibility — of object-oriented database systems are needed to facilitate the development of a versatile WFMS [13], especially with meta-modeling approach. In ADOME-WFMS, we advocate a three-level meta-modeling approach wherein workflows, capabilities, exceptions, and handlers are defined at a meta-level as depicted in Fig. 3.

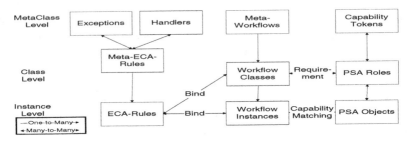

Fig. 3. Three Level Meta-Modeling for ADOME-WFMS

Workflow templates are defined at the meta-level so that workflow definitions can be instantiated for specific applications. For example, a generic requisition workflow template can be declared at the meta-level, so that specific requisition workflow definitions have customized rules and sub-activities can be instantiated for purchasing different category of items. Capability tokens are defined at the meta-level so that they can be combined to form PSA-roles, which capture requirements of task classes (cf. [14]). Exceptions (which are events) and handlers (which correspond to conditions and actions) are defined at the meta-level. Exceptions are associated to handlers in the form of meta-Event-Condition-Action-rules (meta-ECA-rules). Specific ECA-rules can then be bound to workflow for versatile exception handling (cf. [15]).

To illustrate further, the meta-level design for activity schemas is shown in Fig. 4 with the following features. All activity schemas are treated as sub-classes of the meta-class `Activity`. `WFMS_class` serves as the root class of all class definitions in the WFMS for easy maintenance of the classes and objects. The meta-activity schema contains all features for defining activity schemas, such as input/output parameters, and the activity graph, which describes the sub-activities and their incoming/outgoing transitions, join/split types, mandatory/regular handlers. Class-attributes (which is a feature supported in many advanced object-oriented systems [26]) are used for storing either attributes of the class object (such as class description) or attributes of the same value among all objects of the class (such as the input / output specifications). All sub-class objects inherit the definition attributes of the super-class object but each of the classes can have their own value of class attributes. WFMS related events for activities (such as `execute`, `finish`, `abort`), standard workflow exceptions (such as `no_PSA`, `PSA_reject`, `cannot_proceed`) are declared with the meta-class so that these features are applicable to all activities schemas.

When an activity instance is started, it has its own copy of the activity graph and re-execution pattern. This allows both instance and schema level workflow evolution. On the other hand, rule objects can be declared outside of the scope of activities first, and then bound to individual activity schemas (or specific instances) to facilitate reuse. The hierarchical composition is important for encapsulating details of activities and sub-activities to facilitate reuse and to allow the design of workflows in both top-down and bottom-up manners, as detailed in [14]. It further introduced scoping for exception handlers, nested transaction models and localizing failures.

```
class WFMS_class                          class Graph_Node isa WFMS_class
class_attributes:                         attributes:
  Class_Description: string;                Subactivity: Activity;
  Class_Date_Created: date;                 Predecessor_Join: (AND_join, OR_join, NIL);
Attributes:                                 Successor_Split: (AND_split, OR_split, NIL);
  Instance_Date_Created:                  end;
    date;
  Name: string;                           class Activity isa WFMS_class
  Instance_Description:                     /* all activities are sub-classes of this
    string;                                    meta-activity class because each different
end                                            activity class can have multiple instance */
                                          class_attributes:
class Task isa Activity                     Input_Parameters, Output_Parameters,
attribute_initilization:                    IO_Parameters: set of Parameter;
  Activity_Graph = NIL;                   events:
attributes:                                 execute, finish, abort ...
  Task_Need: set of Token;                exceptions:
  Allow_Partial_Match: bool;                no_PSA, PSA_reject, cannot_proceed ...
                                          rules:
          ...                               Manditory_handlers: set of rules;
methods                                     Handlers: set of rules;
  Match_Cost, Partial_Match,              attributes:
  Match_Cost_Ext...                         Activity_Graph:
end                                           (Activity_Node set of Graph_Node;
                                               Transisition set of Arc;)
class Arc isa WFMS_class                   Reexecution_Pattern:
  Source, Destination:                        (optional, repeatable, replacable...);
    Activities;                             /* parameters for execution of instance */
  Transisition_Condition:                   Priority: integer;
    Boolean;                                PSA_chosen: set of PSA;
end;                                      methods
                                            Decomposition, PSA_for_Activity, Execution,
                                          ....
                                          end
```

Fig. 4. Meta-level Specification of Activities and Tasks

In summary, this full object-oriented approach enables full inheritance of various activity properties (such as rules and re-execution mode) down the composition hierarchy and applies to each of the activity / task instances. From this meta-level schema, users can define all other classes for the WFMS, including activity schemas, PSAs, roles, exceptions and handlers. Further, from these schemas WFMS objects (in particular, activity instances) can be instantiated. This contributes a substantial improvement to WFMS modeling based on relational models (such as [28]) because the entity modeling and implementation is tied together in a straightforward manner. Extensive reuse is also facilitated as discussed in [15].

3   ADOME-WFMS Architecture and Activity Enactment Mechanism

The ADOME system was developed to enhance the knowledge-level modeling capabilities of OODBMS models [31] to allow them to more adequately deal with data and knowledge management requirements of advanced information management applications, especially WFMSs. The ADOME prototype has been built by integrating an OODBMS (ITASCA [26]) and production inference engine (CLIPS [23]). Therefore, a WFMS can be implemented on top of it with relative ease. In the case of ADOME-WFMS, the architecture and functional aspects (as depicted in Fig. 5) are as follows.

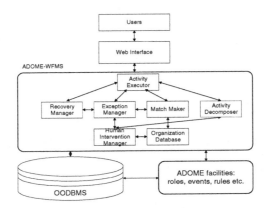

Fig. 5. ADOME-WFMS Architecture

ADOME active expert OODBMS provides a unified enabling technology for the WFMS, viz., object/role database, event specification and execution, rule / constraint specification and processing [31], etc. *Organization Database* manages data objects for the organization, as well as PSA classes, instances and their capability token (role) specifications. Besides maintaining user-specified extensional tokens / roles systematically, intensional token/role derivation for a PSA is also supported (cf. [14]).

Activity Decomposer facilitates the decomposition of activities into tasks. The user provides the knowledge and related data to decompose activities into tasks by a user interface (cf. [14,16]). *Activity Executor* coordinates execution by user-raised and database generated events as explained in the next section. *Match Maker* selects PSAs for executing tasks of an activity according to some selection criteria as explained in [14,11]. *Exception Manager* handles various exceptions by re-executing failed tasks or their alternatives (either resolved by the WFMS or determined by the user) while maintaining forward progress as explained later in this chapter. *Recovery Manager* performs various housekeeping functions, including logging and rollback, to maintain the WFMS in consistent states as explained in [17].

Web Interface allows users and PSAs to access ADOME-WFMS and the database through a web-browser, so that users can be mobile. This supports effective management of Problem Solving Agents, cooperative exception handling, user-driven computer supported resolution of unexpected exceptions, and workflow evolution.

3.1   Workflow Enactment Mechanisms of ADOME-WFMS

In this section, we shall concentrate on using a centralized control and coordination execution model centered on the *Activity Executor* of the WFMS. The *Activity Executor* monitors the task execution status and enforces deadlines. For the normal task life cycle, it initiates the PSAs to be selected by the *Match Maker* to carry out their assigned task and get the response (if any) from the PSA upon task completion. On the other hand, if a task raises exception events or does not respond within the deadline (i.e., *time out*), the *Exception Manager* will respond and handle it.

An event driven activity execution model with meta-ECA-rules has been described in the previous chapter. Moreover, this model provides a unified approach for normal activity execution and exception handling. Now, ADOME-WFMS can support activity execution through the *Web Interface* (cf. [16]). Users can define an activity class with the ADOME-WFMS *Activity Editor*.

With a web-browser, a user can log on to ADOME-WFMS to search / browse for an activity class (by name, department, etc.). The system provides a preliminary checking function, which determines if the required PSA and resources are possibly available. (Their actual availability depends on the execution of other concurrent activities.) Pressing the *Start* button on the web page will trigger the corresponding start-event for the activity through the *Web Interface*. External application software can also trigger the corresponding start-event to start the workflow.

For human PSAs, the selected PSA will be informed via ICQ with the URL of an *Interface Page* generated from a template in the database by the *Web Interface* (cf. [16]). If the PSA is offline or does not reply within a deadline, an electronic mail will be sent instead. The selected PSA can then use a web browser to open the interface page (logging on is necessary) to: (i) accept the assignment by pressing the *Accept* button and then start work later with the *Start Work button*, (ii) accept and start work immediately with the *Start Work* button, or (iii) reject the assignment with the *Reject* button. The *Interface Page* contains also a list of required data objects for the task (such as other forms, voice or typed messages of colleagues, relevant database information). The PSA can then view or update the objects during his work. It should be noted that the PSA may browse the *objects passed* before deciding to accept the task.

After finishing the assigned task successfully, the PSA replies to the *Activity Executor* by pressing the *Normal Finish* button of the interface page. ADOME-WFMS will assume the PSA rejects if no reply can be received within a user-defined deadline. Data objects are passed via the mechanism of web-page forms (e.g., by filling in a web-based requisition form). The *Activity Executor* then carries on with the next step according to the result passed back. The PSA can report failure by choosing an exception type with the help of another pop-up page. Upon failure or time out, the *Exception Manager* will be invoked to handle the exception.

3.2   Detection of Events and Exceptions

Primitive events and composite events are all detected by the underlining ADOME event facilities as described in [10]. Since exceptions are ADOME events, detection of exceptions for ADOME-WFMS is well supported at run-time. External exceptions raised by external entities can be intercepted by the WFMS. Changes in workflow definitions, rules, schema and any WFMS data objects are also detected as update events, supported by the underlying ADOME active OODBMS mechanisms.

Workflow exceptions are raised by WFMS components, for example, PSA not available in *Match Maker*, not enough resources or PSA reject assignment in the *Activity Executor*, data constraint violations upon updating the *Organization Database*, (ignored) failure of task / sub-activity causing exception to its parent in the *Exception Manager*. Moreover, workflow exceptions are detected by automatic ADOME ECA-rules and/or constraints, e.g., activities cannot meet deadline, activities constraint violation (e.g. budget exceeded).

4   Handling Exceptions in ADOME-WFMS

As supported by the underlying ADOME facilities, the following information items are passed to the *Exception Manager* upon the exception detection: source and type of exception, state information of the task / activity [10], and any extra parameters defined by the exception type (e.g., budget value). The *Exception Manager* [15,16] then takes control and carries out the following: (1) Perform notification if necessary. (2) Identify the appropriate exception handler(s) and execute them. Handlers are modeled as sub-activities in ADOME-WFMS. (3) One or more handlers will be executed until the problem is solved. (4) If no appropriate exception handlers are found (i.e., an unexpected exception), or human intervention is specified, the *Human Intervention Manager* will be invoked. The human can then select the appropriate handler and/or perform workflow evolution. (5) If rollback is required, the *Recovery Manager* will be invoked for compensating activities (cf. [17]). (6) Resume / redo execution, jump to the appropriate step as decided by step 2 or 3, or abort the current task / sub-activity so that the exception propagates to its parent for further handling. Though a failure may propagate up the activity composition hierarchy, this approach localizes exceptions and thus reduces loss of work done.

4.1   Identifying and Executing Exception Handlers

One or more exception handlers may be qualified to handle an exception that occurs. The ADOME-WFMS *Exception Manager* employs the following priority order for selecting the appropriate exception handler(s) (cf. [11] for the detailed algorithm):

1. Mandatory ECA handlers - Since the users specify these as mandatory, all relevant handlers (with event matched and condition fulfilled) bound to the current scope (cf. Sect. 4.2) are executed in the order of the task / sub-activity, its parent and all the way up to the *global* activity. These mandatory actions, such as logging and notification, may or may not solve the problem causing the exception. If they cannot solve the problem, other categories of exception handlers will be executed.

2. Procedural handlers - These are extra branches for exception handling. Each procedural handler is specific to a certain task or sub-activity under a particular context for handling specific outcomes. Since they are explicit and context sensitive, they are chosen before (3) ECA handlers. For example, the 'supplier not found' arc (cf. Fig. 1(a)) represents a procedural handler.

3. ECA handlers - These are searched from the current activity up the composition hierarchy to allow special exception handlers to override default exception handlers if necessary. If more than one relevant handler was declared for the same activity, the one(s) for the more specific exception type would be chosen over the more general exception type (as explained in Sect. 4.2).

4. Built-in handlers - For generic exceptions, ADOME-WFMS has built-in exception handlers. For example, if a PSA rejects a task assignment or the best candidate PSA is not available, the WFMS will find the next available PSA. If all PSAs capable of executing the task are busy or the required resources are occupied, the WFMS will either wait or choose alternate execution paths.

5. Re-execution criteria - If none of the above handlers is specified, ADOME-WFMS will attempt re-execution criteria. (Please note that re-execution and re-throwing the exception at the current or parent scope can be specified explicitly in handlers too.) Some measures to prevent cascaded exceptions and loops, mainly related to deadline and budget constraint, can be found in [17]. ADOME-WFMS automatically re-executes the *repeatable* failed activities; choose another execution path for *replaceable* failed activities; skip *optional* failed tasks. This feature can save many tedious explicit jumps and aborts, especially with scoping in ADOME-WFMS (cf. Sect. 4.2). Moreover, this way can resolve many unexpected exceptions if re-execution helps. However, *critical* failed tasks without explicit handlers are unexpected exceptions. Therefore, it will result in human intervention. Upon re-execution, in order to maintain work continuity and save start up overhead, the same agent is preferred unless otherwise specified. The next candidate would be the nearest capable sibling or ancestor according to the organization structure (such as a teammate or supervisor).

4.2   Exception Modeling for Reuse in ADOME-WFMS

The main entities and relationships in ADOME-WFMS with respect to exception handling are all modeled as first-class objects. In particular, the class *exceptions* is a subclass of class *events*. A taxonomy of exceptions and handlers is found in [14]. Handlers are allowed to be sub-activities so that they can carry out any complicated actions; and nested exceptions are supported by recursive invocation of the *Exception Manager*. In ADOME-WFMS, declarative exception handlers in the form of ECA rules can be bound to selected classes, objects and roles, both dynamically at run-time (with *bind* statements) and at definition time. This is because the underlying ADOME supports ECA rules and the above-mentioned dynamic features [10]. Furthermore, handlers can be specified within the scope of different activity and sub-activity levels, i.e., the handler applies not only to the body of the target activity but also to all its sub-activities and tasks. This is the case since handlers can be inherited down the activity composition hierarchy.

The ADOME-WFMS *Human Intervention Manager* supports users to modify all the above declarations and associations at run-time as described in Sect. 4.3. The power of ADOME-WFMS in reuse over other systems (such as [7, 20, 28, 27, 25]) is mainly due to the ability of ADOME in dynamic binding of rules to different dimensions (objects, roles, sub-activities, etc.) at run-time. Since exceptions can be common in a WFMS, reusing exception handlers is vital to the effectiveness, user-friendliness and efficiency of the WFMS. However, a methodology in workflow design to facilitate reuse of exception handlers is beyond the scope of this chapter.

In ADOME-WFMS, some mechanisms for reuse of exception handlers follow from its hierarchy activity structure. For procedural exception handlers, arcs from several peer tasks / sub-activities at the same level (siblings inside the same parent activity) can lead to the same exception handler for some degree of sharing. Because of scoping, only one declarative exception handler is required for each exception type for each activity composition hierarchy (as explained in the previous section). For example, declaring $r2$ at the *requisition* activity level will enable $r2$ for all the sub-activities and tasks for the whole diagram. Similarly, human intervention requirements of exception handling (automatic, warning, system-assisted and manual) and re-execution patterns (optional, critical, repeatable and replaceable) for sub-activities and tasks are specified within the scope of this composition hierarchy, with the lowest level taking priority in specification and thus overriding those of higher levels.

Declarative exception handlers are first-class ECA rule objects. A rule object r is declared and defined once and then can be associated with more than one scope by repeated binding. For example, we can declare r9=(E:All_exception, amount>1000000, CEO.inform) and then bind $r9$ to *payment, requisition,* so that all exceptions in the payment and requisition sub-activities will inform the chief executive officer for transactions greater than one million dollars. Since exceptions are events (which are first-class objects in ADOME), exception classes are also arranged into an 'isa' hierarchy. Thus, an exception handler for a super-class will also handle an exception of a sub-class. (E.g., an exception handler for program_error will handle subscript_out_of_range also.) Extending the event-part with 'or' event composition can generalize exception handlers (e.g., E: program_error ∨ PC_failure, A: EDP.manager.inform), and increase the applicability of the exception handlers. Moreover, meta-level rules can be instantiated through parameters and supplied methods to specify rules, such as budget rules instantiated with actual budget figures.

4.3   Web-Based Human Intervention Manager

Upon *unexpected exceptions* or *manual* exception handling is specified, the *Human Intervention Manager* sub-module of the *Exception Manager* alerts the specified user by ICQ (or if not successful, then by electronic mail), with the URL of an *Exception Page* (cf. [16]) that assists the user to handle the exception. This web page, again generated from a template, offers reuse of existing exception handlers by providing a list of possible resolutions, and relevant data objects to assist the human decision. Moreover, all recent case-by-case resolutions are kept in the database for user reference. Since every scenario may be different, only the user can probably determine what are the most appropriate actions. Some suggested resolution for some exception cases under different situations are presented in [16].

On the other hand, especially when *manual* exception handling is specified, there may exist a list of more concrete exception resolutions, which probably needs the human user to choose since there may not be enough knowledge/experience for the system to totally automate such a decision. For example, when the task „check available funding" in Fig 1(c) fails, the exception would trigger *manual* handling. Here, the user can choose from a list of *suggested resolutions* (with parameters) or browse/edit for other resolutions (such as returning the goods). Before making a decision, the user may browse the *objects passed* for further information or consult the *Decision History*.

Prior to executing the action specified through human intervention, the Exception Manager performs checking to avoid further cascaded exceptions. In addition to generally specified constraints in the ADOME-WFMS, some of its specific ones are illustrated in [16]. Should some constraints be violated, the *Exception Manager* will further inform the user of the potential problem and ask for confirmation. There are often scenarios where one may handle exceptions for a more important task at the expense of sacrificing other less important ones.

4.4   Web-Based Workflow Evolution

ADOME-WFMS has the required facilities for supporting various types of workflow evolution (cf. [14]). In particular, besides conventional exception handling resolutions, the *Human Intervention Manager* sub-module also accepts update of workflow on-line. In contrast, there are currently few WFMSs having such facilities for supporting the whole spectrum of exception-handling resolutions, especially those relating to workflow evolution. In ADOME-WFMS, the user can choose any of the suggested resolutions to be persistent, or enter schema evolution operations, update of workflow and/or enter new ECA rules (but subject to the enforcement strategies as described in the next section). As workflow evolution requires the modification of workflow definitions or adding ECA rules to the system during work in progress, an advanced schema evolution capability is required at run-time. Due to ADOME's support of dynamic schema evolution [31], ADOME-WFMS readily provides exception resolutions based on schema evolution. It should be noted that the resolutions based on schema evolution are general-purpose ones, which can help reduce the occurrence of additional exceptions.

In [7], a complete, minimal, and consistent set of workflow evolution primitives is proposed. These workflow evolution primitives can be used for static and dynamic workflow evolution, including for migration of individual workflow instances. They are divided into two parts: (i) *declaration primitives* modify the declaration of workflow variables (including their default values), (ii) *flow primitives* modify the flow structure of the workflow schema. In [11], we have shown how these primitives are adapted and supported in the ADOME-WFMS framework.

Workflow evolution policies refer to how workflow instances adopt newly evolved workflow schema, while they are executing. Because ADOME-WFMS uses activity decomposition, upon workflow evolution (i.e., modification of a certain sub-activity class definition), the side effects of affecting other activities containing this sub-activity are very much confined. At the time of the workflow evolution, only those activities having the same sub-activity currently executing are affected. Other activities having the same sub-activity but not currently executing are unaffected since the sub-activity is encapsulated, and behaves as a black box to activities at a higher level. In order to allow further control over the semantics and implications of workflow evolution, users can choose the various evolution policies as described in [11]. Furthermore, we support a mechanism called hand-over policy (as motivated by [32]), in which hand-over rules (in the form of ECA rules) are used to specify how individual affected workflow instances adopt the new schema for execution.

We have also designed a web-based interface for workflow evolution. Upon pressing the *workflow evolution* button, the user can access a workflow evolution menu page (cf. [16]), where he/she is presented with a set of possible workflow evolution options.

5   Related Work

Sophisticated programming language features for exception handling date back to the Ada programming language [1]. The feature of exception propagation for resolving exception handlers, generic procedures and generic exception handlers, motivate the employment of meta-modeling of exceptions and handlers for ADOME-WFMS. [3] is a classical article on exception handling but for general database-intensive information system. [34] built a taxonomy and suggested a meta-model on exception handling for office information systems, with handling methods for different kinds of exceptions. HiPAC [9] represents a classic active OODBMS. Many of its features and concepts, such as treating rules and events as objects, ECA rules, composite events, exceptions as events, etc., influence the design of many later systems. A detailed survey on active OODBMS can be found in [13].

Many early contributors in workflow exceptions, such as [2, 20], use transaction workflow models. Earlier OO WFMSs, such as [27] (TriGSflow) and [30] had little support for exception handling. [29] adopts a knowledge-base approach to handle expected exceptions in WFMS in the form of a process handbook with strong emphasis on agent management. OPERA [25] incorporates primitives based on exception handling concepts developed for programming languages coupled with ideas from advanced transaction models. Crossflow [24] models virtual enterprises based on a service provider-consumer paradigm, with contract-based matchmaking between them.

WIDE [5, 7] uses object and rule modeling techniques and suggests some measures in handling exceptions. Exceptions are classified but not handling approaches. Reuse and management of exception handlers are presented with only some implementation details. Workflow evolution primitives are again not at a semantic level. The main drawback of WIDE is missing facilities for coordination of agents and also a lack of a coherent model of various entities and their inter-relationship in a WFMS.

Very few commercial WFMSs provide support for handling exceptions. Even if they do, they only address very basic problems to a slight extent. InConcert, by In-

Concert Inc. [33], supports event-action triggers. Staffware, by Staffware Corporation [35], and Changengine, by Hewlett-Packard [6] support special tasks called event nodes, which can suspend the execution of a workflow instance on a give path until a pre-defined (exception) event occurs, and then can execute an event handling sub-activity in the workflow. [6] discusses how various kinds of expected exceptions can be mapped on top of Changengine. Eflow [8], by Hewlett-Packard, is one of the closest commercial systems with features like E-ADOME in handling e-Services.

One of the earliest work in workflow evolution is [21], but this article describes a limited set of change primitives. Process-centered Software Engineering Environments [22] also adopted several mechanisms to process model evolutions before similar approaches were introduced in WFMS. As mentioned in Sect. 4.4, we apply the techniques [8] and [32] in designing ADOME-WFMS workflow evolution primitives and operations. PROSYT [18] addressed inconsistencies and deviations of task instances in general process support systems, but the contribution was more on the formal modeling than semantic modeling. [4] presented a unified framework for tolerating exceptions for data and processes in WFMS, but without details at the logical and implementation levels. Most related work in workflow evolution addresses exceptions caused by inappropriate workflow evolution rather than how workflow evolution can contribute to exception handling and avoidance.

A more complete survey on „Error Handling in Process Support Systems" is in another chapter of this book. In summary, other workflow systems either do not address exception-handling problems comprehensively or concentrate only on extended transaction models. Furthermore, few systems have advocated (let alone supported) an extensive meta-modeling approach (based on agents, match-making, exception handling, etc.). Compared with the systems close to us, ADOME-WFMS has the most features and can be readily extended to support mobile agents in the Internet.

6   Conclusion

This chapter has presented an overview of adaptive exception handling in a flexible WFMS based on ADOME - an active OODBMS extended with role and rule facilities. Compared with other research on this topic, ADOME provides an improved environment for developing a WFMS, which can adapt to changing requirements, with extensive support for reuse. In particular, the resultant system (i.e., ADOME-WFMS) supports a rich taxonomy of exception types and their handling approaches, and a novel augmented solution for exception handling based on workflow evolution. Effective reuse of workflow definitions, exceptions, handlers and constraints in ADOME-WFMS are also possible. This chapter has also described in detail, how expected exceptions are actually resolved with the ADOME-WFMS Exception Manager, and highlighted how unexpected exceptions are actually handled with the ADOME-WFMS *Exception Manager* through its *Web Interface*. It should be noted that, though exception handling is highly automated in ADOME-WFMS by scoping, binding and reuse, human intervention management must be provided to support for (totally) unexpected exceptions and drastic workflow evolutions. Moreover, the *Web Interface* also demonstrates effective management of human PSAs, especially during cooperative exception handling.

ADOME-WFMS is currently being built on top of the ADOME prototype system, with a web-based user interface to accommodate the whole range of activities [16]. Furthermore, we are developing E-ADOME via a cross-organizational workflow approach [12], which supports an extended set of web-interface facilities for enactment of e-services and e-commerce activities.

References

1.   Ada 95: Language Reference Manual (LRM) - the revised international standard. (ISO/IEC 8652:1995): Information Technology – Programming Languages – Ada (1995)
2.   Alonso, G., et al.: Exotica/FMDC: a workflow management system for mobile and disconnected clients. Distributed & Parallel Databases, **4**(3) (1996) 229-247
3.   Boridga, A.: Language Features for Flexible Handling of Exceptions, ACM Trans. on Database Systems (1985)
4.   Borgida A., Murata, T.: A Unified Framework for Tolerating Exceptions in Workflow/Process Models - A Persistent Object Approach, International Joint Conference on Work Activities Coordination and Collaboration (WACC '99), San Francisco (1999)
5.   Casati, F., Fugini, M.G., Mirbel, I.: An Environment for Designing Exceptions in Workflows. In Proceedings of CAiSE 98, LNCS Springer Verlag, Pisa (1998)
6.   Casati, F., Pozzi, G.: Modeling Exceptional Behaviours in Commercial Workflow Management Systems. In Proceedings of the 4th International Conference on Cooperative Information Systems (IECIS 98), IEEE Press (1998)
7.   Casati, F.: Models, Semantics, and Formal Methods for the Design of Workflows and their Exceptions. PhD thesis, Dipartimento di Elettronica e Informazione, Politecnico di Milano, Milano, Italy (1998)
8.   Casati, F., et al.: Adaptive and Dynamic Service Composition in eFlow. HP Laboratories Technical Report HPL-2000-39 (2000)
9.   Chakravarthy, S.: Rule Management and Evaluation: An Active DBMS Perspective. SIGMOD Record, 18(3) (1989) 20-28
10. Chan, L.C., Li, Q.: An Extensible Approach to Reactive Processing in an Advanced Object Modeling Environment. In Proceedings of 8th Intl. Conf. on Database and Expert Systems Applications (DEXA '97). LNCS(1308), Toulouse, France (1997) 38-47
11. Chiu, D.K.W.: Exception Handling in an Object-Oriented Workflow Management System. Ph.D. Thesis, Computer Science Dept., Hong Kong University of Science and Technology (2000)
12. Chiu, D.K.W., Karlapalem, K., Li, Q.: E-ADOME: A Framework For Enacting E-services. VLDB Workshop on Technologies for E-Services, Cairo, Eygpt (2000)
13. Chiu, D.K.W., Li, Q.: A Three-Dimensional Perspective on Integrated Management of Rules and Objects. International Journal of Information Technology, **3**(2) (1997) 98-118
14. Chiu, D.K.W., Li, Q., Karlapalem, K.: A Meta Modeling Approach for Workflow Management Systems Supporting Exception Handling, Special Issue on Method Engineering and Metamodeling, Information Systems, Elsevier Science, 24(2) (1999)159-184

15. Chiu, D.K.W., Li, Q., Karlapalem, K.: A Logical Framework for Exception Handling in ADOME Workflow Management System. International Conference on Advanced Information System Engineering (CAiSE'00), Stockholm, Sweden, (2000)
16. Chiu, D.K.W., Li, Q., Karlapalem, K.: Web Interface-Driven Cooperative Exception Handling in ADOME Workflow Management System. In Proc. 1st International Conference on Web Information System Engineering (WISE'00), IEEE Computer Society Press, Hong Kong (2000) 174-182
17. Chiu, D.K.W., Li, Q., Karlapalem, K.: Facilitating Exception Handling with Recovery Techniques in ADOME Workflow Management System, Journal of Applied Systems Studies, Cambridge International Science Publishing, Cambridge, England, 1(3) (2000)
18. Cugola, G.: Inconsistencies and Deviations in Process Support Systems, PhD Thesis, Politecnico di Milano (1998)
19. Dogac, A., Ozsu, T., Sheth, A. (eds): Proceedings of the NATO Advanced Study Institute (ASI) Workshop on Workflow Management Systems and Interoperability, Istambul,Turkey (1997)
20. Eder, J., Liebhart, W.: The Workflow Activity Model WAMO. In Proceeding of CoopIS-95 (1995) 97-98
21. Ellis, S., et al: Dynamic Change within Workflow Systems, Proceedings of the Conference on Organizational Computing Systems (1995).
22. Fuggetta, A., Ghezzi G.: State of the Art and Open Issues in Process-centered Software Engineering Environment, Journal of Systems & Software, 26 (July 1994).
23. GHG Corp: Clips Architecture Manual, Version 5.1 (1992) available at http://www.ghg.net/clips/CLIPS.html
24. Grefen, P., Hoffner, Y.: Crossflow – Cross-Organizational Workflow Support for Virtual Organization. In Proceedings of the Ninth International Workshop on Research Issues on Data Engineering: Information Technology for Virtual Enterprises (RIDE'98) (1998)
25. Hagen, C., Alonso, G.: Flexible Exception Handling in the OPERA Process Support System, 18th International Conference on Distributed Computing Systems (ICDCS 98), Amsterdam, The Netherlands (1998)
26. Ibex Corporation. http://www.ibex.ch/
27. Kappel, G., et.al.: Workflow Management Based on Objects, Rules, and Roles. IEEE Bulletin of the Technical Committee on Data Engineering 18(1) (1995) 11-18
28. Karlapalem, K., Yeung, H. P., Hung, P. C. K.: CapBaseED-AMS - A Framework for Capability-Based and Event-Driven Activity Management System. In Proceeding of COOPIS '95 (1995) 205-219
29. Klein, M., Dellarocas, C.: A Knowledge-Based Approach to Handling Exceptions in Workflow Systems, Proceedings of the Third International Conference on Autonomous Agents, Seattle, Washington (1999)
30. Kumar, A., et.al.: A framework for dynamic routing and operational integrity controls in a workflow management system. In Proceedings of the Twenty-Ninth Hawaii International Conference on System Sciences 3 (1996) 492-501
31. Li, Q., Lochovsky, F. H.: ADOME: an Advanced Object Modeling Environment. IEEE Transactions on Knowledge and Data Engineering, 10(2) (1998) 255-276
32. Liu, C., Orlowska, M., Li. H.: Automating handover in dynamic workflow environments. In Proceedings of the 10th International Conference on Advanced Information Systems Engineering CAiSE'98, Pisa, Italy (1998)159-172
33. McCarthy, D., Sarin, S.: Workflow and Transactions in InConcert. IEEE Data Engineering,16(2) (1993) 53-56

34. Saastamoinen, H.T.: On the Handling of Exceptions in Information Systems, Ph.D. Thesis, University of Jyväskylä (1995)
35. Staffware Corporation: Staffware Global - Staffware's Opportunity to Dominate Intranet based Workflow Automation (2000) http://www.staffware.com
36. Workflow Management Coalition: The Workflow Reference Model. (WFMC-TC-1003, 19-Jan-95, 1.1) (1995)

Author Index